"After reading this heart-openir[...]
self approaching my work with ι[...]
ness. No longer do I relate to m[...]
as persons offered a gift: the opportunity to experience
and renew life in a holistically-different way."

> — Yurii Cachero, Client Advocate
> Hospice of San Francisco

"A comprehensive collection of enlightened thinking and
practical wisdom on immune dysfunction. The reader
comes to understand that powerful techniques for the
healing of disease do exist outside the exam rooms of
traditional medicine. My own clinical experience with
persons with AIDS, herpes, hepatitis, Hodgkin's Dis-
ease, and leukemia has shown that emotional and
spiritual factors can have profound impact on our nat-
ural ability to conquer disease."

> — Jeffrey M. Leiphart, Ph.D.
> Clinical Psychologist

"We have here a bold and multi-faceted inquiry into the
nature and 'treatment' of psychoimmune dis-ease. This
book includes successful therapies, self-help experiences,
and life-affirming information. Its excerpts of trance
channeling serve as a powerful intuitive source of un-
derstanding, counsel, and inspiration.
"This outstanding contribution to the literature is
an excellent practical handbook on healing dis-ease. It
focuses on attitudinal and other, mainly non-physical
aspects of a severe individual and social problem, one
typically beset with ignorance, confusion, and fear. The
book also deals sensitively, reassuringly, and fairly with
the delicate issue of self-responsibility for personal well-
being—both the acquisition of dis-ease, as a stimulant
to personal growth, and its subsequent healing."

> — William H. Kautz, Sc.D.
> Director, Center for Applied Intuition

PSYCHOIMMUNITY & THE HEALING PROCESS

A HOLISTIC APPROACH

Psychoimmunity & The Healing Process

TO IMMUNITY & AIDS

SECOND EDITION
Revised and Updated

Jason Serinus, editor

CELESTIAL ARTS
Berkeley, California

A NOTE TO THE READER: No singular system of healing, be it "Western" or "Eastern," has a monopoly on the truth. You are totally unique. No one quite like you has ever existed on this planet before. Acknowledge your special wonder and needs. The program of healing that is right for you can only be determined by communion with your inner self. Please seek guidance in adapting the generalized body of information within this book to your specific health needs. The ideas and suggestions which follow are presented for your education and well-being, and in no way are intended to replace diagnosis and advice from trained and trusted medical and/or healing practitioners. Most cities in the United States offer practitioners skilled in both allopathic and holistic approaches to healing and wellness. You are encouraged to avail yourself of their knowledge and dedication. The references throughout this book to "we," "us," "ours," and so on, refer specifically to either the author of the article, or The Holistic Group. Such references never indicate the viewpoint nor the counsel of the publisher. It is important for the reader to understand that The Holistic Group is positing a *different* interpretation of AIDS and dis-ease than that of the scientific/medical community. The Holistic Group and the Editor and contributors to this book make no claims as to the results of applying this program to any particular case history. The Inquiry of The Holistic Group is presented as a research paper, not as a cure for AIDS.

Celestial Arts
P.O. Box 7327
Berkeley, CA 94707

First Printing, 1986
Second Edition, 1987

Cover photo by Susan Thiele
Backcover photo by Christopher
Cover design by Ken Scott
Chinese calligraphy by Pax Cheng
Typography by HMS Typography, Inc.
Text design by Paul Reed and Nancy Austin

Library of Congress Cataloging-in-Publication Data

Psychoimmunity & the healing process.

Includes index.
1. AIDS (Disease)–Psychosomatic aspects.   2. Holistic medicine.   3. Trance.   I. Serinus, Jason, 1945- .
II. Kübler-Ross, Elisabeth.
RC607.A26P794   1986   616.97'92   86-11701
ISBN 0-89087-461-1

Made in the United States of America

3 4 5 — 90 89 88 87

CONTENTS

PART I: A NEW UNDERSTANDING

PART II: A HOLISTIC APPROACH

PART III: KEVIN RYERSON'S TRANCE CHANNELINGS

ACRONYMS APPEARING IN THIS BOOK:

AIDS – Acquired Immune Deficiency Syndrome
ARC – AIDS-Related Condition
KS – Kaposi's sarcoma
AMA – American Medical Association
HTLV-III – Human T-cell Leukemia Virus-III (the "AIDS" virus)
   Note: In late 1986, the new nomenclature "Human Immunodeficiency Virus (or "HIV") was adopted as the uniform international designation for the AIDS virus, which is designated in this book as HTLV-III.
CDC – Centers for Disease Control

ACKNOWLEDGEMENTS

There are so many people to thank, in addition to our blessed publisher, for making this work a reality. Some are practitioners, others are friends and co-workers. There are even people to thank who will be amazed to see their names below. Mention does not necessarily connote membership in The Holisitic Group which assembled the information contained in the Acquired Immune Deficiency "Inquiry."

Thank you: Jean Sayre-Adams, R.N.; Jim Allen, D.C.; Jim Avila; Luther Balliew; Keith Barton, M.D.; Norman Basye; Thomas Alan Berg; Alan Brickman; Perry and Zirah Brown; Fred Brungard (aka Sister Missionary Position); Denise Buzbuzian of "Au Naturel"; Jose Casamada; E. Kitch Childs, psychologist; Yurii Cachero; Pax Cheng; Elaine Chiodi; Gordon Clark; Richard Cohart; Misha Cohen, C.A., of "Quan Yin"; Ken Coupland of Sentinel USA; Gabriel Cousens, M.D.; Nora Cousens; Jim Cox; Lynn Davis; Tamara Diaghilev, teacher of psychic development; Don Donegan, masseur; Mark Drusin; Robert Raye Ellis of "Live and Let Live"; Feather Singing; Art Fisher; Bob Fogg; John Fox and Deki; The Foxes; Doug Fraser; Anastasia Furst, palmist teacher and reader; Jeanne Garcia; David A. Garfield; Rosemary Gladstar's Rosemary Garden; David Glassberg; Peter Goetz; Kathy Goss; Jim Gottsman, masseur; Susan Green, D.C.; Charles Hall (aka Crazy Owl), Ph.D. and health practitioner; Steve Hanan; Shari Harter; Louise Hay, metaphysical counselor and healer; Joseph Helms, M.D., and acupuncturist extraordinare; Bruce Henderson, artist; Barklie Henry; David Hinds at Celestial Arts; George Jalbert, R.N.; Lola Sybil Jordan; Richard Katz; Mica Kindman; Danaan Lahey; Leon Lashner, D.C.; Ray Legnini; Jeff Leiphart, Ph.D.; Robert Levitt; Robert Hoffman Lin, L.M.T.; Shirley MacLaine; Lin Mazlo; John McLean; Walter Mellon; Alison Moad of 5B; Mary-Sharon Moore; Charlie Murphy; Edna R. Nassberg; Richard Nelson; Irene Newmark, C.A., teacher of breema bodywork and shiatsu, certified acupuncturist, Chinese herbalist, nutritional consultant; Nicolaas and Wildwood Resort/Retreat; Carolyn North; Jarrett Oddo, who's a lot more than a sofabed salesman; Robert Parker, Ph.D., expert on aging and nutrition; Steve Peskind; Al Peterson; Michael Rabinoff, N.D.; Paul Reed, my editor at Celestial Arts; Frank Robinson; Lynn Ryerson; Sa'shwa, healer, reader, founder of Church of the Gentle Brothers and Sisters, of which I am a Minister; Lois Schiller of Aletheia Institute; Jeff Segal; David Sereda; Richard Shames, M.D.; Vicki Smith; Soma; Starhawk; Paul Steutzer, N.D.; Sujata; Bill Teeter, certified acupuncturist and Chinese herbalist; Marvin Tauber; Dana Ullman; Richard Vincent, masseur; Patricia Wilson; and all those loving souls who at one time or another have rubbed my shoulders or held my hand.

Thank you, editors and publications who did not charge for spreading the word about the paper on Acquired Immune Deficiency which preceded this volume: *San Francisco Bay Guardian*; *Coming Up*; *East Bay Express*; *Whole Life Times*; *This Month on the River*; *What's Happening on the Russian River*; the *Pacific Sun*; and *The Well Being Calendar*.

Thank you, managers, owners, workers, and collective members of the following establishments—most of you sold our initial paper on Acquired Immune Deficiency without profit, thereby making it available to the people who needed it most at low cost: A Woman's Place Bookstore; Au Naturel Health Foods; Berkeley Holistic Health Center; Berkeley Natural Grocery; Berkeley Women's Health Collective; Buffalo Natural Foods; Good Earth Natural Foods; Inner Sunset Community Foods; Inside/Out Health Foods of Key West; Living Foods; Oakland Natural Grocery; Rainbow General Store; Santa Rosa Community Market; Shakespeare Books; Shanti Nilaya; Stanyan St. Real Foods; T&T Natural Foods.

Thank you, above all, loving souls whose articles and interviews appear in this volume.

—*Jason Serinus*

PREFACE TO THE SECOND EDITION

The concept of taking responsibility for both our dis-ease and our healing has been one of major contention within the holistic health and AIDS communities. My desire to address this issue—and to explore even further the ways in which we individually and collectively can go about healing AIDS—has led to the addition to this book of a third trance channeling through Kevin Ryerson.

My understanding of the human experience has convinced me that we *do* in fact create our own reality. This means that we create—choose—every single experience that shapes our destiny: our past; our birthdate; our parents; our joys; our sorrows; our relationships; our political system; our dis-eases; our cures; our death; and our future. We create it all.

We usually are not aware of our choices, however, or of the reasons for them. This is because they are often made, even before we inhabit our bodies, by our superconscious self—our spirit—the timeless dimension of our being whose range of knowing extends far beyond the confines of our conscious mind.

Why, you may ask, would anyone create a reality or choose a lifetime filled with experiences as potentially fatal as AIDS or pollution or the nuclear bomb? We have been taught that we must resist such "bad" and "evil" forces so that we do not fall "victim" to them. Assuming we do create our own reality, why would anyone in their right mind choose to experience AIDS?

As the entity John explains in Chapter 15: "All that ye must understand is that ye are part of a greater and infinite sense and order of things...for simply, ye are part of God and God is love. Experience everything uncompromisingly as an opportunity to increase thy understanding and to increase and learn to restore harmony to all things." From such a perspective, there is neither "good" nor "bad," there is only experience. All experience exists for only one reason: to allow us to understand that we are all One, united in love. "God is love, love is harmony, and harmony begets peace." All else is illusion.

I wish that we didn't have to go through so much pain and suffering in our lives. I wish that all my friends who have left their bodies were still with me, still here to experience the joy and the fullness that I am learning that life can be.

If only we would let go of the angers and the fears that separate us one from another—black from white, gay from straight, Russian from American, woman from man. For, as Spirit has taught me, it is only when we finally choose to love ourselves and each other unconditionally that AIDS, war, and human suffering will cease to exist.

My friend Kevin Ryerson has suggested in the Foreword that this book offers us an opportunity to look into the depth and the phenomena of our own souls. If we allow ourselves to drop our judgments about the nature of experience, I believe we will find that AIDS as well affords us such an opportunity.

May the material which follows serve to unite us with the love that is the source of all healing and all creation.

—*Jason Serinus*
Oakland, California
May, 1987

PREFACE

This book demonstrates that holistic medicine is primarily a matter of attitude rather than techniques. The editor is to be credited for interviewing people who have used their encounters with Acquired Immune Deficiency as springboards for self-transformation. I believe that such people have as much to teach us about Acquired Immune Deficiency, and certainly about life, as does medical research.

The specific advice proposed for the treatment of immune dysfunction and of Acquired Immune Deficiency strikes me as basically safe and sound, and should be used preferably in the context of personal oversight by an experienced health practitioner. As Anthony and Richard—two persons with Acquired Immune Deficiency—observe at the outset of this book, each treatment approach must be "felt from the inside" to see if it offers real benefits.

Whatever the treatment plan, it is the attitude that one nurtures and incorporates into its application that makes the difference between vitality and mere survival. Illness is a surprise quiz from the Universe about the purpose and direction of life.

—Keith Barton, M.D.
Berkeley Holistic Health Offices

FOREWORD

by Kevin Ryerson

As I examine the work of the many persons who have created this manuscript, I find herein a common unity of understanding and direction. The material which follows has its roots in the basic conception that we as human beings are more than physical entities; that we consist of three dimensions: mind, body, and spirit. Through an examination of the phenomenon of psychoimmunity and how it relates to each and every one of us, this book ultimately serves to teach us about the nature of human existence. The central message of the contributions which follow is that we as human beings, as we open our hearts and contribute to each other, are the true source of all health and wealth.

It is my belief that as the reader explores the contents of this manuscript, they will find herein a blueprint—a model—which can serve as a means for understanding the nature and issues of their own humanity. Bearing this in mind, do not view these contents as the final and definitive statement on Acquired Immune Deficiency or any other of the other dis-ease states examined herein. It is not the intention of this work to compete with other healing systems, or even to create an exclusive or closed holistic healing system within its own right. Rather, I encourage the reader to allow this material to illumine the methods by which they can develop the life skills to enable them to contribute, not only to personal well-being, but to the collective well-being of all persons.

As I examine my own role in the creation of this book, and review its intuitively-derived contents, I see constantly running through these pages the message that we are the creators of our own reality—our own human condition. It is in the roots of our humanism—our loving essence as human beings—that we find the true foundation for that which is outlined herein and offered up for practical application. As the readers explore the teachings of the many people who have helped create the very human dialogue which follows, let them do so with an open heart and an open mind. Above all else, may they know that they are merely being offered an opportunity to look into the depths and the phenomena of their own soul.

To
Dan, Paliku, Anthony, Richard, Dennis,
Jose, and Edna Ruth Nassberg
whose determination and love
in the face of life-threatening illness
has given birth to this book.

Judgments do not matter.
There is no matter.
All substance is immaterial.
Only love exists.

INTRODUCTION

This book has grown from an initial exploration into the health crisis of our time, Acquired Immune Deficiency, into a thorough investigation of the nature of the healing process. This was not my original intent. The very nature of the dis-ease state (this word is hyphenated to emphasize the psychospiritual disharmony and stress which produce this state), and the particular way in which dis-eases characterized by immune dysfunction have shrouded more and more lives and relationships with fear, disharmony and suffering, has mandated such an approach.

In order to protect and heal oneself from any dis-ease, be it the common cold, herpes, or cancer, one must first understand just what *wellness* and *healing* are all about. The basis for the holistic approach to health is rooted in the understanding that we are more than our physical bodies—that we are composed of mind, body, and spirit. When these three components of our being—mind, body, and spirit—are aligned in perfect harmony, we are free to live our lives in health and in peace. Only when an imbalance or blockage of energy exists on one or more of these levels does dis-ease manifest.

Thanks to the discoveries of medical science, we have been able to identify the germs, bacteria, and viruses which are linked to many dis-ease states. These organisms, however, while contributing to the manifestation of dis-ease on a physical level, are *not* the primary cause of illness. We are hardly sitting targets for, or "victims" of, some army of invading organisms, against which a healthy immune system is our defense. Rather, as the text which follows attempts to demonstrate, it is primarily a "disruption of consciousness," a misunderstanding of our essential nature as radiant beings of love who are here to serve one another, which is responsible for the dis-harmony which contributes to dis-ease. Only when we dwell in the negative and lose sight of the infinite wisdom and love which are our essential nature do we allow ourselves to be "bent out of shape" by the challenges of life, and create the disharmony and stress which may manifest as dis-ease.

Acquired Immune Deficiency, candida, herpes, and cancer are just a few of the diseases which are on the rise precisely during this crucial period of history when the choices we make as human beings are determining the survival of our species and of our planet. Anyone reading this sentence knows that the ability to wipe out the human race lies in the push of a button. Many of us do not trust the people who have access to that button. The toxins that have polluted our food, air, and water—our means of sustenance—are polluting our bodies and taking their toll. Much of what our parents, forefathers, and foremothers saw as the cornerstone of their existence, the foundation upon which they built their lives, now seems as fragile as the California coastline. When even apple pie mix is removed from the grocer's shelf because it may "cause" cancer, we know we are in trouble. It is no wonder that many of us are sick, or sick with worry. Stress is everywhere. Change is everywhere. All of us are affected by new imbalances on the planet which threaten even the biological means by which we maintain and reproduce ourselves.

Jack Schwarz, an internationally respected teacher and healer, suggests in this book that by resisting change—by stagnating our energy and functioning from a stance of defense and reaction—we affect the functioning of our immune systems, and set the pattern for the rise of dis-ease states. If this is true, the choice of health means the choice to move forward, to adapt and change. We are faced with the ultimate challenge of building the harmony and loving unity necessary to preserve all living things on this planet. More and more of us, rather than giving our power over to political, religious, and medical "authorities" are taking responsibility for creating our individual and collective realities. We are choosing to respond to the unknown with open hearts and minds. We are letting go of fear, blame, and the need to judge others. Through our love and determination we are healing the planet, our neighbors, and ourselves.

All healing begins within. Whatever road to health we choose, all systems, substances, and practitioners merely serve as tools by which we can balance and realign ourselves. By taking responsibility for our health and uniting in love and in harmony, we have the ability to live healthy and joyous lives.

We are all one, united by the motivating force of the Universe, which is Love. All health and healing, both within and without, are created as we accept ourselves and each other as unique and perfect manifestations of this Love. The challenges we face, be they nuclear proliferation or cancer, homophobia or AIDS, present us with constant opportunities to transform ourselves and the planet through love and understanding. "Political" issues, "social" issues, and "gay" issues are illusions; there is but one "human" issue, and that issue is Love. It is from such an understanding that the present work arises.

This book is organized into three parts. The first, which begins with a discussion by Jack Schwarz of the relationship between consciousness and the immune system, offers an overall perspective on both the phenomenon of healing life-threatening illness, and the alignment of mind, body, and spirit which is the essence of the healing process. Through the words of some gifted healers and six magnificent men who are experiencing healing, we can hopefully gain a new understanding of the nature of the healing process.

The second part, which concentrates on the specific case history of AIDS, is filled with information applicable to all healing. Articles on the chakras and conscious recovery, followed by specific meditations for the healing of immune dysfunction, afford us an opportunity to put the principles of psychoimmunity into practice within our own lives. By uniting mind with body, we may transcend dis-ease states.

The final part of this book is dedicated to the trance channelings of Kevin Ryerson, Mediator. Kevin has received international recognition as one of the many special contributors to Shirley MacLaine's growth and spiritual awareness, as evidenced by his frequent appearances in her wonderful books, *Out on a Limb* and *Dancing in the Light*. Kevin both appears in her miniseries, *Out on a Limb*, playing himself, and serves as an artistic consultant on the project. Millions have experienced him either on local or national TV or on the radio, including appearances on "The Merv Griffin Show" and "The Today Show." Information channeled through Kevin forms the basis for *Flower Essences*, a fascinating exploration of the healing essences of plants, and *Gem Elixirs and Vibrational Healing*, Vol. I and II, both by Gurudas.

A fully accredited trance channel, working in the tradition of Edgar Cayce and Jane Roberts (*The Seth Material*), Kevin has developed the ability to set aside his normal waking consciousness so that Spirit Entities who have access to higher consciousness and information can speak through him. As a member of the group of holistic practitioners who generated this book's "Holistic Inquiry into the Prevention and Healing of Acquired Immune Deficiency," Kevin has generously contributed three hitherto unpublished channelings to this volume. The first offers much insight into the nature of the healing process; the second, on "Psychoimmunity," contains new information on human anatomy, biology, and mental functioning which may provide revelations to all readers, lay or professional.

A clear understanding of the terms *"stress"* and *"spirituality,"* as well as the concept of *"mind, body, and spirit,"* is essential to a comprehension of all that follows. With the help of Mr. MacPherson and Mr. Webster, we may define *stress* as "basically any outside force or pressure on a living organism that causes atrophy in its normal physiological function." *Spirituality,* "the acknowledgment of the transcendental nature in the human condition," can empower us to eliminate stress and establish harmony and well-being within ourselves and throughout our environment.

Mind can be understood to relate to the Conscious Mind, the intellectual and personal frame of reference that hopefully enables you to comprehend these words. Mind has the ability to extend both into the past and the future. *Body*, often referred to by John as "the body physical," signifies the vehicle which you have created for your current physical expression on the planet. The body corresponds to the Subconscious Mind, lying just beyond the perimeters of the Conscious Mind, in which feelings and traumatic experiences may be suppressed and stored. All the body can experience is the Now—the right-this-minute reality of the earth plane.

Spirit relates to the Superconscious Mind—the part of your consciousness which extends beyond the physical framework—which contains all of your past thoughts and all of your future potential. This intangible realm of spirit can be accessed by such psi phenomena as past-life recall, meditation, telepathy, near-death experience, and premonition. It is through the dimension of spirit that we are affected by such collective and group pressures as cultural, religious, societal and psychological dynamics. Our spiritual range of awareness extends far beyond the limits of the Conscious Mind. By accessing the awareness of our infinite potential—our spiritual dimension—through such a process as meditation, we remember our true identity as God, and gain the ability to *transcend* physical, mental, and social limitations. Through alignment of mind, body, and spirit, we may transcend dis-ease states and re-establish the harmony and inner peace which is our birthright.

Your current identity on the earth plane as a human personality composed of mind, body, and spirit is but one expression of your *soul*, your ability to have a unique individual expression within the all-encompassing consciousness of Love that is called God. The soul's path almost always includes many physical incarnations, during which time we create countless experiences from which to learn all that is, including everything you are experiencing at this very moment, is an expression of God.

Editing this book has brought me in contact with many brave and loving men and women who are transforming frightening diagnoses of cancer and Acquired Immune Deficiency into a determination to live and enjoy their lives in health and in peace. These human beings are a constant inspiration to me. It is a joy and a privilege to be able to witness anger, rage, blame, and helplessness transformed into what some people with Acquired Immune Deficiency have told me is a "spiritual blessing," a "tremendous opportunity" for both individual and collective healing. I thank them, and all of the contributors to this project, for blessing us with the opportunity to share in their love and their insight.

To all of you who wish to add to the growing sense of harmony and purpose in the Universe, and to my friends who are healing themselves of Acquired Immune Deficiency, I dedicate this book.

—Jason Serinus
Oakland, California
May 1986

PART I

A NEW UNDERSTANDING

CHAPTER 1

CONSCIOUSNESS AND THE IMMUNE SYSTEM

by Jack Schwarz, N.D.

In the past sixty years, humanity has been going through very fast transformations, faster than ever before in human history. Figuratively speaking, we could say that we have gone in sixty years from the wagon wheel to satellites oribiting in space. It should not be so difficult to understand that in our current period of fast-moving evolutionary transformation, all living things, especially human beings, are being affected as never before by the profound changes that have taken place in the physical environment.

In this new era—the so-called communication or information era, with its trends and megatrends—we not only recognize the increased speed with which we are bombarded by information, but also the necessity for an equally fast response. We must develop a capacity to adapt immediately to new situations created by the transformational process.

The human being operating and existing in this world possesses a mind to perceive and transmit, and a body to respond and execute actions. The mind in all its stages seems to be able to give directions to the vehicle, the body, by means of an inherent quality called "consciousness." And the body through its immune system seems able to respond to this direction-giving consciousness.

In the early 1920s a theory was developed to suggest that diseases might be caused predominantly by misdirection or misinterpretation of information perceived by the mind, which then manifested itself as malfunction or disease in the body and its immune system. This theory was named "psychosomatics." As years passed even the most organic and mechanically oriented health practitioners could no longer deny the possibility of truth to be found within this theory. Yet even today, more attention is given to the pathological and organic causes of disease than to the state of emotional and mental consciousness within people afflicted by malfunctioning of the body systems, and in particular the immune system.

Scientists throughout the world perceive this universe to be composed of and exist through *energy*, which they state "cannot be created, nor destroyed, but only transformed from one state into the other with constant change of purpose and qualities to fulfill this purpose." Strangely enough, many or most of these scientists seem to exclude humanity from these universal principles, as if humanity exists somewhere beyond this universe.

How different our lives and our health might be if we would just realize that, because we are an intricate part of this universal system—like a cogwheel in a timepiece—any resistance to change or any attachment to the past as well as to the present stagnates the whole, thereby decreasing our mental, emotional, and physical capacities.

What do some of the experts in immunology have to say about the relationship of "consciousness, mental and emotional states" and how they affect our immune system and health?

Research in immunology shows clearly that when microorganisms attempt to invade the body, the immune reaction of body chemicals secreted by the thymicolymphatic system is a significant element in determining the result. Susceptibility and resistance to infectious diseases seem distinctly linked to stress, tension, and emotional states. The well-known microbiologist Rene Dubos has concluded: "There are many circumstances, some of which are of common occurrence in human medicine, where the physical, chemical, physiological, and probably psychological factors which affect the *host* play far more decisive parts in the causation of disease than does the presence of this or that microorganism."

Possible links between stressful experiences and diseases

are found in the production of stress-responsive adrenal cortical steroid hormones (hydrocortisone), which decrease or suppress immunological responses and hypothalmic regulation of the immune response in the thymus gland and the lymph glands. It has been reported in Russia that by electrical stimulation of a specific region of the hypothalamus, antibody responses are enhanced in animals. Destruction of this region of the brain in animals leads to complete suppression of the primary antibody response, and to prolonged recovery from illness which requires intact immune mechanisms. In experimental animals, removal of the thymus at the time cancer-causing viruses are injected into their bodies increases the death rates and rate of growth of tumors. These studies and others imply the existence of a hormone, probably produced by the pituitary gland, controlled by the hypothalamus. Such a hormone may be related to or the same as the human growth hormone produced by the anterior pituitary gland.

It is important to note that mice subjected to persistent forms of stress show enlargements of the adrenal glands, decreased white blood corpuscle counts, decreased functioning of the spleen, thymus, and lymph glands, and an increased susceptibility to a variety of infectious diseases.

Western society seems to be striving to maintain behavioral patterns and systems based on the average, and finds it extremely difficult to deal with those groups or individuals which are either below or beyond these behavioral patterns and systems. It should be clear that groups or individuals adopting behavioral patterns or life styles not belonging to the average will have to deal with a tremendous amount of pressure, resistance, and stress in order to maintain an individual status in life and to survive. As already mentioned, excessive pressure and stress definitely has a detrimental effect upon the immune system and its interactivity with the endocrine system. Individuals subject to such pressure and stress will be faster subject to diseases. Nor can we presume the average person to be automatically free from deficiencies of the immune system—any excess of stress can cause malfunctioning. The "nonaverage" person might attract this faster because of greater stress.

Treatment that attempts to restore only the pathological organic state, without inclusion of mental and emotional therapies, seems to be a waste of purpose, energy, and human life. In order to prevent deficiencies of the immune system, a much more holistic approach needs to be adapted. Of foremost importance are changes in society leading to greater tolerance of those who choose different life styles than the average.

For individuals afflicted by immune deficiencies, it is advisable to be instructed in and shown methods of self-regulation (voluntary controls) in order to increase resistance levels against invasion by foreign microorganisms. There is a variety of methods for acquiring self-regulation, such as meditative exercises, perceptualization through imagery, and biofeedback, among others.

I recommend reading the book *Beyond Biofeedback* by Dr. Elmer Green and Alyce Green, and my work entitled *Voluntary Controls*, which has many exercises for self-regulation.

CHAPTER 2

A TALK WITH ANTHONY
AND RICHARD

It would make sense that if you come down with a very serious illness, an all-consuming illness such as Acquired Immune Deficiency, the changes you would have to make are just as serious and just as all-consuming. It's incredibly important not to think that what you're gonna do is go on a vitamin program and be fine, or go to an average, run-of-the-mill shrink and talk about your mother and be fine. It's my belief that you have to take the whole holistic health framework, which is your body-mind-spirit, and work on all of it. You have to change almost everything in your life when something this serious has come up, because this is a serious challenge to your life, and it has to be dealt with in just as complete a reaction. I don't want to make it sound like you sort of change your job and you'll be all right, or go take a few vitamins. You have to do everything.

—Anthony

"Anthony" and "Richard" are pseudonyms for two men diagnosed with AIDS whom I interviewed in October 1983. When I first met Anthony at a May 1983 San Francisco meeting of AIDS alternative practitioners, I was convinced that this attractive bright-eyed man might very well become the "victor" over AIDS that he declared himself to be. Our paths have crossed on many occasions since, and we have conducted follow-up interviews in February 1984 and in December 1986 (for *Yoga Journal*).

Although Anthony's road to recovery has not been an easy one—he has had to transcend the stress related to diagnosis, loss of a job, death of his roommate, and countless other factors—he has constantly availed himself of his own inner spiritual resolve and the support of a network of healers. I would often see him on the way to healing groups, where he not only received from others but developed his own facilities as a healer and channel. As of May 1987, he had chosen to distance himself from the dramas of big city living, and was thriving in service to himself and others at a school for disadvantaged and disabled children set up in another country by my first spiritual teacher.

"Richard," who at the time of this interview had declared himself totally healed of AIDS, was introduced to me by our good friend "Paliku." (It was my discovery of Paliku's diagnosis that provided the impetus for the beginnings of this book.) Richard struck me as a willful and very talkative man with the kind of insistent personality that just might be able to get him what he wanted. At the time of our interview, he worked in the downtown financial community of San Francisco during the day, and as a healer and reader the rest of the time. A special part of his life was reserved for playing the clarinet in the San Francisco Lesbian/Gay Freedom Day Marching Band.

Although Richard is no longer with us, I am heartened by the knowledge that my first two friends diagnosed with AIDS, Paliku and Dan Turner, have as of May 1987 each lived with dis-ease for a good five years.

Richard: Before, I heard you saying that you were interviewing two people with AIDS. That doesn't support me, because I really consider that I no longer have AIDS; not that it's in remission, but that it is past. I'm totally well, as well as I was before I had it—*better*, even. I asked someone before the AIDS vigil the other night (November 1983), "Are they going to have anyone speaking who's a victor?" He replied that he had *never* thought of that. I know that people who are into a holistic approach supposedly believe it because we believe that it will work. But even of these people, how many are willing to just step forward and claim that it has worked? It's really much simpler than it sounds.

Jason: How forward have you stepped publicly?

Richard: I have not stepped forward publicly and I'm not willing to use my name in this interview. Because I cannot prove my healing according to the AMA, I feel like any good that I could do would be negated by the fact that I can't prove it. My intention is to serve other people just by word of mouth, and by working with people who have AIDS and supporting them in their healing.

Jason: What about you, Anthony?

Anthony: The reaction that people have to a definite AIDS diagnosis or possible AIDS diagnosis is just too bizarre. It's very uncomfortable, and that's not avoidance on my part, or denial; it's just something that I don't want to deal with in its negative aspects. There's a handful of people who deal with it very well, and I don't have any problem discussing my AIDS with them.

Jason: I was at a party last week, and a man came up to me and said hello, because he had recognized me from one of my room-to-room performances on 5A, the AIDS ward at San Francisco General Hospital. And he said, "Shhh, don't tell anyone here at the party that I have AIDS, or they'll freak out."

Anthony: You immediately become the recipient of sympathy, of anger, of fear. It's too emotionally charged, when it's not necessary—in my case, anyway. If I were in a hospital bed, or if I were not able to perform some of my everyday living activities, I might feel differently. The only way I would feel comfortable coming back to AIDS in a public sense is if someone came up with a test that definitely and conclusively said whether someone had AIDS, and if I then took that test and it came out negative. I originally consented to use my name in the interview because I thought there was more support for my state of health. I thought that more people saw me as being healthy than actually did.

Richard: The first thing a friend and teacher told me, when I began to discuss my AIDS diagnosis with her, was, "Don't tell this to *anyone*. . .except healers." My parents still don't know. It's hard for other people to grasp that it's possible actually to heal something like AIDS.

Jason: Yes, even though I do believe that healing AIDS is possible, I still tend to slip into the mindset that it's somewhere in the future. Those thought forms are incredibly powerful. I had to move away from San Francisco because of all the energy surrounding the illness and people's conception of what a person who has AIDS is going to do. The thought forces of other people are so *incredibly* powerful. The community in general is doing all people diagnosed with AIDS an incredible disservice by seeing them as dying.

Richard: Absolutely! It's true we need to get more federal funding for AIDS research. If we can ever find a medical cure, fine, because a lot of people are never going to take a holistic or metaphysical approach to healing. For their sakes, I'm all for getting the money. But I know what has worked for me.

Every time I tell someone about my illness, I say, "Look, I've got an incredible opportunity that's come my way, and I want to share this with you. I want you to support me in seeing AIDS as that, and if anything else comes to your mind, wipe it out of your mind, because that will not support me." Self-pity is one of the worst things. And pitying someone who has AIDS is the worst thing.

Anthony: I've found that most people with AIDS are looking for pity, and have developed a support network amongst themselves which supports further illness and death. It's supporting that weakness within themselves. It's almost like a cycle that goes downwards...

Richard: Yes!

Anthony: ...and that in turn is supported by the rest of the community—by almost everyone. The few people who really do choose not to lock into that form are almost ostracized.

Richard: "Don't tell me any more or your holistic bullshit." That's a direct quote from my doctor.

Anthony: Just the idea that you are going to be healthy, or in fact that you *are* healthy, regardless of your method of treatment, is not accepted. I had quite a few people think that my initial reaction to my diganosis was in fact manic, because I saw it as an *opportunity*. They kept waiting for me to fall apart and dive into a depression because of my original positive reaction.

Jason: You also had a lot of support around you for healing, didn't you?

Anthony: I kept on getting input that I could be well, and that I shouldn't worry. When I spoke to one of my former lovers in New York, he got excited about me having AIDS. He said — he actually said — that it was *wonderful*. "I could never say this to anybody else, but this is wonderful, because it will just cause you to change so much, and you'll be fine. I'm not worried about you at all." Those were the first things he said.

Jason: So some of the immediate input you got from people you knew was positive?

Anthony: Yeah, it was *all* positive. It was very clear. Most of the people that I know are spiritual people, and their reaction was immediately and clearly: "Oh great, this is gonna be fun! Your life is going to change totally, because what you're doing now with your life is not what you're supposed to be doing. You know it. That's why you've been miserable, that's why you got sick, and this is gonna change it. So don't worry about it and just change." I got that from everyone, from all of my good friends.

Jason: Richard, could you tell us something about the diagnosis, progression, and healing of your illness?

Richard: In the summer of 1982 I was doing some introspection, re-evaluating my whole life as to where it was going. I was doing a lot of affirmations, and I just sort of asked the Universe and God for help. I was putting out that I wanted to deal with whatever it was between me and really going for it 100% and getting in touch with my spiritual life purpose,

which for me is to manifest Christ consciousness and to empower other people to experience that. And I was saying that
my strength is sufficient to handle whatever comes my way,
so please show me whatever is in the way.

I was doing all these other affirmations as well. I got a
transfer to another city, with a promotion and raise, and I
manifested $1,000 to get my car fixed. I even got a new ward-
robe. I came up here and lived in the kind of house I wanted
to. Relationships that were not supporting me dropped out
of my life peacefully, and people who supported me 100% came
into my life.

Along with all those wonderful things, about November
of '82 a lesion appeared on my arm...a purple spot. I didn't
think anything about it. My teacher in Los Angeles was telling me this was a year when you can choose to see things as
opportunities and grasp them. She's made a lot of predictions
in my life that were very accurate, and one of the things that
she told me was that I was going to have a tremendous opportunity come up for me in the health field. I've been active
as a psychic healer for about eight years, and I've learned a
lot of things recently from this teacher.

So when I had this lesion, I said, "What if it's KS?" And
I said, "Well, I don't think it is, but if it is, I'll just get rid of
it." And when the doctor told me that's what it was, I said,
"Okay, fine. Just give me some data because I haven't read anything." I was afraid at that point. I began to process through
a lot of stuff, and realized that what came up for me is that
AIDS has a lot to do with past anger and hurt; with unwill-
ingness to forgive others and to forgive oneself; with when
you feel inwardly that someone has done something bad to
you, you're really blaming yourself for it.

Jason: Did you feel ill when you were first diagnosed?

Richard: No. I was doing a lot of real positive things at the time
that this happened, and I believe that by the time I had the
manifestation of a lesion, and discovered it, I was already on
the road to recovery.

Jason: Did you go through the classic first phase of AIDS, which for some is night sweats, swollen glands...?

Richard: I had swollen glands, but not night sweats. I noticed over the few months previous a lessening of energy. A lot of gay men have swollen lymph nodes. My lymph nodes are way down now. I have plenty of energy, and have no other lesions, and no other AIDS symptoms.

Jason: How were you diagnosed with AIDS and KS?

Richard: They biopsied the lesion. I still have the scar from where they biopsied it. Anyway, I just immediately chose to view my diagnosis as an opportunity. When something like this comes up, it's important to see it as an opportunity and grab it. You can take it and you can win with it. I just decided that AIDS was the greatest opportunity in my life. And it *was*, because it got me to examine my priorities. If your life is lined up, whatever your life purpose is, everything you do will work. Whatever you do will just work. And if you're not, it won't. Nothing will.

Anthony: AIDS was definitely presented to me as an opportunity for growth, a motivation for integration of all my abilities.

Richard: Anthony and I have done a lot of the same things: heavy doses of vitamins, a monotropic diet for a while (where you don't combine proteins with starches, you don't eat fruits with anything else but fruits, etc.). I immediately eliminated all alcohol and red meat.

Jason: Had you read a book that told you all these things to do?

Richard: The lady I work with in L.A. recommended this to me. Also, she suggested that I do colonics. I've heard that's pretty controversial. I think colonics were very beneficial for me. I took a week's vacation from my job and followed Dr. Bernard Jensen's book *Tissue Cleansing through Bowel Management,* and I got a colima board so that I was able to do colonics at home. I did two a day, and I fasted for the week, cleansing myself with the preparation of psyllium seed powder mixed with apple cider vinegar—it sounds awful, I know—and wheat grass juice tablets, coffee enemas, clay water, garlic, etc. And when I started back eating, I chose things that were very cleansing, such as aloe vera juice.

Jason: How soon after you were diagnosed with KS did you begin doing this?

Richard: I made the decision immediately. I had trouble finding a colonic therapist who would take me because of the AIDS thing being communicable, or so they thought. [Ed. note: As long as a colonic hygienist follows minimal sterilization procedures, such as those provided in the "Colonics" section of the Inquiry which follows, there is no cause for concern about the spreading of AIDS through colonic irrigations.] So I realized that I had to save up money and get a colima board, which ran about $200. It took me a couple of months.

    The key to my healing, and the thing I want to say to people with AIDS who've adopted a holistic approach, is: Do what you're doing with your colonics, diets, or whatever, but don't see your wellness as being in the future. You may say, "I'm looking at my lesions. How can I say that I'm well?" You can say it. *Say it.*

    I was meditating on: "I am a whole person." "All my body's cells are filled with radiant life divine." "I am well, I am well, I am well." I would say that in the midst of my regular meditations, and all through the day.

    One day I was meditating, and I was saying, "I am well, I am well." And it came to me that I *am* well. I am! I was sort of meditating while I was walking to lunch, and I saw this thing. . .it was like a cell. . .the body cell of me. It could have been all of my body cells. I saw the cell with a dark thing in the middle which was a nucleus, and I just concentrated on that. All of a sudden, the dark nucleus in the middle of that cell changed from dark to blazing white light, and just filled up the whole cell. And I knew that I was well.

Jason: Have you followed a similar visualization process, Anthony?

Anthony: I was utilizing physical visualization as decribed by the Simontons: your body fighting off the cancer cells as such. I was doing these on my own. And I've used a lot of healing techniques, some of which I no longer use. I vary according to need.

Jason: Did you receive medical validation for your healing of AIDS, Richard?

Richard: No. The doctors say, "There's no diagnosis of AIDS apart from its various symptoms." I have no symptoms. I had a positive biopsy over a year ago. My doctor won't approve me to get the T-cell ratio blood test. He says it's not conclusive, and I'm inclined to agree with him, because the T-cell ratio fluctuates so much from person to person, and in a given individual. My blood looks fine. So do all the other tests I get. I go in every couple of months and we chat and he signs me up for a blood test.

Anthony: Yet the blood test isn't conclusive, because I had a blood test that came out normal, and I still have lesions.

Richard: That's why I'm not willing to say my name. Because I can't prove I'm well by the "real world standards."

Jason: Please tell us your basic story of diagnosis, Anthony.

Anthony: I was diagnosed by biopsy in February or March of 1983. I had lesions, fatigue, night sweats, weight loss—just general poor health. I had originally gone to the hospital with swollen lymph nodes and fatigue, and they told me that I was healthy, and not to worry about it. But they wanted to monitor my lymph nodes for about six months. I said I can damn well monitor my own lymph nodes. I'm not going to come to the hospital to have somebody go "uh huh" on my neck. So I did. Subsequently, I got a little worse, and I had a spot on my foot. So I went to another doctor, and he said, "Oh no. You're not well."

Jason: Was this diagnosis also at the first hospital?

Anthony: No, no! I didn't go back there. I wasn't happy with the treatment. I went to another clinic that has a very large gay practice. That clinic referred me to yet another medical center. They did two biopsies, which came back as positive, which is negative as far as I'm concerned. That's *not* terribly positive, is it? And then I was referred to San Francisco General Hospital, where I'm seen about once a month. I go to the basic AIDS outpatient clinic, and they just take blood tests. At this point, I've gained my weight back, there are no night sweats. . .

Jason: What kind of regimen did you follow?

Anthony: Basically a change in diet patterns. Your basic healthy living. A more balanced diet—something close to a macrobiotic diet, but not as strict. Megavitamins, with stress on antioxidants, vitamin C, vitamins E, A, and the B vitamins for stress. Antioxidants are to free the toxins from the system. There was meditation. No alcohol. No stimulants. Herbal preparations. . . It was clear the illness came about because of change in my direction. I was leading both a spiritual and, quote, "materialistic" life. I was a real estate salesman and manager, and sort of spiritual on the side. I was not well integrated. I realized I was here to work spiritually, metaphysically, psychically, but I couldn't figure out how to make money doing it. Part of that came from being raised at a time when people didn't make money doing that. Even as near as ten years ago, people didn't make money doing those things.

Jason: What were those things you might have done? Tell us something of your past.

Anthony: I was brought up in Manhattan, then Queens, 26 years ago. The only avenue to any sort of philosophical or religious feeling seemingly open to me then was the priesthood.

I explored that for a while. I even thought of becoming a monk. And then I went from organized religion to spirituality. AIDS gave me the kick to balance and integrate my life. The message was: "Okay, fine. If you're not going to do what you're supposed to do, we'll let you leave. You can go now. Or you can stay and do what you're supposed to do."

When I was first diagnosed, I didn't have a problem with the possibility of dying. My big decision, and my problem, was: "Alright. Are you going to stay, or are you going to go?" I've had a number of near-death experiences before. I drowned once, became very ill a couple of times—and this was another "stay or go; come on, decide" situation.

Jason: For both of you, your consciousness around life and death, and your ability to decide which path to follow, is very clear. It sounded earlier, Anthony, as though you believe that most people with AIDS are not that conscious of their ability to make a choice.

Anthony: No, no they're not. When I was asking myself which to choose, I asked for some kind of sign or affirmation about which way I was supposed to go. And it became very, very clear, because I was just *overcome* with indications that there were things I was supposed to do, changes I was supposed to make. This was evidenced by my own spiritual awakening.

Richard: Approximately 100% of the people on this planet walk around not aware that they have made a *choice* to live. They have chosen to live, and at some point they give up on that choice. I realized last summer that if I choose to line up my life around my spiritual life purpose, then everything in my life will simply work; and if it isn't lined up with my higher purpose, nothing will work. It's that simple. And for me, my life purpose is spiritual. My work is manifesting Christ consciousness, healing, loving and unity, empowering others to experience their own godliness, lovingness, and magnificence. This lifetime my mission is to spread joy, to teach, to heal, and to forgive. I am able to work in the business district by day and go home and do healings or readings or whatever at night.

It's appropriate for me to do both. And I support Anthony in his decision to leave his old world entirely.

Anthony: I could not possibly continue to work as before, not only because I was too ill, but because I was too conscious all the time. And it kept getting worse and worse and worse. I was just too overly conscious of the ridiculousness of what I was doing. It's necessary for the running of the planet—everybody has to do something—the whole thing is very valid. But me balancing books, ordering employees about, and looking neat in a little suit and perfect hair—I couldn't deal with it any longer.

Jason: What I'm hearing is that for both of you, AIDS has been a chance to integrate and change directions.

Richard: I don't think it's any accident that I moved to San Francisco and got diagnosed with KS two months later. I was meant to be here.

Anthony: The few people I do know who are getting better have had to make total life style changes in *everything* that they do.

Jason: What do you see as your life direction, Anthony?

Anthony: I'm becoming more involved in healing, various methods of healing utilizing vibrational remedies, flower essences, aroma therapy, gem therapy. . .I'm considering going into business, dealing with healing gemstones. I'm doing some channeling. I'm channeling a book now. Much to my surprise, it just came through. I was just sitting down writing and it came through, by some combination of clairvoyance and automatic writing. Two days later a publisher called me and said he would publish it. So my work involves consultation, healing of the mind, body, and spirit. Mostly focusing on vibrational remedies seems to be my direction. And that includes trance work.

Jason: Has the transition, and your healing, been difficult for you, Anthony?

Anthony: It varies between being incredibly exhilirating, because I'm doing new things and rediscovering things that I thought I wanted to do as a child—you can imagine the excitement—and incredibly difficult. After all, this is something I'm doing in a period of crisis. When I was first diagnosed, I was just too sick to work, or to do much of anything. My experience goes back and forth—it's extremes. It is at times apparently difficult, and then at other times remarkably easy.

The only way I got through the not-having-money problem was knowing that in a reasonable amount of time I would, because I was healing and going back to work. If I thought it was a dead end, and if you attach yourself to the idea that you're going to live on public support for the remaining three or four years of your life [Ed. note: People with AIDS and other debilitating diseases often receive public assistance and social security when they can no longer work], it can be a terribly depressing situation. I can't say how one would get out of it.

Jason: But you never attached yourself to that?

Anthony: No, public support is a temporary situation. I needed not to work for a short amount of time—I couldn't. That involved the difficulties of living on a little bit of money. But I was getting other things done at the same time. I was going through a lot of internal changes, questioning my entire life. I tackled what I'm doing for a living, what sort of person I am, where I'm going to live, and what sort of people I'm going to have around me.

Jason: What brought you to a holistic approach, Anthony?

Anthony: That's basically my philosophy to begin with. And considering they didn't know anything about AIDS at all, and still know very little, it was rather foolish to be experimented on.

Jason: Richard, you had a teacher with whom you remained connected after moving to San Francisco, and she gave you direction.

Richard: I only knew my teacher for perhaps four months when I was first diagnosed. She was one of the things that came into my life among all the other positive things.

Anthony: My information came from, and always comes from, all over. I just asked questions, and the answers came. When I had medical problems, there was a homeopath, a naturopath, someone around to offer assistance. When I had spiritual questions, the spiritual answers came from various people, or from signs. And since I decided that I needed support, I found those people, and those people found me. The people around you are a good reflection of where you are.

Jason: Both of you were willing to stop, to question what you were told, and to make decisions without anyone in a traditional position of medical authority supporting you.

Richard: Well, it's either do that or get ready to die.

Anthony: Even with holistic treatments, you have to be very much in touch with yourself.

Richard: What's right for somebody is not right for somebody else.

Anthony: I was presented with many different programs at different times, and I've had to sift through them all, pulling out what is best for me. In holistic treatment, people should realize it's just slightly different angles on the same path. The things that are always going to be in common include cleansing, a change of diet, eliminating chemicals, getting to some level of purity, and something along the lines of meditation, visualization, affirmation. There has to be emotional, psychological, and physical change. You could do biofeedback if you're not into meditation, or you could tack affirmations onto your refrigerator. People should keep in their mind that all these things are together. It's not just 25 people around them giving them different programs; it is the *same* program. Don't separate them all up, because then you'll get confused. Just calmly pick up the information that's being offered, and look inside. Try some things, and see how they feel.

Richard: Some approaches are mutually exclusive. That doesn't mean that they invalidate each other. For example, if you're doing macrobiotics, you don't take vitamins. You have to look at each approach as a whole thing. The macrobiotic approach as a whole works.

Jason: One could do macrobiotics, and acupuncture, and ayurvedic herbs—those would go together.

Anthony: Or you could take the macrobiotic diet *and* do your megavitamins. Be eclectic. You have to pull aspects out of whatever systems are right for you.

Richard: The process immediately makes you more introspective. If you just open yourself to the various forms of information and just stay tuned to what comes to you, your inner self will tell you what's right for you.

Jason: Do you feel there's some kind of support network growing for this holistic approach? Or do people mainly have to rely upon themselves when they are diagnosed?

Anthony: I think this decision has to start *within* the individual. Organized holistic support groups do not yet exist. Support exists in New York and San Francisco; once you are firm in your conviction, you find yourself in that support group. But it's not organized. It's just something that you attract to yourself. You may have to change a great deal of your environment, because your old environment is part of what created the disease state. You may have to stop looking for support in your old environment.

Richard: Right. If you just artificially change something in a state of panic, you're still operating out of the same fear and negativity that created the disease in the first place. So whatever you do probably won't be very effective. You have to trust yourself, and come from a conscious decision to live.

Jason: I'm hearing from both of you: "Slow down, don't panic! Stop, look, and examine."

Anthony: Absolutely. One-on-one support does exist. And organizational support will exist when people are willing to accept the fact that it's possible to be well.

I founded an organization, Life Support, to provide the kind of support needed for people pursuing an alternative path. And I found there was not enough call or support for it, both from the medical community and the patients. That may change, but when I started the organization in the spring of '83, the time was not right. Healing had not yet been accepted as a possibility. It's taken a while for people to get over the initial shock of the AIDS phenomenon.

Richard: If nothing else, when people get hopeless enough, when they've tried a lot of things and nothing works, sooner or later they'll start listening to alternative information.

[Ed. note: In San Francisco at least, many large symposia on alternative methods of healing AIDS and other life-threatening diseases are frequently held, sponsored by health food stores and AIDS organizations. A referral system of alternative practitioners working with people diagnosed with AIDS and ARC has been set up by the San Francisco AIDS Alternative Healing Project. Teachers such as Louise Hay, Sally Fisher, Elisabeth Kübler-Ross, Irene Smith, Jack Schwarz, and myself (see Resources section) present programs around the country. And an international network of AIDS alternative healing organizations and practitioners is developing.]

Jason: Of course, neither of you came out of a sense of hopelessness. For both of you, this disease has been empowering.

Richard: Oh, absolutely! It's the best thing that ever happened to me. AIDS is the biggest *gift* of my whole life. And it's this wonderful opportunity to use all the healing energy I've devoted to other people on myself.

Jason: What, Richard, has made you a survivor?

Richard: I define willingness as the awareness of the power to choose. If you are willing to come from being well, then you are aware that you have the power to choose that for yourself.

Jason: And where did you get the idea that you have the power to choose?

Richard: First of all, I have been motivated by a desire to live. And I had the feeling when I was diagnosed that there was something more to my life—that I wasn't finished with it.

Anthony: I got the idea that I have the power to choose life and death basically from my spiritual background. I view death as something that we do, that our souls do consciously in order to change. When we have exhausted what is best for us to do in this lifetime, we make a dramatic change by dying and being re-introduced to a different set of circumstances. It would be next to impossible to introduce every set of circumstances into one lifetime. We are all just here to experience, to learn, and to grow—the idea of the soul journey. Given what things are like here, it would be difficult to learn everything that you have to learn in one lifetime.

Jason: What do you think made you a survivor, Anthony?

Anthony: There's a basic rebellious personality trait of mine that manifests as if you say, "Do it," I'll say "No!"; if you say "Don't do it," I say "Yes!" That has helped me a lot in this illness. I try to do things differently, and that's just basic to my personality.

Coming upon the decision as to whether or not I was supposed to be alive or not was the main crisis. It did occur to me that AIDS and dying were fine and almost a gift, and I was just supposed to go on my way to my next lifetime—I do believe in reincarnation. But after I decided that I was supposed to be here (and there were many, many signs that I was supposed to be here), I realized that I had to do different things—that I had to change my entire life.

Richard: Anthony talks of his religious background, which in time translated into his current spiritual perspective. I first got into healing eight years ago, when something told me to put my hand on the face of a person who had a toothache. The toothache went away in five minutes. I don't know where that came from. But I was led to this ability, and I was told to be of assistance to others. AIDS is such an opportunity to help others.

Jason: The practitioners and healers who put together the information in the Inquiry of this book believe that stress is the key critical factor in determining whether or not the AIDS virus will take hold of someone after it enters the system. You told me, Anthony, that when you get into stressful situations, your healing process slows down.

Anthony: As a matter of fact, at one point it reversed. My lesions were going away, and I was in a stressful situation, which included problems with my disability checks, securing a place to live, my belongings, and my truck, and there was a marked change in my physical state.

Richard: Yes. I had been in a real stressful period in every area of my life recently when I noticed another little spot on my arm, and I said, "Oh, God!" I realized that I was attached to being right about having healed myself, and I wasn't seeing this new spot as an opportunity, until I finally turned it around and discovered it was just a scratch. But it gave me a good opportunity to re-examine and ask, "Are you sure you're on the right path?" and the answer I got was "YES!"

Anthony: I think that everyone, healthy or not healthy, should be monitoring their body a little better. I think you can detect and deal with AIDS before you're up in a hospital bed.

Jason: But, of course, you didn't.

Anthony: I thought there was something wrong before I had the "classic symptoms," and I went to a doctor and he told me I was healthy and fine and not to worry about it—and I mistakenly took his word for it. It took six or nine months before

I went back again with one spot on my foot, and said, "There *is* something wrong, I *know* there's something wrong. What is wrong here?" It was a weakness in me that decided to believe in the doctor. It was a psychological relief valve: "Oh, okay, the doctor says I'm fine."

I see a lot of people who are not well, who are just not healthy, and they go to the doctor and the doctor tells them that they don't have AIDS, and they think they're fine. That's ridiculous! You can't just wait for a diagnosis. Allopathic medicine gives you a diagnosis when there are severe symptoms present, and then is *not* the time. Your body knows. I knew when I was sick, and the doctor told me, "No." If you feel like you're ill, and you think there is something wrong, that's when you have to follow through.

Jason: And listen to your own inner voice.

Anthony: Right. Most people I know who are concerned about AIDS are concerned because they're not feeling well. And when the doctor tells them that they don't have AIDS, they let themselves go on not feeling well. They think, "Okay, it's fine. I can *not* feel well, but I won't die," which is ridiculous.

Jason: Because they are off balance, and their dis-ease is a message that something's fundamentally off balance in their life.

Anthony: Right. Had I started acting when I first visited the doctor, this would've been much easier for me, because I wouldn't have had to deal with a health crisis at all. Or I don't believe I would have. You can't say for sure.

Jason: Maybe the whole thing happened to enable you to go through all the incredible changes you're going through now. Has your work become more concretized in terms of reaching out with your spiritual work?

Anthony: Yes, much. I have spiritualized my life. I'm going more towards "right living." Another thing that's incredibly important is that if you are going to make a decision, are leaning towards it, or have already decided that you can make the necessary changes to get better, you have to insulate yourself *against* the AIDS mainstream. You have to insulate yourself against rap groups, *against* other AIDS patients. *Don't* read the newspapers, because all you'll get is negative feedback. It's entirely negative in the way of a decision to get better. They can be very helpful if you're thinking that you will probably be sick and die in three years, or if in fact you welcome death. That's fine. That's okay. But if you've made the other decision, the decision to live, you're not gonna get that support anywhere from the mainstream.

Jason: Well, there are groups like the Shanti Project (not connected with Elisabeth Kübler-Ross's organization, Shanti Nilaya), which counsels people coping with AIDS and other life-threatening diseases, which have a broad base of support within the community. I met some of Shanti's volunteer counselors at one of their in-house briefing sessions, and discovered that many of them are discouraged and turned off by allopathic medical treament of AIDS. I think many of these counselors are looking for ways to share alternative information with their clients, but are hesitant to push their holistic advice on them.

That briefing was a very heavy experience. We kept on hearing one account after another of the horrors and tribulations of chemotherapy and experimental drugs, until I could no longer stand the mounting despair and gloom in the room. Being who I am, I stood up, begged the speaker's pardon for interrupting him, and shared my feelings with the counselors present. My assertion that a diagnosis of AIDS does not imply an inevitable progression from dis-ease to dis-ease, from milder forms of chemotherapy to more drastic ones to an inevitable and painful death, was met with relief and gratitude by those present—it transformed the feeling in the room. Thank goodness the final medical speaker never showed up, and that Jean Sayre-Adams of the Alternative Therapies Unit at San Francisco General arrived early. Everyone welcomed her presentation on healing with open hearts and arms.

Anthony: Yeah, and I think that's rare. I have yet to meet any-one in or through Shanti who is thoroughly committed to someone being able to take charge and get better. I haven't found *one*. I found a number who *said* that they are, and who feel that holistic methods are fine; but I think that's lip service or intellectualizing, and I can tell intellectualizing from what's in the heart.

Jason: I have heard many stories of people deciding to attend rap groups, only to discover that those present were all talk-ing about how they could forestall dying, rather than how they could go about healing themselves and go on living. The thought form that people diagnosed with AIDS will eventu-ally die from the dis-ease, whether articulated or not, certainly affects the nature of any counseling/support relationship. I can only pray that more individuals working with people diag-nosed with AIDS or ARC will allow themselves to explore the possibility that healing this dis-ease *and* remaining in the body is possible.

The Shanti Project has changed its emphasis to support-ing people to *live* with dignity. This signals a fundamental change in consciousness, and a move towards accepting the reality that people can heal themselves of AIDS. I've heard many wonderful stories of the total and unconditional love and support between Shanti counselors and their clients. Despite our reservations, I must say that I respect and am grateful for the commitment and love of the staff and of the organization. Working with people facing life-threatening illness requires a tremendous amount of love, compassion, and selfless serv-ice. The extent to which we all have opened our hearts to peo-ple who are coping with AIDS is extraordinary.

I'm wondering if either of you has any additional thoughts you'd like to share?

Richard: I want to say again that if someone is diagnosed with AIDS, you have to *stop* and look at your whole life rationally. Try to see the opportunity in it. Slow down, get in touch with yourself through whatever works for you, and get in touch with what your life purpose is—what you're here for. Line yourself up with that, and really allow your own inner direction to come forth. When you avail yourself of treatment, don't come from the place of "I'm doing this because I hope I'll get rid of it, I hope I'll get rid of it" in a state of panic. Healing happens just like a snap of the fingers. Wellness happens *in the present*, because all there ever is, is present.

Jason: So "wellness" is a decision that one makes.

Richard: And it's in the present. If your wellness is in the future, it's going to stay in the future. Ten years from now, it will still be in the future.

Anthony: When you go into your period of thinking about what you're going to do, it's very easy for a lot of people to go into seclusion and do their introspection in a dark, almost morbid kind of way: "Oh, I've got to stop work, and...let me think...I've got to be introspective. I read it in this book. I have to sit down right now and I have to think about what I'm all about." For some people, that may be right. But for others, it might be best to do your introspection in an atmosphere that re-affirms your joy of life.

Instead of taking time off and being in your apartment and being introspective, you can take a vacation. Go do something. Go buy a car. Do something new! Stimulate your life, and re-affirm that you *want* to be here. Become more in touch with what you really enjoy about being here.

Richard: It may sound like a cliché, but you've got to learn to love yourself. Louise Hay has just made a meditation tape for AIDS people in which you visualize yourself as a little boy not getting enough love, and then looking at that little boy and saying, "I love you." A counselor friend of mine believes that a lot of AIDS people really want a loving relationship, but what they're doing instead is going out to the bars, and places where that's probably not going to happen. And when that doesn't happen for them, they get to feel rejected, that they're not worthy of having a relationship. It just leads to an incredible amount of self-loathing and self-resentment, which is that stress of the self-against-the-self which can be so critical in determining whether or not you'll develop AIDS.

Editor's Note: For a good two years after this interview, Richard lived a healthy and full life convinced that he had totally healed himself of AIDS. During this time period, he became the drum major of the San Francisco Lesbian / Gay Freedom Day Marching Band. One of his most applauded acts occurred at one of the annual Lesbian / Gay Freedom Day Parades, where he directed the band to play a glorious triumphal march in front of a bunch of bullhorn-toting Fundamentalists, thereby succeeding in completely drowning them out.

In the autumn of 1985, Richard re-experienced the symptoms of AIDS. Despite renewed attempts to heal himself, he died (left his body) in August, 1986.

In retrospect, it is clear that Richard had succeeded in rendering the AIDS virus into a dormant state, only to have it resurface during heightened periods of stress. His story is similar to that of William Calderon, whose smiling face graced the March / April 1985 cover of *New Realities* magazine. William courageously declared that he had achieved the "first complete recovery of AIDS," only to leave us a year later on May 10, 1986.

When William Calderon first visited his physician, the brilliant Richard Shames, M.D., he was a very ill man with KS lesions all over his arms, legs, chest, and back, as well as internally in his rectum and esophagus. By the time of his *New Realities* cover story, William had so succeeded in restoring his immune system that, according to Richard Shames, "All his lesions were gone. That he was in remission was beyond a doubt. That he was cured seemed a real possibility."

After the publication of his interview, William began a non-stop schedule of serving others through speaking, interviews, facilitation groups at the Center for Attitudinal Healing (See Resources), and so forth. Often his phone would ring in the middle of the night, revealing the voice of a fearful man just diagnosed with AIDS and desperate for support. Despite repeated warnings from his physician to slow down and eliminate stress, William continued his "immune-suppressing" regimen of working non-stop for the healing of his brothers. The stress of all this, feels Shames, was the cause of the resurfacing of the AIDS virus and of his death.

The death of these beautiful men in no way shakes my faith in the ability of people diagnosed with AIDS not only to render the AIDS virus into a dormant state but to heal themselves totally. It does, however, underscore the truth behind the assertion of The Holistic Group in Chapter 8 which follows that heightened degrees of internal and external *stress* lie at the root of, not only AIDS, but *all* dis-ease. I am certain that, had each of these men gotten to the root of their emotional and spiritual dis-ease which had manifested physically as AIDS, they would still be with us in their bodies today.

Healing AIDS requires a 100% commitment to transformation. Living not only with but beyond such a life-threatening dis-ease demands more than simply detoxifying and rebuilding the body, fighting the virus and restoring the immune system; it asks that we learn to unconditionally love ourselves.

We are all engaged in healing, both individually and as a human species; we are all learning to love ourselves. May we learn from the examples of these brave men, and serve ourselves and our neighbors with equal devotion.

I strongly recommend the July / August 1987 *Yoga Journal* article, co-authored by Susan Jacobs with myself, which further develops these ideas, and contains further word from Anthony.

CHAPTER 3

THE VITAL ROOTS OF IMMUNITY

by Paul Lee, Ph.D.

My interest in herbs and the immune system began with a book written by my teacher at Harvard—Paul Tillich. The book was entitled *The Courage to Be*. Tillich traces the history of vital self-affirmation from the early Greeks (Homer) to the modern period, and discusses the various notions of anxiety that each period faced: the anxiety of fate and death (the ancient period), the anxiety of guilt and condemnation (the Reformation period), and the anxiety of meaninglessness and emptiness (the modern period).

The basis of his discussion is an old Greek word which he translated as the courage to be—*thymós*. It is a word frequently used in the *Iliad* of Homer, and it means "courage," "vitality," or "spirit," in the sense of biological spirit, as in a spirited horse.

Tillich wonders about this measure of biological spirit meted out to everyone, some receiving an enormous endowment, others less, as though it were central to the riddle of inequality. Why do some have the courage to surmount any of life's adversities while others are crushed by them? This is the mystery of the courage to be. It is the old question of Hamlet, "to take arms against a sea of troubles, and by opposing end them."

Tillich's book touched a nerve in Americans. Even though it is a difficult book to read, full of philosophical ideas strange to most readers, it has gone into repeated printings.

It touched a nerve because of the American difficulty with

affirmation of self. We don't know who we are, or we flee from finding out, seeking every escape possible, from alcohol to drugs to neurosis. Life does us in. We fail to muster the reserves to cope.

With Tillich's discussion in mind, I discovered two subsequent derivatives of the word *thymós*, words that name an herb and a gland. The herb is *Thymus vulgaris*, popularly known as the herb thyme, and the gland is the thymus, the master organ of the immune system, located just below the cleft in the neckbone.

I began to appreciate how the herb and the gland carried through Tillich's discussion of vitality and courage. The herb has always been associated with courage and is thought to confer courage, partly as an implication of its germicidal and disinfectant properties. It enhances and protects life—in other words, augments courage—because it defends against germs and pathogens, whatever would defeat life by causing disease and illness.

The thymus gland is the organ of courage. It is the basis for the dynamics of vital self-affirmation as the center of our immune system. The thymus gland *is* our vital center. Therefore, it is the appropriate place to tap when we confess our sin and guilt as in the Roman Catholic practice, *mea culpa*.

I was able to put herbology and immunology together on top of Tillich's courage to be, as though he had written the philosophical/theological basis for the two fields. It is extraordinary to think that herbalism was about to be revived and the thymus gland only then discovered in terms of its function and structure when Tillich wrote his book, in the early 1950s.

Now, in the 1980s, the immune system is the hottest topic in the medical sciences, tantamount to an information explosion, where even researchers in the field are lost in the mass of detail. The herb renaissance is clearly upon us in terms of the recovery of the botanical basis of health care, as evidenced by the remarkable growth of the herb industry and the increasing interest in herbal products by the health consumer.

The revival of herbal health care, however, has not occurred within the ranks of professional health care training and practice. Instead, there is a deep-seated prejudice against herbs as something left behind by the advance of modern medical health care and the triumph of synthetic drugs.

Here is what happened. In 1828, a German chemist by the name of Woehler artifically synthesized urea, the nitrogen waste part of urine. He made urea without a kidney, by heating up ammonium cynanate, which he could get from *inorganic* substances. At a certain temperature, he was able to simulate (artificially synthesize) an organic substance.

Woehler's experiment heralded the origins of biochemistry. It was now possible to isolate the so-called active constituent of a medicinal herb, determine its chemical structure, and then derive that same chemical from inorganic sources through artificial synthesis. Medicinal herbs were *supplanted* by synthetic drugs. Modern industrial medicine and health care superseded traditional herbal medicine, which fell into neglect, especially the more industrialized the society. In industrial society, factories are called plants.

This trend became overwhelming. The trend in the history of science is called physicalism. It is the reduction of all entities to their physical and chemical constituents. The view that was refuted—and with it, medicinal herbs—was vitalism. Vitalism was the defense of the integrity of organic entities and their *irreducibility*. As chemicals are chemicals, regardless of their context, it was an indefensible argument, especially in a physicalistically determined advancing industrial society. Herbs were rejected as the botanical basis of health care.

This trend has now peaked. The realm of herbs is being rediscovered, and sooner or later, even the medical, nursing, pharmacy, and nutrition professions will reincorporate medicinal herbs into the curriculum of health professional training.

So, health consumers are left to their own devices in attempting to find out what herb is good for what, where that stupid slogan of the health professional still lurks in the precincts: "Whoever self-medicates has a fool for a doctor."

This historical state of affairs will have a short term, the more the word gets out that there is an herb good for whatever ails you. But it is the context in which those of us who are responsible for advocating the use of herbs have to make our pitch. I, for one, am tired of the grimace on the face of a health professional when I talk about herbs being good for the immune system. It is time they sat up and listened.

But what can you do when even vitamin C is a controversial topic in the treatment of AIDS? You do everything possible to get the information out anyhow and mark time waiting for the day when all Americans wake up to what is growing under their noses for their benefit and use. It is my prediction that herbs will re-enter professional health care under the auspices of immunology and the herbs good for the immune system will herald the return of herbs generally.

It is now the case that converging lines of international research on immunostimulating herbs confirm this prediction. Germany, Russia, China, France, and Japan all have teams engaged in determining the chemical constituents of medicinal herbs that augment human immunity. A growing repertoire of herbs are now identified according to their immune-enhancing potential. It is important for the American health consumer to know this information and to begin using the herbs that increase and defend immunity to illness and disease, especially so in the case of those who suffer from immune deficiencies. AIDS is the tip of the iceberg in terms of immune diseases, a tragic and awesome tip, and one that has alerted everyone to the necessity of a healthy immune system.

What follows is a discussion of herbs that are now known to influence the immune system, and the country in which research is being conducted. Special attention is given to *echinacea* as the herb of choice for treating immune deficiency. [Ed. note: See Chapter 12.]

Early research on herbs that stimulate the immune system was done in Russia by I. I. Brekhman of Vladivostok. He uses the term "adaptogen" to talk about the facility of adaptation to stress, the increase of stamina and endurance, as well as concentration and performance, based on extensive testing done on Olympic athletes and astronauts, who uniformly functioned better when given herbs with adaptogenic properties, conferring what is called "nonspecific resistance" — namely, immune enhancement. Ginseng and *eleutherococcus senticosus* (popularly known as Siberian or Eleuthero ginseng, although it is not ginseng) are the herbs of choice in Russian research.

In China, the herbs of choice are *Astragalus* and *Ligustrum*, although there is a host of Chinese herbs that could be considered immune-enhancing. Dr. Sun Yan, of Beijing, conducted strict Western scientific analysis of these herbs at the University of Texas Medical School at Houston, on a three-year grant, with excellent results. In fact, Dr. Baldwin Tom, an immunologist, who was part of the research team, has stated, "In the next ten years the cancer field and the biological response modifier field (immune enhancement) are going to really explode, and within that explosion will be herbal medicine" (*Medical Tribune*, March 28, 1984).

In France, remarkable research and product development on herbs that enhance immunity is being done by Dr. Jacques Vernin, president of the Vernin Laboratories.

In Germany, extensive research has been done by Dr. H. Wagner at the University of Munich, investigating the chemical properties of herbs that stimulate immunity. A new therapy has developed in Germany based on this work, known as *umstimmungstherapie*, namely, *retuning* the immune system. *Echinacea* is the herb of choice for this therapy and the products developed for it, as well as *Aristolochia, Thuja, Baptisia*, etc. The list numbers some twenty herbs.

In the United States, the Platonic Academy of Herbal Studies, in Santa Cruz, California, is developing herbal immune programs for health care.

It is important to know that certain foods, minerals, amino acids, vitamins, and herbs, all considered as nutritional supplements, can become part of an immune-enhancement program. Anyone suffering from AIDS or at risk in terms of AIDS would do well to familiarize themselves with such a program and implement it into their health care regimen.

It is hoped that in the next decade immune enhancement will become the catchword in American health care and not immune deficiency. The faster the reception of medicinal herbs and their reintegration into modern health care training and practice, the sooner this will come about.

Reviving the Mithridate

There is a 2,000-year tradition in the West of an herbal formula to enhance immunity to poisons. This tradition bears the name of an ancient king of Asia Minor. Mithridates Eupator VI gave the name "mithridate" to an herbal combination he concocted with the help of his court physician, Krateuas. There are recipes that are extant, one at the University of Strasbourg, dating from the 18th century.

Mithradatism is the practice of the form of immunization through herbs.

A review of the new botanical basis for immunization is now in the planning stages, with a view toward correlating the ancient recipes with the modern ones. This is now possible through THEOREMA, a computer data base of ancient and historical recipes, at the University of Liege. *Aristolochia*, for instance, a main herb in the Mithridate, is now being used in *umstimmungstherapie*.

It is possible to posit "an herb code in the immune memory of DNA" as an heuristic notion for exploring herbs for their immune-enhancing factors and the susceptibility of various organ systems, with the immune system as a basic model, for herbal health care. The odd linguistic connection between *Thymus vulgaris* and the thymus gland provides a conceptual basis for such a consideration. As a potent germicidal and disinfectant, *Thymus v.* is an obvious immune enhancer.

In this way, immunology can be utilized, along with molecular biology, as a new conceptual foundation for a revived science of herbology and a restoration of *materia medica* as an important subject matter for health professionals with a new appreciation for the botanical basis of health care.

For further information, and an herbal formula for psychoimmunity, please contact Paul Lee directly (see Resources Section).

CHAPTER 4

MY WORK WITH PEOPLE WITH ACQUIRED IMMUNE DEFICIENCY

by Elisabeth Kübler-Ross, M.D.

The workshops we have been doing with AIDS patients were really initiated when we realized that not only people, but a lot of institutions reject AIDS patients—not only hospitals, but even hospices and funeral parlors. We have always had AIDS patients in our other workshops; we just had so many AIDS patients that we couldn't handle it, so we squeezed in an extra workshop at Wildwood Resort in Northern California just for the AIDS patients who could not attend our regular scheduled LDT (Life, Death, and Transition) Workshops.

I think that what impresses me the most is the common denominator of all these people—it's a total feeling of not only confusion about their whole identity, but a lot of guilt, shame, fear, isolation, and rejection—about ten times more than our average workshop population. Nonetheless, I find that we are able to teach them how to learn to accept themselves and love themselves. That's the hardest thing for these patients to learn. Anytime you are full of self-hate, or negativity as we call it— "fear shame guilt" which are really the only enemies of man— you *cannot possibly* become whole, no matter what you do to your physical body.

So we decided to work with these people, not only with the physical quadrant but with the emotional quadrant, to get them back to natural emotions. The agony and pain those people share is absolutely overwhelming. I have never in my life heard so many dramatic stories of rejection and isolation. And we find that the few who have a support system, such as a partner who really stands by them in spite of the disease, do much better than those who are rejected and don't have a support system.

At the end of one of my LDT workshops—one man was beaming through the whole workshop—I asked this man what made him look so happy, knowing the fact that he was imminently dying. He replied that he had learned for the first time, *because* of his illness, what unconditional love is all about. He had called his parents in North Carolina during his hospitalization and told them that he was in a hospital in San Francisco with cancer. He didn't dare to tell them that he had AIDS. And he told us that he had felt the necessity to go back and say goodbye to them and tell them once more that all the significant moments in his life had to do with them, whom he had previously rejected because of their conservative kind of background. It seems that his parents had been looking forward to his visit, in spite of the fact that he hadn't seen them or communicated with them for many years.

As he approached the log cabin where they lived, he was petrified of seeing them come out on the porch, because he was afraid that if his mother would see his face, her outstretched arms would drop down and she would not even be able to touch him. He had horribly visible lesions, a purple nose, and holes in his cheeks. For most people, seeing him would be very repulsive. His Mom came out with her arms outstretched, still wearing the same apron that she wore when he left her years and years ago, and the closer she got the more panicky he became—until finally she reached him, and put her arms around him, and his cheeks on her cheeks, and whispered in his ear, "It's okay, son, we know that you have AIDS, but it's okay with us."

Everybody was crying. He spent the weekend there, and then returned to his home in San Francisco to attend the workshop to share this whole thing with us. And that experience touched probably more of the people attending the workshop than any lecturing or experimental work we could have done with them; just to know that there are people who know what Unconditional Love is all about.

And I think that if people accept those people with AIDS in workshops like our LDT workshop, real change can occur. The first day nobody wanted to sit with him, the next day more and more people sat next to this man during the meals, and then the last day everybody hugged the AIDS patient and were no longer afraid of being contagious. These people with AIDS have really enriched the lives of our workshop patients, and helped us all to grow enormously.

CHAPTER 5

A TALK WITH CHUCK MORRIS AND TOM CHAUDOIN

Participants in Elisabeth Kübler-Ross's
Life, Death and Transition Workshop
for People with Acquired Immune Deficiency

When Charles Lee (Chuck) Morris, former publisher of the San Francisco gay-oriented newspaper *Sentinel USA,* and himself a man with AIDS, participated in one of Dr. Elisabeth Kübler-Ross's five-day Life, Death and Transition (LDT) workshops, he was so convinced of the value of the experience that he asked Dr. Kübler-Ross if she could devote some time specifically to people with AIDS. The result was a three-day LDT workshop, held November 2-4, 1983, in the Russian River area north of San Francisco. Thanks to the dedication and generosity of the San Francisco AIDS Fund and the staff at Wildwood Ranch/Resort, and the contributions of many individuals and businesses, tuition, food, and transportation were offered free to all AIDS attendees in need of assistance. Three days after returning from the workshop, participants Chuck Morris and Tom Chaudoin met with me to discuss their experiences. A follow-up interview was held with Tom in January 1984.

Chuck explains that his first LDT workshop in San Diego "was such an uplifting experience...one of the greatest I've ever had in my life...and it helped me tremendously." In the middle of that workshop, knowing that the time Elisabeth was booked up perhaps two years in advance, he asked her if she might come up to the Bay Area to spend either an afternoon or evening with people with AIDS. Her response was not only an emphatic "Yes!" but the commitment of her staff to a three-day workshop, with Kübler-Ross leading and facilitating the work on the final day.

Chuck had experienced over three years of AIDS-related illnesses and crises by the time the workshop was held. He experienced his first AIDS symptoms in the spring of 1980, but was not officially diagnosed as having the disease until May 1982, when the term AIDS was coined to describe his condition.

Tom Chaudoin, an artist with a strong interest in metaphysics, taught art in public schools in Indiana and Arizona before moving to San Francisco to establish a freelance career in advertising illustration. Though having experienced some staph and yeast infections, psoriasis, and dermatitis, Tom first learned he had AIDS on his 34th birthday, July 19, 1983, after being diagnosed with pneumocystis pneumonia. His condition was considered so severe that the doctors in charge abandoned hope for his recovery and discontinued administering antibiotics. Tom had resigned himself to death and composed his Last Will and Testament before he decided, somewhere in the middle of his doped-up haze, that it was not his time to check out. With the aid of several psychics and healers, information channeled through Kevin Ryerson, massive doses of vitamin C, and the prayers and support of many loving friends, Tom remained with us.

In the following year, he finished his wondrous set of color pencil and pen-and-ink illustrations, "Rock and Roll the Stars," an homage to rock and roll stars of the '60s, and organized a psychic development class for people with AIDS led by Tamara Diaghilev. He also introduced me to the work of metaphysical teacher and healer Louise Hay, aiding my own process of growth, affirmation, and self-love. Tom returned to San Francisco General with pneumocystis on July 19, 1984. Two days after celebrating his 35th birthday, lying in the same bed in the same hospital room where he had been diagnosed the year before, Tom Chaudoin, surrounded by much love and light, chose to leave his body.

The following interview with Chuck Morris and Tom Chaudoin was conducted in November 1983.

Chuck: We let people with AIDS know about the workshop by composing a letter which the San Francisco Department of Public Health confidentially mailed out to everyone with AIDS who had been reported to them. We also allowed some time for word of the workshop to get around in the community, so that individuals with AIDS who had succeeded in keeping their identities out of the Health Department and government computers could take advantage of the offering.

The thing that concerned me most about the announcement was that people might presume that the workshop was about death and how to die. I think that Elisabeth's primary connection in the public eye has been as a thanatologist—death researcher. I was concerned that people receiving the letter might think it was a "Let's all get together and learn how to die" workshop. And the focus of her work, and the focus of that workshop, was really on *how to live*. It had very little to do with death.

In the LDT workshops, "death and dying" is not really talked about as a workshop topic until the last day. Most of the workshop is really about: How do we live now? How do we live a fulfilling life? How do we get rid of unfinished business? And most importantly, how do we learn to love people unconditionally? That's Elisabeth's work in a nutshell. The LDT workshop is not just for people who have life-threatening illnesses.

Jason: What, Tom, were your expectations when arriving at the workshop?

Tom: Well, I really didn't have too many. . .because the only thing by Elisabeth Kübler-Ross that I was familiar with was an article in the *Berkeley Holistic Health Handbook* that I read about a week before attending. I thought it was going to be an opportunity to deal with some of my feelings, particularly anger and discouragement. Those are two things I had been feeling a lot.

Chuck: It came out at one part of the workshop that somebody expected we were going to be confronting each other. . .an Encounter Group or one of the old T-Groups. And that isn't what happens. I mean, there is a great deal of encountering. . .but what we are doing is *encountering ourselves*. Nobody is throwing things at us.

Jason: Were there people who had fear of each other because they had AIDS?

Chuck: Sure. And people who were afraid of themselves because they had AIDS.

Because this was a shortened version of the Life, Death and Transition workshop, some things normally contained in the five-day experience were modified or omitted. On the first day, the workshop began with people standing up and introducing themselves. After the facilitators gave a rundown of what was going to happen, everyone stood up and walked around without touching, silently making eye contact with every other person in the group. Then everyone was asked to scream, about which Chuck says, "I think everyone felt a tremendous sense of relief after that first scream." That evening, everyone drew and discussed pictures, a process which helped reveal where people were at, and what fears they were holding. On the second day, the "mattress work" began.

Chuck: We started with breakfast at 8:00 A.M. Every hour and a half we would take what Elisabeth calls a "physiologic break." For her it's a cigarette break. Besides breaks for lunch and dinner, we worked til as late at night as we had to.

Jason: Were people able to do it?

Chuck: Almost everybody was. You're on such a tremendous psychic and spiritual high that you're not even aware of being in your body at that point. There is some other energy that is propelling you. You're aware that your body may be tired, but it doesn't make much difference.

Tom: Especially the second day, when we started doing the matwork. It was so intense, and I was so *there,* that I didn't even think about being tired, or how I was feeling physically.

Chuck: The matwork is pounding, beating up a phone book with a hose, screaming, holding a pillow and crying. Basically the matwork allows us to get in touch with both the Hitler and the Christ (or the Mahatma Gandhi or the Martin Luther King) in us...

Tom: Or the Mother Theresa.

Chuck: Oh, yes. Elisabeth is very fond of talking about the Hitler in us. And we all have a Hitler in us. We also all have a Mahatma Gandhi in us. But we can't keep in touch with that Mahatma Gandhi because so often people press buttons that bring out the Hitler. And those are all things that go back to our childhood. Somewhere in our childhood something happens to us...garbage that we carry with us for ten, twenty, forty, sixty years. The purpose of the matwork is to get back to that initial experience and get rid of it, so we can stop reacting to people in that old way. We get rid of that unfinished business so we can get back in contact with the Mother Theresa in us. Because that's our natural state.

Jason: How did that work for the two of you? Did you get back there?

Chuck: Yes, I got back there.

Jason: Did it work for you, Tom?

Tom: Oh, absolutely. I was very apprehensive about the entire process. I'm very self-conscious. It's very hard for me to scream in front of everybody...but I did. I felt very uncomfortable about getting up in front of a whole group of people and letting them see my anger and my sadness and my fear. That was hard. But when I sat there with other people while they were going through those processes, it got me started, and made it possible for me to do that too. I couldn't have done it without those other people. But the whole object is that we're in a group, and it is a group process.

Chuck: And the more people, the better. One of the ground rules of the matwork is that the person working is not allowed to touch or be touched by anyone else in the group. You see people in this tremendous pain, and I think our very human response is to want to help and to do something. It's very difficult to sit there and say to yourself that the best thing I can do to help this person is to do nothing, and let them feel this. Because the effect sometimes of helping people is to shut them down. If Tom were sitting here now and started to get really upset and cry about something, if I put my arms around him, and held him close, and said, "No, it's okay," the effect of that is to play rescuer and to say everything's going to be okay and I'm here to help you...when what he *needs* to do is to experience that pain and get through it and put it behind him. The more I comfort him, the stronger the temptation is to just stifle the emotion...which sooner or later is going to blow.

Tom: ...Umhum...

Jason: So you get no support for your resistance, and every support for letting go.

Chuck: Precisely. The last day (day 3) is the *gorgeous day.* After all of the shit that you have been through, the last day is getting rid of all this shit. You make a conscious decision. This is what I have learned. This is who I am now. This is the shit that I'm going to get rid of. This is the unfinished business that I am going to finish and leave here. And this is what I'm going to take home with me. And it's also the saddest day, because it's the day of saying goodbyes.

Tom: One of the things we did the last day was to make a shit-list of what we were going to leave behind. And we also made a list of what we were going to take with us from the workshop. I wrote my list on a page out of my diary, and tied it up with a ribbon that was part of my diary's bookmark. I said when I threw it into the fire we built that I was leaving behind the part of me that isn't strong enough to conquer this disease. And I also was leaving behind the part of me that was sick.

Chuck said something about how the love between everybody there was very tangible. Well, it was with me for some people, and it wasn't with other people. *But,* the amazing thing is that when the whole experience was over with, I knew, I knew deep down that I had received love from *every single one* of those people in that workshop. Even though I wasn't able to feel it with everybody, and was able to connect with some people more than others, I *knew* that I felt love from every single person in that room. And I knew that I felt that for everybody there, too. And it gave me a lot of *hope.* It gave me a whole lot of hope. And I think I also realized that *death is my choice.* You know, it's *really* my choice.

Jason: And *life* is your choice.

Tom: Right. I believed that before I went to the workshop, but I believe it more now than ever.

At the end of the third morning, right before Elisabeth Kübler-Ross came to speak, we each chose a partner and formed two facing circles, positioning ourselves so that partners in the inner circle faced their partners in the outer one. We joined hands with the people in our circle, and had to communicate a nonverbal message—whatever we wanted—to our partner opposite us. The facilitators started playing music and every so often they would ask the inner circle to move one person to the right, so that we ended up being able to look into the eyes of every single person in the other circle. Talk about love! I can't tell you what I got, and what I felt for those other people as that was happening, it was so great! And my message to those other people was that I wasn't going to die of AIDS, and that I didn't want them to die of AIDS either. I don't know whether they got that message from me or not, but I know that there was such a tremendous amount of love going back and forth and around that circle that I can't even *begin* to describe it.

One guy there who's very sick—I know a lot of his background and what he's been through and everything—I looked into his eyes and it was like staring into the face of death itself, but his eyes were filled with love. And it was very powerful.

Jason: Was there talk of afterlife, the next lifetime, reincarnation?

Chuck: Yes, Elisabeth talked about it.

Jason: What percentage of attendees do you think came to a realization, Tom, of being able to make a choice of either life or death?

Chuck: I would say 90%.

Tom: Yes.

Chuck: I think that almost everybody that took that workshop would come out of it, if they were open enough to it, with a realization that living or dying is a matter of our choice.

Jason: Were there people who came there who were angry at themselves for being gay because they had AIDS? And were they able to deal with that?

Chuck: Oh, yes.

Tom: Oh, yes, *very much.* Me included. Some of them dealt with it beautifully. At first I thought people were kind of drama queens when they were going through their processes, and I sort of thought, "Oh, this is an exaggeration." And then I realized that even if they were drama queens it was okay because they were really putting themselves out there. And that was beautiful. I was being judgmental in the beginning. You heard such incredible things from these people that in another circumstance you might have thought it was an exaggeration, but it wasn't.

Jason: Well, judgments are a real good way to protect yourself and keep your heart closed.

Chuck: You learn very quickly into the workshop not only to suspend judgment but just how *foolish* and unuseful judgments are. They serve *no purpose.*

Jason: I had a real fear that because of all the judgments out there from the Moral Majority, and all the negative stuff around homosexuality, and because so many people who are gay come from homophobic family and religious backgrounds, that people would fall for the sin and guilt line, seeing their AIDS as a punishment for their homosexuality, and hate themselves.

Chuck: Some people with AIDS have experienced that. The lovely thing about these workshops is that you find a way to get past that, and to let go of it. You come to a realization that (homophobia) is something that people are putting off on you. What I discarded at the workshop is how people view me or see me, and what they think of me, because it has nothing to do with the reality of me. It was one of the items on my shitlist. And I think that a lot of people attending who felt that AIDS is punishment for something—for being gay—dropped that belief and left freer of other people's judgments of who they are.

Jason: What did you get out of this experience, Chuck, that differed from your first LDT workshop?

Chuck: In the workshop I'd done before, I dealt with having AIDS. The biggest thing that I got out of this workshop was letting go of a lot of grief. I met somebody who also had AIDS, and we fell madly in love. He died in the early part of September. And what I was able to do through this workshop was first of all to come to terms with that grief and *experience* it, which I had refused to let myself do. I cried the night he died and hadn't cried since then. In this workshop I dealt with that grief, let go of it, and also let go of my guilt around his death. There was a *lot* of guilt there.

He had been taken into an intensive care unit. I flew down to Los Angeles where he was hospitalized, and the minute I walked into the unit, I knew I should just reach over and disconnect his respirator. And I didn't do it. I had a lot of guilt around that, because he suffered a *horrible* death for ten days. So a lot of my work was letting go of that. And I hope that people who are dealing with AIDS on any level out there, or *any illness,* or have lost anybody, would take advantage of one of these workshops.

Tom: Oh, really! You know, I was sort of very composed at the beginning of the workshop. . .

Chuck: . . .Weren't we all!. . .

Tom: . . .then one person got up who did not have AIDS and started going through her process. . .there were a few special guests who didn't have AIDS. . .and I don't know what it was that she said or even did, but that is what got me going. It wasn't even one of the people who had AIDS that really touched that deep deep part of me first. And I know that person's experience was every bit as intense as any of the people there who had AIDS.

Especially the second day, the things that I was really able to let go of most were anger and sadness. I have a fear of this disease, but I don't have a fear of death. I didn't even before I went to the workshop. So that's not a huge issue for me. But I have a lot of anger. And I was really able to let go of a lot of that, at some very specific people, and in a more general way as well.

Jason: What about Kübler-Ross's approach to change?

Chuck: Elisabeth and her staff select workshop leaders very carefully, making sure to put people in charge who have dealt with their own unfinished business, so that nothing gets in the way of their helping and sticking with the participants. The beauty of all this is that one half hour on the mat doing mat-work is worth twenty years of psychotherapy. It cuts out the bullshit. It gets right to the very basic problem. The beauty of the group experience—we had thirty people in the room, but in her usual workshop you have eighty—eighty people focusing tremendous energy that gets through to everybody. There's no way you can resist it, try as you like.

Tom: It absolutely got through. I've been in psychotherapy for the last three and a half years, and I got more out of watching, just watching one person up there on that mattress than I have in all those years of therapy. Group interaction adds a very human and spiritual dimension that I haven't experienced in my years of psychotherapy, or in my reading of books on healing.

Chuck: In the group process, as followed in this workshop, every time you do it, it works. Because you're so isolated in doing it, and yet so surrounded by love.

Jason: Do you have any concluding thoughts for our readers?

Chuck: I have one message, which is, I hope, the same message that I've given to people over the last year and a half wherever I've spoken or done an interview. If we as people are doing anything other than giving people love, and getting love from people, we're fooling ourselves. *We have nothing to give anyone else other than love.* Anything else is an illusion. Spending time doing anything else is an illusion, and foolhardy. And the only way we can give people love and experience it is to do it *unconditionally.* No "I'll love you *if*" or "I will love you *when,*" but just simply, "I love you."

Tom: As much anger as I've experienced, and as much sadness as I've experienced since I found out that I have AIDS, this illness has been an incredible opportunity for me to do exactly what Chuck just said.

Jason: To get in touch with the love.

Tom: Oh, yeah. And I mean from every person in that workshop. One of my best friends and I went out to dinner last night to the Sausage Factory on Castro Street, and we both broke down in tears right in the middle of dinner at the Sausage Factory.

Jason: It wasn't because you were eating sausage? (laughter)

Tom: Really. I'm vegetarian. . . .What Chuck said is absolutely right on. All there is is love.

Jason: Thank you both.

My follow-up interview with Tom occurred several weeks after a benefit showing of his artwork, which drew 75 people and raised $2,000 to enable him to pay off some of his medical expenses and explore holistic and alternative means of treatment. An eye infection which had kept his eye "running and running and running" through his illness—"it's kind of me not being able to cry or something, and I got to cry a lot while I was at the workshop'—had healed, his complexion had improved, he'd gained more weight, and the tone of his voice was freer and more alive. He had also completely rearranged his apartment.

Jason: Now that two months have passed, what can you say you gained from the workshop that still affects you and how you relate to your illness?

Tom: We have organized a support group of people who attended the workshop, which meets twice a month, as a very real way to do something with what we have learned. It's an opportunity for externalization every time we meet...a continuation of the work we started together.

The main thing I got from the workshop was the ability to release a lot of negative feelings that I had not released before. That just cleared me out, so that there's more room for positive feelings. I realize, and I *really believe* that illness is very much affected by a person's emotional state...including susceptibility to illness. Part of the reason I believe that so strongly is that I saw people in the three days of that workshop get better.

Jason: Have they continued to get better?

Tom: I certainly have. And a lot of those people are doing very well. But the most important part of the workshop for me was the spiritual aspects: *hope* and *love*. And those are things that just don't disappear when you leave the workshop. I think that love, "unconditional love" as Elisabeth Kübler-Ross would say, is a very, very powerful healing tool. I said to a friend recently, "All of a sudden I feel a lot of love for other people, but I don't really know how to express that or give that to them." And my friend said, "By letting other people love you, you're giving love!" That happens a lot more in my life than it used to. And I feel very hopeful and optimistic.

Jason: Tom, do you pray?

Tom: I would prefer to say that I "communicate." I do meditation every single day. I visualize health, not every single day, but a lot. I have found when I'm feeling ill or not very good that creative visualization has been very helpful to me.

Jason: Is there anything else you want to add?

Tom: I think the most important thing was that I was able to release and externalize so many feelings that I hadn't been able to do before, and to share so much with the people attending. *I have never experienced so much love, or felt more alive, in my entire life.* I feel very much alive right now. I've got some physical ailments, yet in many ways I don't feel like I even have AIDS. You know, the doctors have more or less told me that I have a terminal dis-ease. And I do *not* believe that. *I do not believe there is such a thing as a terminal dis-ease.* I've known people who have had cancer and were going to die and are still alive and healthy and don't have cancer anymore. I've known people who've had other horrible dis-eases—a woman who has lupus and who was supposed to die years ago—and she's still living and going to nursing school. So I don't accept that there's such a thing as a terminal dis-ease.

Since the workshop, I have come to *totally accept* that life and death are a person's *choice*. The bottom line is not whether medical science is going to find a cure for AIDS. It's whether or not I'm going to choose to live or die, and whether or not I'm going to choose AIDS as the reason for my death.

On July 18, 1985, a letter from Charles Lee Morris appeared in the *Sentinel USA* in response to an article reporting that, except for Bobby Reynolds, publisher of the *People with AIDS* newsletter, all the speakers at San Francisco's first "Fighting for Our Lives" AIDS march of May 2, 1983, were now dead. Below are excerpts from Chuck's response.

Not so. At least, I don't believe I'm dead quite yet; just out of sight.

Some people who have taken comfort in the fact that I have survived with AIDS for slightly more than five years now and who remember that I spoke at that very first AIDS march may have been disheartened to learn, although prematurely, of my death in such a roundabout way.

For the record: Charles Lee Morris, former publisher, gay activist, and longtime AIDS survivor, is alive (though no fool would also add 'and well'), and for the first time in my life, living a quiet nonpublic life with my wonderful lover of almost two years. . . .

I am marvelously happy with one of the world's most extraordinary men. Two months ago I experienced another bout of pneumocystis pneumonia and I wish to publicly thank all those who phoned or sent cards or notes. That, coupled with my mate's unending love, proved to be a strong antidote for the bugs ravaging my body. Bless you all.

On January 6, 1986, close to six years after he first came down with AIDS, Chuck Morris left his body.

If you are interested in attending an LDT workshop, contact: Workshop Coordinator, Elisabeth Kübler-Ross Center, South Route 616, Head Waters, VA 24442; or call (703) 396-3441. LDT workshops and similar workshops specifically designed for people with AIDS are coordinated on the West Coast through Hal Frank, San Diego AIDS Project, P.O. Box 81082, San Diego, CA 92138, (619) 294-AIDS; they also offer workshops for health professionals working with AIDS. Additionally, readers are referred to the entries on Da Free John, Stephen Levine, Ram Dass, and Elisabeth Kübler-Ross in the Resources section.

CHAPTER 6

IRENE SMITH SHARES
HER INSIGHTS

Irene Smith is a massage therapist who views her craft from a perspective of sharing and healing. In 1980, at a pivotal time in her life,
she was introduced to the work of Elisabeth Kübler-Ross through
attending a series of Life, Death and Transition workshops in the
United States and Canada. So transformative was her experience that
she decided she wanted to touch people going through life-death
transition. In April of 1982 she approached the Hospice of San Francisco to propose what was then an unheard of service in San Francisco: massage for terminally ill hospice clients. Irene initiated that
service, and in 1983 began visiting San Francisco General Hospital
weekly to offer massage to people with AIDS.

Irene's letter to the *Bay Area Reporter* (B.A.R.), published September 13, 1984, was so moving that I decided to visit Irene and learn
what else she might have to share with us. Her letter and interview
follow.

Letters to the Editor: Bay Area Reporter (9/13/84)

*At this time I work primarily with people with the condition of AIDS.
I have a positive view on this condition that I'd like to share with you.*

*What I believe we are dealing with here is a condition of fear,
negativity, guilt, and anger that has come to a head. We are being
forced to see it manifested in the physical body, that we might begin
to learn to grow, to sort out and confront the conditions that we have
set up for ourselves at this time. We are being forced to grow to love
and to share our fears and hopes with others, and to come to the aid
of our brothers. We must look at the positive growth that is going*

on, and put our focus there. We must learn from this if we are to correct it.

The fear, sadness, and horror of this dis-ease must be overcome if we are to overcome the dis-ease itself.

If you have had a friend who died of AIDS who you stayed close to during this dis-harmony, think of how you grew with the experience. Think of the love you shared with this person. Think of the growth this person had to confront in order to live with this disease and to die with it. Think back to the precious moments of love and growth you experienced with this person and share this with others.

If you are a person who has this condition, focus on the lessons you are learning and the love and support you are generating.

I have been a massage therapist in Unit 5B for one year and have gone once a week with very few exceptions. I go from room to room where there might seemingly be sadness and horror, only to hear from the occupants of these rooms, "I can't believe this place. Everybody here really cares." "I've never experienced such love and care in my life." "This place feels like home—everyone really loves me." These people are the healers of our times. They are forcing us to grow.

What greater memorial than to look at the lessons we are learning, the love we are sharing, and to continue to grow with it. We are being forced to reach the truth of our very existence. Love. Love in its purest form. That which is other than the physical body.

Our losses, our fears, and our horrors are our tools for learning. We must experience these losses, let them go, and get on with what we have gained from these losses. Only by creating a positive learning experience from this can we heal it. We are the healers of our times.

I hear over and over again, "I am afraid to live without this condition because I have never experienced such love in my life." Last night a friend told me, "I would rather live one year more with this dis-ease than 50 years of my previous lifestyle. I have never been so loved or closer to my purpose in life. I have learned more in the nine months since I've been diagnosed than in the 30 years prior to this condition."

We must learn from this and set up positive, loving conditions in which to live. People are actually dying for love. We need to take a good look at what is going on here.

We are constantly looking to other responses to satisfy our internal needs, and this is not working. Yes, I believe AIDS means death. Death of an old lifestyle and creation of a new one. This is the full circle of life.

The Gay community is the healer of our times, because of your total freedom to be creative, your joy in living, and the enormous opportunity to love yourself and others at this time. This is the healing of our times.

This is total freedom to create a healing *community. Be Proud!*
—*Irene Smith*
San Francisco

Jason: Irene, when we spoke previously by telephone, I mentioned a person diagnosed with AIDS whom we both knew who made the decision to pass over. We were both shocked by his death, because he had seemed so clearly aligned with the healing process.

Irene: Yes. I worked with this gentleman for about six months, and I had known him about six months prior to our working together. I knew him to pursue all different modes of healing throughout the year. He went to spiritual healers, psychic healers, physical healers, emotional healers—he made a 24-hour a day process out of healing. At one point during this process he was quite radiant; to be with him I actually felt that this man was healed.

During one of our visits, I asked him why he could not accept the fact that he was healed. He looked at me and very honestly stated that he was afraid to live. And I believe that this comes up for a lot of people. I believe that during a life-threatening illness we are so loved and so supported that *we are afraid to live* without our dis-ease.

I also see, as in the case of this gentleman, that he reached a point where if he could have clearly sat down and given *thanks* for the healing that had already come his way—and been able to accept his healing and to accept further love on this plane—he would still be with us. I believe that what happens to a lot of people, not just with life-threatening illnesses but in the process of healing anything, is that they get wrapped up in a pattern of "more"—just like we live today. We want more cars, more clothes, more sex, more highs, more relationships— we're in a pattern of "More." And when we run up against something that needs healing, we seem to follow in the same pattern. We go from one healer to the other healer to the other healer to the other healer, staying within the pattern of more and more and more, never sitting down and acknowledging the healing that we have, and giving thanks for it.

So what we do is actually *run past the point of our healing.* We overheal, which is another way of being off balance, which is staying within the pattern of dis-ease.

Jason: Did you ever discuss this with him?

Irene: The only thing that I discussed concerned why he could not accept the fact that he was healed. He said it was because he was afraid to live. And I asked why he had not given thanks for the healings, or just slowed down to pray, and given thanks for the healings he had already received. He came to the point of telling me that he was both afraid to live and afraid to be with his dis-ease. So there was a very uncomfortable point there at which he could give no thanks.

Our talk took place two months prior to his death. And I must tell you that being with him in the hospital in the process of his dying was like being with a person who was totally whole and healed, dying, which was very different for me. I believe it was most different for most of the people who surrounded him at that time.

Jason: How does your experience working with people with AIDS who seem to be making the choice to die differ from working with people with other life-threatening illnesses who seem to be on that path?

Irene: My personal experience seems to be that I have a harder time accepting the death of someone in the prime of their life rather than someone in their 50s or 60s.

Jason: Among people of the same age bracket, have you come across differences between what people with AIDS are holding onto and have to get rid of, and the stuff that people with other life-threatening illnesses are dealing with?

Irene: Due to the fact that we're working with people in the prime of life, there is more of a holding on to a physical existence on this plane. There seems to be a greater will to live. There also seems to be a much greater sense of lowered self-esteem. Possibly from a life style of being a suppressed minority and partly from having a dis-ease which can carry isolation and rejection.

Jason: That really supports what The Holistic Group states about the psychospiritual nature of AIDS in the book's Inquiry. We believe AIDS attacks members of culturally isolated minorities who experience both great internal and great external stress. You're talking a lot about that kind of oppression and alienation that gays buy into. Do you spend much time talking to people when you massage them?

Irene: Everybody's different. I try to be there for whatever the person needs. Some need to talk and some need to be quiet. When I work in the hospital, understanding that the patients may have spent a day filling out forms, having tests, or talking to counselors, I simply go in and ask if there's anything I can do in the way of touch today, and they either answer "yes" or "no." I end my conversation there. A lot of times the entire visit is in silence.

Jason: In this past year, have people with AIDS been more open to holistic alternatives, and to seeing this dis-ease as something that must be approached fully on all four levels?

Irene: Definitely. AIDS seems to be about growth, exploration, and openness on all levels and a more total approach to healing. But I must tell you that I don't think in terms of alternatives. I'd rather think in terms of *additives*. One of the greatest healings we're experiencing at this time is recognizing that healing requires the best from both worlds. I think if you can come from a standpoint of adding to the culture that has already been set up, we will come to a very comfortable place of healing in our society. I believe that one of the reasons AIDS is here is to bring all healers together.

Jason: Would it be fair to use the word "balancing" instead, as in balancing a medical approach which might advocate "fighting fire with fire" through chemotherapy, with an alternative approach which might say "all you have to do is take vitamins"? The Chinese, for example, combine Western surgery, which is a wonderful thing when it's called for, with acupuncture.

Irene: I see what you mean, and it is a matter of balancing. However, with our already set-up culture, I use the term "additives" because that's what we're doing. We're adding to the pattern that is already created. That's the way a lot of people structure their consciousness.

Jason: In addition to your work with Hospice and on the AIDS ward, you've been training with Elisabeth Kübler-Ross. What led you to that?

Irene: I was fortunate, so very fortunate, to have been allowed to go through a process of healing with Elisabeth, that I decided that what I want to do with my life is help other people become aware of this process, and experience it. If not to reach out and love and help one another grow, why else are we on this planet?

What I've realized is that you just can't heal the physical body without coming to grips with the pattern that created the symptoms of your dis-ease in the first place. You need to work with the emotional pattern, with the totality of being, and with your spirituality. When your physical quadrant, your emotional quadrant, your intellectual quadrant, and your spiritual quadrant are in balance, then you are in harmony. It can be any one of these four things that is off balance, and it is only by delving into your total being that you can come to grips with your dis-ease, and embrace your healing.

Jason: Do you have a set goal around working with Elisabeth in the future, such as leading and facilitating her workshops?

Irene: It's a totally open goal—whatever she needs from me, or however I can serve best through her Center. I feel the best way to be with her is to be open.

Editor's Note: In 1985, Irene Smith was awarded the "For Those Who Care" award by the San Francisco NBC-TV affiliate KRON for her humanitarian service to the community. In addition to her consistent personal service to people in need, she has so far trained over 200 massage practitioners in her work. As of April, 1987, she had twelve active hospital volunteers massaging people diagnosed with AIDS in five clinical settings in San Francisco, including Letterman Army Hospital! It is no wonder that she has been termed "beloved" by Van Ault, holistic editor of the San Francisco *Sentinel*, and by the thousands of people whose hearts she has touched.

I cannot put into words how much I have learned from Irene Smith, both from her words and her example. More of her wisdom can be found in the July/August 1987 *Yoga Journal* article "Living with AIDS" co-authored by Susan Jacobs and myself. For information on Irene's trainings for bodyworkers caring for people diagnosed with AIDS and other dis-eases, and on her booklet *Guidelines for Massaging PWAs*, please see her listing in Resources at the back of this book.

CHAPTER 7

LISTENING TO THE INNER VOICE

The Test of AIDS: A Letter from a Friend

This letter was received by me on May Day, 1986 in response to my article "Permission to Heal," also titled "We Are Healing AIDS," which has appeared in several regional and national publications.

About 8 months ago my lover told me he had tested positive for HTLV-III. I was deeply shocked, as I had assumed that since we had been monogamous for 4 years we had escaped the threat of AIDS. I was also shocked because both of us were in perfect health, and I had no idea that my lover was concerned or worried.

When he told me I felt like I had been slugged in the solar plexus. I withdrew into myself watching carefully how I was responding. About half an hour later, I felt a warm breeze caress my face and I knew it was the kiss of Quan Yin (the Chinese goddess who symbolizes compassion and mercy—"the mother of all beings").

I came out of this trance meditation and told my lover that, no matter what happened, I had no regrets.

Several weeks later I went to San Francisco to take the AIDS antibody test. The hospital setting was almost guaranteed to produce negative energies. I did my best to bathe the waiting room in healing golden light, but I found my efforts constantly thwarted. I became exhausted just waiting.

The group taking the test was ushered into a room where we watched a video which is used by an AIDS organization. In the video they show a cartoon of someone being invaded by the unconquerable AIDS virus (depicted as nasty triangles). I was horrified! They didn't seem to understand that they were projecting the same fatalistic im-

age the world presents about AIDS, and that, since the imagistic level
of the brain lies deeper than the discursive, they were affecting people at a subconscious level.

I became very angry and told them that I refused to take the test.
They interpreted my response as emotional fear (not true). Finally,
one of the people in the program said that he really needed statistics
for his work, and he wanted me to take the test. I felt some honesty
in his request, and agreed to take it. Several weeks later I received
the results—positive.

I began going to AIDS support groups, but I found the energy
so negative that I would have to spend three or four days in concentrated meditation just to shake off the negativity. I know that the
leaders of these raps are well-meaning, but "support" is hardly what
I received.

Finally my lover and I sat down and agreed that we had to take
this thing into our own hands. Every evening, before going to sleep,
I would say, "I am filled with Golden Healing Light. Every part of
my body streams with Golden Healing Light. As I enter dreamtime
I will enter the world of Golden Healing Light." Similarly, upon
awakening I would request that the Golden Healing Light fill me during the day.

One day, while taking a shower, a golden light surrounded me
and suffused me. I could feel it coursing through my body.

In addition to the healing light invocation I have used megavitamins. At first I also drastically changed my diet. Though I have been
vegetarian for many years, I never followed a specific plan or philosophy. This time, following an herbalist's advice, I conciously restruc-
tured my diet. In two weeks I had gained over fifteen pounds—nor
was I thin to begin with! Finally, when hardly any of my clothes
would fit I said to myself, "Listen to your own body. Trust it." I
returned to my original diet with some modifications. The extra fifteen pounds dropped off and my weight stabilized.

As of now, both my lover and I are of excellent health. We are
both optimistic and have plans for a long life together.

I believe something very profound is happening in the gay community. We are becoming intimately and deeply aware of our
body/mind in its many dimensions. Does it sound callous to say that
AIDS, in the end, may be a blessing?

A five-minute meditation dedicated to the healing of AIDS happens every day at 7 P.M. Observed in accordance with local time zones, it allows healing energy to flow in waves around the planet.

The term "meditation" connotes any process by which one may allow the body to relax so that the mind may explore the full dimensions of self. If adding your loving energy to this world-wide meditation is harmonious with and appropriate to your life and schedule, please feel free to join in in whatever way(s) you choose, silently or otherwise.

LISTENING TO THE INNER VOICE

Dr. Paul Dague was a San Francisco Bay Area psychologist, noted for his work with gay and lesbian service organizations. He worked as mental health director at the Pacific Center and as executive director of Operation Concern. As staff psychologist at the Kaposi's Sarcoma Clinic at the University of California at San Francisco, Paul helped the Shanti Project establish the first support group for people with AIDS in November 1981. In June 1982 Paul was diagnosed with Kaposi's sarcoma. He died the morning of January 20, 1984. He gave this talk to a group of Shanti counselors shortly before his death.

For all of us with AIDS, how we go about the issue of treatment plays a major role in our lives. I was on interferon for seven months, and then I no longer qualified for the program because I had gone from seven lesions to thirty. Within three weeks of the time I was off interferon I had over 200 lesions. You can guess just how freaked out that caused me to be. Now I've stopped counting.

I spent a month in a metabolic nutritional hospital in Mexico. I felt a lot better but I kept getting new lesions. Two months after that there were still more lesions coming, and so we tried a high-powered chemotherapy. The major effect of that was goodbye beard and hair. I'm currently undergoing thirty-six treatments of full body radiation.

In addition, I have used visualizations, prayer, meditations, all the homeopathic and vitamin kinds of stuff. From the very beginning I've taken the most active role I can in managing my own therapeutic treatment program. Not knowing what remedies might work to counteract the syndrome, I've made the most reasonable choices I could, trying each possible solution, one after the other.

My initial goal was naive—to restore my faulty immune system and achieve complete remission. Bitter failures along the way have forged more realistic benchmarks. Yet at the same time I am moving toward the same goal—total cure, not remission but *total cure.*

Patients, more often than not, have a decent idea of what they need for themselves. The psyche, I believe, takes care of us in terms of coping. When we are able, we handle some of the deep-seated feelings that come from dealing with the prospect of death, which is essentially what AIDS is all about—dying a helluva lot sooner than you had planned and having lots of time to think about it.

I'm fed up with hearing, "We all die. If it's not AIDS, you could walk out into the street and get run over by a truck." That's a crock of manure. I've had 17 months to contemplate my potentially early death. There is time to do a lot of thinking and a lot of fearing. There is absolutely no denial that death is one of the possible outcomes for me. I am intimately aware that I could be dead within six months, a year, or two years. The men in my family live into their eighties—what a cheat! There's not denial; it's more like an acceptance of the variety of possibilities which exist and working with that and finding your peace with it.

The diversity we bring to thinking and feeling about AIDS is incredible. And it is important to honor that diversity, to have a sense of love and caring. One of the most important therapeutic interventions is to be there with them, not to go digging for their feelings. For almost everybody the deep feelings will come up. For some it takes longer.

Some days I feel together. I just feel good, alive, vibrant. I feel closer to myself, to God, to my 18-year-old daughter. But there are days when if the Buddha would come to visit I would find something wrong. None of us knows what tomorrow's going to hold.

I live in fear of pneumocystis. I've had a cough for over two weeks. The X-rays show clear, but my fear about pneumocystis is very high. I don't like coughing; I find it upsetting. But in general I've moved from more time being scared to more time feeling at peace with myself.

In the aftermath of one of the most severe dislocations of my forty-six years, I find myself able to weather the storm with fortifying doses of humor, screaming fits, meditation on the positive forces around me, crying, and the support of children and loving friends. My friends have opened their arms to me in love in ways that before they hadn't. Plus my clients have hung in there.

I've come to know some of the other people with AIDS, and friendship has developed there—deep, caring kinds of friendship. I've discovered an amazing reserve of equanimity and tenderness in the face of terrifying pain and isolation. I'd even call it courage. These are the qualities I share with a surprising number of people with AIDS. It is this kind of sharing that helps sustain me, as I hope I can contribute to helping sustain them through our common tribulation.

Three weeks ago a rather close friend who had AIDS died. But the times that we had together were good for both of us. I've really just discovered what a community is all about, and it's the most delightful realization to know you are able to rise up from the bitterness and hopelessness of your circumstances to help others discover the rare and essential beauty of life.

Impending death is a reality for us all. But to me it has become far less important to dwell on that fact than to address the tragedy of living life burdened with fears, lies, or indifference in all the stunning variety of forms that these take—like perpetrating a negative self-image, doing a job that one hates or making oneself hostage to the rules of the jungle at the expense of all else in life. Since contracting AIDS I've been trying not to accept my unconsciousness as I did before. In fact, I'm trying to see everything I say or do in the light of the underlying truth or lie I'm creating for myself—because I can't afford the cost of allowing anything but that reality to guide me now.

Because nobody can tell me what's causing AIDS, I have

to listen much more closely to my inner voice than I have ever done before. I have to listen to my body tell me what it needs. I have to listen to what my spirit says it needs. And I have to have the courage to follow my inner voice even though it may differ from medical advice.

In the words of Dr. Richard Alpert/Ram Dass, and this is my statement, too:

> *My goal is to be Free,*
> *to be Truth, to be love,*
> *to be God.*

PART II

A HOLISTIC APPROACH

CHAPTER 8

A HOLISTIC INQUIRY INTO THE PREVENTION AND HEALING OF ACQUIRED IMMUNE DEFICIENCY

by The Holistic Group

Editor's Introduction to the Inquiry

At the beginning of the 1980s, while the medical profession and the media were prematurely declaring that AIDS, a life-threatening illness of which they had the most limited understanding, was irreversible and fatal, there existed in the United States many strong and courageous individuals who refused to accept that their life-threatening dis-ease was an automatic death sentence.

Turning off the TV set, ignoring their doctor's dirge that they had at most two years to live, and separating themselves from the belief systems which sentenced them to permanent "victim" status upon the appearance of one purple spot, these individuals chose to journey within to the root of all healing—the love of self.

Because healing of AIDS cannot yet be "medically verified," and because the general mindset of the American public is that such healing is not possible, most of the people diagnosed with AIDS or ARC who are experiencing remission feel that it is perhaps better to keep their healing to themselves than to open themselves further to the undermining misunderstanding that healing AIDS without a medical "cure" is an impossibility. Nonetheless, that they keep themselves under cover for the sake of their own healing does not alter the reality of their existence.

The very concept of "cure," as defined by Western allopathic medicine, excludes virtually all individuals diagnosed with AIDS or ARC from its ranks. To be declared "cured" requires that one remain symptom-free with normal blood levels for a period of five years. While such a position may seem medically reasonable in an age of media sensationalism, races for the Nobel Prize, and pronouncements of overnight success or failure, it does not always serve people diagnosed with dis-ease.

How is one to declare oneself "cured" of a dis-ease that was first documented and identified only in 1981 and 1982? The time factor alone defeats almost all hope of a positive declaration. What's more, medical science has yet to develop a test for AIDS that identifies the "syndrome" apart from its manifestation as either the cancerous Kaposi's sarcoma or one of a host of opportunistic infections; not even the controversial AIDS-antibody test is a test for the dis-ease itself. How can one declare oneself "cured" or even in remission of a "new" dis-ease which medical science cannot yet accurately identify or test?

Recognizing the catch-22 nature of their situation, more and more people diagnosed with AIDS and other life-threatening dis-eases are simply opting out of the allopathic system of rules and regulations. They know that they are ill; they know they can die. They also know that they—not their doctors—are responsible for their own health, and that they can take their power to determine whether they will live or die from AIDS. They refuse to see themselves as "victims." Rather than giving over responsibility for their healing to Western medicine, they have chosen to go within, listen to their own inner voice, and find their own solutions.

These people diagnosed with AIDS have replaced medical pessimism, chemotherapy, and dangerous experimental drugs with affirmation, self-love, and a determination to achieve a new balance of mind, body, and spirit. Some of them consult nutritionists and psychic healers, while others combine Western and Eastern healing approaches. Some go to clinics in Mexico, others to yoga and meditation groups; still others choose to go dancing. Whatever their path, they refuse to succumb to the climate of fear and reaction. They listen to themselves. Some have stabilized their conditions or are in remission. Many are in the process of healing. And more than you will read about in the newspaper have journeyed deep within themselves, on pathways uncharted by medical science, and have found that they have healed themselves.

To comprehend what these people diagnosed with AIDS are doing, it is necessary to understand that the Western rational model of thought and reality does not have the corner on truth in the Universe. Human beings and their surroundings are composed of more than atoms, matter, flesh, and bones. We are more than our physical bodies. There is a part of each and every one of us that is eternal: our Spirit, our God-Essence—our Soul. That spirit gives us more power and strength than the hydrogen bomb, the Pentagon, and the Kremlin, because it gives us each the power to shape our own realities. In the realm of the Spirit lies the power to determine the course of our lives.

It has been written that freedom is the recognition of necessity. To be free to heal, it is necessary to step outside the materialistic framework that confines our imagination to what can be rationally demonstrated and proven, and to have faith in our own power and potential. Science cannot ultimately explain, for example, why the universe exists, why all the atoms that comprise our bodies come together, or even why sperm + egg + 9 months = baby. One cannot dissect the human body and find the acupuncture meridians; yet the Chinese have been healing people for thousands of years through this "invisible" system based upon energy and inner balance. There is more to our existence than the rational mind can either explain or grasp. Through a willingness to embrace Ultimate Truth, the mind and the spirit can work with the physical body to overcome this dis-ease.

A diagnosis of AIDS is not necessarily a death sentence; but transforming that diagnosis into an opportunity for healing demands a total commitment. Precisely because the disease is so insidious, and attacks people on the three levels of mind, body, and spirit, it must be approached simultaneously on all three levels. The decision to live must be total, involving every thought, every cell, every habit and belief. With support systems and defenses undermined, AIDS represents a real test of who one was and who one chooses to be. The holistic approach enables one to prevent and start healing AIDS precisely because it operates on all levels of one's being.

Holism deals with the total human organism—an integrated whole which is greater than the sum of its parts—rather than just with symptoms, viruses, and illnesses. Holism understands that a person whose mind, body, and spirit are in harmony, whose energy is in balance, does not manifest dis-ease. Holistic healing thus focuses not on getting rid of symptoms but on empowering the individual to establish a state of mental, emotional, physical, and spiritual harmony and wellness in which health is a constant of life.

Given that AIDS is such a total challenge to a person's existence, a holistic approach affords one the power and the means to address the entire problem. Those who embrace the holistic path believe that in order for a virus or "bug" to take hold in the body, there must exist a condition of imbalance and disharmony that leaves one open to the dis-ease in the first place. Holism goes to the root of the problem, healing the mental, emotional, and spiritual—as well as the physical—disharmony within the individual. Once mind, body, and spirit are aligned in harmony, the healing process is allowed to manifest. A person whose mind, body, and spirit are in harmony heals themself.

To my thinking, examining the many documented cases of near-death experience affords one insight into the experience of coping successfully with AIDS. The classic near-death experience involves someone who on a physical level has died, but who on the level of consciousness approaches the tunnel leading out of the body and then decides to return. Often such people hear a strong voice asking them whether they want to live or die, or declaring "It is not yet time" or "You still have work to do." Profoundly affected by this experience, they frequently return to life with an altered and expanded sense of consciousness. Aware of the changes they must make, and of their unfinished business, many take control of their lives as never before, often dedicating themselves to "right living" and to a positive and healing path. There is nothing like physically dying and immediately being born again to alter one's direction and sense of purpose.

Healing AIDS demands the same kind of total commitment to change as afforded by the near-death experience—except that the message to change may not be so graphically clear. Surrounded by contradictory belief systems, people diagnosed with AIDS must see beyond the tunnel vision of medical/media/mass-myopia which views them as "victims" in order to make contact with the capacity to heal. These people's challenge is a complete one, because, of their own volition, they must move radically inward, beyond any pre-established definitions of who they are and who they should be, to connect with the unconditional self-acceptance and Love which are the essence of all healing. They must literally be "born again," not into the false truths of Fundamentalism, but into the true spiritual understanding that all human beings are children of God and manifestations of Divine perfection and order.

Many people diagnosed with AIDS are engaged in this process. It is working for them. These people are at the forefront of the change in consciousness which is transforming our planet in our lifetimes. And we, by supporting their decision to heal—and giving them our love—heal ourselves as well.

A brief analysis of how AIDS has been approached in the United States will help us understand the tenacity of the thought forms and expectations which surround the dis-ease. When health authorities first took notice of the syndrome of immune dysfunction which they later termed Acquired Immune Deficiency Syndrome, it appeared to be new to planet Earth. Observing that this collection of hitherto rare opportunistic infections seemed rapidly to be killing most of the people it affected, and that most of those people were gay men, some of these authorities at first thought that they might be dealing with a sexually-transmitted "Gay Related Immune Deficiency." For reasons that some observers may be inclined to term homophobic, medical authorities, the media, and finally the general public leaped to the conclusion that the dis-ease was not only mysterious but absolutely fatal. Rather than stating the incontrovertible truth that AIDS was and still is at best a hazily understood life-threatening dis-ease, the medical authorities and media prematurely declared that a host of frightening unknowns meant that the dis-ease was incurable.

People diagnosed with AIDS prior to 1983 were in some respects treated as are many individuals who are presumed guilty until proven innocent: they were condemned to death by the system that claimed to offer them their only hope for healing, and given—*at most*—two years to live. Close to four years later, this situation has hardly changed. For example, one woman diagnosed with AIDS whom I visited on the most progressive AIDS ward in the country in late 1985 was told by her doctor that she could expect to live ". . .at best, no more than two years." A man who came to me in 1986 for an alignment and healing session was told by his doctor that he had never seen anyone with his condition last ". . .more than seven months." And a third client was asked, shortly after recovering from a bout with Pneumocystis pneumonia, if he had "made out [his] will yet." Being stigmatized as a "victim" while one is still alive and kicking can hardly be interpreted as support for the possibility of remission and healing.

While public understanding, support, and compassion for people diagnosed with AIDS is growing—witness the impact of Rock Hudson's AIDS diagnosis on our collective consciousness or, for that matter, the impact of this and other works on our psyches—the first people diagnosed with AIDS were afforded virtually no organized community support, and had to cope with an incredible wave of AIDS hysteria that frequently cost them their jobs, homes, and friends. Rather than being offered hope for recovery and cure, these people diagnosed with AIDS—at least 75% of whom were gay men—were treated to stories of irresponsible hospital authorities shipping their critically ill brothers off on long death trips to San Francisco, nurses and hospital personnel refusing to work with them, and funeral parlors refusing to embalm their bodies. No wonder that, facing fairly universal affirmation of their impending demise, a large number of people diagnosed with AIDS over three years ago bought into that death sentence and died.

What exactly are the underlying assumptions behind the

fatalistic approach to AIDS? Why was AIDS declared incurable, and even a "plague," before doctors and scientists knew very much about it? Is it possible that even the medical community is afflicted with the tendency, common to the American psyche, to label anything foreign, unknown, or just plain different as threatening, destructive, and even evil?

To what extent does homophobia lie at the root of such hopeless conclusions drawn from such inconclusive evidence? Might it even be possible that those amongst us who consider homosexuality itself as a "plague" simply projected that belief onto a dis-ease which seemed primarily to affect gay men?

It is important to acknowledge that AIDS can be both life-threatening and psychologically overwhelming. The AIDS virus strikes at the heart of the immune system, leaving one susceptible to any number of hitherto rare and potentially overwhelming opportunistic infections. Because chronic immune dysfunction means that health is no longer something that can be taken for granted, or even expected, people diagnosed with AIDS often feel stripped of their usual means of keeping themselves together physically, mentally, and spiritually. Quite suddenly, sometimes with the barest of warnings, they must cope with a diagnosis that implies that they are ultimately defenseless against a syndrome of dis-eases that seems capable of surfacing at any moment to destroy them.

To compound the personal reality of the dis-ease, the social and collective reality which greets people diagnosed with AIDS, as described above, is hardly conducive to inner peace and affirmations of healing. Changes in income, living situations, and friendship can be profound and traumatizing. While many wonderful organizations and individuals have come forth to help people diagnosed with AIDS, most of these still orient themselves, consciously or unconsciously, around support for "dying with dignity" rather than supporting the possibilities of remission and healing. The message is everywhere, and the message is clear: People diagnosed with AIDS are fated to die of AIDS, most probably sooner than later.

This message first hit home to this writer in February of 1983, perhaps three months after sharing in the death of my mother from cancer. Lying in bed at 1:30 A.M., resisting meditation by reading a respected magazine which featured a cover story on AIDS, I discovered two pictures of a friend of ten years being examined for his swollen lymph glands and KS lesions. Shocked by the revelation of his AIDS diagnosis, which was preceded not only by my mother's death but by the AIDS diagnosis of another man whom I knew and respected—I chose not to despair, but rather to take a leap of faith. Sensing that the conclusions I was reading about AIDS' absolute fatality were premature and just plain ridiculous, I left the oft-repeated mantra, "There is no known cause, there is no known cure," to the realm of the six o'clock news. My meditation of the evening became a resolve to access some higher source of knowledge about the dis-ease, and to investigate the possibility of its healing.

Many phone calls later, in April 1983, a research group of 18 highly dedicated and educated individuals—The Holistic Group—assembled in my crowded North Oakland cottage to get to the bottom of the AIDS phenomenon. Out of that meeting came the research paper "AIDS & KS: A Holistic Approach," which I edited and distributed. Thirty-seven months later, I can say with certainty that we did something right. Not only are the public and medical professionals beginning to take note of reports of the possibilities of healing AIDS, but both of my friends, God Bless 'em, are still alive.

This Inquiry is an outgrowth of that 20-page paper titled "AIDS & KS: A Holistic Approach," which was first distributed by The Holistic Group in June 1983 at the annual San Francisco Lesbian/Gay Freedom Day Celebration. Our research group—composed of holistic practitioners with backgrounds in traditional and alternative medicine, physiology, and therapy—assembled to disseminate positive alternative information on the prevention and healing of AIDS. After completing the first phase of our research, we submitted our findings to a sympathetic group of holistic practitioners for criticism and review. The final consensus was edited into printable form, advertised through Letters to the Editor in several gay, alternative, and health-oriented publications, and sold at minimal cost by mail and at supportive San Francisco Bay Area health food stores.

In 1983, when we first published our paper, the only other voices to be heard amidst the dirge of despair were those of the Macrobiotic Centers and Louise Hay, the metaphysical counselor and teacher who created the tape "AIDS: A Positive Approach" (see Resources section). People were searching for life-affirming information; many perhaps were dying for lack of it. The speed with which our thousand copy run was snapped up and passed around demonstrated the need for an expanded Inquiry into the dis-ease. In the fall of 1983 I began to "flesh out the paper a bit." Thanks to the dedication of countless individuals, many of whom are acknowledged at the beginning of this book, the following Inquiry, and this entire book, began to take form.

Most of the research of The Holistic Group remains not only valid but prophetic. (Our paper is again available—see Resources section). For example, in April 1986, three years after The Holistic Group came together, press reports began to surface concerning a man who at first tested positive for HTLV-III antibodies, and who was later shown to have eliminated them without medical treatment. Dr. Jay Levy, a leading AIDS researcher at the University of California at San Francisco, disclosed this information at a meeting of the American Society of Microbiology in Washington, D.C. As quoted in the *San Francisco Chronicle* (4/15/86), Levy said, "We don't know whether this will turn out to be an unusual case or a common one. Nevertheless, it is encouraging and may offer some hope that changes in lifestyle may help the immune system recover [from the assault of the AIDS virus]." This information supports what The Holistic Group first asserted in its June 1983 paper.

Throughout the Inquiry which follows and throughout this book, the point is made that healing AIDS and other life-threatening illnesses is possible. The emphasis is on achieving an alignment of mind, body and spirit which allows one to attain a balanced and whole state *and* remain in the body.

Two gatherings I attended in the first half of 1986 have clarified my consciousness as regards the healing process. The first, "Healing in the Heart of AIDS," involved a joint presentation by Stephen Levine, author of *Who Dies?*, and Ram Dass, author of *Be Here Now, Grist for the Mill* (with Stephen), and *How Can I Help?* (with Paul Gorman) (see Resources section). The second, "In the Heart Lies the Deathless," was a two-day workshop with Stephen Levine. The teachings of these men, as well as teachings through Kevin Ryerson and Louise Hay, have taught me that the true essence of *all* healing is opening our hearts and our consciousness to love.

Stephen Levine has stated that "healing may not well be changing the nature of the body...Some of the most miraculous healings I've ever experienced are of people who died with no unfinished business. They had healed their lives." [Note: "Unfinished business" is a term coined by our contributor Elisabeth Kübler-Ross, M.D., who has profoundly influenced Stephen Levine and Ram Dass.] He spoke of people with whom he had worked who had managed to "lick" their terminal dis-ease—to get rid of the tumor or whatever—yet who remained some of the angriest and most spiteful people he had ever encountered. These people, in his opinion, had not healed themselves; they had simply removed the symptoms of physical illness from their bodies. Their true healing, which allows one "to touch with love and mercy that which we have so often touched with anger and confusion," had not yet occurred.

Stephen has helped me recognize that there are many people diagnosed with life-threatening dis-eases such as AIDS who, despite every attempt to heal their dis-ease by holistic or allopathic means, have watched themselves move slowly or rapidly towards death. Some of these individuals, who may be reading these words at this moment, may tend to "blame" themselves for their apparent "failure," feeling that they did not do a good enough job with their healing work. Others may remain angry until the bitter end, venting their rage, not only at the dis-ease which they have constantly fought, but at themselves and those around them.

My heart goes out to you, my friends. I ask that you read the following Inquiry, and especially the material in Part III of this book, without judging yourselves. There is no right way or wrong way, there is no success or failure; "there is only experience." Who are we to judge either ourselves or another human being, or to pretend that we can fully comprehend the miraculous order of our Universe? What matters in *all* our lives, whether we have a life-threatening dis-ease or not, is that we open our hearts to ourselves and other human beings. In doing so, we open ourselves to God. God is love, love is harmony, harmony begets peace. By opening our hearts to love, we open ourselves to the essence of all creation, and to the essence of ourselves. What experience can be more complete, than embracing fully in the moment the very essence of all there is? By opening our hearts, we remember fully who we are. This expansion of consciousness—this transcendence of separateness—is the essence of the healing process. It is also the essence of this entire book.

The dis-ease under consideration is most frequently termed "Acquired Immune Deficiency Syndrome" or AIDS. The Holistic Group believes that such terms as "Acquired Immune Deficiency," "HTLV-III Acquired Immune Dysfunction," or "HTLV-III Related Immune Dysfunction" are more appropriate descriptions of this state. There is a commonly encountered misconception which asserts that one does not die from AIDS itself, but rather from the "syndrome" of opportunistic infections which are "acquired" from it. Such a misunderstanding might in part be avoided if the term used to describe the dis-ease were changed. Nontheless, recognizing that "Acquired Immune Deficiency Syndrome" is what the dis-ease will undoubtedly be called for a long, long time, The Holistic Group has chosen to stick with that term.

Some readers may wonder about the process by which The Holistic Group has arrived at its conclusions. The basis of all scientific investigation, and all of its discovery, is intuition. An inventor or scientist first has a "hunch"; they then develop research models and plans of investigation by which that hunch may be investigated. This process of intuition is "the phenomenon of direct knowing," enabling us to access "information that bypasses the normal rational or logical thought processes." Intuition is a phenomenon of memory, and is always stimulated by human need that is usually rooted in the *now.*

When I first recognized the horrors of the AIDS epidemic, and sensed the power of the thought forms underlying the dis-ease, I stopped long enough to breathe and to begin to remember what human beings are really about. This is the process of meditation—allowing the body to relax so that the mind can explore the full parameters of self. I remembered that dis-ease is more than a physical phenomenon—that we are more than physical beings. I looked at the members of my community who were being condemned to death, and I determined to act. Thus was The Holistic Group convened, and so did the material which follows begin to come together. Three years later, after countless people diagnosed with AIDS or ARC have asserted their ability to achieve remission and/or total healing, scientific research has progressed to the point that we are beginning to unravel the physical mysteries of this dis-ease; research projects are finally being initiated to confirm what our intuition, and the wisdom of the people diagnosed with AIDS whose interviews appear in this book, had already suggested. Is there any question but that the appropriate action on the part of The Holistic Group was to put out their research, much of which was based upon already accepted holistic practice, when it was most needed? We sensed the need; we chose to serve. What else is there to do in life but serve other people and thereby serve ourselves?

While the Inquiry which follows pays special attention to the risk of AIDS transmission to women and bisexual and heterosexual men, The Holistic Group has chosen to focus a large part of its attention on the singlemost group of individuals in the United States who are experiencing the challenges of AIDS: gay men. For reasons that will be explained in the text, the Group believes that, in the United States at least, gays will continue to comprise the majority of individuals contracting the dis-ease. Every observation which The Holistic Group makes about the physical, mental, emotional, and spiritual nature of the dis-ease and of the healing process remains valid for *all* individuals. Since all women, men, and children do run some risk of AIDS contagion, it is hoped that all readers, regardless of sex or sexual preference, will approach the discussion which follows in a spirit of love, unity, and self-interest.

A HOLISTIC INQUIRY INTO THE PREVENTION AND HEALING OF ACQUIRED IMMUNE DEFICIENCY

by *The Holistic Group*

What Is AIDS About?

Our approach to AIDS is rooted in the basic assumption that we are more than our physical bodies. We are all composed of mind, body, and spirit. We all have the potential to achieve the harmony and balance of mind, body, and spirit which is the basis of all health and inner peace.

Most so-called "physical" dis-ease, as defined by Western medical science, is actually symptomatic of a deeper dis-ease—a fundamental imbalance on the levels of mind and spirit. Only by examining AIDS in all of its aspects—mental, emotional, spiritual, and physical—can we begin to develop a full understanding of its nature, and the methods for its prevention and healing.

On the level of the body, we believe that AIDS is transmitted by the HTLV-III virus, and that it travels between individuals primarily through the blood and the semen (see Chapter 19 for a discussion of vaginal secretions). Examined solely from this perspective, gay men in particular, who frequently engage in sexual activity in which semen may enter a partner's bloodstream through microscopic fissures in the skin tissues, are likely and frequent targets for the AIDS virus. Similarly, intravenous drug users, hemophiliacs, and recipients of blood transfusions are also at high risk for exposure to the virus through the bloodstream.

But coming in contact with the AIDS virus is only one reason, and *not* the main reason, for the spread of AIDS among "high risk" groups, and among gay men in particular. Viruses, germs, and bacteria cause dis-ease, but they are not the sole cause, or even the primary cause, for someone contracting a given dis-ease. The germs that cause the common cold, for example, are routinely spread throughout the population; yet only some individuals who come in contact with them come down with a cold. The same holds true for the AIDS virus.

Far more people have come into direct contact with the virus than ever have or ever will come down with cases of AIDS.

We believe that the physical models thus far generated to explain outbreaks of AIDS among high-risk groups such as homosexual men, IV-drug users, and hemophiliacs, as well as among Haitians, Africans, and other isolated groupings, present only a partial understanding of the nature of this dis-ease state. Every illness has its psychospiritual aspects—factors which make some individuals more susceptible to it than others. After thoroughly examining AIDS, we have concluded that the psychospiritual nature of the dis-ease is the key to understanding its current manifestations within the United States and abroad.

Psychospiritual Nature of the Disease

We believe that the AIDS virus particularly strikes individuals and groups who have been isolated by the dominant culture — *culturally isolated minorities* who are forced to express their emotional, physical, and spiritual nature apart from the community at large — and individuals within those isolated communities who experience undue psychological and/or socioeconomic hardship. Societal isolation places unusually heightened degrees of stress upon the individual and collective mind, body, and spirit of its outcasts. It is this isolation, often internalized as self-hatred or lack of self-acceptance, which allows the AIDS virus to begin to incubate once it has entered the system.

The place in the physical body where a dis-ease manifests can help us discover the deeper dis-ease which resides on mental and spiritual levels. The concept of "psychosomatic ailments" evidences an understanding of the connection, for example, between suppressed feelings or unresolved emotional trauma and subsequent physical dis-ease.

The physical key to understanding AIDS lies in its association with the complete collapse of the thymus gland. The thymus is the central factor of the immune system, and is responsible for producing those T-cells we hear so much about. From a metaphysical perspective, it is associated with the heart chakra, the spiritual energy center that radiates harmony and love within and without our being. The thymal dysfunction which lies at the heart of AIDS is connected to the deeper disharmony at the core of this dis-ease, the lack of love from without internalized as a lack of self-love.

North American gay men, intravenous drug users, and Haitian refugees are the three culturally isolated groupings hardest hit by AIDS in the United States, with gays accounting for the vast majority of reported cases. Gays in particular, whose current wave of liberation began with the 1969 Stonewall Rebellion, have seen the blossoming and growing tolerance of their lifestyle threatened by the rise to power of the fundamentalist Christian right and conservative political administrations. Fostered by John Briggs, Anita Bryant, Jerry Falwell, and Lyndon LaRouche, social pressures upon the gay community have increased to the point where fear can be felt in the air. It is no coincidence that the rise of AIDS has to a large extent coincided with the recent upsurge of right-wing political and religious repression of gays.

We consider the stresses placed upon gay individuals since childhood, combined with the recent upsurge of anti-gay judgment and oppression, to be the *key causal element* of the rapid rise of AIDS in the 1980s. Stresses placed upon gays have only increased since the introduction of AIDS into the public consciousness. While for many—regardless of sex or sexuality—AIDS has presented a tremendous challenge and opportunity for unity, love, and compassion, for others it has furthered division and alienation, not only between gays and heterosexuals, but within the gay community itself.

Internalized homophobia—negative feelings about self because one is gay—has been exacerbated by the cries of fundamentalists that AIDS is a manifestation of sinful homosexuals reaping their own reward. Many gays now look upon their brothers not as sources of love and support but as potential infectors. The gay bathhouse controversy in particular, initally fueled by the demands of Reverend Falwell to close the establishments, reflects the negative political, social, and moral judgments cast upon sexually active gay men. And the tendency of the media to assume anything but a holistic and healing approach to the AIDS phenomenon has only increased negativity and alienation.

Lesbian women and gay men have always played an important role in the growth and health of the larger social fabric. They are an integral part of society despite society's attempts to disown them. Among the homosexual population is found an unusally large number of artists, sensitive individuals, and creative geniuses. Gay people constantly bring to the fore the need for acceptance of the full range of artistic, social, and sexual expression. By cutting off gays and stigmatizing them, society denies itself access to much of its sexual, artistic, and spiritual creativity. The alienation that gay people experience hurts not only gay people, but society as a whole.

Acceptance of the unique contributions that gays make to society and to life on this planet is essential to halting the spread of AIDS. We are all parts of the whole of creation, bound together by the motivating force of the Universe, which is Love. We are all brothers and sisters. Only by uniting, loving one another, and celebrating our common humanity will lesbian women, gay men, and their open-hearted supporters be able to reverse the new wave of repression in the United States. With gays as a group under more scrutiny and pressure now than at any time in recent history, self-love, unity, and positive collective action are the basis, not only of individual and collective freedom, but of the reduction of the pressures which are the central cause of the rise of AIDS.

Stress: Lifestyle, Diet, Drugs
The alienation that gays, the socially disadvantaged, and other minorities experience as a result of cultural disinvestment—which gays may experience and internalize as homophobia—has set the stage for the rise of AIDS. Those individuals within the culturally isolated homosexual minority most likely to come down with AIDS, should the virus enter their systems, are those who have both internalized their oppression, and who are experiencing heightened degrees of internal and external stress. These additional stresses may be related to high-pressure lifestyles, socioeconomic isolation, severe childhood trauma such as coming from a "broken home" (see section entitled

"Additional Factors Contributing to Susceptibility to AIDS" which follows), poor nutritional patterns, the intake of chemicals and/or major stimulants, environmental toxins, and so on. When the stress of being part of a culturally disinvested minority is exacerbated by such deeply-rooted patterns of stress, the conditions are ripe for the successful incubation of the AIDS virus within the system. While the specific stress patterns will vary from individual to individual, it is the debilitating weakener of the immune system, the stress of the self against the self, which creates the imbalances lying at the core of Acquired Immune Deficiency.

Societal alienation, a highly competitive lifestyle, social pressures, poor diet, radiation, overindulgence in alcohol and caffeine, drugs, harmful chemicals, and synthetics all potentially overstimulate the adrenals, thus affecting the functioning of the central nervous system. The adrenals control the "fight or flight" syndrome. If they are continually overstimulated through years of unhealthy living and abuse, the central nervous system will experience undue stress and eventual breakdown (burnout). In such a state, clear communication of nerve impulses along the central nervous system to the body's internal organs is prevented; this results in the tendency of the endocrine system (of which the adrenals are a part) to atrophy. In the simplest language possible, stress affects the immune system; chronic stress can lead to immune dysfunction.

It is speculated that, at an earlier stage of human evolution, our ancestors did not have an immune system *per se.* What we now term the immune system once aided in the proper digestion of nutrients, and, particularly through aiding the assimilation of proteins, helped to maintain an individual's well-being. Food, bacteria, and viruses were all digested, as the human being in ancient times was immune to everything. The skin, for example, was probably originally a digestive organ, not an eliminative one.

At our current stage of evolution, we still experience the affects of our earlier evolutionary make-up. For this reason, neurological impulses not only communicate sensation and pain impulses to the brain, but are connected with cellular rejuvenation. (For example, it has been demonstrated that a mild current of electricity stimulates cell rejuvenation and promotes healing, particularly in cases of broken bones.) Chiropractic theory affirms that the low voltage electrical charge generated in the central nervous system not only is registered as pain, but is actually critical to the functioning of the endocrine system. Too little or too much nerve supply and electrical charge can affect or even atrophy the endocrine system, thereby affecting the immune system and leaving one open to dis-ease.

Synthetics taken into the system—including food colorings and preservatives—overstimulate the adrenals, and contribute to central nervous system burnout. The spleen, which is part of the endocrine system, is especially affected by the intake of synthetics. Equally damaging are most recreational drugs, and overindulgence in alcohol. The maximum "safe" level of alcohol we can sanction is a glass or two of beer, one or two glasses of wine, or "two to three fingers" (one shot) of hard alcohol.

We do not recommend the eating of heavy red blood meats, as these are saturated with adrenalins stimulated by the animal by the fear generated at the point of slaughter. These adrenalins create heightened degrees of stress in the endocrine system.

Pesticides have had a damaging effect on much of our population. Even such a "mild toxin" as malathion, which is sprayed to eradicate certain insect infestations, may have long-term health risks. Especially when inhaled and accumulated on the parasympathetic ganglia, we believe that this pesticide can affect the central and parasympathetic nervous systems, contributing to possible immune dysfunction.

Marijuana?
We have chosen to single out this one substance, which is often lumped together with such potentially damaging drugs as cocaine, amphetamines, and heroin, because the politics surroundng its legality and use only obscure its positive effects as both a stress reducer and medically valid adjunct to many allopathic and "alternative" forms of treatment.

Viewing marijuana as objectively as possible, we have mixed feelings about its long-term use. While it must be acknowledged that some people are allergic to the substance, and that THC, the active component of marijuana, can have a temporary dulling effect on the white blood corpuscles, we believe this effect is benign, and is more than compensated for by the positive attributes of marijuana as a medically validated tool for stress reduction. We know of one man, for example, who was medically issued a "you're not going to live much longer" verdict due to his chronic high blood pressure, and who credits the stress reducing benefits of marijuana with keeping him alive. Other reports exist of its value in treating glaucoma, and in combatting the nauseous side effects of radiation therapy and interferon.

While neither recommending nor endorsing its use, The Holistic Group strongly believes that marijuana can help reduce stress in a person with AIDS, especially if consumed in conjunction with visualization exercises. Were we presented with a case history of a long-term marijuana user who had been subsequently diagnosed with AIDS, we would first investigate whether or not that individual had used marijuana as a tool for stress reduction; our intuitive "hit" would be to suggest that the long-term psychospiritual stress of the individual, rather than the marijuana, was ultimately responsible for their weakened immune system and dis-ease. We would further suggest that this individual's continued use of marijuana, combined with visualization exercises, stress reduction techniques, and other work whose goal was the re-establishment of harmony in mind, body, and spirit might prove preferable to the stress encountered by eliminating marijuana from their lifestyle.

For those who do elect to use marijuana, we suggest that they consult with a trustworthy health practitioner to make sure that they do not harbor allergies to the substance. Because of potential damage to the lungs caused by the inhalation of smoke (compounded by the possible inhalation of smoke laced with paraquat and other toxic substances used in marijuana eradication programs), we strongly recommend that marijuana be consumed as a tea, and ingested at the minimal levels necessary to achieve the desired effect. Assimilating THC through the intestinal tract is far healthier than absorbing it through the lung tissues. (A recipe for marijuana tea, especially effective in countering interferon therapy side effects, can be found in the "Interferon" section of this Inquiry.) For those readers who currently use marijuana, but who are experiencing fears around its use because of AIDS, we recommend visualizing the weed as having only a positive effect.

Lest there be any question about psychedelic drugs, we do not believe that psyllocibin mushrooms and peyote are immunosuppressant when consumed in their organically bound form. LSD and ADAM/Ecstasy, as well as cocaine, most certainly are immunosuppressant.

Psychoincubation of AIDS
Jeff M. Leiphart, Ph.D., a Bay Area psychotherapist, published an article in the San Francisco newspaper, *The Bay Area Reporter* (9/29/83) that supports our beliefs that stress is a key critical factor in the rise of AIDS. Dr. Leiphart spent a year and a half in extensive psychotherapy with 26 men diagnosed with either AIDS or pre-AIDS conditions. In each one he found an unresolved "emotional emergency" relating to survival and safety, usually dating from early childhood. Each man held within himself the sense that his survival was always in jeopardy. Blocking rage, holding back anger, and avoiding confrontation by adopting a "Mr. Likeable" nice-guy coping personality was the common defense mechanism used by these men.

Examining theories which link mental and emotional states with the functioning of the immune system, and citing Steven E. Locke's *Mind and Immunity: Behavioral Immunology,* Leiphart emphasizes that the constant threat of survival experienced by these men and their common adaptive responses can, over a period of time, lead to a pronounced exhaustion and weakening of the immune system: "Psychoimmunology research suggests that if these bodily preparations by the 'threat-emergency system' (the endocrine system and adrenals) operate on high for months or years, rather than in the 'quick-use style' (the fight or flight syndrome) for which they were designed, the consequences on the body and the immune system can be harsh."

Happily, Dr. Leiphart reports that by employing techniques to bring long-suppressed anger and rage to the surface, he has succeeded in holding AIDS in check. Many of his patients diagnosed as suspected developers of AIDS stopped manifesting symptoms and those with KS developed no new lesions. Months after publication of his findings, his patients remained stabilized.

Further support for this approach to psychoincubation of AIDS can be found in the work of Dr. O. Carl Simonton. One of the pioneers in the use of visualization techniques for healing oneself of cancer, and author of *Getting Well Again*, Simonton suggests four personality characteristics that may make one prone to malignancy:

(1) a tendency to harbor resentment;
(2) a tendency toward self-pity;
(3) difficulty in developing and maintaining meaningful, long-term relationships; and
(4) a poor self-image (lack of self-worth/esteem)

* * * *

When Richard Brian Herbaugh, 29, hung himself in San Francisco's Golden Gate Park soon after being diagnosed with Kaposi's sarcoma, this note was found near his body:

> *Maybe this wouldn't have happened*
> *if I had liked myself more.*

* * * *

AIDS in Haiti, Africa, and Other Communities
We believe that our analysis of the psychospiritual nature of the AIDS virus explains not only its manifestation among gay men, but its occurrence among homosexuals and heterosexuals in Haiti, Africa, and other communities. Coming from Haiti, for example, can be understood as equivalent to being born on the wrong side of the tracks. Politically, socially, and

economically, Haitians, both in their native country and as expatriates in the United States, represent a distinctly oppressed culturally isolated minority. In Haiti, superstition is consciously fostered by the government as a means of denying social and political freedom to the populace, poverty is extreme and grinding, and tension a constant of life. Such overall impoverishment and politically induced stress lowers the general Haitian immunity to the point where the AIDS virus can be passed among both heterosexuals and homosexuals by means of semen or blood entering the body through fissures in the skin. The cultural, social, economic, and political isolation and oppression experienced by native Haitians establishes the preconditions for both weakened immunity and the incubation of the AIDS virus.

Many individuals of African origin are raised with a sense of "cultural castration," with many parallels to that of Haiti, resulting in a depressed sense of self-direction and self-esteem. Africa is a continent so broken up and oppressed by racism and imperialism that attempts on the part of its people to assert independence and autonomy frequently degenerate into military dictatorships which thrive on such psychological and spiritual fragmentation. In the specific case of Zaire, where AIDS approaches epidemic proportions in both white and black communities of heterosexual orientation, we believe that close examination will reveal that the white people with AIDS feel colonized within a black continent, while the black people in turn feel colonized by the white rule of First World countries. The high percentage of African AIDS cases among black heterosexual women can be traced to lacerations in the vaginal tissues acquired from penetration by the male before full clitoral or other stimulation or adequate lubrication on the part of the female, as well as to the higher degree of stress experienced by these sexually oppressed members of culture. In all such cases, the experience of being culturally isolated and disinvested is the key factor.

The highest AIDS rate in the United States may be found not in San Francisco or New York City, but in Belle Glade, Florida. Characterized by Dr. Mark Whiteside, co-director of Miami's Institute of Tropical Medicine, as a "little piece of Haiti right here in America," this dense pocket of rural poverty lies in the heart of the Everglades, 85 miles northwest of Miami. In April 1985, Belle Glade had 41 AIDS cases among its 24,000 residents, a rate five times higher than that of San Francisco or New York. While 16 groups of the cases were intravenous drug users, 7 were gay and bisexual men, and 10 were Haitian—a group that has recently been eliminated as a "high risk group" by the Centers for Disease Control—Belle Glade contains 8 other cases with no current prior connection to designated high risk groups.

In our estimation, examining the social, political, and economic situation in Belle Glade not only explains its high rate of AIDS, but adds credence to our thesis. Belle Glade is characterized by poor sanitation, rodents, slums of Caribbean refugees and migrant workers, a high tuberculosis rate, fecal contamination, malnutrition, and many endemic dis-eases which are manifestations of a weakened immune system. Most of the cases of AIDS in Belle Glade originate among men from these depressed slums. While the local landowners cheerfully refer to the town as "the Winter Vegetable Capital of the World," Edward R. Murrow exposed the oppression of its population 25 years ago in a program entitled "Harvest of Shame." Is it necessary to discuss Belle Glade in greater detail? Here we have yet another example of a culturally isolated population, experiencing great internal and external stress, whose lifestyle promotes a weakened immune system, infection, and, to borrow a phrase, the "dysfunction of consciousness" which sets the stage for the rise of AIDS.

One final note: Some investigators, discovering that many of the gay men in the United States have histories of IV-drug use, have questioned whether or not the categories established by the Centers for Disease Control for high risk groups fairly represent the population groupings most affected by AIDS. Their argument is that when an IV-drug user is discovered to be gay, that man is classified not as an IV-drug user with AIDS, but as a gay man with AIDS. If IV-drug users, whether homosexual or heterosexual, were classified as "IV" cases as opposed to "gay" cases, they believe that gay men would appear to be at much smaller risk for AIDS contagion than is currently accepted.

While it is possible that most of these gay IV-drug users could have contracted AIDS through the use of shared needles, we feel that the *primary* cause of their addiction is their oppression as a culturally-isolated minority. It is this oppression, when internalized as a lack of self-love, which encourages their dangerous drug use in the first place. We would even speculate that a close examination of the economic profile of these IV-drug users will reveal that the majority of them are from lower economic brackets. Certainly in the case of the heterosexual IV-drug users, for example, who during certain months in New York City have accounted for more new AIDS cases than have gays diagnosed with the dis-ease, cultural and economic disinvestment lies at the root of their diagnosis.

Additional Factors Contributing to Susceptibility to AIDS

We believe that people whose childhood was characterized by coming from a "broken home" (for want of a better term) can experience heightened susceptibility to the AIDS virus. This includes both orphans and other individuals who have experienced extreme emotional and even physical trauma during childhood due to their parents' separation, death, or disappearance. For many such individuals, this separation or loss becomes internalized as a message that they have been rejected and are unworthy of love.

It is interesting to note that there was an outbreak of pneumocystis pneumonia in European orphanages among infants during World War II. Undoubtedly this was related to the immune-suppressing stresses of separation from their mothers combined with the stresses of war. It is also important to note that Rock Hudson, the man whose AIDS diagnosis and subsequent death literally brought AIDS into the conscious minds and living rooms of the American public, was both the product of a broken home and a gay man. Certainly the stresses of having his father abandon his family when he was four, his mother remarry and divorce, and growing up to lead one of the most notorious "double lives" in Hollywood took their toll on the immune system of this courageous man.

As will be discussed in the section entitled "Development and Progression of the Syndrome" which follows, the AIDS virus may remain dormant in the body for many years before manifesting as the immune dysfunction known as AIDS. The key critical element in determining whether or not the immune system will successfully rid the body of the virus, render it dormant, or be rendered dysfunctional by it relates to the patterns of stress discussed in the sections above. In addition, we believe there is an entire sequence of behavior and disease, starting in infancy, that can lead to heightened susceptibility to the AIDS virus. No single individual, of course, fits the following profile; we offer it mainly to help diagnosticians, therapists, and other professionals involved in AIDS research and treatment.

The presence of any three of the following factors, combined with a high-stress lifestyle in adulthood, can indicate heightened susceptibility to AIDS:

(1) The experience in infancy of susceptibility to parasites in the intestinal tract, or mild allergic reactions, such as rashes, to mother's milk and mucous-producing substances;

(2) shortness of breath, which may be related to allergies and afflictions of the upper bronchials;

(3) the subject might experience remission of the above between the ages of 3 and 7, only to find these symptoms reactivated between 12 and 15 years of age;

(4) high susceptibility, ages 12 to 21, to pneumonia and viral infections of the body;

(5) between 12 to 16 years, experiencing lockjaw once, or even twice;

(6) unusual difficulty with digestion;

(7) hyperacidity in the abdomen;

(8) forms of extreme hyperkinetic behavior, especially in early childhood;

(9) unusual degrees of sugar cravings, developing between the ages of 8 and 15, and then dropping off. These would correspond to a history of hyperkinetic behavior;

(10) unusual degrees of anxiety as the subject leaves adolescence and approaches early adulthood. (A trained and sympathetic therapist can distinguish between the anxiety that most persons have experienced during this period, and the heightened degree of anxiety which indicates emotional disturbance on some level);

(11) early development of sexual awareness, probably between the ages of 8 and 10, which a professional would term "acute prepubescent sexual response."

The AIDS Virus

Our initial research paper, "AIDS & KS: A Holistic Approach," published in June of 1983, stated our belief that the causative agent of AIDS was probably human T-cell leukemia virus, or a parallel or mutated form of that virus. We also noted during that time period that the AIDS virus was a parallel virus to the herpes virus, and that it shared with it a tendency to mutate. Subsequent scientific investigation has confirmed many of these findings. The AIDS virus, variously identified as HTLV-III and LAV, is a member of the same family as human T-cell leukemia virus. The reason that it took scientists as long as it did to isolate and identify HTLV-III or the AIDS virus lies in the fact that it does mutate in the body to the point where it may become unrecognizable. It is because French researchers intuited this possibility, and looked for it in a different stage of its development and progression than did the Americans, that the French discovered it first (see section which follows).

We feel certain that cytomegaloviris, or CMV (a lengthy virus of the herpes family, very difficult to throw off, whose extended symptoms include muscular discomfort and even sweats), is a parallel virus to the AIDS virus. Some confirmation for this point lies in the fact that CMV has been found in many people diagnosed with AIDS, and specifically in people who have succumbed to the AIDS opportunistic infection pneumocystis pneumonia. In our opinion, any course of treatment successful for herpes or CMV will prove beneficial in the early stages of AIDS. Such treatment could possibly hold the progression of AIDS in check until adoption of the detoxification and healing programs described later in this Inquiry might render the virus dormant, or even rid it entirely from the body. To be specific, a homeopathic preparation of CMV, which is harmless, might be successfully incorporated into a holistic treatment program to achieve this effect. Many homeopaths have the equipment necessary to prepare the 30X or 10mm potency of CMV which we believe would prove beneficial. (See discussions on CMV and homeopathy which follow for more information.)

[Ed. note: Several members of The Holistic Group have suggested areas of study and experimentation which might yield important information pertaining to the development of an AIDS vaccine. If herpes is in fact a parallel virus to the AIDS virus, is it not possible that people infected with it may have a higher resistance to HTLV-III than do other members of equivalent populations? Were this the case, individuals diagnosed with herpes who test positive for the HTLV-III antibody might evidence less of a tendency to develop full-blown AIDS than others who test positive for HTLV-III antibodies.

More provocative is the suggestion that since both HTLV-III and viruses of the herpes-like strain are parallel viruses which share the potential to mutate, might it not be possible that by manipulating the structure of the herpes virus through the process of genetic engineering—artifically mutating it, as it were—to move closer to an understanding of the AIDS virus and its mutations? This same procedure could be applied to a substance such as acyclovir, which has demonstrated success in the treatment of herpes. If genetically manipulating the herpes virus might move us closer to the mutations of HTLV-III, perhaps genetically engineering acyclovir in parallel fashion could lead to the development of an AIDS vaccine.]

As noted in our original paper, published in June 1983, we wish to suggest that the origins of the AIDS virus eventually may be found to exist, not in Africa as commonly believed, but in areas of Cambodia, Vietnam, Korea, and India. We speculate that there's a band spanning between Southeast Asia, India, and Africa, in which many common dis-ease organisms will be found to incubate. AIDS has undoubtedly existed in Asian cultures for a very long time, but has gone virtually undocumented due to the low level of medical research, technology, and practice in those countries.

While the HTLV-III virus has clearly incubated in Africa and Caribbean countries, we believe that the physical origins of this current epidemic are in Southeast Asia. AIDS has not stricken U.S. Asian refugee populations as a whole due to the maintenance of strong family and cultural ties within these groups, and a dietary regimen/lifestyle considerably less stressful than the high-stress, alcohol- and drug-dependent patterns of the majority of those currently diagnosed with AIDS.

While some researchers have suggested that the African (or Southeast Asian) strains of HTLV-III are different than the one in the United States, we believe that they are substantially the same. What divergencies that do exist stem from the fact that this particular virus undergoes mild mutations from one generation to the next.

Development and Progression of the Syndrome
We wish to present below a model for the incubation of the AIDS virus within the system, and the eventual manifestation of the opportunistic infections connected with AIDS. Although this model may differ in parts from current understandings, we feel confident that further research will eventually validate our findings.

We believe the incubation period for the virus is 8 to 22 months at most, depending upon the individual. Some isolated cases will exist where an infected individual's immune system will rally to the point of holding the virus in a dormant stage, while not entirely eliminating it from the system. Reports of cases where the virus has seemed to incubate for up to 5 years are due to the immune system's ability to hold the virus in this dormant stage. AIDS is most transmittable in the early period of infestation, beginning about 14 days after contact, and terminating with the manifestation of the dis-ease's opportunistic infections. We do not believe that the virus is transmittable if the immune system has rendered it dormant, but hasten to note that the virus can remain dormant for an indefinite period of time. The program of detoxification, cleansing, and balancing which follows has been designed to strengthen the immune system to the point of completely cleansing the body of the virus and its toxic effects.

The first AIDS symptoms, manifesting by the eighth month, include certain forms of minor lesions, sweats, chills, fevers, and temporary blisterings—in some cases herpes-like in nature. Unusual tremblings and, in some cases, muscular contractions and shortness of breath may also manifest as evidence of the virus's interplay in the central nervous system. Both the immune system and the nervous system, particularly in the high-stressed individual, focus their entire attention on the invading virus. The effort to fight off the invader heightens the stress on the already overworked adrenals; blood analyses of AIDS patients taken at this time would indicate the presence of epinephrine (adrenalin) as evidence for this assertion. The long period of resistance, during which the immune system is sorely overtaxed by its fight and by the stress and diet of the individual, eventually brings about the collapse of the immune system itself.

The virus centers its continuous overstimulation between two critical reflex points: the coccyx and the medulla oblongata. These points may already be overtaxed by the tendency of impurities and synthetics to congregate there; autopsies of high-stressed individuals evidence this fact. The continuous reflex alarm passing between the coccyx and the medulla oblongata will overstimulate the adrenals; this leads to either an over- or understimulus of either of their functions, and eventually to the imbalance and breakdown of the adrenals and the endocrine system. The swellings frequently observed in the lymph glands result from the immune system's attempt to alleviate the stresses placed upon the kidneys, as the kidneys seek to eliminate excess adrenalin (and other products of adrenal overstimulation) from the system.

By the eighth month of incubation, the DNA of the AIDS viral pattern will begin to integrate into the connective tissues, and particularly into the skin tissues. Lesions which may appear at this time are comparable or similar to those in advanced states of certain syphilitic disorders. As the viral-like nature of the disease begins to break down, it is carried through the genetic molecules of the infected individual in a truly cancerous manner. It is likely that by this time the AIDS virus will have mutated to the point where it is no longer traceable in the body; it thoroughly hosts the body by virtue of its ability to alter the cellular memory (DNA code). Many of the difficulties encountered while conducting scientific investigation and laboratory analysis can be linked to this phenomenon.

[Ed. note: The Holistic Group first published this model in June 1983; 18 months later, facts such as the rapid mutation of the AIDS virus have been scientifically validated.]

Stresses upon the immune system, particularly after about the twelfth to fourteenth month, allow the body to be opened in varying degrees to other forms of inflammation; this hastens the arrival of opportunistic infections, particularly those pneumonia-like in nature.

It is important to note again that factors such as the fear and suddenness with which AIDS strikes, constant and frightening media reports, the increasing psychic pressures upon the gay community, political pressures exerted by the fundamentalist Right to withhold research funds for AIDS and herpes (as though attempting to introduce a biological system of morals into the American lifestyle), and the superstitious and paranoid fears bandied about because of the "plaguelike" quality of the disease's spread (which is regarded by some as a form of punishment for sinful acts) all contribute to the increased stress upon even the most sober individuals within the gay and heterosexual communities. This stress, when internalized, makes an individual more susceptible to the AIDS virus, and facilitates its progression into such opportunistic infections as pneumocystis pneumonia and the cancer called Kaposi's sarcoma.

One of the most puzzling aspects of AIDS has been the specific choice of esoteric opportunistic infections through which it may eventually manifest. From our perspective, it is vital to comprehend AIDS as a progressive syndrome of toxicity, which can eventually overwhelm the body's immune system and eliminative processes. As the body attempts to eliminate the toxic effects of the AIDS virus, it calls upon its primary eliminative organ, the skin; the skin in fact is often the *last* means of elimination of toxins from the body. Upon examining Kaposi's sarcoma and some of the most common AIDS opportunistic infections, e.g. pneumocystis pneumonia, tuberculosis, herpes, candida, and CMV, one discovers that they are all dis-eases of the skin tissue or of the lungs. Noting that Chinese medicine views the skin as the external organ of the lungs, and that both skin and lungs are composed of connective tissue, we have concluded that the various opportunistic infections cited above, in combination with the night sweats and the swollen lymph glands, represent the final attempts by the body to throw off toxins. It is only natural that when the virus progresses into its final phases, it should manifest in the last eliminative tissues to be called upon, namely the lungs and skin.

Once we understand the nature and progression of the disease, we can see that the body is clearly crying out for help in eliminating the toxic effects of the virus by utilizing all means available to it. Aiding the body by instituting the holistic program of detoxification and cleansing which follows offers a viable means of furthering this eliminative process. A holistic approach to healing AIDS makes plain good sense.

Another phenomenon puzzling researchers is the observation that while KS frequently strikes gay men, it usually does not manifest in nonhomosexual hemophiliacs. We believe this is because the immune system of gay men is more stressed due to the isolated social pressures placed upon them, paving the way for the insinuation of the virus into the tissue and its eventual manifestation as cancer. While these men's widespread use of "poppers"—inhalants usually containing amyl, butyl or isobutyl nitrate—to enhance the sexual experience has been implicated as a possible cause of this phenomenon, this drug use, as discussed above, may in itself be traced back to the deep sense of alienation from society and self experienced by many gay men.

What Constitutes a Diagnosis of AIDS?

As of this writing, no test for AIDS exists. The blood tests developed to ensure the safety of the nation's blood supply only indicate presence of antibodies to the AIDS virus; they do not indicate whether or not a person has or will ever develop AIDS. Lacking a foolproof test for AIDS itself, the Centers for Disease Control in Atlanta, the government organization responsible for keeping track of the "epidemic," has drawn up a list of opportunistic infections which it uses as indicators of AIDS. This list, which is reproduced below, represents a noble attempt on the part of medical and scientific investigators to diagnose a dis-ease which they find easier to observe than to understand.

Opportunistic Diseases Used as Indicators of AIDS

The diagnostic methods (with positive results) required to fit the case definition are shown in parentheses.

A.   *Protozoal and Helminithic Infections:*
  1.   Cryptosporidiosis, intestinal, causing diarrhea for over 1 month, (on histology or stool microscopy);
  2.   *Pneumocystis carinii* pneumonia, (on histology, or microscopy of a "touch" preparation, bronchial washings, or sputum);

3.   Strongyloidosis, causing pneumonia, central nervous system infection, or disseminated infection (beyond the gastrointestinal tract), (on histology);

4.   Toxoplasmosis, causing infection in internal organs other than liver, spleen, or lymph nodes (on histology or microscopy of a "touch" preparation)

B.   *Fungal Infections:*

1.   Candidiasis, causing esophagitis (on histology, or microscopy or a "wet" preparation from the esophagus, or endoscopic or autopsy findings of white plaques on an erythematous mucosal base, but not by culture alone);

2.   Cryptococcosis, causing central nervous system or disseminated infection (beyond lungs and lymph nodes) (on culture, antigen detection, histology, or India ink preparation of CSF)

C.   *Bacterial Infections:*

1.   *Mycobacterium avium* or *intracellulare* (*Mycobacterium avium* complex), or *Mycobacterium kansasii*, causing disseminated infection (beyond lungs and lymph nodes) (on culture)

D.   *Viral Infections:*

1.   Cytomegalovirus, causing infection in internal organs other than liver, spleen, or lymph nodes (on histology);

2.   Herpes simplex virus, causing chronic mucocutaneous infection with ulcers persisting more than 1 month, or pulmnonary, gastrointestinal tract (beyond mouth, throat, or rectum), or disseminated infection (but not encephalitis alone) (on culture, histology, or cytology)

3.   Progressive multifocal leukoencephalopathy (presumed to be caused by Papovavirus) (on histology);

E.   *Cancer:*

1.   Kaposi's sarcoma (on histology)

2.   Lymphoma limited to the brain (on histology)

F.   *Other Opportunistic Infections with Positive test for HTLV-III/LAV*:*

In the absence of the above opportunistic diseases, any of the following diseases is considered indicative of AIDS if the patient had a positive test for HTLV-III/LAV*:

1.   disseminated histoplasmosis, (on culture or histology)

2.   bronchial or pulmonary candidiasis, (on microscopy or visualization grossly of characteristic white plaques on the bronchial mucosa, but not by culture alone)

3.   isosporiasis, causing chronic diarrhea (over 1 month), (on histology or stool microscopy)

G.   *Chronic lymphoid interstitial pneumonitis:*

In the absence of the above opportunistic diseases, a histologically confirmed diagnosis of chronic (persisting over 2 months) lymphoid interstitial pneumonitis in a child (under 13 years of age) is indicative of AIDS unless test(s) for HTLV-III/LAV are negative.* The histologic examination of lung tissue must show diffuse interstitial and peribronchiolar infiltration by lymphocytes, plasma cells with Russell bodies, plasmacytoid lymphocytes and immunoblasts. Histologic and culture evaluation must not identify a pathogenic organism as the cause of this pneumonia.

H.   *Non-Hodgkin's Lymphoma with Positive Test for HTLV-III/LAV*:*

If the patient had a positive test for HTLV-III/LAV*, then the following histologic types of lymphoma are indicative of AIDS, regardless of anatomic site:

1. Small *non*cleaved lymphoma (Burkitt's tumor or Burkitt-like lymphoma), but not small cleaved lymphoma,

2. Immunoblastic sarcoma (or immunoblastic lymphoma) of B-cell or unknown immunologic phenpotype (not of T-cell type). Other terms which may be equivalent include: diffuse undifferentiated non-Hodgkin's lymphoma, large cell lymphoma (cleaved or non-cleaved), diffuse histiocytic lymphoma, reticulum cell sarcoma, and high-grade lymphoma.

Lymphomas should not be accepted as indicative of AIDS if they are described in any of the following ways: low grade, of T-cell type (immunologic phenotype), small cleaved lymphoma, lymphocyte lymphoma (regardless of whether well or poorly differentiated), lymphoblastic lymphoma, plasmacytoid lymphocytic lymphoma, lymphocytic leukemia (acute or chronic), or Hodgkin's disease (or Hodgkin's lymphoma).

---

* a positive test for HTLV-III/LAV may consist of a reactive test for antibody to HTLV-III/LAV or a positive culture (isolation of HTLV-III/LAV from a culture of the patient's peripheral blood lymphocytes). If multiple anitbody tests have inconsistent results, the result applied to the case definition, should be that of the majority done by the ELISA, immunofluorescent, or Western Blot methods. A positive culture, however, would over-rule negative antibody tests.

Kaposi's sarcoma, a rare form of cancer marked by the presence of external and/or internal frequently purple skin lesions; pneumocystis carinii pneumonia; and a host of opportunistic infections (e.g. toxoplasmosis and cryptococcosis) complete with qualifications as to location, severity, and duration are considered as official indicators of AIDS. Many of these infections, such as candidiasis, CMV, and herpes simplex, are of course found among many people who have not been infected by HTLV-III. In an attempt to clarify the situation, the CDC has attempted to establish exactly when the presence of these infections in people at high risk for exposure to HTLV-III may be justifiably considered due cause for an AIDS diagnosis. When a person in a high-risk group for AIDS infection (e.g. gay men, hemophiliacs, IV-drug users) is diagnosed with one of these potential opportunistic infections, but does not evidence it to the degree stipulated on the official list, that person is considered diagnosed with AIDS-Related Condition (ARC).

This list does evidence an attempt on the part of the authorities to light a single candle rather than, as it has been written, to curse the darkness. Nonetheless, the reality of the situation is that, in the absence of a medical test for AIDS, it is impossible scientifically to determine by allopathic means the exact nature of one's dis-ease condition. (Chinese medical diagnosis, observation, case history, inner search, and intuitive techniques may in fact prove the most reliable methods for diagnosing the dis-ease in its early stages.) There is no Western medical way to determine whether or not someone diagnosed with AIDS-Related Condition has or ever will develop AIDS. The situation is so unclear that we do not even have a way of determining the actual number of AIDS cases in the United States or abroad, or of estimating how far off the current tally is.

The real problem is felt in terms of the human suffering that a diagnosis of AIDS or ARC may bring to an individual. People diagnosed with ARC live in a grey zone, unclear about their health status. Often ineligible for government and private financial, health, and counseling services, these individuals are prime candidates for the stress which opens one to susceptibility to the AIDS virus in the first place.

The only solution to this catch-22 dilemma is for everyone involved to take full responsibility for the situation at hand. On the levels of financial, health, and emotional support services, this means granting everyone in need of assistance full access to the resources at hand. Were only a small portion of the funding available within the federal government channeled instead into human support services, all people diagnosed with either AIDS or ARC could easily be cared for.

Most importantly, people diagnosed with either condition must realize that beyond the maze of arbitrary definitions, uncertainty, politics, bureaucracies, and human ego lies their ability to take full responsibility for their bodies and their lives. What matters more than medical "diagnosis" or "prognosis" is the determination to live life to the fullest in health and in peace. By moving beyond all of this mess and resolving to establish inner harmony and balance, people diagnosed with disease can heal themselves.

If you are experiencing any of the infections associated with any kind of immune dysfunction, allow yourself to know that you *do* have power over your dis-ease state. Healing is possible. You can begin now, by reducing stress in your life, and adpoting the principles of psychoimmunity and healing offered throughout this book. There is a powerful and ever-expanding network of love and support which you can tap into. Regardless of the seeming obstacles at hand; no one is a victim of anything. By joining together with all of the people who are committed to transformation on this planet, you can work to heal yourself and all of us.

Transmission of AIDS

We believe that the AIDS virus is so strong that it remains alive and transmittable in bodily fluids up to 48 hours after excretion. Similarly, we believe it can be passed from one infected party to other individuals after about 14 days of incubation. This means that host individuals who are the picture of health, and who have no inkling of the presence of the virus in their systems, are capable of unwittingly transmitting AIDS to others.

The dis-ease is most highly contagious during the first 6 to 8 months of the incubation period, especially when the first stage symptoms manifest around the eighth month. While much hoopla has been made around the presence of HTLV-III antibodies in the blood of large numbers of gays and straights, we do not believe that the presence of these antibodies necessarily connotes either the presence of a case of AIDS, or even of prior direct exposure to HTLV-III. We predict that further research will eventually bear out that the body can develop HTLV-III antibodies, not only from exposure to the virus itself, but from exposure to (1) a sister virus of the HTLV family, (2) one of the genetic evolutions of HTLV-III as it insinuates itself into the body's tissues and eventually mutates, (3) someone else's HTLV-III antibodies (which in turn may be produced through any of these associations). The net result of all this is that a significantly smaller percentage of individuals than is currently predicted who show evidence of HTLV-III antibodies may eventually develop AIDS.

We believe further research will show that since the antibodies themselves can be transmitted in bodily fluids, it is very likely that many sexually active gay men, as well as heterosexuals of both sexes, harbor these HTLV-III antibodies without even having encountered the virus itself. Depending upon the length of time that these antibodies have been in the system, they may register at weak levels in the AIDS-antibody blood test, or even avoid detection entirely. To the extent that antibodies acquired from simple exposure to someone else's antibodies do register positive in the test, so in turn will the estimates of the number of individuals exposed to the AIDS virus be inflated.

We believe that no more than 1% to 2% of individuals exposed in some way to the AIDS virus or its antibodies may actually harbor the virus in an active or dormant stage. This belief, combined with our understanding of the psychospiritual aspect of the dis-ease, leads us to conclude that we are not about to experience the worldwide devastating epidemic of AIDS predicted by the proponents of Viral Armageddon.

We concur with much of the information disseminated by public health departments and medical authorities concerning the transmission of the AIDS virus. AIDS is transmittable through bodily fluids, and particularly through the blood and semen. The microscopic tears or fissures in the lining of the rectum which can occur during anal intercourse can allow infected semen to enter the bloodstream of a carrier's partner; hence, this act without condoms is a risky and health-threatening form of sexual/love expression. Similarly, oral sex (fellatio) which includes ejaculation into the partner's mouth is of risk, as the semen can enter the bloodstream through ulcerations in the mouth or gastrointestinal tract; ingested semen which survives the gastrointestinal tract can also enter the bloodstream. It is also possible that infected semen or blood can enter the partner's bloodstream through cuts on the hands or other surfaces of the body.

We strongly believe that dry kissing and French (wet) kissing pose virtually *no danger* to most parties. Further research will eventually confirm that when the AIDS virus is present in saliva, it is usually of such a weakened state that it poses a threat only to the most sensitive of individuals—those whose immune systems are already in a severely weakened state. We believe, for example, that an individual with an already weakened immune system could conceivably get AIDS if continuously exposed to infected saliva for a period of *almost a full year*—but both preconditions of an already weakened immune system *and* continuously lengthy exposure would be necessary for infection. Kissing many different people, in our opinion, poses no risk unless all of these are carrying the AIDS virus. Were kissing a viable means of AIDS transmission, the AIDS virus rates among homosexuals and heterosexuals would be astronomically higher than at present.

Much has been written about the so-called "promiscuous nature" of gay male sexual encounters. We are very uncomfortable with such moral judgments. A large number of gay men spend most of their adult lives in monogamous relationships. What we will acknowledge is that the gay male community is a rather closed community in which "incestuous relationships," i.e. sexual encounters among a whole group of people who know each other or who frequent the same bars, baths, or social circles, are not uncommon. How many gay men reading this have discovered that they share mutual sexual partners with their friends? Unfortunately, when it comes to diseases such as VD and AIDS, this potentially liberating mode of behavior heightens the risk of transmission.

"Safe Sex," Condoms, and Lubricants

"Safe sex" means safe sexual conduct. This involves modification of one's sexual appetite, and establishment of long or longer-lasting relationships. Mutual masturbation and the use of latex condoms during anal intercourse are practices we encourage between people who are not 100% certain of their partner's active sexual history. Latex condoms greatly reduce the environment in which the AIDS virus can live, and are effective in inhibiting the spread of AIDS. Men using them for the first time are encouraged to read the instructions for their use, and to employ only water-soluble lubricants.

While it is an established fact that only water-soluble lubricants are safe to use with latex condoms—others can contribute to unsafe rapid deterioration of latex—the oil-based composition of most water-soluble lubricants has been brought into question. Preliminary research indicates that the

hydrogenated fat globules present in many water-soluble lubricants may enter the body through the anus and vagina and
lodge in the lungs and heart, thereby potentially contributing
to eventually serious health problems.

The safest way to use condoms and to enjoy anal and/or
vaginal intercourse is to employ only water-based (non oil-
based), water-*soluble* lubricants. The water-based lubricants we
recommend are *Probe* or *OXY-C2*. *OXY-C2* consists of chlorine
peroxide in a base of aqueous carboamers. While preliminary
research indicates that it may be effective against Epstein-Burr
virus, candida, and even HTLV-III, The Holistic Group believes
that its value as a lubricant resides in its absence of
hydrogenated fats, rather than in its possible antiviral properties. "Safe sex" with *OXY-C2* gel also implies following safe sex
guidelines, which include the use of condoms in sexual intercourse. The safe nature of *OXY-C2* and *Probe* relates to an absence of fat molecules that might clog up the lungs or heart.

The following suggestions will enable you to get maximum
protection and maximum satisfaction while using condoms:

(1) Store latex condoms in a cool, dry place. Latex eventually disintegrates, so if you haven't used your condoms after, let us say, six months, it would be wise to discard them
and buy new ones;

(2) do not test condoms by inflating or stretching them;

(3) open the package carefully, watching out for long or
jagged fingernails. Tearing open the package may damage the
condom;

(4) gently press the air out of condoms having recepta-
cle tips before putting them on. Air bubbles can cause condoms to break. If you are using a plain-ended condom, leave
about a half-inch free at the tip to catch the semen;

(5) make sure the anus or vagina of the receptive partner and the outside of the condom are well lubricated with
a water-soluble lubricant before entry. If the anal sphincter is
too tight, the condom may rip during the initial entry;

(6) use only water-soluble lubricants. Non-water-soluble
lubricants cause condoms to deteriorate quickly, sometimes
during intercourse;

(7) hold onto the base of the condom when necessary
so that it won't slip off;

(8)   after ejaculating, the penetrating partner is advised to withdraw his penis gently before he loses his erection, at the same time holding onto the condom around the base. This ensures that the condom will not slip off, and that semen will not seep into the anal or vaginal canal;

(9)   use condoms only once, and never with multiple partners;

(10)   experiment with different condoms to find the one(s) best suited for you. If you try them first using safer sexual activities, such as masturbation and rubbing between the thighs, you'll get a sense of how much stress they can take before breaking;

(11)   some users prefer the more expensive condoms made of sheepskin, often called "natural" condoms or "lambskin." Several studies indicate that the walls of these condoms are of unequal thickness, due to the variations in space between the cells which comprise the animal skin. These "natural" condoms therefore do not always offer adequate protection against leakage or breakage. Excepting an allergy to latex, latex condoms are the ones to buy. If you are allergic to latex, and hence choose to have intercourse using sheepskin condoms, take responsibility for educating both yourself and your partner of the possible risk involved;

(12)   some condoms are lubricated with nonoxynol-9, a very mild soap which kills sperm, prevents common venereal disease, and has been demonstrated to kill the AIDS virus in laboratory test tubes. While many studies indicate the safety record of the spermicide for vaginal use, none have been conducted for use in anal sex.

The Holistic Group does not endorse the use of nonoxynol-9 in either vaginal or anal sex. We believe that, when combined with a hydrogenated fat-containing lubricant, it may have a tendency to promote rupture of the anal and vaginal membranes, thereby leaving a person even more susceptible to penetration by the AIDS virus, should any semen enter these ruptures. We suggest instead that you follow safe-sex guidelines, educate your partner, and have sex in a loving and responsible manner. We are inclined to believe, however, that the potential danger of nonoxynol-9 is significantly decreased if it is included in water-soluble lubricants which do not contain potentially-dangerous fat molecules.

Further research will clarify some of the issues discussed above. Certainly, the clearest response to all these concerns is not to forego the joys of sexual intercourse, but rather to follow safe-sex guidelines, advocate and support research into lubricants and condoms, educate your partners, and allow yourself love and pleasure by having sex in a loving and responsible manner.

Cultivating the ability to achieve dry climax, or learning to withdraw the penis from the anus or vagina before orgasm, are honorable and healthy practices. Much has been written about exploring the joys of creative "safe" mutual masturbation and erotic play, and we encourage you to explore the literature and the act itself.

The belief exists in many cultures that ejaculation "weakens" men. Perhaps this belief has its roots in the fact that the immune system can be subtly affected by excessive ejaculation, in that both zinc and the protein contents contained in semen, which are necessary for the body's maintenance of its white blood cell count, are reduced. Men who are extremely active sexually may compensate for the loss of zinc in semen by taking zinc supplements.

We believe that abstinence—certainly when it comes to one-night stands and casual sex—is beneficial for people with AIDS. If someone with AIDS is blessed with a steady sexual partner, it is best to develop the ability to achieve dry climax without ejaculation, and to approach intercourse, both anal and vaginal, with condoms and caution. Zinc supplementation and additional protein may be in order if a man with AIDS chooses to ejaculate during sexual activity (see "Amino Acid Treatment" section which follows). If one is experiencing extreme phobia around sexual activity due to fears of AIDS contagion, we recommend abstinence for perhaps 30 to 60 days, and massage therapy to reduce stress.

AIDS calls for discretion and love in sexual relations—not for celibacy. Sexuality is a positive force in human interaction. The sexual act not only discharges tension and stress, but draws people together and unites them in love. Wilhelm Reich, although antihomosexual, in fact laid the groundwork for gay liberation and sexual liberation by revealing that procreation is only one "natural" motivation for the sex act. Sex brings us in contact with other human beings, so that we may explore our commonality and oneness; it is about much more than having babies. While some human beings may create other human beings through sexual activity, this merely assures that the cycle of love and unity may continue to evolve to higher and higher levels.

Taking responsibility for one's sexuality by honoring both one's highest self and the health and welfare of one's partner is of the utmost importance. Sexual activity is a powerful and potentially transcendent channel for love and unity; it achieves its highest expression when based upon mutual attraction and respect.

Transmission to Heterosexuals and Bisexuals

Research and somewhat sensationalistic press reports in the past year have revealed cases of AIDS transmission in America to heterosexual and bisexual men and women. While we recognize that knowledge of the possibility of heterosexual transmission is important, and that additional funds for research and treatment may be freed once those who hold the purse strings finally realize that it is in the interest of both "gays and straights" to do so, we do not believe that a widescale outbreak of AIDS among non-IV-drug-using heterosexuals in the United States is just around the corner.

The psychospiritual nature of the dis-ease is the main factor at work here, and explains why AIDS has been so slow to spread outside the culturally oppressed gay minority (and IV-drug-using community) within the United States. Heterosexual men and women are not an oppressed minority within this country; they are much less open to succumbing to the virus. And while some bisexual men assert that they are as oppressed as their gay brothers, and of course engage in the same male-to-male sex practices as do gays, their ability and frequent choice to "pass" makes them less susceptible to the AIDS virus than are exclusive homosexuals.

Gay men have tended up to now to have more sex with more partners, within a relatively closed community, than do heterosexual women and men. This again heightens the risk of AIDS transmission among gays. When heterosexual women choose to have many different sexual partners, their encounters frequently include the use of condoms, which greatly reduce the possibility of semen entering the bloodstream. Certainly those heterosexuals and bisexuals who have sex with many partners, who hold deep-seated negative feelings about their sexual interactions and themselves, and who share the additional factors of susceptibility outlined earlier in this Inquiry, run the greatest risk of both exposure to and contraction of AIDS.

Transmission to Women
Given that the AIDS virus is transmitted through the blood and the semen, and that it attacks culturally isolated minorities, approximately 75% of all officially reportable United States cases of AIDS involve the people in the highest risk group, namely, sexually active gay men. A significant number of women in the United States, however, have been diagnosed with the dis-ease. These cases appear mainly within the category of hemophiliacs, IV-drug users, Haitians, and recipients of AIDS-infected blood transfusions. Nonetheless, women do run risk of AIDS transmission while engaging in sexual activity.

Because of the nature of their sexual interaction, lesbians who exclusively relate sexually to other exclusive lesbians run the least risk of coming in contact with AIDS through sexual activity. The only possibility for sexual transmission of AIDS between two exclusive lesbians is through the entrance of infected blood into the uninfected partner through either cuts in the mouth, hands, or other body parts. (Transmission of course is also possible through blood transfusions or the sharing of IV-drug needles.)

Women who relate sexually to men can conceivably come in contact with the AIDS virus through any of four circumstances: swallowing semen during oral sex, allowing semen to come in contact with open cuts in their mouths or on the hands or other body parts, experiencing anal fissures during anal intercourse, or experiencing tears in the vaginal wall during vaginal intercourse. Swallowing semen is therefore discouraged, and condoms suggested as a means of protecting women who relate sexually to sexually nonmonogamous men.

While the women and men within our group acknowledge that United States women suffer greatly from sexual oppression and sexism, sexism affects women and their immune systems differently than does the sexism and homophobia directed at gay men. Gay men in general are far more publicly identified as social outcasts and as a sexual minority than are lesbians and women in general. When bigots speak of "gays," it has been frequently observed that they are usually referring to gay men, ignoring the "homosexual threat" of lesbianism. This phenomenon has usually been attributed to the fact that friendship and physical displays of affection among women are far more socially acceptable, and consequently less threatening, than are similar displays of affection among American men.

Women, though divided socially, politically, and economically, comprise over 50% of the United States population, and do not experience the specific quality of oppression which affects the gay, culturally isolated minority. Surely "tomboys" and stereotypically identifiable lesbians are the women who have experienced the most antihomosexual oppression among women, but few have experienced that degree of alienation common to the many gays who in their younger days believed that they were the "only" homosexual in their community. Women certainly experience many dis-eases, especially of the genital region, which can be linked to their oppression within a patriarchal culture; we do not believe that AIDS will become one of these dis-eases.

We also wish to point out that research indicated that women process stress on a much more intuitive level than do men, and are more in touch with their bodies. Men who accept the social conditioning of "manhood" tend to mask their feelings, divide their minds from their bodies, and hold onto their stress. This again makes women open to a different set of dis-eases than those found in men.

But the role of women in society is changing. The traditional societal model has subjected men more than women to severe performance pressure in the workplace, requiring them constantly to "prove themselves" and their "manhood" through their social and professional roles. Women's traditional workplace—the home—subjects them to a different distribution of stress peaks than does the male "job," allowing them to handle their stress in a more effective manner. (We wish to suggest that the key to the longevity of women lies in their natural superiority in handling stress and in the specific set of traditional expectations which declares that "women's place is in the home.") Now that many more women than ever before are entering blue- and white-collar professions, and abandoning this traditional role, many have taken on all the competitive pressures associated with the traditional competitive "male" workplace. Especially for professional women in business and industry, the pressure to prove themselves the equals of their usually chauvinistic male associates has taken a terrible toll on their health. Consequently, the incidence of stress-related dis-ease among professional women, such as heart attacks, which have always been more common among males, is accelerating alarmingly. To the extent that a woman, or a man for that matter, accepts the rules of the game by buying into the roles and demands of the competitive, production-oriented marketplace, vigilance and care with regard to stress and health maintenance is essential.

"Social" Transmission

Transmission of AIDS is possible when bodily fluids—blood and semen—infected with the AIDS virus enter one's system during sexual contact, blood transfusion, or the sharing of IV-drug needles. Neither medical research nor circumstantial evidence indicate that AIDS can be transmitted by touching, sitting next to, or sharing the same space as a person with AIDS. You will not get AIDS through eating in "gay" restaurants, using public hot tubs or saunas, or shaking someone's hand. AIDS is not casually transmittable. We encourage readers who harbor deep fears of contracting AIDS to use their anguish as a stepping stone into self-examination. For example, if you are gay and have stopped having sexual contact because of the AIDS epidemic, you might examine your feelings of being potentially defenseless and victimized. Similarly, if you are heterosexual and want to feed your gay dinner guests from paper plates, you might care to examine your feelings about gay people and about your own sexuality on the deepest levels.

Rooming with a person with AIDS poses no real problem; in fact, it offers a tremendous opportunity for expressing unconditional love. AIDS is most contagious in its early phases, most specifically at the point where it has been recognized but remains untreated by holistic methods. As soon as someone takes the steps outlined below to rebuild the immune system, the risk of contagion drops. Roommates need only observe normal patterns of cleanliness and hygiene. There is no reason to isolate a person with AIDS.

When personal choice or social circumstance indicate its need, we support the idea of common living facilities for people with AIDS. The Shanti Project in San Francisco, for example, has been funded by the city to manage residences for such individuals.

Maintaining Good Health
We believe that probably 65% to 73% of "healthy" individuals who come into contact with the AIDS virus have the ability to throw it off. AIDS is not a plague that you are guaranteed to get if, for example, you've had "unsafe sex" with someone who is eventually diagnosed with AIDS. The key elements in the prevention of AIDS are the reduction of external and internal stress, and the promotion of a positive and healthy outlook.

Examined from a holistic perspective, a healthy individual is one who:

(1)   Exercises regularly (aerobic exercise, such as jogging or swimming, strengthens the heart; this in turn helps stimulate the thymus gland, which is a key regulator of the immune system);

(2)   maintains a healthy diet, free from drugs, alcohol, caffeine, stimulants, and unnecessary red blood meats;

(3)   employs cleansing practices such as sweats and saunas;

(4)   develops means to minimize physiological and emotional stress; and

(5)   thinks positively.

Such a healthy individual, after coming in contact with the AIDS virus, may display symptoms which are herpes-like or syphilitic in nature; the immune system, however, can rally and throw off the virus before it spreads throughout the connective tissues and develops into any of the AIDS opportunistic infections. As mentioned earlier, it is possible for the virus to remain dormant within the body, only to surface during a period of heightened dietary, chemical, or emotional stress. Maintaining a state of wellness is possible when one adopts a healthy lifestyle as a way of life.

A Cleansing Diet for the Worried Well
The term "worried well" has been coined to describe the large number of individuals who display no AIDS symptoms, but who fear they may be harboring the AIDS virus. If you are such an individual, the following diet is offered for your benefit. We urge you to listen to your body's messages about the appropriateness of this diet for you, and to consult with a health practitioner when necessary.

For a minimum of seven days, and ideally for a period of three weeks or longer, we suggest:

(1)   Fruits in the morning. The best fruits for this cleansing are papaya, pineapple, strawberry, and black cherry, if available;

(2)   *steamed* vegetables in the midday, as these are the most cleansing. Most recommended are asparagus, spinach, collard, beet, and root vegetables (e.g., potatoes, carrots, etc.).Consume the steaming water as well;

(3)   a mixture of rice and beans, which together form a complete protein, for the evening meal: ¾ cup uncooked rice to ¼ cup uncooked beans is the best combination. Soaking beans overnight, and then discarding the water, cuts down on cooking time and helps eliminate gas. Any bean is okay, with kidney and lima the most highly recommended. Brown rice requires 3 cups water to each cup of rice for cooking to a soft consistency;

(4)   for additional protein, consume bean curd, plus nuts and seeds, specifically pecan, walnut, macadamia, sunflower, and pumpkin. (Pumpkin seeds are high in zinc, and help

cleanse the intestinal tract.) Eliminate all blood meats, fish, and chicken for the duration of this diet. Hypoglycemics will benefit from eating small amounts of nuts and seeds throughout the day. If possible, save your tofu or tempeh for the evening meal;

(5)   eliminate all salt from the diet;

(6)   consume 3 to 4 cups a day, hot or cold, of teas rich in vitamin C, such as rose hips and hibiscus. Whole rose hips need to be boiled and simmered;

(7)   fast 1 day out of 7 on melon. Any one form is okay, with canteloupe most highly recommended when available. If you cannot obtain melon, eat cherries, or simply fast on pineapple juice;

(8)   increase your garlic intake by consuming either 2 to 6 cloves per day raw garlic, or 2 to 5 capsules per day of the scentless and equally potent liquid Kyolic™ garlic extract. If you choose raw garlic, you can chop it up into small pieces and swallow it with water. (One of us almost drove off the highway trying to eat a particularly potent clove.) Eating parsley will help neutralize the smell of raw garlic on the breath;

(9)   when coming off this diet, reintroduce fresh vegetables, as well as fish and chicken, if they are a normal part of your diet. Chicken is recommended boiled, baked, or broiled, not fried.

Although it is neither necessary nor likely, this cleansing diet may bring about a homeopathic cleansing of the lymphatic system, which could manifest as swollen glands, a sore throat, or other signs of "sickness." When one member of The Holisitic Group tried this diet, he misinterpreted his laryngitis as "getting sick," rather than comprehending his "symptoms" as evidence of detoxification and cleansing. Since he was consulting a Chinese doctor and herbalist at the time, he described his symptoms and his diet to him and asked for help. This respected practitioner, usually right on the mark, intoned that garlic should only be consumed in cold climates such as Alaska. He even dared to say that the cherries our friend was reveling in for breakfast were a "no-no," and that homosexuality was a reversal of yin and yang energies! Our group member was of course angered by the doctor's homophobia, and equally upset by the potential loss of his beloved cherries.

We reject outright such absolute statements. Our holistic approach is an eclectic one, eschewing hard and fast rules in favor of honoring whatever seems most appropriate at a given moment to promote balance and harmony in mind, body and spirit. With this (or any) diet or program of detoxification and healing, the only hard and fast rule is that one take full responsibility for one's health through honor, love, and self-respect.

While this cleansing diet may prove beneficial for people diagnosed with AIDS, it is not specifically recommended for them. The dietary regimen for AIDS which follows is in itself cleansing.

What if I am Diagnosed with AIDS?

AIDS is not necessarily an inevitable progression from one opportunistic infection to another to a helpless and painful death. The key to your healing is stress reduction, positive thinking, and the establishment of harmony and balance on *all* levels of your being. Upon diagnosis of AIDS we urge the immediate institution of the following programs and therapies:

(1)   Stress reduction techniques, such as biofeedback, visualization, and meditation;

(2)   therapeutic massages and other techniques which can educate your mind and body to relax and heal;

(3)   detoxification techniques, including colonics, plus foods which increase bulk and encourage elimination; oxygenation of the colon; saunas and sweats;

(4)   a detoxifying natural-foods, vegetarian-style diet which concentrates on those foods which help build up the immune system. It is especially recommended that the diet include ample whole grains;

(5)   add to the dietary regimen: mineral supplements, particularly those rich in zinc, calcium, iron, iodine, and selenium; vitamins, specifically vitamins C and the B complex (to help alleviate stresses upon the neurological tissues); antiviral and immune-enhancing substances such as Kyolic™ garlic and Blue-Green Manna; homeopathic substances and flower essences as needed;

(6)   elimination of all stimulants from the system;

(7)   chiropractic alignment of the physical form, which

purpose is to alleviate stresses and tensions placed upon the medulla oblongata and the coccyx.

As the first and key critical element in healing AIDS is stress reduction, we wish to begin our discussion of the various elements outlined above with a look at biofeedback.

Biofeedback

Through biofeedback, conscious circulatory control can be developed. It is possible to learn to send the blood flows to each of the critical portions of the endocrine system, particularly to the spleen, the lymphatics, the thyroid, and the pancreas. We urge that this process be combined with a series of therapeutic massages and saunas, re-educating the deep tissues of your body to relax. Connected breath is also important in oxygenating and purifying the blood, and in developing the conscious ability to achieve deep states of relaxation.

Practitioners of biofeedback can easily measure blood flows to the internal organs through observation and thermographs. For example, if one observes that the temperature of the throat rises, or that the area is flushed, one can presume that extra blood flows are being sent to the thyroid. In addition, thermographs can monitor a person's ability to surround the pancreas and other areas of the body with blood.

It is possible to develop conscious circulatory control through meditation, visualization, hypnosis, and self-hypnosis, should these be the methods you prefer. Certainly visualization and affirmation are critical to the healing process (see the contributions of Margo Adair and Kevin Ryerson, and the Resources section of this book).

Colonics

Colonic irrigations have long been recommended in cancer detoxification programs, and may be credited with contributing to the healing and recovery of more people than is currently considered medically or socially acceptable. [Ed. note: Louise Hay, the healer whose write-up begins the Resources section of this book, employed colonics as one aspect of the nutritional detoxification/fortification program which contributed to her swift healing of "operate or die" vaginal cancer.] This method of colonic cleansing circulates water throughout the entire large intestine in a controlled manner, removing fecal matter and toxic debris from the colon's walls. Administered by skilled and loving practitioners, colonics can be pleasant and energizing; they are certainly easier to experience and far more effective than an enema. Not only to colonics cleanse your body, they also stimulate reflex points in the colon which help balance the body's energies. Do not be surprised if you find yourself relaxed and glowing after a colonic.

Though it will vary from individual to individual, our general recommendation is to do colonics twice a week, combined with the ingestion of psyllium seed to temporarily increase bulk. Try this program on a bimonthly schedule of 1 month on, 1 month off, as necessary.

A colonic implant combining wheatgrass juice and acidophilus can prove beneficial for all individuals. To 4 oz. of wheatgrass juice, add either 4 oz. liquid acidophilus or ½ tsp. of the high potency dry form. Irish moss is another frequently used colonic implant with soothing and demulcent properties.

It is essential to patronize practitioners who employ certain minimal standards of sterilization. Though apparatus and techniques will vary, we recommend that practitioners have several stainless steel insertion devices on hand, to be used in rotation while the sterilization procedure is followed. If the practitioner does not own expensive sterilization equipment, we recommend that they first steam or boil the insertion apparatus 5 to 10 minutes to weaken the virus. Then expose it to ultraviolet light for another 5 to 10 minutes to kill whatever virus may remain. To help the ultraviolet light reach the interior of the apparatus, put it in a stainless steel bowl, or a concave surface covered with tinfoil, to reflect the ultraviolet rays into the interior cavities.

We encourage colonic practitioners to work with people with AIDS, and in the same breath assure their other clients that, once sterilization procedures are followed, they are in no danger of contracting the disease from the apparatus. The design of colonic apparatus allows fecal matters and toxic material to pass only through the insertion apparatus and the waste tube; viruses and fecal matter do not back up into the machine itself. Thus, when the apparatus is sterilized, the possibility of AIDS transmission through it is eliminated.

While coffee enemas are beneficial in some detoxification programs, we do not recommend them with AIDS because of the increased neurological stress brought upon the system by the introduction of caffeine.

Saunas

Saunas form an important part of our detoxification program. The choice of taking either steam saunas or dry saunas can be determined by one's condition. Steam saunas are easier on the lungs, but are sometimes not beneficial to individuals sensitive to bronchial infection during the cold and damp months. The converse may be true in your case for dry saunas. Certainly those of a weakened constitution are wise to stay in a sauna only a short time. Following saunas with a dry brush massage can further stimulate the skin and remove toxins. If you are unsure as to which program of saunas and sweats is best for you, consult a qualified health practitioner, nutritionist, or acupuncturist.

Detoxifying Diet

The diet which we recommend is similar to the basic health-promoting diet advocated by most health food oriented nutritionists. Such a diet is harmonious with basic body chemistry; it promotes, rather than interferes with, basic digestive and energy-producing processes. A balanced diet is by definition a detoxifying one, and reduces stress on the system. It can even help mitigate some of the side effects of prescribed medications.

Try to obtain organic and/or unsprayed foods whenever possible. Whole grains are especially important: most people will benefit from eating whole cooked grains twice a day. Both steamed and raw vegetables are permitted, as are, when desired and easily digested, eggs and dairy. If you are indeed lactose-tolerant, try to emphasize raw and cultured dairy products, such as yogurt, kefir, and acidophilus cottage cheese. If you are accustomed to eating flesh, lighter fish and fowl may be consumed 2 to 3 times per week.

In general, people diagnosed with AIDS may benefit from up to 40 grams of protein per day. (This figure includes both complete and incomplete proteins.) Those who choose to get their protein exclusively from whole grains, beans, soy products, nuts, seeds, and vegetables are encouraged to consult the guidelines for protein combining found in Frances Moore Lappe's classic *Diet for a Small Planet*. It is neither beneficial nor healthy for the average individual to consume vast amounts of protein each day.

It is important to eliminate all red meat from the diet, for reasons discussed earlier. Try to eliminate coffee, because of its effect on the nerves; certainly limit its intake to 2 cups a day. Similarly, black tea drinkers who cannot shake the habit are advised to drink no more than 3 cups per day, weakly brewed. Avoid chocolate because of its high sugar content and possible negative effects on the liver. It is best to avoid MSG because so many people are either allergic or sensitive to it; patronize Chinese restaurants that will cook without it. Fried foods are also no-nos, as are, of course, sugar, white flour, "unbleached flour," and any grain substances which do not contain the whole grain. Avoid all preservative, chemical additives, food dyes, and, in general, anything you can't pronounce.

It is important to begin to learn the basics of a healthy, truly natural diet, and to patronize food stores committed to protecting the consumer. The Food and Drug Administration (FDA) is now allowing laboratory-proven "mild carcinogens" in food and food dyes, and has given the go-ahead to life energy destroying irradiation of certain foods. Carefully reading the label on any product you buy for consumption or cosmetic use, *especially* when it is labeled "natural," is encouraged. Such commercial euphemisms as "natural," "100% pure vegetable shortening," "cooked with honey," and "whole wheat" often conceal "natural" white sugar, glucose, fructose, high-fructose corn syrup, white flour, and hydrogenated vegetable oils or shortening.

A few more guidelines: Use virgin olive oil or, when not available, cold pressed oils derived from other foods for cooking and salad-making. Avoid iced or cold food directly out of the refrigerator, since the cold sedates the digestive juices.

(While ice-cold food may be great near the equator, for most of us it is detrimental, because it makes the body work extra hard to maintain normal body temperature.) Cooking with ginger, on the other hand, has a warming and stimulating effect on the digestive system, and can help neutralize toxins in food. Finally, paying attention to basic food-combining principles, such as those advocated by Dr. Herbert Shelton, can greatly improve digestion and absorption of nutrients.

Supplements

AIDS frequently manifests as the cancerous opportunitistic infection Kaposi's sarcoma. Since cancers leach nutrients out of the body and inhibit their proper assimilation, a comprehensive program of vitamin, mineral, and food supplements is recommended for a person diagnosed with AIDS. After carefully examining the needs of people with AIDS, we have concluded that the four most active and crucial supplements for recovery are vitamin C, garlic, zinc, and calcium.

Vitamin C strengthens the body's general resistance to viruses, and stimulates the eliminative process. Much excellent literature exists about the power of this vitamin as a free radical scavenger, and we encourage you to investigate the work of Dr. Linus Pauling and others. Vitamin C is not a panacea— it does not always work. We do not even believe that it is always essential to healing the common cold. But much evidence, research, and living examples attest to its potentially central role in the healing of AIDS.

We recommend that someone with AIDS begin taking vitamin C in dosages of 25 gm./day, increasing the amount until they reach the maximum dosage their body can absorb. Urine tests of people with AIDS reveal that they can ingest 50 or even 80 gm. of vitamin C per day without excreting any excess: this means that their bodies are needing and using vast quantities of vitamin C! Large doses of vitamin C can upset the stomach, frequently resulting in diarrhea. Though diarrhea can signal that the body has reached the maximim dosage of vitamin C required, in the case of AIDS it frequently indicates the need to switch from the most commonly used form of vitamin C, sodium ascorbate, to the vitamin C available as calcium ascorbate or mixed ascorbates. Calcium ascorbate in particular is not acidic as is sodium ascorbate, and can be tolerated in large doses by the stomach. What is most important, especially in the case of pneumocystis pneumonia, is to begin to take vitamin C in *whatever* form is the most accessible and convenient, and in large quantities.

We urge you to obtain your vitamins from natural sources (see discussion which follows). In the case of vitamin C, however, the bulk of the natural material is so great that taking more than 1000 to 1500 mg./day of the totally natural substance is impractical. We therefore suggest that you try to obtain some of the natural material, from sources such as rose hips or sago palm, to balance out the large quantities of ascorbate you may be taking. It is also recommended that you take some bioflavanoids, herperidin and rutin to aid in proper assimilation. But if these are not available, affordable, or practical, do not hesitate to take as much vitamin C in the form of sodium, calcium or mixed ascorbates as is necessary. Readers who choose to use straight ascorbic acid powder are encouraged to mix in some powdered rose hips to increase its life energy. Putting a quartz crystal on top of the closed mixture may also prove of benefit.

Garlic is a time-honored antiviral agent, and receives our highest possible recommendation. Should you choose to consume the raw, ideally organic, cloves, 5 to 15 at the most are suggested, daily, combined with generous amounts of parsley to absorb the smell. It is fine to chop the cloves into small pieces, and to swallow them down like mini-vitamin pills.

Garlic may also be consumed in the scentless and odorless Kyolic™ format, with the liquid being our first preference. Manufactured in Japan, Kyolic™ garlic retains all the life energy and beneficial qualities of raw garlic, without any of the alienating odor. Certainly hospitalized individuals who consume large quantities of raw garlic may find that the resultant mouth and even body odor may seriously isolate them from medical personnel who look askance at such behavior to begin with; Kyolic™ is indeed a "sociable alternative."

Kyolic™ garlic is the form we specifically recommend for

people with AIDS. This is because, speaking from the vantage point of Chinese medicine, people with AIDS will often develop a tendency toward yin deficiency, and will find Kyolic™ garlic less heating to the system. We suggest taking 2 to 6 capsules of liquid Kyolic™ twice a day as needed. The liquid may be purchased by itself, or in a twin package that includes a bottle of empty gelatin capsules. These capsules are filled right before ingestion, preventing the liquid from dissolving the gelatin before it is consumed.

Zinc is essential in rebuilding the immune system. We suggest 25 to 35 mg. daily, since it can be toxic when consumed in large doses over extended periods of time.

Calcium soothes the nerves, and is important for stress reduction. Unless you are working with a nutritional consultant, who is tailoring a program of diet and supplements to your specific needs, a general rule you might follow is to take twice the Recommended Daily Allowance (RDA) of a given vitamin or mineral supplement. In the case of calcium, for example, this translates into 2000mg/day.

The *B vitamins* are also important in times of stress: high-stress individuals may require many times the RDA of B complex. One of the Bs in particular, *Pantothenic Acid,* can both reduce stress and make vitamin C more assimilable.

Vitamin A can also be useful for people diagnosed with AIDS, because it promotes repair of the neurological tissues. Beta-carotene, the Vitamin A precursor which has with Vitamin C the ability to act as a free-radical scavenger, is found in ample supply in *Blue-Green Manna,* a fresh water algae discussed later in this inquiry.

Blue-Green Manna, and several key amino acids can also positively affect the neurological pathways often targeted by the AIDS virus. These amino acids include:

(1) *L-Glutamine,* which helps maintain nervous system function. Take 500 mg. 3 to 4 times/day, incorporating it into the regular program of supplementation;

(2) *L-Phenylalanine* (not the D-form), a natural precursor to neurotransmitters, which is necessary to the manufacture of neurotransmitters and hormones; it also gives support to the glandular system. Take 500 mg. 2 to 3 times/day as part of the general program;

(3) *L-Arginine,* which causes release of growth hormone which stimulates the immune system, helps in healing and regeneration of the liver, and is helpful to the nervous system. Take 500 mg. 3 times/day as part of the general program. While this

amino acid is beneficial for people diagnosed with AIDS, do not take it if experiencing herpes or viruses of the herpes family, such as CMV or hairy leukoplakia (see section on herpes which follows for more specific information);

(4) *L-Gamma Amino Butyric Acid (L-GABA)*, which is potentially useful for its tranquilizing affect. Take 500 to 1000 mg. 3 times/day when experiencing neurological difficulties.

Pancreatic glandular substance is valuable in restoring the atrophied aspects of the pancreas. A complete collapse of the pancreas may be found in 25% of people stricken with AIDS, rising to 35% if the disease is allowed to spread unchecked. Practitioners will find this manifesting as an almost diabetic-like condition, particularly after the period of sweating and muscular discomfiture. Pancreatic enzyme has played a key part in the cancer treatment programs of Dr. William Donald Kelley, as it can help destroy foreign protein (tumors) in the body.

Selenium is recommended to help reinforce the cell walls. It might also prove wise to explore *royal jelly, propolis,* and *bee pollen,* as these are natural supplements to and strengtheners of the immune system. *Saw palmetto,* favored by one of our group members, has been used successfully in hormone balancing, but will probably have benefit in only 10% to 15% of AIDS cases.

We believe that *BHT,* an antioxidant widely used in foods because it prevents spoilage by delaying degradation of lipid components, has the ability to slow the progression of AIDS. Research has shown that BHT can destabilize the hydrogen bonds and strip the lipid covering of retroviruses, thus allowing white blood cells to attack them more effectively. One study, in fact, reprinted in the *Journal of Infectious Diseases* (Vol. 138, No. 1, July 1978), specifically focuses on the ability of BHT to inactivate human and murine CMV. BHT can be harmful to some individuals; consult a nutritionist or health practitioner before taking it. (See section on herpes.)

Anything that is applicable toward alleviating herpes-like symptoms is applicable toward treatment of AIDS. *Lysine,* for example, is often successfully employed in herpes treatment, and we endorse its use by people with AIDS (see section on herpes). As mentioned earlier, a homeopathic preparation of CMV could prove of enormous benefit in the treatment of both herpes and AIDS.

As some holistically-oriented chiropractors believe that iron deficiency is linked to the T-cell failure common in AIDS, we have considered the use of iron supplements. We believe that a lack of iron in the system relates to a lack of the magnetic influences critical to cell regeneration. This is not unlike the discovery of extra molecules of magnetite within cancer cells which cause an imbalance within the cell memory based on the more magnetic levels; this results in T-cell fatigue which manifests as a breakdown in the immune system. (See Kevin Ryerson's "Psychoimmunity" channeling for more information.)

Synthetic Vitamins and Antibiotics

Try to obtain high quality natural vitamins when possible. As the holistic health movement has stressed for many years, the life energy of vitamins and foods is vital to our well-being; chemical analysis does not take this into account. We encourage you to consult with someone in a health food store you trust, who is familiar with the manufacturing processes employed by the various vitamin companies.

While we do not deny that some synthetic vitamins—vitamin C, for example—have proven beneficial to human health, many synthetic substances can, over a period of time, collect in the body and damage the adrenals. FDA regulations are disturbingly lax in terms of vitamin fillers, potency, and labeling. A product can be labeled "natural" vitamin E, for example, when only 10% is natural and the rest is synthetic. Similarly, synthetic vitamins A and D may be labeled "100% fish liver oil" when only 10% of it is the natural substance. Lax legislation also allows manufacturers to sell products at 10% to 15% below the stated potency. And, worst of all, mass production may significantly lengthen storage time, resulting in a 50% loss of potency by the time the supplement is ingested. Some vitamin brands are definitely better and more reliable than others.

Raising children on a daily regimen of synthetic vitamins is to be avoided, as the constant dose of synthetics, as mentioned above, can, over time, damage the adrenals. Many of us, aware of the depletion of our nation's soil and the proliferation of toxins in the environment and food chain, have attempted to protect ourselves by downing massive quantities of vitamins on a daily basis. We believe that further research will show that the body is in fact able in some degree to manufacture and synthesize nutrient substances, and that a general physical dependency upon supplements may discourage the body in its role of nutrient production and assimiliation, eventually leading to chronic imbalances. We urge you to examine the degree to which you need to supplement your body with natural vitamins before you initiate their wholesale consumption.

Occasional use of antibiotics to supplement the work of the immune system can prove beneficial, notwithstanding their negative effects upon the body. We affirm the use of penicillin or other antibiotics in cases of venereal dis-ease; we do not believe that their use in recurrent cases of syphilis, for example, might result in so serious an impairment of immune system function as to justify their consideration as a possible co-factor in the spread of AIDS. (See discussions of syphilis and homeopathic substances which follow.) The main problem with antibiotics arises when they are continuously dispensed within the system, particularly to the elderly. Long-term reliance on either vitamins or antibiotics to do the work for which the body was designed can have deleterious results.

Chiropractic
Chiropractic alignment of the body, specifically to alleviate stress and tensions placed upon the medulla oblongata and the coccyx, is important in cases of AIDS and immune dysfunction. Adjustment of the medulla oblongata allows for clear flows of energy along the neurological pathways which help stimulate the immune system. Correct alignment of the coccyx, which is a reflex point for the adrenals, helps with proper functioning of endocrine system and nervous system; by helping to "ground" and center an individual, it promotes calm and reduces stress. (For more information, please refer to the article on the chakras as well as to the "Psychoimmunity" channeling.)

To alleviate stress upon the medulla oblongata, we suggest alignment of the entire cranial area—in particular loosening and alleviating tension at the saginal suture (the uppermost point where the cranial plates attach to the cranium) and the temporal mandibular joint (where the jaw attaches to the cranial points). Many chiropractors have experience with nutritional supplements, colonics, and other aspects of our program.

The Thymus

The thymus gland, situated at the top of the breastbone above the heart, has a direct relationship to the immune system and to AIDS. The thymus is most active in the first seven years of life, atrophying 50% by adulthood. In people with AIDS, the normal decline of the thymus is exacerbated, and the gland functions on a very low level. Undue stresses placed upon an individual in early childhood may also render the thymus dysfunctional, bringing about atrophy of a major portion of the endocrine system and a weakening of the body's resistance to infection. We believe that research will eventually prove that the thymus may be one of the most central elements responsible for continued functioning of the endocrine system, and that any program that might stop its shrinking or serve to reanimate it could strengthen the immune system, adding longevity to the human body and preventing degeneration of the physical form.

The thymus has several major functions in relation to the immune system. Most importantly, within it B-lymphocytes— cells which form antibodies and attach foreign invaders—are converted into T-lymphocytes, which specifically attack microbes and some cancers. There are two classes of T-cells: helpers and suppressors. Helper cells (T4) promote antibody production by B cells and enhance surveillance and destruction; suppressor cells (T8), in general, dampen these activities and prevent overstimulation. The normal ratio of helper to suppressor cells is about 2:1.

In people with AIDS, the normal ratio of T4 to T8 cells, which is 2:1, is usually reversed, often registering around .8:1 or even as low as .1:1. This reverse ratio is also found in more than 80% of urban gay men who register no AIDS symptoms. Given that some AIDS patients maintain a "normal" ratio of 2:0, and that medical research has arrived at no satisfactory explanation of this phenomenon, the T-cell test used by many doctors to determine the presence of AIDS is of questionable value. What we can nonetheless state with certainty is that the return of the thymus to its normal production of T-cells would help in healing AIDS.

Research will eventually bear out that one of the functions of the thymus in adults is the assimilation of vitamin C and the B vitamins. It also assimilates and produces extra elements involving supplementary forms of hemoglobins, adding to a secondary form of oxygenation in the body. In an earlier state of our evolution, it is probable that the thymus manufactured substances similar to hemoglobin.

Yet another function of the thymus is the production of the hormone thymosin. While thymosin's function is not yet entirely understood, we believe that it is currently being synthesized in laboratories for use as an immune enhancer. What is clear is that the thymus may be called upon to give its all in the fight against the AIDS virus, and may thus become atrophied or destroyed in the process; this would at least greatly diminish the production of thymosin. We can even project a possible sequence in which, at the beginning stages of AIDS infection, a sharp increase in thymosin might be observed for a short period of time, followed within three months by a radical decrease. Such a phenomenon would indicate that AIDS is in an incubation phase. We encourage research to see if this pattern is a universal one, since its detection could prove useful in AIDS diagnosis. Supplemental thymosin might bring about a regeneration of the immune system in AIDS patients— we strongly encourage testing of its use in healing AIDS. We suspect that thymus gland extract is a valid source of at least a small amount of thymosin.

When the thymus gland is in an atrophied state, it might be best stimulated through the use of organically-bound iodine, iron, and mineral substances which would stimulate the level of hemoglobin. Chlorophyll, similar in structure to hemoglobin, could also be ingested to stimulate the thymus, as could the pure isolated plasma substance of hemoglobin itself. Eating seaweed can help the thymus. Similarly, wheat grass juice and barley green, rich in chlorophyll, can underwrite or enhance, but not completely replace, thymus activity. It is even possible that regular ingestion of wheat grass juice or barley green during the first seven years of life, or at least before puberty, could prevent the atrophying of the thymus, thus contributing to healthy longevity.

Research has already shown that mother's milk contains substances which contribute to immunity and protect an infant from infection. We believe that the thymus will prove responsive to a rather unusual combination of chlorophyll and powdered mother's milk of the same genetic extraction and ancestry as the individual being treated. The following protocol is suggested: Take 16 oz. of mother's milk and reduce it to powder. Add 4 oz. of distilled water to the powder, followed by 3 Tbsp. of chlorophyll concentrate derived from alfalfa. Take 1 to 2 fluid oz. of this mixture every 3 hours, 4 times a day; continue this dosage for a minimum of 3 months, and up to 6 when necessary. The mother's milk in this formula may be supplemented with goat's milk, providing that the diet of the goat consists of brown rice, barley, millet, comfreys, oats, alfalfa, and sea kelp. Admittedly, obtaining mother's milk of the same genetic extraction and ancestry as an individual may prove difficult, especially when issues of the parent/child relationship remain unresolved between grown-ups. Colostrum, the mother's "first milk" and therefore strongest in antibiotic properties, has been obtained from cows and processed for human use; it may be used in place of mother's milk in this formula. Colostrum is available in various formulations and strengths from a select number of supplement manufacturers; experimentation with dosage is suggested.

Among the naturally derived substances available for stimulating the thymus are thymus extract of animal thymus gland, homeopathic thymus extract, thymosin, the injected "Thymus-an" (not currently available in the United States), and the algae marketed as Blue-Green Manna. We believe that, from a holistic standpoint, consuming Blue-Green Manna, and accompanying it with visualization, meditation, and/or biofeedback with the goal of stimulating and rejuvenating the thymus, is the most effective and preferable approach.

Blue-Green Manna

Blue-Green Manna, *Aphanae klamathomenon flos-aquae,* also marketed as Super Blue-Green, is a blue-green single-cell algae which abundantly grows during late spring, summer and fall in only one place in the world, the pristine waters of unpolluted Klamath Lake in Oregon. All attempts to reproduce it in other natural environments and in the laboratory have so far proven unsuccessful. It is believed that this algae is one of the oldest and simplest life forms on the planet. A true breatharian organism, it grows and reproduces itself prolifically by photosynthesizing the nitrates and nitrites from the air.

It is estimated that the mix of hot springs, cold volcanic mountain streams, and two pure rivers that feed into Upper Klamath Lake has produced perhaps 200,000,000 pounds of the algae for at least the 10,000 years since the retreat of the West Coast's ice cap. Much of this algae has remained within the lake system, creating a nutrient-rich layer of sediment covering the lake's floor that reaches 35 feet in depth. It has been calculated that the top one inch of existing sediment contains enough nutrients to support the algae's growth for another 60 years. This fact alone may account for the algae's identity as one of the most elemental and complete naturally-occurring nutritional foods on the planet. Because Blue-Green Manna poses no toxic hazard to human beings in its natural state, it may be harvested for human consumption through the simple process of freeze-drying. While Spirulina, another blue-green algae, must be high-temperature spray dried in order to destroy a bacterial sheath which interferes with human consumption, Blue-Green Manna's ability to be harvested through freeze-drying retains all of its life energy and nutritional elements. Were mass production to be employed in its harvest, we believe that it could indeed serve as a prototype for solving world food and nutritional difficulties.

Blue-Green Manna is rich in chlorophyll and the eight essential amino acids, as well as naturally occurring vitamins, organically bound (chelated) minerals and lipids. Vitamin-wise, it is particularly rich in B vitamins, including B-12 and beta-carotene, the vitamin A precursor which shares with Vitamin

C the ability to act as a free radical scavenger (neutralizer). One gram of the algae contains about 1400 micrograms of beta-carotene. To obtain this much of the substance from other food sources, one would have to consume 14 grams of liver, 70 grams of carrots, 14 eggs or 5 quarts of milk.

Much has been written about the importance of beta-carotene in anti-cancer diets and its relevance for people concerned with AIDS. Not only does it function as a free radical scavenger, but it seems to positively affect immune function. It has been demonstrated that absolute numbers of T4 lymphocytes (helper cells), which are essential to immune functioning, have been increased with oral administration of high doses of beta-carotene without toxic side effects. Furthermore, the frequency of T8 cells was unaffected by its addition to the diet. Thus, the intake of beta-carotene demonstrably improved the T4:T8 ratio which is a measure of immune function.

The algae contains as much as 60% pure protein, with a remarkably balanced amino acid profile. Most importantly, its proteins are glyco proteins, as opposed to the lipo proteins found in most vegetable matter and beef. In glyco proteins, where the glucose molecule is already attached to the amino acid molecule, the human body's natural process of converting protein into glucose has already begun. As a result, the nutritional contents of Blue-Green Manna are highly assimilable and more readily available to the body than in the case of most other foods.

While some degree of laboratory research and controlled experimentation has been performed on Blue-Green Manna and other blue-green algae, much of the following discussion of Blue-Green Manna's unique food value is derived from a combination of personal testimony, observation, muscle-testing, intuition, and work with intuitive Kevin Ryerson. We are well aware that in the winter of 1985, the FDA attempted to stop distribution of this algae on the grounds that unwarranted medical "claims" had been made for its nutritional value. (To some health-oriented observers, the FDA is often perceived to have a penchant for suppressing the value of nutritional substances and medical/nutritional research which may threaten the medical status quo.) We thus feel compelled to assert that The Holisitic Group makes no "claims" for the medical value of either

Blue-Green Manna or any of the food products or cosmetics derived from it.

Though ample personal testimony exists as to the positive nutritional effects of the algae, FDA regulations prohibit the printing of such testimony, considering it tantamount to "making claims." (For this reason, companies which manufacture and market vitamin C cannot quote the research of Nobel Prize winner Dr. Linus Pauling in their literature.) Though constrained by government regulation to limit our discussion of this naturally occurring complete food to the most carefully chosen of phrases, we nonetheless wish to emphasize our belief that the extraordinary nutritional properties of this algae deserve the attention of *all* nutrition-conscious individuals.

We believe that Blue-Green Manna can help rejuvenate the thymus gland—the central factor of the immune system—and positively effect its function; it also appears to stimulate the spleen and other specialized factors of the immune system. The algae seems especially to affect the upper energy centers and glands of the body, perhaps helping to correct imbalances of the pituitary and pineal glands as well as the thymus. Some sources have even suggested that it can help rebalance the body's physiology, even to the point of balancing left-right brain function. All of this is of great import to anyone concerned with immune dysfunction or AIDS.

Preliminary research indicates that Blue-Green Manna may be one of the greatest sources of energy to the brain yet explored. People taking it report an overall increase in mind-brain function, including an increase in mental alertness and stamina, clarity, short- and long-term memory, problem-solving ability, intuitive perception, and creativity. This seems to be due to its content of "essential neuropeptides," short chains of amino acids acquired only through dietary intake, which help the brain initiate certain functions. It is speculated that many of the neuropeptides contained in Blue-Green Manna were by the process of evolution eliminated from the present biochemical pathways in the brain, and that they are responsible for "essential" mental functions, not usually expected by the consumer.

Neuropeptides function as either neurotransmitters or hormones in the human body. In the case of Blue-Green Manna, its "essential neuropeptides" seem capable of crossing the blood-brain barrier and directly stimulating the neurotransmitters in the brain. This phenomenon appears responsible for its observed ability to aid the creative visualization process, balance moods, counteract chronic fatigue, lift many individuals out of depression, and create a greater sense of centeredness and well-being. Its neurotransmitter effect, combined with what seems to be its effect on the upper energy centers of the body, may contribute to what some have termed its potential as a tool for psychic development, dream recall, and spiritual unfolding.

It is important to note that the algae's neuropeptides may affect both the nerve synapses in the brain and the flow of nerve impulses along the neurological pathways. Blue-Green Manna seems to *promote a more even flow of nerve impulses throughout the body.* Recent studies have demonstrated that when the neurological tissues are restored in the body, they are then able to stimulate the body's cells and *promote healing.* This apparent boon to the nervous system and the healing process is of great importance to people diagnosed with AIDS and ARC.

Blue-Green Manna appears ultimately to *stimulate the cellular memory,* or the genetic code (DNA) of the more specialized cell tissues in the body, helping to promote mitosis and extra cell generation which is central to the healing process (see discussion of cellular memory in "The Nature of the Healing Process" section). Its positive nutritional effects on the body thus seem to include abilities both to stimulate the immune system and to provide the appropriate antibodies in the system.

When Blue-Green Manna has been given to people with Alzheimer's disease (presenile dementia) and normal senility in a formulated and controlled manner, it has usually either stopped the progression of or at least partly reversed their symptoms; a significant return of memory and overall restoration of central nervous system function have been among the observed results. (See the article "Report of Treatment of Alzheimer's Disease with Aphanae Klamathomenon flosaquae" by Gabriel Cousens, M.D., in *Ortho Medicine*, Win-

ter/Spring 1985, Vol. 8, Nos. 1 and 2.) Physicians and chiropractors giving it to the elderly report a rejuvenation of the
circulatory system and an increase in vitality and youthfulness.
When administered in powder and spray form ("Mannastat")
to 350 lepers in India, 95% went into remission.

Blue-Green Manna seems to be a powerful detoxifier, especially affecting the liver. The Japanese, for example, have used
blue-green algae to successfully detoxify people of cadmium
poisoning. Blue-green algae also seems to remove heavy metal
deposits of lead and mercury. Others have successfully employed it in the treatment of allergies, ranging from milk allergies in infants to hay fever, not only removing the symptoms
but even the allergies themselves. It has also been used to treat
sickle-cell anemia and rheumatoid arthritis with impressive
results.

Research has even shown that while Spirulina's cellular
structure is affected by the same radiation levels as are harmful to human beings, Blue-Green Manna's cellular structure
remains stable at such levels, and only begins to mutate when
exposed to 100 times that amount of radiation. What is even
more astounding is that after only two generations of reproducing itself in mutated form—it reproduces many times a day—
the algae bounces back and continues to reproduce itself normally. This indicates a remarkably high level of life energy, or
life force, and suggests that Blue-Green Manna can both contribute to increased cellular stability in the body as well as protecting the body from and removing deposits of radiation.

Japanese biochemists have labeled the factor in blue-green
algae responsible for an increase in sustained physical and mental energy, and for rebalancing cellular metabolism, the controlled growth factor (CGF). The CGF is not only a general tonic
which especially seems to affect the body's upper glands such
as the thymus, but has specifically evidenced power as a tonic
for life extension, increasing the life span of laboratory mice
by 50%. This is perhaps due to the algae's effect on the thymus (which we believe will be revealed by further research to
hold the key to longevity in the body) and/or due to its stabiliz-
ing influence on cellular structure. Whatever the exact reasons,
Blue-Green Manna's effects on the lifespan of mice, on the

elderly, on moods, on the brain, and on toxicity lead us to conclude that it may prove to a powerful tool for human life extension.

We believe that Blue-Green Manna can be added to the program of a person diagnosed with AIDS at any time. Because it seems to improve the assimilation of megadoses of vitamins, one may not need to take the vitamins in such large quantities. Furthermore, except in rare cases of allergies, we believe that *almost everyone* can benefit from the potential for mind, body and spirit alignment which this algae seems to possess. Using it for at least 4 months seems to allow for its effect on the entire cell cycle to transpire.

Blue-Green Manna and Super Blue Green come in many combinations and forms. By consulting with someone familiar with the different algae products, working intuitively or experimenting with different products and dosages, one can determine which product(s), in what amount(s), may prove most beneficial for a given individual. In the absence of personal consultation, we would suggest taking 2 to 3 capsules of the basic Blue-Green Manna, or 3 to 4 capsules of Super Blue-Green Alpha-Sun, twice daily for at least 4 months. We especially suggest that Blue-Green Manna or Super Blue-Green be used in conjunction with visualization and, if appropriate, flower essences, as these will enhance its potential healing effects.

Both brands of the algae harvested from Upper Klamath Lake are only available from distributors familiar with their nutritional properties.

You cannot purchase Blue-Green Manna or Super Blue-Green in stores. For information on obtaining them, please contact the editor of this book at the address included in his listing at the end of the Resources section.

Flower Essences

Flower essences as a form of healing were first developed—at least in our current period of history—by the English Dr. Edward Bach between 1928 and 1936. Bach taught that "the basis of disease is to be found in disharmony between the spiritual and mental aspects of a human being." Exploring the vibrational essences of flowers, trees, and plants, Bach developed

38 "remedies" from a similar number of species to treat the emotional disharmony which saps vitality and allows dis-ease to spread. Prepared by either floating flower petals on water under the bright sun, or by boiling parts of the plant in water, flower essences are best understood as homeopathic dilutions which help balance the mental, emotional, physical, and spiritual aspects of the individual. Since these essences in no way contradict other herbs, medicines, or modes of treatment, it is fine to take them either alone or as part of any comprehensive program of healing.

Dr. Bach's concept of using the vibrations of flowers as "remedies" has been greatly expanded by the work of such contemporary healers as Richard Katz of the Flower Essence Society, Kevin Ryerson, Gurudas, and Irene Newmark. After being introduced to the 38 Bach remedies in 1976, Richard Katz began to explore the properties of California wild and garden plants. Desiring to find out how and why flower essences have such powerful effects on human beings, Katz began a program of observation, attunement, meditation, and visualization to enable him to have an inner dialogue with flowers and plants. This was followed by careful observation of the effects of flower essences on himself and others.

Katz explains that "each plant represents what we could call an archetypal pattern of life energy. Similar archetypes are found with our own being and consciousness. By distilling these patterns of energy into flower essences, we can use them as catalysts to awaken our own capacities and qualities which are either undeveloped or blocked in their development. By working with flower essences, we can help attune our individual human natures with the harmony and spiritual perfection of the consciousness of which we are a part."

A most important aspect of the work of these contemporary healers is a reinterpretation of flower essences, not merely as "remedies for negative states of mind," but as positive tools for growth, cleansing, harmonizing, and protection on all levels of one's being. There are currently over 200 flower "essences" available, which can be mail ordered in individual and kit form (see Resources section of this book). The Flower Essence Society even has available a reprint, *Qualities of the Bach Flower*

Essences, by Suzanne Garden, which reinterprets the 38 Bach Remedies in terms of positive "quality," "pattern," and "lesson."

We recommend essences that reduce specific phobias and "fears in general," such as Rock Rose, Walnut, and Black Cherry, for people with AIDS. Combining the use of essences with stress reduction techniques such as biofeedback, meditation, and visualization may prove especially powerful—Thousand Petal Lotus would work well here. And the Rescue Remedy, a Bach first-aid combination of five of his flowers, is highly recommended, not only for people with AIDS, but for anyone concerned about possible contagion, or stressed out by the realities of life after 1984. Composed of Star of Bethlehem, Rock Rose, Impatiens, Cherry Plum, and Clematis, the Rescue Remedy as a first aid tool restores confidence and calmness when faced with "shock, fear, terror, panic, severe mental stress and tension, a feeling of desperation or a numbed, bemused state of mind." In more gentle and positive terms, Rescue Remedy is great for smoothing out the highs and lows that can hinder growth and development, and for understanding and facilitating the ongoing process of emergence in our lives.

Interferon
Interferon helps restore the body's natural abilities to resist viruses, and has proved effective in halting the progression of AIDS in a significant number of cases. Were the following suggestions regarding protocol adapted, we believe interferon would prove effective for 40% of the people receiving it. With optimal usage, interferon can throw AIDS into suspension, and in many cases into complete remission.

We believe interferon works best at the early stages of the dis-ease, when AIDS may *first* be detected; we urge that it be administered even before KS develops. We recognize that the treatment is very expensive and only selectively available; we also understand that it is usually not administered until KS manifests. But we are convinced that further research will substantiate that genetically-derived interferon (as opposed to any synthetic form that may be developed), most effectively in the gamma-form, could prove beneficial to a large number of people diagnosed with AIDS or ARC if it were administered earlier and in larger doses.

One major difficulty in administering interferon, especially in large doses, has been the nausea it produces. To remedy this, we suggest the detoxification program described earlier, with an emphasis upon colonic cleansing, saunas, and supplements which aid elimination through the kidneys. In addition, marijuana is a natural substance which has been shown to reduce nausea in cancer therapy, and will certainly prove effective with interferon.

Marijuana tea does not harm the lungs. It can be brewed effectively, providing that the plant is *not* exposed to boiling water, which can alter its chemical make-up. Using a glass or porcelain pot, allow boiling water to cool 25 to 30 degrees before adding the marijuana (you can brew all parts of the plant). Let it steep 25 to 30 minutes, during which time the temperature can drop another 10 degrees. Ingest this brew as necessary.

In cases where interferon is suspected to have played a negative role in treatment, we suggest that the entire case history and treatment of the person be examined before conclusions are reached, as other factors may actually be responsible for a worsening of the condition. Should the decision be made to discontinue treatment, drop the level gradually, reducing it by tenths over a period of 100 days. Much promising research with interferon is transpiring. A nasal spray of interferon, for example, has been shown to prevent infection by one of the viruses that causes the common cold.

Opportunistic Infections
While the general program of healing described above is recommended for all manifestations of AIDS, we would like to offer some additional healing approaches for KS and some of the opportunistic infections most frequently associated with Acquired Immune Deficiency. These supplementary approaches will act as *catalysts* to the general program, enhancing its healing effects on the specific infection as well as the entire mind-body-spirit.

When healing is instituted in one part of the body, the defense system is stimulated for healing *throughout* the body. Conversely, anything that weakens one part of the body will have negative effects on the entire system.

As has been suggested earlier, we believe that chemotherapy and radiation suppress the overall immune system; we do not advocate their use with people with AIDS. Many of the drugs used to fight specific opportunistic infections are indeed beneficial; the detoxifying diet offered earlier can help mitigate any of their potentially negative side effects. Other drugs may appear to "conquer" a specific symptom, but in fact will work in a manner similar to chemotherapy and radiation, paving the way for further progression of Acquired Immune Dysfunction through the additional stress they place on the immune system. While it is not our desire to comment on any of these drugs, or to contradict anything that your doctor may recommend, we do wish to urge caution in the choice of drugs employed in the "fight against AIDS." Some holistic medical doctors prefer to strengthen the overall immune system rather than to treat specific opportunistic infections with immune-suppressing drugs, because they discover that the candida and other parasitic infections that may emerge as a result of that treatment only exacerbate the underlying problem.

Kaposi's sarcoma (KS). This form of skin cancer attacks the blood vessels, creating a type of hemorrhage which manifests as purple lesions. It has recently been demonstrated that KS will go into remission and even resolve itself when the immune system is restored. This supports our assertion, included in our original paper of June 1983, that the best way to approach KS is through an immune-enhancing holistic approach whose goal is to detoxify the body, fight the virus, and rejuvenate the immune system.

Several treatments have already been offered for KS, skin lesions, and skin cancer in general. These include interferon, interleukin II, and such homeopathic preparations as periwinkle, mistletoe, and phytolacca (poke root). In addition, we would like to offer a number of novel formulas for healing these conditions.

Each of the following formulas can be enhanced by applying a solution of hydrogen peroxide to the lesion prior to their application. Use traditional stock bottle strength, available from pharmacies, cutting it by ⅓ with distilled water. Apply the peroxide to the lesions for one minute, then wipe it off. While the peroxide will not by itself heal the lesions, it may prevent AIDS-associated parasitic inflammations from manifesting. In addition, the formulas themselves, when applied following the use of hydrogen peroxide, may also help prevent these parasitic infections.

Each person with AIDS may find a different formula or combination of these formuals beneficial. We suggest that you experiement with them on a controlled basis, rather than trying all of them at the same time. Positive results can generally be noted within 6 to 12 weeks. The formulas include:

(1)   A selenium solution composed of aloe gels, selenium, and organically bound silicon. Organically bound silicon is available as either a tincture of silica or horsetail, or in the form of Dr. Barmakian's ALTA-SILIX silica, which is derived from silica. To 4 oz. of aloe, mix 1000 mcg. of selenium (pulverize mineral supplement tablets of selenium), either 50 drops of silica or horsetail tincture, or 8 pulverized tablets of Dr. Barmakian's product. Apply to the lesions twice a day for at least 3 months, and take 1 tsp. internally twice a day;

(2)   combine 3 fluid oz. of aloe vera with either 3 to 6 gms. of dried kelp or dulse (powdered), or ½ fluid ounce of liquid dulse. Mix well and apply to the lesions, as well as consuming internally. If using the powdered kelp plus the aloe vera gels, allow it to dry;

(3)   either of the above two aloe formulas may be complemented by the use of "Yunnan Paiyao" powder, a Chinese patent medicine and secret formula, relatively inexpensive, which we believe contains radix pseudo ginseng. Used in Vietnam to heal deep lesions, Yunnan Paiyao is a hemostatic, and helps stop bleeding into tissues. The instructions on the package suggest that it can be useful in "arresting hemorrhage, curing wounds, activating blood circulation, dispersing blood clots, decreasing lymphatic inflammation and swelling, as well as expelling pus and counteracting toxins." We suggest that it is best taken internally, according to the directions on the package, with 1 oz. of warm wine. (The warm wine increases circulation and helps carry Yunnan Paiyao out to the skin.) Be sure not to consume the safety pill in the bottle. We suggest

that one try the average dose of .25 to .5 grams per day. Yunnan Paiyao may especially prove beneficial with internal lesions;

(4) a mixture of 8 oz. aloe vera, 1 oz. pure cajeput essential oil, and 1 oz. St. John's Wort tincture. Apply twice a day for 3 months. It is best to use this at a different time of day than Yunnan Paiyao.

[Note: "cajeputi" is a genus name, which may include any one of perhaps 300 varieties of cajeput tree, punk tree, or tea tree. In developing this formula, we have drawn upon the cajeput oil available from Tiferet Essentials (contact the editor for more information). Since we believe that melaleuca veridiflora, also known as nialouli, is the cajeput oil most effectively incorporated into this formula, we suggest that you obtain pure niaouli. Niaouli seems similar in properties to eucalyptus. Among its reported uses are as a urinary antiseptic, tissue stimulant, intestinal antiseptic, and application for skin ulcers and fistula. Used in Africa to purify water, it reportedly neutralizes the tuberculin bacillus at .4%. It has been suggested that it has properties as an endocrine system and leukocyte stimulant. The Holisitic Group makes no claims as to the medicinal value of niaouli or the above formula.]

(5) another method for treating internal as well as external lesions, when one is of sufficiently strong constitution to fast, is to institute a 3 to 7 day grape fast; combine this with the ingestion of 4 Tbsp. aloe vera gel mixed with 8 oz. distilled water, taken 2 to 3 times daily. Organic concord grapes are most preferable, although this is not critical; you may eat as many as you want. Repeat this cycle every 120 days, adhering to the basic vegetarian diet described earlier in the interim;

(6) castor oil packs, as described by Edgar Cayce, also appear to be of great benefit here. (A complete discussion of their use is found in "The Nature of the Healing Process" channeling in Part III of this book);

(7) a bath including the essential oils of tonka bean, tea tree, niaouli, thyme, juniper, hyssop, cypress, and angelica is included in the Cleansing Baths section of Chapter 12. This healing, tonifying and detoxifying bath may prove of benefit to anyone diagnosed with AIDS or other immune dysfunctions.

Pneumocystis pneumonia. Pneumocystis is the most fright-ening complication of AIDS, in that it comes on the fastest in a potenially overpowering manner. People with AIDS who adopt a program of adequate vitamin C supplementation run much less risk of coming down with this pneumonia. Should you have pneumocystis, we endorse the current use of the an-tibiotics such as pentamidine and DFMO *in combination with* megadoses of vitamin C. Begin with 25 gm. daily, and increase the dosage as necessary, following the guidelines provided earlier. This is one opportunistic infection where vitamin C can mean the difference between life and death.

Candida albicans. We believe that candida, CMV, and a host of other fungal infections are actually present in the bodies of most individuals, but are ordinarily held in check by a healthy immune system. Only when the immune system is severely depressed, as in the case of AIDS, do these dis-eases surface.

Candida tends to surface, not only in people diagnosed with AIDS, but in a host of other individuals experiencing im-mune dysfunction. Diagnoses of candida have become com-mon in the United States because of the frequent and prolonged use of broad spectrum antibiotics (first introduced in 1947), oral contraceptives, and the nearly universal overcon-sumption of sugar. As these fungi thrive in warm, moist tis-sues saturated with sugar, they discover welcome hosts in women who may be combining an unhealthy diet with either broad spectrum antibiotics prescribed for bladder and genital infections (which can knock out the healthy bacteria which keep the fungus in check) or regular use of "the pill" (which can increase susceptibility to fungal dis-ease).

Much evidence already exists to back our assertion that, when the immune system is restored to its normal function-ing, an almost automatic resistance to candida and other fun-gal and parasitic organisms will be set in motion. If the central immune system is restored by following the general outlines of the program offered in this Inquiry, these infections will tend to resolve themselves.

Candida is a potentially serious dis-ease, with the capac-ity of invading tissues and organs, infecting the blood, and even aggravating the system while lying dormant. Because much valid information already exists in printed form on holistic approaches to candida and other parasitic infections, we encourage you to explore it and the anti-candida diet with the help of a nutritionist or other health practitioner. It is of essential importance to approach parasitic and fungal infections in a manner that enhances, rather than further suppresses, an already weakened immune system.

People diagnosed with either AIDS or ARC are encouraged to adopt the mind-body-spirit approach to healing offered in these pages. To catalyze the effects of our general program, and of *any* anti-candida regimen you may adopt, we suggest that you drink chapparal tea. Add between 1 tsp. and 1 Tbsp. chapparal to 1 quart of water, bring it to a boil, and steep below boiling temperature for 30 to 60 minutes. Understood from the perspective of Chinese Medicine, the sharpness and acuteness of the chapparal contains both yin and yang properties; it has both a cooling effect and an influence upon the Triple Warmer meridian. These two intense polarities can be balanced by the addition of boiled honey, which also has mild antibiotic properties.

Garlic is extremely effective against candida. So are other natural antibiotics such as cherry bark teas, ginseng, apricot teas, and goldenseal; these must always be taken in consultation with an herbalist, and never consumed casually. In addition, sources rich in iodine, iron, selenium, silicon, and vitamin C have antibiotic properties when introduced into the system.

A gargle of hydrogen peroxide can help heal both candida and oral thrush (candida of the mouth). Experiment with stock bottle dilutions from 20% to 10%, diluting it even further as necessary. (You don't want it to burn you.) Do not swallow the peroxide after gargling.

American Biologics in Tijuana has had positive results experimenting with C-3, a form of OXY-C2 prepared as a mouthwash. We are certain that many other organizations and practitioners have developed other beneficial treatments.

The Australian Tea Tree Oil specifically derived from melaleuca alternifolia warrants mention here. The therapeutic properties of this oil as a very strong fungicide and antiseptic have been acknowledged and verified in many different controlled situations. It is speculated that perhaps because it has not been previously used in the modern world, viruses and fungi have not yet developed resistance to its therapeutic properties.

Certificates of testing available from Australia, not yet recognized by the FDA in the United States, have indicated that melaleuca alternifolia may be helpful in healing candida, staphylococcus infections of all sorts, athlete's foot, acne, tinea, and cold sores. Some have used it to prevent infections in cuts and abrasions, insect bites, boils, and minor wounds, citing its bacteriocidal properties. In the context of this manuscript, we are especially intrigued by its potential use in the healing of candida.

Only a few companies import melaleuca alternifolia into the U.S. It is important to obtain the highest quality tea tree oil, one that has not been over-distilled for cosmetic use or cut with other oil. (As of this writing, we are still investigating the strength and purity of various sources of melaleuca alternifolia. Please contact the editor for more information.)

After successfully cleansing the body of candida, avoid such fermented foods as yeast, tamari, and tempeh for a period of 6 to 12 months. We believe, however, that such foods, as well as sweeteners such as honey, can be safely consumed by most post-candida-ites if boiled first.

Cryptococcus (a meningitis-producing fungus). This dis-ease represents a wearing away of the central, sympathetic and parasympathetic nervous systems, and is one of several Central Nervous System disorders affecting a small percentage of people with advanced cases of AIDS. Bolstering the neurological synapses is key to the healing of such conditions, and of AIDS in general; hence the importance of Blue-Green Manna and supplementary amino acids in our program. Kyolic™ garlic intake plus medicinal levels of chamomile and comfrey teas will further help catalyze the healing process. Make an equal mixture of both teas, brewing 2 to 3 tsp. in a cup of water, and drink 3 cups daily.

Toxoplasmosis (an organism affecting the brain). In addition to the sulfur antibiotics usually prescribed for this dis-ease, strengthen the overall immune system through our general program.

Cryptosporidiosis (infection of the bowel). The most effective natural treatment we can suggest is at least 4 to 5 capsules daily of Kyolic™ garlic. We know one physician who has successfully employed the Gumbie Pepper bush, native to the Virgin Islands, in cases of AIDS-related diarrhea and colitis. We would like to offer a less esoteric natural antidote which we believe will curb the diarrhea and help stop the concomitant dehydration process. Blend a "smoothie" from 4 to 5 oz. bananas, mashed into a palatable paste, thinned with 2 to 3 fluid oz. aloe vera juice. Drink this, wait 30 minutes, and then consume 8 oz. dried apples (for pectin content). Comfrey/pepsin tablets may also help heal this infection.

Lymphoma. This cancer of the lymph system calls for, first and foremost, a lot of detoxification. Lymphatic massage is recommended to keep things moving through the ductless gland system. Maintaining a higher cardiovascular rate through intake of niacin will help keep the capillary actions open; iodine is also recommended to slightly elevate the metabolism. Finally, psychoimmunity techniques such as creative visualization will certainly prove of benefit. (See Resources section for a host of possible visualization tools to explore.)

We are well aware that many individuals choose to combat lymphoma with radiation, despite its immune-suppressing effects. We urge these people to adopt the detoxification procedures suggested earlier in conjunction with their medical treatments.

Sometimes cases of lymphoma are in places such as the anus, where lymphatic massage might prove a rather provocative procedure. In such a situation, yogic practices of tightening and loosening the anal sphincter will serve the same purpose.

Hairy Leukoplakia. This virus, which lives on the tongue, can result in a very sore and enlarged tongue, including ulcerations and bald patches. We believe that it is similar to the herpes virus. Adopt the suggestions for combatting herpes which follow.

Cytomegalovirus (CMV). The presence of CMV in so many people diagnosed with AIDS, and of CMV antibodies in a large number of gay men, has been the cause of much concern. We believe that CMV, a lengthy virus of the herpes family, is actually a very common virus which is present in large numbers of individuals. Ordinarily held in check by the immune system, CMV will tend to surface in cases of immune dysfunction or AIDS. That CMV antibodies have been found in so many gay men is due to the fact that so much intensive research has been focused on this particluar segment of the community. As research progresses on the presence of CMV and CMV antibodies in the community as a whole, we believe that our hypothesis will be validated by the discovery of these antibodies in wide segments of the general population.

As mentioned earlier, we believe that CMV is a parallel virus to the AIDS virus. Any course of treatment successful for combatting herpes will, in our opinion, prove beneficial in the early stages of AIDS. Such treatment could possibly hold the progression of AIDS in check until the general program of healing described above could render the virus dormant, and even rid it from the body.

A harmless homeopathic preparation of CMV in potencies of 30X or 10MM is also suggested as a treatment for, not only CMV, but for AIDS itself. Many homeopaths have the equipment to prepare such potencies. These are both neutral potencies, with very few "provings" or side effects. Since 10MM is a fairly new principle in homeopathic circles, we refer practitioners and readers to information on the subject in the text *Flower Essences.*

An outbreak of CMV in a gay man or any other member of an AIDS "high-risk" group is indicative of a weakened immune system, and may indicate a predisposition to AIDS. The treatment described above, as well as our general program, is offered to individuals who wish to protect themselves from developing full-blown cases of AIDS.

Sexually Transmitted Diseases (STDs)
Syphilis. We include a discussion of this dis-ease in our Inquiry thanks to the research of Joan McKenna at the Institute

of Thermobaric Repatterning (see Resources section) who has discovered a high degree of heretofore "undetected" syphilis in people diagnosed with AIDS. Recognizing that venereal diseases such as syphilis are endemic among both gay and African populations, speculation has arisen that the persistence of undetected secondary and tertiary syphilis among these populations may be a possible co-factor in the rise of AIDS.

Noting the high degree of antibiotic use among gays and IV-drug users so far diagnosed with AIDS, McKenna has suggested that "subcurative doses of penicillin" and other antibiotics may mask the primary symptoms of syphilis, forcing it into a latent secondary and finally tertiary stage. Because no foolproof test yet exists to detect latent syphilis in an individual with a known history of syphilis, McKenna has suggested that in fact many individuals with secondary and tertiary syphilis have so far registered false negative on syphilis tests. Noting that many people diagnosed with AIDS also have a history of syphilis, she has hypothesized that their undetected latent syphilis, combined perhaps with their frequent use of antibiotics, may be a strong immuno-suppressant factor in their development of AIDS.

We would like to offer an alternative analysis to explain this phenomenon. We believe that what has really been detected here is, in classic homeopathic terminology, the syphilitic miasm.

A miasm is an inherited genetic predisposition to a disease which develops in the following manner. Let us suppose that your great grandmother has syphilis. During the slow progression of her dis-ease, way before her death, she gave birth to your grandfather. According to homeopathic theory, while your grandfather never came down with syphilis—it is not passed down to children during pregnancy as is the AIDS virus—he nonetheless inherited the syphilitic miasm. This miasm has in turn been passed down to you. This miasm is an "unfinished dis-ease," not completely eliminated from your ancestor's system, which has been passed on to you in a miasmic state.

Miasmic dis-ease is normally benign. In most cases, individuals will simply pass the miasm down from generation to generation. The syphilitic miasm, however, while normally benign, can surface in the body as a case of active syphilis when the immune system is severely stressed. In this manner it works similarly to candida and other fungal infections which, as noted earlier, are present in most individuals but are normally held in check by a healthy immune system.

Homeopathic theory thus leads us to conclude that what is being detected here is not "undetected syphilis" masked by the use of subcurative dosages of penicillin, but rather the surfacing of the syphilitic miasm in individuals with severe immune dysfunction. We do not believe that latent syphilis is rampant in the gay community. Furthermore, we reject speculation that penicillin and other antibiotics are a significant cofactor in the rise of AIDS. Unless allergies are present, both we and McKenna affirm the use of penicillin in the treatment of syphilis. People diagnosed with AIDS in whom the syphilitic miasm has emerged are urged to combine this penicillin treatment with a holistic program of detoxification and healing.

Many case histories exist which indicate that homeopathic treatment in and of itself may at times prove an effective treatment for syphilis. Nonetheless, homeopaths within the United States are legally forbidden from advocating homeopathic treatment as a cure for syphilis. Without advocating such a position, we wish to observe that any homeopathic treatment for syphilis would have to be totally tailored to the individual client. Syphilinum might be effective for one individual, mercury for another, a homeopathic preparation of penicillin for yet another. The use of autonosodes, homeopathic treatments made specifically from cultures of the affected individual's own dis-ease toxins, might prove especially beneficial, not only in the case of syphilis, but in the treatment of AIDS. Equipment for the generation of autonosodes is for the most part available in Europe and South America.

The section on herpes which follows contains information on one possible homeopathic follow-up to penicillin treatment.

Herpes. A general program to follow in outbreaks of herpes and viruses of the herpes family would include dietary changes plus the use of Lysine and perhaps BHT. Because the amino acid L-Arginine feeds herpes, eliminate such arginine-rich foods as peanuts, almonds, chocolate and citrus. In acute cases, we suggest you try up to 2000 mg. Lysine 4 times/day, for a period of 5 to 7 days. Follow this up with a maintenance dosage of 500-1000 mg./day. In addition, for those who are not sensitive to BHT, taking it in various amounts may prove beneficial. Some individuals have gained benefit from using the oil form as a mouthwash.

Much excellent literature on herpes and other STDs already exists. Because it is beyond the scope of this Inquiry to attempt a complete discussion of the subject, we refer you to it. (Some have suggested that the mental pattern associated with herpes relates to a suppression of creativity.) We do, however, wish to share some additional information not usually encountered in the standard literature.

The Platonic Academy of Herbal Studies, in Santa Cruz, California, has been successfully putting herpes into remission using a 100:1 extract of the red algae *dumontiaceae*. This algae is an immune enhancer, as are many spectrums of algae. We are encouraged by such work, and believe that the algae as currently employed is a good base formula that needs to be individualized in each case.

We learned about the work of the Fryer Research Center in New York City from a letter on holistic approaches to AIDS in the *New York Native*. We wish to share their approach in treating STDs by quoting from the correspondence sent us by their medical director, Dr. Richard Ribner:

In addition to a full Preventive Medicine regime, I use Homeopathic preparations to cleanse the body of residual toxins of Gonorrhea and Lues. Back in 1790 Dr. Hahnemann predicted that something of this nature would occur. The modern treatment—the established treatment—with antibiotics is okay, but he stressed that the body must be fundamentally detoxified. The frequent episodes of nonspecific urethritis and herpes I believe are due to the residual strains of Gonorrhea. So when I treat for herpes, I am not interested in an ointment to get rid of the skin lesions. The skin lesions are telling me that there are toxins in the body. The way to get rid of the lesions is by getting rid of the toxins in the body.

I use the homeopathic preparations of Medorrhinum, Lycopodium, and Thuja in such cases. I usually double check myself by mus-

cle testing the patient with the homeopathic preparation I think is indicated, and then choose the one that tests best. Usually it is the Medorrhinum. Subsequent to that, just to be sure, I use remedies to detoxify for Lues: Syphilinum, Mercurius vivus, and Aurum. (Further information on homeopathic approaches to the treatment of AIDS and its opportunistic infections may be found in the channeling, "The Nature of the Healing Process" in Part III of this book.)

Intestinal parasites. Intestinal parasites (amoebas) are often transferred through sexual contact, and can prove very difficult to remove from the system. They have been experienced by so many individuals who have later been diagnosed with AIDS that many practitioners have posited a direct connection between the two.

We do not accept that parasites themselves are a direct cause of AIDS, but we do believe that people who have a predisposition to stress are most likely to come down with them upon exposure. Once you do have parasites, both their effects on the body and the treatments frequently prescribed to get rid of them will tend to increase the stresses placed upon an already stressed immune system, especially in the commonly encountered case of recurrence. This weakening of the immune system by parasites will render an individual highly sensitive to the AIDS virus—hence the frequent concurrence of AIDS and intestinal parasites.

Many medicines commonly prescribed for parasites and vaginal infections may do more harm to the immune system than to these tenacious little buggers. Flagyl may be carcinogenic. We have heard several stories of people taking more and more flagyl to fight one, two, then three bouts of parasites, only to finally come down with AIDS. Carbarsome contains arsenic, and equally should be avoided. And while we are unclear regarding the effects of diiodohydroxyquin (diodoquin), since they vary so much from person to person, we can say that traditional antibiotics are the least harmful medicinal remedy.

We would like to offer, as an alternative approach, a simple formula which we believe will prove most effective in most cases of inner-lunum and extra-lunum parasites. Make an herbal compound of the following:

1 part dried cabbage leaves,
½ part Kyolic™ garlic,
⅓ part Korean ginseng,
⅓ part organically grown tobacco.

Take 2 tablespoons twice daily, separated by at least 6 hours; it is not critical to coordinate this with mealtimes. To optimize the effects of this formula, eat a minimum of 8 to 16 oz. daily of boiled or pickled cabbage in the form of sauerkraut.

We suggest that you try this approach by itself, without the addition of antibiotics, for at least 7 days. If after 2 weeks there is no improvement, it might be wise to seek more conventional modes of treatment. Should the treatment work, as we expect it will, continue it until the body is *totally* cleansed of parasites.

Tests for parasites are of questionable accuracy. We have met one man who insistently told his physician that he had parasites, even though his tests repeatedly came out negative. It was only when he entered the hospital with pneumocystis that the parasites were finally discovered in his system. The final test of whether or not you have parasites, and of the success of your cleansing, is how you feel and how you continue to feel. (The Sept. 23, 1983 issue of *Science* magazine contained an article by Frances D. Gillin, David S. Reiner, and Chi-Sun Wang, reporting that an unusual lipase present in human milk kills *Giardia lambia*, the inner-lunum parasite, and *E. histolytica*, the dysentery amoeba. The authors speculate that mother's milk serves to protect infants from these parasites. We are very encouraged by this research, as we mentioned in the "Thymus" section of this Inquiry that another of mother's milk's remarkable functions is the ability to stimulate the thymus.)

Body lice (crabs). We include these little buggers under the STD category because of their intimate mode of transmission. Although many over-the-counter pyrinate-containing preparations are readily available to kill crabs, these are not always 100% effective. Kwell, the prescription medication often resorted to when these critters proliferate, has been implicated as a possible carcinogen. To those readers who wish to honor the sacred nature of both human and animal life, we would like to offer a simple natural formula to transfer these little lice intact to the far reaches of your sewage system.

Intermix equal quantities of oil of pennyroyal and oil of garlic, cutting them with an equal quantity of distilled water. Put this mixture in an atomizer, and spray it on the infested areas. Leave it on for 24 hours, and then shower. Towel dry— put the towel and all infected sheets and clothing in the laundry—and repeat the procedure 2 more days in succession for a total of 3 applications. While the solution will render the eggs dormant, it is necessary to remove them from the body to prevent reinfestation. Try enlisting your sexual partner or your next door neighbor to aid in the egg hunt.

[Editor's Note: The following systems and approaches are among many entertained by those on the healing path. We include them herein because of their potential benefit to people diagnosed with AIDS and others.]

Homeopathy
The science of "homeopathy" is discussed in various parts of this Inquiry. Dana Ullman, M.P.H., co-author of *Everybody's Guide to Homeopathic Medicine,* offers the following definition:

> *Homeopathic medicine is a natural pharmaceutical science that uses various plant, mineral or animal materials in very small doses to stimulate a sick person's natural defenses. The medicines are individually chosen for their ability to cause in overdose similar symptoms to those the person is suffering. "Homoios" in Greek means "similar" and "pathos" means "disease" or "suffering". Since symptoms are actually efforts of the organism to reestablish homeostatis or balance, it is logical to seek a substance that would, in overdose, cause similar symptoms. The medicines, thus, go with, rather than against, the person's natural defenses.*
>
> *Homeopathy is composed of two highly systematic methods: toxicology and casetaking. First, homeopaths find out the specific physical, emotional, and mental symptoms that various substances cause in overdose. Homeopathic texts have more detail on toxicology than any other source. Second, homeopaths interview their patients in great detail to discover the totality of physical, emotional, and mental symptoms. The homeopath seeks to find a substance that would cause similar symptoms and then gives it in small, specially prepared doses.*

In summary, then, one may say that homeopathy is based upon the principle that a substance which produces symptoms in overdose in a healthy person cures those symptoms in micro-dose in an ill person.

Acupuncture

Acupuncture is part of the venerable system of Chinese medi-cine for which we have the greatest respect. As a complete holistic system, Chinese medicine asserts that when an in-dividual's physical, emotional, mental, and spiritual energies are in balance, dis-ease does not manifest; it is geared far more toward achieving and maintaining health and well-being than toward treating symptoms and dis-ease.

Chinese doctors measure the vital energy, or chi, flowing through the 12 pathways or meridians of the body by meas-uring the "pulses" in the wrist, and by noting, among other things, the condition of the tongue and the appearance of the face. Whether or not individuals feel themselves "ill," the Chi-nese understand that any chronic imbalances in this vital energy will eventually manifest as dis-ease. These imbalances may have genetic, internal, or external causes, and may result in physical, emotional, or mental illness. By correcting the im-balances, the Chinese believe that the body will right itself, and the dis-ease will be replaced by harmony and well-being.

Acupuncture, as part of this system, involves insertion of, for the most part, very thin needles into the skin. This proce-dure is relatively painless and often unnoticeable; lying down on a back full of needles and falling asleep is not uncommon. Some practitioners employ electroacupuncture, putting a mild electrical pulse through the needles to enhance their effects. If you are not familiar with acupuncture, or are frightened of it, you may want to refer to an excellent introductory article in the September 1983 *Whole Life Times* (Vol. 29), which relates one woman's experience of her first acupuncture session.

If you are drawn to Chinese medicine as part of your treat-ment for AIDS, we must emphasize that it is *not enough* just to have needles stuck into you. In order to reap the full benefits of acupuncture, and to balance successfully the body's ener-gies through this system, you must combine the needles with Chinese herbal medicine, right diet, stress reduction, and posi-tive thinking.

We believe that acupuncturists can achieve a 65% to 70% rate of accuracy in diagnosing AIDS through skilled observation, case history, and the tools of pulse and tongue diagnosis. A symptom picture including alternate swelling and receding of lymph nodes, a marked or acute shortness of breath, marked imbalances in the spleen chi (energy), and imbalances in the kidney chi involving deficiencies of kidney yin with hyperactivity of kidney yang would suggest a possible case of AIDS. (We note here that it is also possible to verify elevated activity in the adrenals by administering a blood test to measure the degree of adrenalin present in the system, or by noting unusual quantities of adrenalin stored in the fatty tissues.) Acupuncturists will find that the root of the dis-ease (the original problem) will show up in kidney chi imbalance, and the stem (where the problem manifests) in the heart chi. The governing vessel relates to the coccyx and medulla oblongata, whose importance was discussed earlier (see "The Nature of the Healing Process" channeling for more information on diagnosis).

Because Doctors of Chinese medicine always determine the exact course of treatment by noting the imbalances of the specific individual, it is neither possible nor wise to attempt to outline a complete Chinese medical approach to AIDS. What is important to emphasize is that the knowledge, sensitivity, and diagnostic ability of the practitioner are crucial to successful treatment. You will probably find that acupuncturists will choose to deal with the night sweats that manifest in the early phases of AIDS by animating the Triple Warmer Meridian.

Practitioners of Chinese medicine may wish to consult several articles in the *Journal of the American College of Traditional Chinese Medicine* which address immune dysfunction and AIDS. Issue number 2, 1983, pages 12-22, contains three articles, translated by C.S. Cheung, M.D., and Howard E. Harrison, C.A., which discuss specific Chinese herbs and decoctions and their relation to immune responses and AIDS. Issue number 2, 1985, pages 20-29, features an article by Reece Smith entitled "AIDS Prevention: Preliminary Considerations on the Management of the Prodrome Symptoms Using the Concept of Traditional Chinese Medicine." (The address of the journal is 2400 Geary Boulevard, San Francisco, CA 94115.) (For comments on the usefulness of Yunnan Payiao in healing KS, refer to the section on Kaposi's sarcoma above.)

Practitioners may want to employ figs as an aid to detoxification of people with AIDS and of the worried well. Steam the figs, as this makes them more palatable and more easily assimilable by the body, as well as increases their effects as a mild diuretic. The vapors of the figs, combined with eucalyptus vapors, help drain the sinuses and break up mucus. Eating the steamed figs (making sure they do not come in direct contact with the eucalyptus leaves or vapor) will help revitalize the body's ability to assimilate nutrients and to eliminate toxins.

Short grain brown rice, steamed or cooked slowly into conji, helps relieve stress upon the body, and aids in restoration of the nervous system and of the immune system. Brown rice is a nutritious grain, rich in carbohydrates and fiber, and perfectly balanced between yin and yang (feminine and masculine) energies. Gay readers may safely reject theories prevalent in some macrobiotic circles that brown rice will "cure" homosexuality. Since homosexuality is a purely natural and healthy phenomenon, it does not represent a reversal of yin and yang energies, an energy imbalance, or an arrest of sexual development. Homosexuality cannot be "cured," because all it is is an expression of love, and love itself *is* the cure. Eat all the brown rice you want; whatever your sexuality, you'll be able to express it in a more healthy way as a result.

Doctors of Chinese medicine, as discussed earlier, may prescribe dietary regimens which contradict the suggestions of our group, or the advice of other practitioners. Each system has its own rules and protocol. Our eclectic approach to healing emphasizes that only you can be the final judge of the right path to follow.

Noteworthy Institutes and Individuals
The important work of Louise L. Hay, Russell M. Jaffe, M.D., Ph.D., Emanuel Revici, M.D., The Garson Institute, and Joan McKenna's Institute for Thermobaric Repatterning deserves your consideration. Please see the beginning of the Resources section.

Macrobiotics

Macrobiotics has certain parallels to traditional Chinese Medicine, in that it is a closed system—complete unto itself—which attempts to balance the body's yin and yang energies by focusing on strict adherence to a dietary regimen. For those who can *faithfully* follow the program and practice self-discipline, macrobiotics offers a potentially effective means of treatment for AIDS and other imbalances. Our group is inspired by the commitment and healing of a vocal San Francisco proponent of this route, whose KS lesions as of this writing are in remission.

Treatment in Mexico

The American Biologics facility in Tijuana has shown promising results researching and treating AIDS from a comprehensive holistic perspective. Going the Mexican route is a viable choice, but we must emphasize that it is not necessary to go south of the border to heal AIDS.

Amino Acid Treatment

This treatment, described in *The Cancer Survivors* and practiced by Dr. Burton at the Rand Memorial Hospital in the Bahamas, involves injections of amino acid proteins 8 to 12 times daily. As has been mentioned earlier, the loss of protein through semen can lower the body's natural immune resources, and may in fact be a major factor for some people with AIDS. As this treatment can replenish that loss of proteins, we endorse it for those for whom it is appropriate.

Herb Teas

We do not wish to attempt a full inquiry into the various herbal teas and compounds that can be useful in the prevention of and healing of AIDS and other immune dysfunctions, as this would require a separate treatise in its own right. Certainly *echinacea*, which is discussesd by our friend Paul Lee in this book, has great validity here. We also wish to mention Pau D'arco, the Argentinian tea with definite antiviral and anticancer properties; Chinese herbology; chapparal, which is a blood cleanser; hibiscus and rose hips, which are natural sources of vitamin C; and ginseng, which tonifies the body. While cayenne can induce elimination through the skin tissues, we do not believe its use is critical for people with AIDS. (See Native Herb Co. listing under Resources for more information.)

Taoist System

Dr. Stephen Chang of San Francisco has been working with this system of Taoist healing, which includes herbal formulations based on the five-element theory. This is another closed system—complete in its own right—whose explorations we can endorse for those individuals naturally drawn to it.

Total Body Modification

This system, developed by Dr. Viktor Frank, is in our belief effective in the treatment of AIDS. The practitioner should work on levels which affect the skin's tissues, the pancreas and the thymus, and those parts of the vertebrae which affect these specific organs. The reflex points should be those which in the system of kinesiology are connected to the above areas and organs; this is also true for working at the base of the feet.

Urine Therapy

Urine represents the body's own natural system of homeopathy, and its careful utilization can build the immune system. Many practitioners and proponents of holistic health have healed themselves of a variety of ailments and dis-eases by systematically ingesting and/or applying externally homeopathic dilutions of their own urine. While this is not our favorite system of treatment, one member of our group particularly swears by this approach.

Drinking one's urine straight should be attempted only under the advisement of someone skilled in its use for healing. If, for example, the elimination system itself is debilitated, adding toxins to the body by drinking toxic urine would not be recommended; a homeopathic preparation of the urine would be appropriate for such an individual. Those who choose to apply urine externally, or to bathe in it, are advised to cleanse with castile soap afterward.

Conclusion

The Holisitic Group has attempted to touch upon many different holistic treatments and approaches, all of which may have validity in the prevention and healing of AIDS. It has been neither our intention nor our purpose to provide a complete blueprint for a program which you or anyone should follow—we in fact reject the notion of "should," and have done our best to expunge it from our thinking and from this Inquiry. The decision as to what to do, we know, can be a difficult one, especially when you are faced with such a life-threatening illness. Allow yourself to be guided by love—love of self and love of your sisters and brothers. Love is the key.

Undoubtedly there exist among our readers many practitioners and people with AIDS who have successfully employed substances and techniques which we have unintentionally overlooked. We encourage and request that all individuals with healing experiences they wish to share with the larger community send their information and case histories to the editor of this book (see Resources section). Through future articles in gay, New Age, and holistic health publications, we will attempt to spread word of your successes. As more and more positive stories of transformation are shared among us, we will be able to hasten the healing of AIDS.

We regret that neither members of The Holisitic Group nor the editor of this book can make themselves available for consultation or diagnosis by mail or by phone. We urge you to consult your local and trusted health practitioners and healers for treatment and support in the prevention and healing of AIDS. Should you not be in contact with such individuals, you can usually locate them by consulting health food stores, chiropractors, New Age and health food publications, the alternative press, centers of yoga and meditation, and even the Yellow Pages.

* * * *

None of us exists as a separate entity independent of one another; each of us is an expression and manifestation of the living organization called humankind. While AIDS is unique neither to the lesbian and gay community nor to this period of history, its manifestation during the crucial 1980s is significant to current collective consciousness of humankind. The disease has centered itself in the United States, a country which claims to be the most evolved upon the planet, a nation held up by many of its political and even religious leaders as a Light to the World. That this country up to now has stifled research for AIDS, running from this challenge and test with homophobic hysteria and blatant bigotry, shows how far this nation has moved from the simple and universal truth: "I am my sister's and my brother's keeper."

In all religions and philosophies based upon truth and love, it is taught that if you wish to know God, you must look to the natural order of things. Homosexuality is found throughout nature; it is a natural expression found within God's creation. For society to wall off and persecute homosexual women and men is to deny its own nature and essence, which is love. The humanity of all is lessened by homophobia and prejudice and loss of life due to AIDS.

AIDS offers an opportunity for all people of concern to bind together and make the statement that overcoming AIDS is a *human* issue. Those among us who say that AIDS is punitive in nature immediately show their own inhumanity. Those who show fear of these issues lessen their humanity. And those who bind together to work toward consensus and healing demonstrate their humanity. We are all sisters and brothers.

Spirit is the common thread that flows through all women and men, binding us together and making us one. Spirit is the thread that holds together each pearl that is precious and dear to the One, the Universal Spirit, the Om, the All, the Father-Mother-God that encompasses us all. Without that thread, the pearls fall and have no order. And what is that Spirit, if not simply love—love which extends to all elements of culture. Only the lack of love brings disharmony and disease to the planet as a whole.

CHAPTER 9

MEDITATION
UPON THE CHAKRAS

THEIR RELATION TO HEALING AND IMMUNITY
by Jason Serinus

During one of my channelings with Kevin Ryerson, I asked the Spirit Entity Tom McPherson if there was anything I might add to this book to further aid readers in strengthening their immune systems. Spirit suggested a spiral chakra meditation, an ancient practice described in detail and diagrams by W. Brugh Joy, M.D., in his much respected book *Joy's Way*. Because this meditation centers upon the heart chakra, the spiritual energy center of love, harmony, and peace which corresponds to the thymus gland, it is of great importance to readers concerned with immune dysfunction, AIDS, and individual/planetary transformation. After leading thousands of individuals through it, both in private practice and in seminars around the country, I can testify to its power to align mind, body, and spirit.

The spiral meditation is only one of many valid approaches to meditation upon the chakras. Rather than reprint it herein, I offer in its stead some basic information on the chakras—our spiritual anatomy—and their importance to the healing process.

Most present-day Western spiritual teachings focus upon seven major chakras, or energy centers, in the body. Just as the bones, muscles, organs, and glands compose our physical anatomy, so do the chakras comprise our spiritual, or "ethereal" anatomy. Best visualized as *radiant spheres of light energy,* these seven chakras, and the many other energy centers associated with them, are the points and regions through which the soul and spirit integrate into the physical body, and serve to animate our being. (Please refer to this book's Introduction for definitions of the terms "mind," "body," "spirit," and "soul.")

The chakras enable us to form our individual earth-plane identities as mind-body-spirit. Through the chakras, both the consciousness and the personality find their focus in the body. The chakras are literally the points through which the soul and spirit integrate into the physical form, and the personality in turn radiates energy out into the Universe. They enable our God consciousness—our soul—to express itself in the physical realm, and to relate to other souls and other expressions of the Universal Consciousness.

The chakras are common to all cultures and expressions of thought. In the Judeo-Christian system they are referred to as the Tree of Life. They are the seven churches in the Book of Revelations. They are the chakras or wheels of the Eastern systems of thought. In Toltec/Aztec mythology, the chakras appear as the seven serpents of Quezalcoatl. And throughout all cultures, they are the seven lights spoken of in context of the seven spirits contained within the individual.

An individual whose mind is not still is often trapped by the "illusion" of the five senses and seduced into believing that gross physical reality is "the" absolutely reality of all existence. Meditation—the process of stilling the body so that the mind can explore the full perimeters of self—allows us to move beyond the dramas of day-to-day existence to explore our true identity as expressions of God. Chakra meditation in particular facilitates our awareness of the infinite wisdom and loving energy that is constantly channeled into the body and coordinated through the chakras. By attuning ourselves to this energy and aligning ourselves with it, we achieve the balance and wholeness which *is* the healing process itself.

Meditation on the chakras allows the alignment of mind, body, and spirit which is synonomous with health and well-being. When the subtle anatomies are aligned through alignment of the chakras, the life force itself is capable of pouring directly into the physical body, completely rejuvenating the body's tissues. Meditation thus allows us to explore the higher dimensions of self—our unity with the love and perfection which is God—and to live as God on the earth plane.

Through meditation on the chakras, one receives revelation and insight, as one aligns oneself within to receiving and transmitting higher energies. When one is in a state of harmony and balance, when stress is eliminated and the mind is at peace, illness and dis-ease do not exist. When the chakras are aligned, healing is the natural state of one's being, for alignment of the chakras represents just that state between yin and yang, male and female, active and passive, acting and feeling, giving and taking, which is the state of optimal health and well-being.

The chakras are open at all times. If they were not open, the personality reading this would cease to inhabit the physical body with which they are now associated (i.e., you'd be dead). It is a misconception that the chakras are sometimes closed, and must be opened through meditation. While the chakras remain open in a misaligned individual, the closed or cluttered mind which corresponds to this state inhibits the free flow of energy through them, resulting in disharmony and eventual dis-ease. Thus the goal of meditation is not the opening of the chakras, but the bringing of them into alignment, by opening the mind to their perfection, so that health and finally a universal consciousness of love and harmony can radiate throughout one's being and all of humankind.

In a discourse on consciousness and the immune system, Jack Schwarz recently noted that "holistic" means that one is not just a body but an entire energy field. Healing is accomplished, not just by merely focusing on the physical symptoms of dis-ease, but by rebalancing the entire human personality. This can be accomplished in part by meditation on the seven chakras. Through focusing extra attention on those chakras where energy seems most blocked, we can allow God's healing energy—our *own* healing energy—to flow unimpeded throughout the body. A healthy person is a radiant person, one whose entire being is full of energy and life, who does not feel stagnated or stuck in life. Such a person does not have to worry about immune dysfunction. The capacity to excite one's own radiant energy, to still one's mind through meditation and allow radiant energy to enter through the chakras, is the key to health.

The Seven Chakras
The First Chakra is located at the tip of the spinal cord, at the tailbone or coccyx. The base chakra, it symbolizes *grounding* and *understanding*. It also relates to the adrenals, which affect the flight/fight syndrome, and relate to one's state of balance. Over-stimulation of the adrenals is a continuous source of anxiety or ungrounding. By meditating on the coccyx and grounding oneself, one can either stimulate the adrenals if one is lethargic, or destimulate to remove anxiety. The color of this chakra is red, and its musical keynote is C.

The Second Chakra is located between the belly button and the genitals, and relates to the testicles in men and the ovaries in women. This chakra is the source of *creativity* and *creation*, including creating all levels of *relationship* by drawing us in contact with other human beings through human sexuality. Meditation on this chakra empowers self-actualization, helping us to form who we are as individuals through intimacy and association with others. Its color is orange, and its keynote is D.

The Third Chakra is in the solar plexus and the stomach, and relates to the *emotions* (gut feelings), as well as to the spleen and the pancreas. Meditation on this chakra helps translate emotions into feelings, which in turn can be translated into *sensitivity*, enabling us to hear another person's needs, and to give of ourselves appropriately. Thus, meditation on this chakra enables us to remain balanced by being sensitive to both ourselves and others. (When we overeat and stuff ourselves, we tend not to deal with our emotions.) Its color is yellow, and its keynote is E.

The Fourth Chakra is the heart chakra—the *heart center* or great balancer—where all the lower chakras are integrated into *love*, which is harmony. Here the loving nature is expressed; here meditation promotes not only love, peace, and harmony, but stimulation of the thymus. The thymus, the original central activator of the entire endocrine system and immune system, is located at the top of the sternum, below the thyroid

(Adam's apple), and relates to the heart chakra. When one's heart is open, the thymus and the immune system function properly. Its color is green, and its note is F.

The Fifth Chakra is the throat chakra, the seat of *expression*. Through meditation on the throat chakra we can personally express who we are, and share this essence with others. This chakra relates to the thyroid and the parasympathetic ganglia, which affect all portions of the immune system. Its color is blue, and its keynote is G.

The Sixth Chakra is the center of the forehead, and is referred to by some as the Third Eye. It represents *vision* and *inner vision*, helping you to fulfill yourself as a human being. It relates to the pituitary, which in turn stimulates the dream state, a state which affords us vision beyond the realms of ordinary waking consciousness. Its color is indigo, and its keynote is A.

The Seventh Chakra, or crown chakra, is at the top of the head, and represents *purpose* and *divine purpose*. The seventh chakra represents the final integration of our being, and our connection with what is beyond the limited consciousness of the body. This chakra allows us to bond intimately with others on all levels, and to express ourselves on higher spiritual levels. It relates to the pineal gland, which can produce visions in the dream state. Individuals who have their right and left brains in balance tend to have slightly enlarged pineal glands. Its color is violet (it is sometimes visualized as a purple lotus at the top of the head), and its keynote is B.

Some systems which describe the chakras refer to an Eighth Chakra, or star chakra, located above the head, where all the other chakras, and the emotional, mental, etheric, and astral bodies resound in tune. This merger of these different bodies of the subtle anatomy at the Eighth Chakra allows one to move beyond personal issues into more cosmic ones.

Certain systems ascribe different names, organs, glands, and locations to the seven points, e.g., calling the Second Chakra the spleen chakra—daintily stepping over the genital area—or saying that the Seventh Chakra relates to the pituitary gland. What is important is not the differences between systems, but rather their shared affirmation of the importance of chakra meditation in achieving health and well-being. As John has stated through Kevin Ryerson in one of his many discourses on the chakras: "For removal of all stress, and the proper alignment from the crown chakra through meditation, which is achieved by first stilling the conscious mind and then stimulating the pineal gland, acts as an anchoring for the life force into the body physical, reanimating the whole of the tissues."

If you refer to the colors and keynotes which represent each chakra, you will find that the seven chakras reflect the seven colors of the rainbow—they are components of the Light— and that they represent the notes of the major scale, beginning with the base key C. The chakras truly are the windows through which enter the light and harmony of the universe.

There are many different and valid techniques for meditating upon and energizing the chakras. Brugh Joy does a spiral meditation, centering upon universal and unconditional love by beginning with the heart chakra (an important matter for people with any sexually transmitted dis-ease). Others begin with the crown chakra; still others with the root chakra. Some meditators visualize golden light at each chakra, others roses of various colors; some even focus upon both color and sound, singing, humming, or, in my case, whistling the appropriate note.

Spirit has connected me with a Steven Halpern tape entitled "Zodiac Suite" which goes up the scale by half-steps from C to B, enabling me to focus my mind and my tones upon the various chakras and points in-between. I have also been directed to attune my first chakra, not to "C" of the major scale, but to "B," and to proceed up the scale from there to A flat. This pitch is closer to the "A" of 438 vibrations per second, which is the note that is sounded if one strikes the sarcophagus in the King's Chamber of the Great Pyramid. It seems that this is the original pitch to which many classical instruments were and still are tuned. This is certainly an area worthy of lifetimes of further exploration—or at least a lot of quiet meditation.

Which chakra meditation is right for you? Only your higher self knows for sure. Give yourself permission to accept the fact that you always know what is in your best interest—you just have to go deep enough to get the answers. Remember that when you get to the Heart Chakra, which relates to the thymus, you can stimulate the thymus by visualizing and experiencing love, and then sending that love out unconditionally to others and to the planet. When you are in a state of unconditional love, you can no longer be offended by anyone or anything. In such a state, you need no defenses—there is nothing to be immune against. In a state of unconditional love, nothing interferes with the flow of your being, because everything is balanced and in harmony. In fact, when love flows fully and unconditionally among all without boundaries or limitations, there is no need for any of the techniques or substances which are described in this book.

Excerpt from Kevin Ryerson's Group Channeling, "Sexuality and Relationships," 6/16/84

Question: *What is the Kundalini?*

John's Answer: *When Understanding begets the desire to bring about Creativity, and Creativity begets the desire to be Sensitive, and when Sensitivity begets the desire to be in Harmony or Loving, and when Lovingness begets the desire to Express, and when the desire to Express creates Vision, and when the Vision expresses sense of Divine Purpose, then all the chakras are open, and ye transcend all the others to the point of the transpersonal, where ye become androgynous and natural in all thy acts. This then is the opening of the Kundalini.*

Question: *Is that really hard to achieve?*

Answer: *Is it hard to be loving?*

Question: *No.*

Answer: *Is it hard to be expressive?*

Question: *No.*

Answer: *It is more difficult to open the Kundalini than it is to know God; and God is simply love. For love is that which unites all the chakras.*

Excerpt from Kevin Ryerson's group channeling, "The Soul's Path," 11/2/85

John: *...for without love, all things come to naught. Love's focus is the heart chakra, the balance, the immaculate heart, for, divine purpose without love has no anchor on the earth plane. Understanding without love is* *but as dry knowledge, and returns to dust. Creation without love lacks sensitivity, so therefore cannot be communicated to others. Sensitivity without love is merely emotionalism. Expression without love is merely the articulation of one's own limited opinion. So thus, the heart chakra is the immaculate balance to all the chakras, where they merge and take wings to set all free.*

Information on the relationship of specific chakras to AIDS is discussed in Gurudas' *Gem Elixirs and Vibrational Healing, Vol. 1,* pages 64-65. Included in that book's extensive bibiography is a section on "Chakras and Kundalini." Among the books on the chakras recommended by Kevin Ryerson are: *Joy's Way* by Brugh Joy; *The Chakras* by C.W. Leadbeater [please ignore the anti-sexual prudery which covers up the relationship between the sexual organs and the second chakra by calling it the "spleen chakra"]; *Kundalini in the Physical World* by Mary Scott; and *Life Arts.* To this may be added *Voluntary Controls: Excercises for Creative Meditation and for Activating the Potential of the Chakras* by Jack Schwarz.

CHAPTER 10

CONSCIOUS RECOVERY

by Margo Adair

Being told that you have AIDS, or any life-threatening illness, may for you become synonymous to being told you will die way before you are ready—unless medical research finds "The Cure." Putting your only hope in medical science is a risky proposition. Medical science understands the progression of many, many dis-eases for which the doctors still have no cure. There is no guarantee they will discover a cure at all—much less inside the limited years you think you have left.

There are people walking around alive and well who were put in their graves years ago by medical prognoses. You *can* choose to live. Medicine has always been a study of *dis-ease*, not health. If you choose to live, the choice must be a *total* one, one in which every aspect of your being is engaged with the process of discovering health. You cannot expect to live—that is, heal yourself—without diligent and constant work. It is by no means something that will happen *to* you; it will only be accomplished *by* you.

If self-pity is an emotion you allow yourself, you are taking the position of being victimized by something happening *to* you; a posture of total powerlessness is something you cannot afford.

To whatever degree you disidentify with what is happening to you—to your body, or any aspect of yourself—you give up part of your power. As your consciousness is an integral part of yourself, it too must be engaged in healing. It is not enough for it simply to react to what is happening. When you have any life-threatening illness you need to dedicate your *whole* self to the healing process—every thought, every feeling, every cell of your body must be involved in the discovery of health. In this article I am addressing the question of how to harness consciousness as your ally in the struggle to recover or to die with dignity. This is sometimes simplistically referred to as visualization.

What is health? As defined earlier in this book, it is the state of being one attains when one's body, mind, and spirit are in perfect harmony, or put another way, when one's personality is aligned with one's higher purpose. In order for this to occur, you must be in harmony with the world around you.

The idea of being in harmony with our world has become ludicrous, for it may blow up in nuclear holocaust at any time, and every day the environment is pumped full of more and more carcinogens. Compounding the problem, our culture is fully fragmented—our bodies are separated from our minds, our work from our pleasure, our private lives from our public lives; and for those of us who are homosexual, our sexuality, the deepest expression of the self, is ostracized altogether.

The result of all this is *stress*—and chronic stress suppresses the immune system. So to heal yourself, you need to remove stress from your life. Obviously easier said than done—but certainly not impossible.

Throughout the ages people have turned to spirituality to muster the courage to face their lives when in crisis. Spirituality is that part of ourselves that is at "one" with all that is. (We are all spiritual whether or not we use that word to describe our experience.) It is the calm sense of connection to all life, the merging of the existential "I" into the whole, the transcendence of the self into something greater. Some people experience it through prayer, some through a walk in the woods or meditation, and others through orgasm. It is the source of creativity, intuition, psychic awareness, and healing powers. It is understandable that people turn to it when in crisis.

I teach people how to use the meditative state of mind for problem-solving, for it is there that we can tap our intuitive/creative knowledge at will. It is there that we experience spirituality. Psychic awareness is only "paranormal" because of our cultural world view. In our secular society we are taught to ignore the awareness that comes when relaxing; instead we learn that all that is out of control originates in the "subconscious" and that if we don't know *why* we know something, we really don't know it. We are taught that the imagination, by definition, is unreal. Compounding it all we are taught that what goes on in our minds has nothing to do with what goes on in our bodies and vice versa. All of this adds up to makeing us suspicious of our own inner experience.

In the trainings I conduct, students do a psychic diagnostic reading of someone whom they know nothing about. To do a "case" they simply enter a meditative/receptive state of awareness and are given *only* the name, age, and address of a person with some physical disability. How do they describe someone about whom they know nothing? All they can do is to use their imagination—*just make it up.* In so doing, they are always able correctly to describe the case they are given in full detail. The interesting thing is that what is most accurate is always what is most discounted by them. However, they discover that their imagination is quite *real.* If you make up a story about someone you don't know and then find out that all you have described is accurate, it necessitates a reevaluation of the nature of reality and the power of consciousness.

Intuitive knowledge is available to all of us; all we need do is learn how to tap it. The intuition and the imagination are intimately connected. The intuition uses the content of the imagination to clothe itself, thereby making itself visible. When you trust your imagination, and work with it, your intuitive knowledge becomes fully accessible.

Intuition differs from the intellect, which is critical, linear, and makes everything complex. It is also different from the emotions which are always forceful and wanting something. Our intuition is simply a quiet knowingness, easy to ignore but impossible to argue with. Unlike other aspects of ourselves, the intuition will never deceive you.

The imagination is the medium of psychic awareness. Consciousness is like a flashlight beam: wherever you direct it is the spot you see. The question itself is what directs the light to illuminate that particular area of the collective unconscious, thus making it consciously known to you. We all have access to information beyond our experience. My life changed profoundly when I learned how to direct my innerconsciousness: I'm now at the controls rather than a mere victim of random events. The lives of people who take my training change immeasurably, for they suddenly find out what needs to happen to resolve problems that have been with them for years. This occurs not because my training is so extraordinary, but because consciousness is so potent when one learns how to tap it. What's most powerful about it is that people learn that they have their own answers and need not be dependent solely on a doctor or therapist. All they need do is learn to recognize their own knowingness.

It is when you are relaxed that your imagination becomes fluid and free. You've probably experienced being stuck on some kind of problem. As soon as you let go of it and relax, the solution dawns on you—Aha!—that light bulb above your head goes on. Imagination is the home of creativity, the medium through which you give your expectations form. By directing your imagination, you can give life to your attitudes and insights.

Your innerconsciousness is what is predominantly present whenever you are not engaged with thinking about what to do next, but instead are relaxing or doing something rhythmic. So, to work with that part of yourself, simply lie back and focus on breathing calmly and deeply with your abdomen and let the rhythm of your breath soothe you. Soon you will find yourself in a state where your thoughts seem to meander, as opposed to rushing through your mind. At this point your innerconsciousness is predominant and your imagination is fluid. It is important to understand that your body is always responding to whatever you are imagining at *every* given moment. For instance, if you want to relax, all you need do is imagine yourself at the beach. Conversely, if you're afraid of heights, you needn't be on a high ledge to get your adrenalin pumping; all you need do is imagine yourself there. At every given moment, our bodies are continually responding to the messages of our minds. So what messages is your mind giving your body? In this society we are taught to distrust the body's own ability to heal itself. This is good business for the drug companies. We're led to believe that the innate wisdom of the body/mind simply doesn't exist.

So, if you're struggling to recover, strive at all times to experience yourself as healthy in the present. Wishing yourself well in the future is not a message your body will respond to. You want it to hear "wellness"*in the moment* as much as possible.

For me, doing a case taught me that consciousness transcends the material world. When one experiences something like this it is no longer just an idea—an intellectual possibility—it is unquestionably real. Knowing that consciousness goes beyond matter is an essential element in being able to grapple with death, for it means that the death of the physical body is not the death of consciousness. In other words, death is not the end, and consciousness is not dependent on the electrical impulses of your brain cells. (I recommend Raymond Moody's *Life After Death*, which is a compilation of the experiences of people who were clinically pronounced dead and then came back to life.) Facing death is not the same as facing nothingness.

Scientific thinking focuses only on the observable, rendering invisible much that is mysterious or unreasonable. The regenerative healing process is one of life's greatest mysteries. Trying to understand it rationally is like trying to understand colors with your ears, but just as your eyes can know color, your deeper self can know healing. Shamans throughout the ages have used the trance state—simply that calm, receptive state—to understand and heal ailments. It is in our interest to stop regarding such behavior as primitive. To mystify the innerconsciousness is to kill the mysterious. When we dip into our psyches we are no longer victims but participants, for there is where true knowingness resides.

With the mystification of innerconsciousness came the mystification of healing powers. When we repossess our innerselves we will repossess our healing powers. How do you do this? What does your inner voice sound like? Because of the mystification most people expect spiritual work to be surrounded with lights, colors, and whispering voices. There is nothing exotic about it. All there is to it is that you begin to take *very seriously* that aspect of yourself that, in all likelihood, you have ignored up to now. The experience itself rarely feels profound; what *is* profound is what happens when you begin to recognize your intuitive inclinations and respond to them.

Being diagnosed with AIDS or any life-threatening illness may in all likelihood catapult you into a tumultuous sea of confusion and screaming feelings. To come to terms with it you must bring yourself to a state of peace. In our secular society we are given two options: be rational or be emotional. Neither alternative by itself will enable you to come to terms with any life-threatening illness; only your spiritual/intuitive self can. This you can accomplish through meditation which takes you way below the surface craziness into a calm state where you can acknowledge on a deep level that you are ill; in so doing, you will get a handle on your life. This doesn't mean that you throw out your rational and emotional processes, but only that they are put under the guidance of your own intuitive knowingness. Your feelings and thoughts can get you in trouble; your intuition never will.

Ill health, on any level, is an invitation to introspection. Being diagnosed with AIDS makes it imperative. For only through introspection can you come to terms with your life and your death. Introspection is not a rational process; to be rational is to be objectively, emotionally neutral and capable of separating yourself from the situation by drawing "reasonable" conclusions. You cannot separate yourself from your recovery process any more than you can separate yourself from your death.

Our automatic reaction when sick is that something is wrong with our bodies rather than our lives. This is an incredible discount of our bodies, for they act as our early warning system and know just what is healthful. If being sick is thought of as wrong, we give away part of ourselves, allowing illness to be forever out of our control. To repossess our healing powers we must repossess our illnesses.

We've got to be careful neither to blame ourselves for getting sick, ignoring the conditions of our lives that need change, nor to blame the conditions entirely, leaving us in a powerless, victimized position. The best way out is to discover how it is that we each *collude* with the detrimental influences. Your internal response to an event is as important as the event itself. For example, two people experience their clothes catching fire: one panics, runs, and fans the flames, incurring severe burns; the other remains calm and consciously chooses to roll on the ground, thus smothering the fire and ending up with only minor burns.

The environment increasingly is filled with substances that are hazardous to our health. Not everyone exposed to carcinogenic substances develops cancer. (This doesn't mean that it is okay to continue to pollute the atmosphere.) No matter what is going on, despite how you feel, you are a *participant* and not a victim.

Sometimes it becomes apparent that you are getting more out of holding onto a problem than you do from being healthy. In other words, the problem itself provides a solution for something else. So ask yourself what it is that made *you* come down with this life-threatening illness. What are you getting out of it? Your immediate reaction to this question may be to be defensive, but blame is not the issue here. Even the worst of things have their positive side. If you allow yourself to look under the surface, you can answer the question. Maybe it is a much needed rest, or alleviation of overwhelming responsibility, or a way out of a seemingly irresolvable situation. Maybe, in the case of AIDS, you feel you deserve it because of your own internalized homophobia. When you find out what the advantages are for you, you can take steps to get your needs met in healthful ways. Then you will be able to focus your energy on healing yourself.

When you're meditating on healing, you need to give your body a clear message of what you want. Imagine what it would be like to be healthy in the particular areas that are afflicted. If you can't experience yourself healthy, then imagining talking to the ailment will move you forward. Your body may not be ready to heal yet—there is a message that needs attending to. Our bodies are barometers keeping us on course toward leading harmonious lives. There is *always* a message there. If you tune in, get the message, and respond to it, you'll find that your life changes profoundly. With any illness or pain your body is talking to you—you just need to listen.

When concerned with health, as with any other issue, your innerconsciousness flows in one of two directions: active or receptive. When you can imagine what you want, and know what it feels like—that is, *feel* what it would be like—then you can project it. When you can't imagine it, an insight is called for: ask your body questions, tune in to your inner self, and then respond to the information you get. Your body can respond to the messages you give it; you can respond to the messages your body gives you.

People think they can imagine anything they want to. This is not the case—you can think it but you cannot always imagine what it would feel like. For example, if you are trying to heal yourself of KS, go into a relaxed state and imagine one particular lesion. Then try to imagine it clearing up. If you can't, then you need to dialogue with the area and discover what it needs. The imagination is the medium through which your intuitive knowledge makes itself known. How you imagine it symbolically reflects what in fact is going on, enabling you to know what is true for you. The imagination reveals the essence of what is occurring. *If you can imagine healing, then you are capable of it.* Your imagination will never deceive you; instead, it will reveal what is going on in your body. Knowing what is true, you can choose how to deal with it.

A burning question for you may be, "Am I going to recover, or am I going to die?" Each of these opposites seems to require a different course of action. The very nature of life itself is the struggle to survive—a struggle that penetrates every level of your being, that resides in every cell of your body. The choice to live—to deny medical prediction—must be a *total* one, one in which you engage every thought, feeling, and cell of your being. What do you do with that voice that may haunt you saying, "They say I'll be dead inside of two years?" That voice is real: you can't pretend it is not there; you can't deny it. If you do so, you relinquish part of your power. One thing about what it means to be human is that we *can* live with contradiction. I suggest that you find out what that voice needs so it doesn't take over. You do this by contemplating what you need to do to die with a sense of completion, and at the *same* time you begin doing those things which will engage you in your struggle to live. You can prepare for the possibility of death in the same way you use your seatbelt in a car as a matter of course—not really expecting to need it.

If you feel increasingly wretched—your recovery feels beyond your grasp—and you are no longer able to experience your healing process, then you need to begin the process of overcoming your fear and choosing how you want to live the life you have left, at the same time readying yourself for the death of your body.

If you can imagine—*feel*—what it would be like for you, for your body, to recover vital health, then it is possible. The voice that says you will die will be around less and less often as you recover, regain your strength and heal yourself.

Each of the above experiences is likely to happen; one when you are feeling low, and the other the rest of the time. Your intuition will tell you, in time, which way you are headed. One side or the other will predominate.

Since your body is always responding to whatever is in your awareness at every given moment, it's important to monitor your thought processes as you move through your daily activities. Notice whether you're spending more time and energy thinking of the problem by being irritated and victimized by it, or spending time moving the problem into a state of harmony. *Do you spend more time thinking about the problem or about the solution?* Your body simply is going to respond to the strongest messages you give it. Whatever you spend the most time on will hold the most energy. It's hard to put more focus on the solution when you're experiencing the problem, but the most important thing is the prevailing last message whenever your affliction comes to mind. When you think of the problem, always have your last image be your recovery— your sense of power and change—and that will be the direction your body takes.

With any constant health problem, tell yourself that it is imperceptibly getting better, and over time the problem will be gone altogether. This way you haven't let your experience of the problem become a reflection of your inability to heal it;

instead, you've allowed yourself to experience the problem while *knowing* that it's continually getting better.

The vital thing to understand is that the last and prevailing message must be a positive one. Expect what is wanted, trust the body and its power to maintain itself, and leave *no* space for the idea of being victimized and out of control. When doctors refer to the placebo effect, they are talking about the belief in the efficacy of treatment. *The agent of change is belief.* In a study of 152 cancer patients, the most significant finding was that a positive attitude toward treatment was a better predictor of response to treatment than was the severity of the dis-ease. The Simontons, who conducted this study, pioneered working with healing cancer by visualization. Their patients have a survival rate twice the national norm. (I recommend *Getting Well Again* by O. Carl Simonton, Stephanie Matthews-Simonton, and James L. Creighton.)

Effecting change with the power of consciousness works in direct proportion to how strongly you believe that it will work. The more you believe something is going to work, the less confusing your inner messages will be; clear messages are directives to which your body can respond. The catch is this: your belief comes from your experience of it working. So I recommend doing little experiments, ones that do not have a lot of emotional charge, like telling yourself exactly what time you wish to awaken in the morning, or picturing in detail reducing any side effects you might be experiencing from medication, while at the same time imagining each of your treatments being effective in the long run. The more you experience success, the stronger your belief in the power of your body/mind becomes. The stronger the belief, the more powerful you are. The agent of change is belief itself.

In beginning to use your consciousness for healing, you must cultivate patience. Just as it took time for your problems to develop, it will also take time for your body to develop and maintain healthy habits. Your body has become accustomed to the problem, and it will now need time to become accustomed to the solution.

As you know all too well, as far as AIDS and many other life-threatening dis-eases are concerned, the medical odds are against you. So it is going to take work—constant, diligent work—to live and to defy medical prognosis. You need to train your consciousness to work with you. Consciously give your body the message of healing, and constantly cultivate your faith, your belief in your own inner healing powers; surround yourself with people who believe you can heal your condition; read books about those who have cured themselves of a so-called terminal dis-ease.

These healing powers are not exotic; it isn't as if only exceptional individuals are endowed with them. These powers are sleeping inside each of us and any one of us can awaken them. We have the power—we just need to *use* it. So-called miracles can become commonplace if we choose to take responsibility. The choice is ours.

CHAPTER 11

APPLIED MEDITATIONS FOR HEALING

by Margo Adair and Lynn Johnson

The introduction and meditations which follow have been prepared by Margo and Lynn for people concerned with AIDS and other life-threatening illnesses, and are available on cassette along with complete instructions on Applied Meditation. They are included in this book because they are models of their kind, and can prove of great value in composing and recording your own meditation and affirmation tapes.

Many teachers of visualization believe that the most effective tape is one that you record in your own voice. By studying the different meditations which follow, and understanding how to structure your personal journey into inner consciousness, you can develop the ability to make your own recordings. The key point to remember is that because the nature of inner consciousness is holistic, it is necessary to translate linear two-dimensional information into a three-dimensional scene. An example of this can be found in the AIDS meditation.

The Resources section at the end of this book contains a list of various recommended relaxation/visualization tapes, including information on Margo's tapes and book. The meditations contained in her book will also be available in cassette, including some which specifically deal with the body and healing. The AIDS tapes especially are now available at low cost, in consideration of the financial pressures facing the people who need them most.

Each of the meditations will generate clear channels for your imagination to move along throughout your day-to-day life. It is good to work with the images and the sensations they evoke when you are not listening to the tapes. Your body responds to whatever you have in your mind, so if you are able to occupy your imagination with positive images and sensations, you help your body in its struggle. When the problem comes to mind, try to move your awareness to any solution you found while meditating. It is also good to meditate on your own without using the tapes. You can do this for as little as 5 minutes or for half an hour or more. When you do meditate on your own, you can go through the same processes the tape offers; or, if you prefer, create your own journey inward.

It is important to aspire to take action on any insights you gain in meditation. Application is more difficult than receiving the insights, but if you don't act on your insights, they will make no difference in your life. In meditation, people become clear about many changes that are needed, resolve to do them all, only to find a few days later that they have not been keeping the agreements they made with themselves. Inside ourselves there are no limits to space and time. The inner-consciousness has access to universal knowingness so it comes up with *everything* — bar nothing — that is needed. Life presents many limitations, so be patient with yourself; move a step at a time. Don't try to eat a banquet in one mouthful.

Most people believe they need total peace and quiet to meditate. It is nice to have peace and quiet, but it is not necessary. You can choose to focus inward on a rush hour bus or a bustling hospital ward. There may be noisy people around you but that doesn't mean you have to listen to them. Instead, choose to ignore them and suggest to yourself that the noise will cause you to be even more focused on your inner process. What you do need is to not be disturbed, so unplug the phone and ask those around you not to interrupt you for a half hour.

Also, you needn't be totally relaxed to meditate; again, this is helpful, but not always necessary for your inner work. When you find yourself tense or in pain, visualize a masseuse working on the afflicted area and then focus on your choice of inner work. One of the great characteristics of inner awareness is that it is childlike, literal, and suggestible. If you have a scratchy throat, pretend you are drinking some soothing cough syrup, which is very different than wishing you had some. If you do this, you'll find your throat feeling more comfortable. Whatever discomfort your body is having, if you literally imagine alleviating it in whatever manner occurs to you, your body will follow suit. When you do this, set up the scene in your imagination and then *assume* it continues on as you move your awareness to other concerns. You'll discover later that it worked. Don't keep checking to see if the situation is getting better; that will only perpetuate the discomfort (comparing necessitates dwelling on the problem). Instead, when the problem comes to mind, simply move your awareness to the scene you set up in your mind's eye to alleviate it. You can use this same technique to alleviate discomfort at any time; you needn't reserve it solely for your meditation session. Remember the placebo effect. *Belief is the agent of change.* All of this works in proportion to how much you expect it to. What is important about small successes is that they increase your faith in the efficacy of your inner work. The more you experience small successes, the more you'll believe in the power of your mind, and the more you can rely on it to work the next time.

As you work with Applied Meditation, your intellectual mind is likely to discount the process and tell you that you are not doing it right or that you're wasting your time. Although your rational mind will find lots to criticize, don't worry—the process works anyway. In fact, the more meditation works, the louder your rational discounts will be. Don't try to argue with your inner critic; just let it take a back seat while you continue with your inner work. Only your own experience in life will reveal how your mind feels while you meditate. If you don't think that you're doing it right, *pretend* that you are. If you do, you will find that although you feel you are not doing it right, the process will nonetheless begin to work for you.

While your intellect is discounting, your imagination is likely to bring irrevelant imagery, or you'll find yourself "spacing out." There is no need for concern—the imagination is extremely fluid. When you find yourself off on some tangent, just bring yourself back to where you left off and continue your inner work.

There is much more emphasis on visualizing—as opposed to feeling or sensing—with this kind of meditation. Some people visualize while others feel things or sense things. Don't worry if you see pictures—however you imagine things is what is right for you.

In meditation you are often directed to ask questions of physiological parts of yourself. Usually people find themselves knowing the answer as they are formulating the question. Time is simultaneous for the imagination; if I say "apple," you don't have to go find it in your awareness to imagine it: the sense or picture of an apple is in your awareness the moment you hear the word. When you ask questions of yourself simply be receptive to your experience at the moment (the awareness) and you'll find yourself with a sense of knowingness. Don't wait for this sense to come to you; instead, give yourself full permission to make it up, for your fantasies will reveal the answers to your questions. Often the answers people come up with seem corny or cliché. The important thing is that they are probably right. The intuition comes up with such answers because it resides in the realms of universality. What's important is not whether these answers are unique, but whether they are helpful.

The following meditations are designed to help you open doors inside yourself to release your own creative and restorative abilities. You can use these meditations to get to know what you already know deeper inside, to facilitate your relationship with yourself. You need not meditate in the "right" way, or for that matter, be ill in the "right" way, die, or even recover in the "right" way. You don't need to perform for anyone. Do only what feels right for you. If meditation is good, use it; if it doesn't, forget it and pursue what does work for you. Only you know what you need.

These meditations are designed to help you regain balance. Through them you can gain insight into what your body wants, and intuitively sense the best treatment course for you. They will help you imagine the choices best for helping your body regain strength. You needn't imagine the internal workings of your body literally. To illustrate, it has been discovered that warming one's hands relieves migraines; you can simply imagine this taking place and the hands will follow suit. Some imagine a little sun in the palm of their hands, while others imagine blood rushing down into the hands; either way, the hands warm up. What is important is that you allow yourself to imagine *in detail,* as if you were creating a movie in your mind's eye. When you do this, strive to see/sense yourself well. It is often helpful, though not necessary, to know the physiology and anatomy of your body because it gives your imagination more to work with.

The first meditation, A Vision of a Healthy Immune System, can be used by anyone working to heal immune dysfunction. The second, Treatment Choice, will help facilitate access to that part of you which always knows what healing path is best for you at this time. The third, Choosing the Best Life Style for Yourself, is designed to help you examine your daily patterns, and to choose which ways of living your life are most conducive to health and well-being.

The Wise Self meditation is designed to enable you to come to peace with the process of dying. Each of us has a peaceful side that we may experience when going for a walk or on a vacation, but which frequently gets lost in the shuffle of our stressful lives. In this meditation you can evoke that quality of quiet knowingness inside of you, and in so doing, you will be better able to ease yourself through your changes. This meditation will help you transfer the feeling that dying is a reflection of failure into the feeling that dying can be part of healing your being, for death can be seen as an enriching experience. I think it is important in coming to terms with death to understand that death is *not* the ultimate end, but a transition of your being. I used to believe that when one died, that was *it;* but in my exploration of consciousness I have discovered beyond any question of doubt that consciousness transcends the material world and continues on. Whatever your belief, this meditation hopefully will enable you to feel somewhat more peaceful amidst your dis-ease.

The Respite meditation is designed to give you relief from your struggle. It guides your imagination through some of the pleasures life offers. This meditation will help you become more comfortable in your body, especially if you are in pain. It is good for your healing process because being lighthearted helps the body. In the book *Anatomy of an Illness*, Norman Cousins recounts how he helped cure himself of a terminal dis-ease with the simple application of laughter.

Each meditation begins with a set of instructions, referring to a basic Induction and other sections which are included beneath the final Respite Meditation. Always begin each Meditation with this Induction, unless you have inductions of your own with which you are most comfortable. The Induction process enables you to enter the relaxed state of awareness key to the successful use of Applied Meditation and all other visualization techniques.

Some of the Meditations include a Vitality of Life section, which is printed after the basic Induction. Gay people will find the Affirmation of Gay Lifestyle appropriate to employ in those Meditations so indicated. Finally, each Meditation ends with a Return to Waking Consciousness, which appears at the very end of these insertable sections.

Meditations

1. A Vision of a Healthy Immune System. This meditation was composed specifically for people concerned with Acquired Immune Deficiency Syndrome, and may be adapted to benefit all those concerned with immune dysfunction.

Begin with "Induction" (page 203).

Gay people then use "Affirmation of Gay Lifestyle" (page 206).

All people then use "Vitality of Life" (page 207) then the following meditation:

Now focus on your bones. . . Penetrate your awareness inside of your bones, imagine the marrow inside of your bones. The marrow is a factory keeping your blood nourished, fluid, balanced. . . Just as your blood nourishes your whole body, your marrow nourishes your blood. As though the marrow were like underground springs feeding the rivers of blood that move through the landscape of your body. . . Your blood is full of richness, of nutrients. Your blood is full of all kinds of cells. There are T-cells and B-cells that flow through your blood, traveling throughout the landscape of your body. They are your body's army of defensive guards. Imagine them. Imagine each and every T-cell and B-cell strong, armies of them flowing through your blood on guard against any foreign agents, any foreign viruses, and foreign invaders, on guard against them, watching for them, recognizing all foreign invaders. The T-cells are the generals, and whenever they discover any foreign invaders, they instruct your B-cells to produce antibodies, and these antibodies flow into your blood and kill anything, any life that should not be there. Imagine the T-cells flowing throughout your body, on guard, recognizing all foreign invaders and appropriately fighting them. Antibodies being produced, sent out into the blood from the B-cells and killing any foreign agents, any foreign viruses. Imagine this now.

* *

And when the invaders are killed off by the antibodies, you have monocytes in your blood, traveling throughout your body, traveling through the tissue, and the monocytes clean up all the debris of the dead cells. Imagine the monocytes traveling throughout your body cleaning up all the debris left behind by the successful fight of the guards, the antibodies. Keeping the landscape of your body clear so all the cells in your body, in every area in your body, in every part of your body are able to do their own job easily, clear of any problems.

* *

You have lymph nodes throughout your body. The lymph nodes are like sentry posts; that's where the T-cells and B-cells live and reside. As the lymph nodes cleanse the lymphatic fluid they recognize when more T-cells and B-cells are called for. And whenever more are needed they multiply and go back out into the blood, taking care of any problems wherever they happen to crop up in the landscape of your body. Imagine the sentry posts, imagine each of your lymph nodes where the T-cells and B-cells live, where they multiply whenever more are needed. Whenever an infection appears in your body these cells come out of your lymph nodes in even greater numbers. Armies of cells flow through your blood going right to wherever the infection is, antibodies being produced and killing the infection, killing any viruses. Then the monocytes come along and clean up all the debris. Imagine this now, however you like. Imagine all this. Feel it. . . .Know that this is so inside your body. Your body has cared for itself in the past, your body cares for itself now. You heal yourself.

* *

Your T-cells and B-cells guard you well, each cell surrounded by a strong membrane keeping the internal body of each cell intact and strong. Imagine each membrane around each of your cells and all of your cells strong, like armor around a knight. Imagine these armies of strong, vigilant cells moving through your body, producing antibodies wherever necessary, destroying any foreign invaders, crushing them, repelling them, recognizing every single foreign invader. These T-cells are extremely aware and perceptive. They recognize any disguises. They know what your body needs and they know what threatens your body. They successfully launch the antibodies who crush any threat to the landscape of your body. Imagine this now. Feel it, sense it, create it in your mind's eye.

* *

This army is vigilant, activating your immune system and successfully destroying infection. All infection destroyed, leaving only what your body needs for its health, for its nourishment. Leaving health wherever this army of cells travels. Imagine these cells knowing well how to recognize what disturbs the balance in any area. There are two kinds of T-cells: the helper cells which activate your immune system as you've been imagining, and the suppressor cells. You only have half as many suppressor cells, you only need half as many suppressor cells. . . .They complement the helper cells, the helper cells that direct the killing of foreign viruses. The suppressor cells let the helper cells know when they can relax, take a break from their vigilance because they know when they've done their job well. The suppressor cells tell the helper cells when they can relax until once again they're needed to eliminate anything that disturbs the balance of your body.

Imagine both kinds of cells. . . .Imagine just the right proportion of the helper cells directing the killing of the foreign agents, and the suppressor cells letting the helper cells know when all's well again and they can truly rest.

* *

All of these cells clearly communicate with each other, knowing just what is needed and responding appropriately for whatever is happening inside your body. Every cell knows its job well, it's never fooled. Imagine, sense the keen awareness of each of these cells distinguishing between what's needed and what's not, recognizing all foreign invaders no matter what their disguise, keeping the whole landscape of your body clear, clean, healthy. . . .Sense it, however you like. Imagine it.

* *

The cells and antibodies flowing throughout your blood, throughout the landscape of your body. This army is just the right size you need. The army's always well-balanced, having twice as many helper cells as suppressor cells, and antibodies produced in just the right numbers necessary to kill off any foreign invaders, and monocytes cleaning up the debris, keeping your body clear and cleansed. Imagine every cell of which you are physically composed in the whole of your body surrounded by strong membranes, absorbing only nourishment, repelling anything that it doesn't need. . . .Each cell strong. Your whole body regaining, maintaining health. If you sense any imbalance in the makeup of your army or in the lymph nodes, if you notice any imbalance anywhere, imagine asking the cells what is needed to regain balance. Let your imagination make up what they tell you. Trust it. . . .

* *

Imagine how you can compensate so your body can regain, maintain its health. . . .Imagine sending vital healing energy to this army. Now travel with the army with your awareness, and notice if there are any foreign viruses in your body, and imagine the antibodies attacking them, killing them, monocytes clearing the debris and your body returning to a state of health. Imagine all this ocurring, as in fact it is. Imagine the army of cells and antibodies attacking, defeating all foreign agents and the landscape of your body returning to a state of harmony, protected from any foreign invaders.

* *

Begin to finish what you are doing. Acknowledge the powers you've become attuned to. Know that the very fact that you've imagined these things makes them possible, makes them probable. Know that you are now aligned with powerful harmonizing energies and you will intuitively act in accord with them. You have evoked healing powers. . . .Know that your body will continue to respond to these healing energies.

Give yourself permission to believe in yourself, to believe in your body, to believe in life itself. And now, return to feeling your whole body intact, healing and in harmony.

* *

End with "Return to Waking Consciousness" (page 209).
[Ed. note: Please see editor's note at the end of this chapter, page 210.]

2. Treatment Choice. *This meditation is applicable to any serious life-threatening disease.*
   Begin with "Induction" (page 203).
   Use "Vitality of Life" (page 207), then the following meditation:

If you have any disturbances in your body, choose one. Work on a single problem at a time. You can work on other problems later. Know that you can communicate with any area of your body. Now imagine the area you have chosen, and let your awareness penetrate into this area. Visualize this disturbed part of your body. Imagine what it looks like, what it feels like. Feel the area of difficulty. Sense its condition. . . .Be aware of the atmosphere in which it lives. Be aware of the quality of energy present in this part of your body. What mood is it in, if it has a mood? What color would this mood be? . . .What sounds or vibrations are present in this part of your body? Know that you can hear this area's messages, gaining insights to problems, discovering what you need to do to heal yourself. You can put in new messages and this area will respond to what you tell it.

Imagine this area having a consciousness of its own, an intelligence of its own, as indeed it does. Imagine that this part of your body sends out a messenger that represents its consciousness, for in fact, this area does have a consciousness. And talk to the messenger. Listen to what it has to say about the mood of this part of the body. Ask it how it feels. . . .Imagine what it would tell you. . . .Use your imagination. Pretend you are having a conversation with the area. Make up a story. Let the child within you make up this conversation. Imagine what the two of you would say if you were to talk.

* *

Trust what happens, even if it feels simplistic. Ask the messenger what is going on. Be receptive to the area's experience. . . .Ask if there is anything this problem is defending you against, anything in your life this ailment is protecting you from. . . .Be receptive to whatever you sense, for it may not answer you verbally. Trust your sense. Imagine what is so. . . .What does the messenger have to tell you?. . . .Imagine what you need to do, what the area needs to do, so that you can both live in harmony together and cooperate in the healing process. Make agreements with one another.

* *

Imagine carrying out these agreements.

* *

Imagine your breath bringing healing energy into this area, however you imagine this to occur. Feel it, sense it getting better.

* *

Now let your awareness expand, and sense how your whole body is doing. . . .Imagine asking your body how it feels about the different *kinds of treatment you have chosen, or are considering. Bring each treatment to awareness separately, and sense how your body responds to each one.*

* *

Imagine receiving one of the treatments now. . . .Notice how your body responds. . . .Ask it how it feels about it. Imagine how this treatment helps your body heal. You may want to ask the messenger you spoke to earlier how it feels about the treatment. Trust your imagination. It will reveal to you what your body knows.

* *

Now take time to imagine any of the other treatments, and your body's response to it. Focus on one treatment at a time. Sense what your body needs to heal itself. Feel your body's response.

* *

Now finish what you are doing. Choose the treatments that are right for you. . . .
If there are any side effects for any treatment that you choose, warn your body about them, and ask your body what you can do to compensate or protect it. Trust your sense. . . .Your body knows what it needs. Be receptive to your body's wisdom. . . .
Talk to your body. Send prospective energy to the areas that need it. Expect your body to respond only positively.

* *

Ask your body if there are specific exercises, foods, or anything in particular it may wish to help it heal. Ask what it wants. Sense what it has to say. . . .Trust your sense.

* *

Decide if you're willing to give it what it wants. Decide if there is anything you want from your body, and ask for it. You can tell your body how you feel, what you want. . . .Sense if it's willing to give it to you. . . .What kinds of agreements might you make so that you can cooperatively take care of one another?. . . .Compromise when need be. . . .Ask your body what you can now expect of it. . . .Tell it what you're willing to do. Come to agreements with your body, and when you come to agreement, imagine acting on it. Notice what that feels like. Imagine your body healing. Breathe in healing energy. Feel your breath carry this healing energy to any and all parts of your body that need it.

* *

If you have any rage, if you have any anger, imagine it forming a flame, and let it burn away anything that doesn't belong in your body, purging your body, cleansing your body.

* *

Imagine what it is you need to do to take care of the aspect of yourself that does not want to heal. . . .Ask this part what it wants, what it has to offer you. . . .Endeavor to make friends with this part of yourself. Decide how to care for this part of yourself, and imagine doing so.

* *

Acknowledge the hard times you're going through. Acknowledge your perseverance. . . .Imagine the vitality of life, and let it pour its healing energy into your body. . . .Or you may wish to focus on a healthy area of your body, and let that area's health spread out and into the ailing area. . . .Feel vital, healing energy, energy flowing, life forces moving. You may want to bring in light, heat, coolness, sound, water, air, whatever is needed. Trust your inclination. . . .Imagine your treatments working. . . .Let the areas receive as much of this energy as they're willing to at this time. Endeavor to be patient with your healing process. Sense the areas, over time, returning to a state of harmony. Experience what this would be like. . . .See it. . . .Feel it.. . . .Know that it can be so. If you cannot imagine being fully well, be sure you have cooperative agreements, so that you and the

*ailment can live in relative harmony for the time being. . . .Imagine
yourself following through on any agreements you've made. Experience
what your life will be like when a state of well-being has returned.*

*   *

*Begin to finish what you are doing. Go over any insights you've
gained, lessons you've learned, choices you've made, the powers you've
become attuned to.*

*   *

*Know that the very fact that you've imagined these things makes them
possible, makes them probable. Know that you are now aligned with
powerful, harmonizing energies, and you will intuitively act in accord with them. You have evoked healing powers. Know that your
body will continue to respond to these healing energies. . . .Give yourself permission to believe in yourself, to believe in your body, to believe in life itself.*

*   *

*And now, return to feeling your whole body intact, healing, and in
harmony.*

*   *

End with "Return to Waking Consciousness" (page 209).

3. Choosing the Best Lifestyle for Yourself.
   Begin with "Induction" (page 203).
   Gay people use "Affirmation of Gay Lifestyle" (page 206).
   All people then use the following meditation:

*Be aware, acknowledge, know that your body is the home of your
life, the home of your spirit. Only you can care for your body, honor
your body, honor your life. . . .You know what's right for you, what
your body needs to maintain its health, to provide a good home for
your spirit. You are now going to take an exploratory journey, and*

*in doing so you'll come to a deeper understanding of your life, of what
your life needs to maintain health, harmony, and vitality. Know that
you are the only one that can fully care for your life, for your body,
for yourself. Acknowledge how all this is so. . . .You know what is
right for you.*

* *

*By exploring your lifestyle with your imagination, you can discover
what is healthy in your life and what is not. . . .In this meditation
you are going to envision the life that is right for you. . . .In so doing, you align your energies and empower yourself to live a lifestyle
that honors your life. As you explore your activities, notice which
aspect of yourself you are acting out of, which aspect is in command:. . . .Your centered self?. . . .Your compulsive self?. . . .Your
anxious self?. . . .Your loving self?. . . .Your lazy self?. . . .Your creative self?. . . .Another part of yourself?*

* *

*Begin by imagining waking up on a current weekday in your life,
preparing for work or any activities of your day. . . .Notice if you're
in a hurry. . . .Notice what you eat and how you feel about
it. . . .what you drink. . . .how it goes through your body. . . .Notice
everything that you ingest. Notice how your body feels about each
thing you put into your body. . . .how your body reacts. . . .You know
what's right for you. . . .Be receptive to your body's experience. . . .*

*See yourself arriving at work. . . .See yourself at work. . . .If
you don't work, imagine your average day. . . .Notice the atmosphere. . . .Notice the people around you. . . .How do you feel
about them?. . . .How does your workplace feel?. . . .Your
breaks?. . . .Notice what you enjoy. . . .See yourself at the end of
your workday. . . .*

*As you go through your day appreciate what feels good to you,
where energy flows freely in you. . . .and in the world around
you. . . .Let yourself appreciate the small things. . . .*

*Notice the things that don't feel so good, where your energy is
shut down. . . .Notice what you can do to make it feel better. . . .Know that you can change the activity. . . .or your atti-*

tudes. . . .or both. . . .You know what's right for you. . . .Imagine how you can change the negative feelings or aspects of your daily life to positive experience. . . .Imagine the negativity soaking into the ground and transforming itself. . . .Feel yourself open to positive changes in your life. . . .Feel the changes already beginning to occur.

* *

With any part of your weekday that feels bad, imagine, create a way you can make it better. . . .imagine it improving. . . .Let your imagination create positive experiences and enjoy how that feels in your life. . . .Know you can create these changes. . . .

Notice your activities after work. . . .what you do. . . .who you're with. . . .what you put into your body. . . .Are these activities good for you? . . .What part of you is in control? . . .What needs to be adjusted for your own well-being? . . .What are you willing to change?. . . .Imagine making the changes. . . .doing what you want to do. Imagine that your sleep fully replenishes you.

* *

Imagine now waking up on your day off and trace your activities in the same way throughout your day off, noticing how you feel about what you do. . . .how you feel about who you're with. . . .what you eat. . . .what you drink. . . .what you smoke. . . .Which aspect of yourself is in control? . . .Notice what feels good. . . .With any part of your day off that feels bad, notice what you can change to feel better and imagine changing that.

* *

As you go through your workday and your day off, notice the exercise you get, and how your body feels about that. . . .Imagine doing enjoyable exercise that maintains the health and vigor of your body.

* *

Bring to awareness all the areas of stress in your life, the places that have hard edges, the activities in your life, the relationships in your life that bring up anxieties, that make you feel stretched, taut, uncomfortable. . . .Notice how you feel about each stress point. . . .Is it a high? . . .Do you want it otherwise? . . .Discover what you want to change to make your life easier. . . .Know that in reducing stress and creating an easier life, you strengthen your immune system. . . .

Notice, now, your sexual activities during the day and the night. How do you feel about them? . . .Are they full. . . .sensual. . . .sensitive. . . .sharing? . . .Are they protective of your health? Do they honor your body? If you would like any changes, make them now. Imagine them already changed.

* *

Notice what you need to do to bring the changes about. . . .Decide if you're willing to. . . .Tell yourself what you're willing to do, and imagine doing so.

* *

Now go back to any areas you did not have time to finish earlier. Choose how to create health in your life. . . .You know what's right for you.

* *

Or you may want to imagine a particular time in the future that concerns you. . . .Discover what's healthy. . . .Choose that future. . . .Remember, you are the only one who can provide care for your body, care for your life.

* *

Feel your lifestyle supporting your whole being in health and joy. Ask your deeper self for concrete ways to bring harmony into your life, and make agreements with your self that are right for you. . . .You are the one that knows what's right for you.

* *

If you have any residual anxieties, imagine them draining away from you. . . .soaking into the ground. . . .knowing they will be transformed into new and positive energies. . . .Know that you are making your life whole and healthy.

Now review all that you've become attuned to in this meditation, affirming yourself and your commmunity. . . .How it is you spend your time. . . .How you treat your body. . . .Sexuality in your life. . . .The choices you've made to honor your life, honor your health, to take care of your body. . . .You choose what's right for you. . . .Know that you have the will, the strength, the support you need to bring about these changes in your life, to maintain health in your life. Feel how this is so. . . .Feel your own power, feel the support there is for you to make these changes. . . .Expect to remain healthful and vital in your whole being.

Imagine yourself surrounded by protective energy, whatever that means to you. It may be light. Create a protective shield around you, and know that it protects you from stress, protects you from detrimental influences, protects you from infection and illness, protects you from viruses. . . .

* *

Feel the goodness of yourself, strong and healthy in a strong and healthy body. Know that it is an established fact that you have full power to live in health and harmony. Feel how this is so, and it will increasingly be so as time moves on. . . .Trust yourself. . . .Trust your body. . . .Trust your mind. Trust nature.

* *

End with "Return to Waking Consciousness" (page 209).

4. Meeting Wise Self: Gaining Courage and Letting Go.
This meditation is designed to help you gain the knowledge needed to come to terms with your life-threatening illness. It supports either

your decision to further your healing process, or your ability to accept your death with ease and dignity.

Begin with "Induction" (page 203).

Proceed with the following meditation:

In a moment, you will hear a bell (Note: Reader may prefer to substitute "In a moment I will snap my fingers"), and at that moment you're going to meet an aspect of your knowingness, an aspect of yourself, which may manifest in many ways. This aspect of yourself is very, very wise, all-knowing. This aspect of yourself may come to you in the form of light, an imaginary being, an animal, a spirit, or maybe another you.

(Bell rings.) Imagine this aspect, very, very wise, very gentle, and yet very powerful and strong. This is your wise self. Meet this part of yourself, very wise and all-knowing. Create, imagine the wise, compassionate self. . . .Imagine it in detail.

* *

Ask this aspect of yourself, how it is that the rest of you can gain the courage you need either to keep up the fight or to move on, to trust the future. Imagine what this aspect would tell you. . . .Sense your own knowingness. Trust yourself. You may receive answers in energy form, they may not be verbal. You may simply find yourself knowing, feeling, having the courage that you need to move on, to trust the future. . . .Imagine asking your wise self what you need to move on. . . .Trust yourself. . . .Give yourself permission to make up what your wise self has to say. . . .Imagine this. . . .Discover your courage. . . .Receive wisdom. . . .Feel the strength of your spirit. . . .Let yourself be empowered. . . .

As you breathe, imagine breathing in this new knowingness. . . .Imagine breathing in this courage. . . .Breathing in strength so that it spreads through every cell of your being. Every cell of your body receiving this strength. . . .Every thought in your mind filled with knowingness. . . .Every feeling in your emotions soothed with wisdom. . . .Your whole being vibrating with courage, with patience, with knowingness. And you become as wise as this aspect you've been communicating with. Imagine this.

* *

Notice what you need in your life to be able to come to completion, move on, to move forward. Talk to your wise self about it. . . .What do you need to feel whole again?. . . .Now imagine receiving what you need. . . .Imagine as though what you need is happening. . . .Imagine doing what you've wanted to do. Feel it. . . .Imagine doing those things you're still able to do. Imagine how and when you'll do these. . . . .Know, if you choose, you can come to peace or gain the courage to continue healing your mind and body.

* *

You may want to imagine doing some kind of ritual or ceremony or dance with your wise self. As you imagine this, you empower yourself, trust the future, let go. You evoke the deepest knowingness of your being. You are courageous, and at the same time compassionate for yourself. . . .Imagine performing a ritual with yourself, a ritual that acknowledges your life, expresses any rage you may feel, transforms any blame, and acknowledges your power. All that you've done. Letting go, and moving on. You can create this ritual in your mind's eye, in whatever way occurs to you, however you are inclined. This ritual can bring you peace or, if you like, it can give you the strength to continue healing.

* *

Begin to finish what you're doing. Feel yourself empowered, stronger. . . .And bring your attention back to my words. You may want to take time to ask your wise self how it is you can take charge of your life now. . . .How you can make your life easier. . . .How you can create peace in your life. . . .You may want to ask your wise self how you can be more comfortable in your body.

* *

If you're in pain, imagine your lungs bringing in lots of oxygen, your breath spreading through your whole body. With your breath, you can bring in whatever qualities will soothe you, maybe a color. . . .maybe coolness, maybe warmth. Imagine the quality you need. . . .Imagine something that has this quality. . . .Now imagine breathing in this quality. . . .Imagine your breath carrying relief through your body. Each breath massaging the whole of your body with relief, with calming effort. . . .Send your breath to wherever your body needs it. Let the quality soothe you. . . .With your wise self you may want to imagine creating a channel, a channel down into the ground to let the pain begin to drain out. . . .Breathe out the pain. Expect the pain to lessen over time. Expect it to be a little easier, a little more comfortable, as time passes. . . .

Imagine the pain lessening, more and more.

* *

Notice whatever may be holding you back from coming to peace with yourself, with your life. Anything that's bothering you. Imagine talking to whatever concerns you. . . .Discover what you need to do to come to peace with yourself, with your life.

* *

Imagine the trouble being transformed. You may want to imagine it soaking down into the earth, you may want to imagine doing something, taking care of something, allowing yourself to move forward. . . .You may need to imagine doing something or saying something you never had a chance to. . . .You may want to take time simply to remember your life, taking time to focus on any concerns you may have, communing with your wisest self.

* *

Begin to finish what you're doing now.

* *

Bring your attention back to my voice, back to my words. Go over all you've come to know in this meditation, all you've experienced in this meditation, any choices you may have made. . . .Imagine setting the stage for this day and the next, where you can carry this energy you experienced in your meditation out into your life, acting out of it. . . . .Knowing that it is there for you always, that it transcends time and space. . . . .And making yourself ready to come out to outer conscious levels. Acknowledge your wise self, knowing your wise self is always with you. All you need is to tap into your deeper self.

* *

End with "Return to Waking Consciousness" (page 209).

5. Creating a Respite for Yourself. *This meditation is designed to offer relief to people in pain.*
    Begin with "Induction" (page 203).
    Then proceed with the following meditation:

Now with your imagination, recreate an event in your life that you thoroughly enjoyed. Pick a particular time that made you happy, or create a time that would have made you happy. . . . .Imagine the details of the scene. . . . .Be aware of others with whom you shared— Imagine the sounds. . . . .the atmosphere. . . . .the colors. . . . .Let yourself enjoy it. Feel it as though it's happening now. What's said. What you're doing.

* *

Enjoy it. . . . .Let it warm you inside. . . . .Recreate another time, maybe a celebration of some kind, in which you had, or could have had, a very good time. Imagine a time when you celebrated, thoroughly enjoyed yourself, shared with others. Let yourself recreate all the details of the scene.

* *

The people. . . . .the place. . . . .the qualities present, the music, the laughter. Enjoy it. Imagine yourself immersed in the scene.

* *

Recreate another time, a time you shared love with another. Feel the warmth, the softness, the excitement, the sharing. Relive times of love, or create times that may have never happened, but had they happened they would have felt wonderful. Create loving scenes in your mind's eye. Immerse yourself in loving energy. Feel yourself appreciated. Feel yourself being loved. Let your heart be warm, be soothed. . . .Imagine the details of the scene. Create the scene. Create loving energy.

* *

Let your heart be warmed again. Create touching moments in your life. . . .Recreate times of laughter, times of play, times your heart was light. Your life felt easy. Recreate the lightness, the humor. Let yourself laugh a little inside. . . .Recreate the laughter.

* *

Remember times you have given to another, times you have been appreciated. Let yourself receive the appreciation once again. Draw it into yourself.

* *

Remember times you have created or accomplished something and you felt fully satisfied with yourself. Feel the satisfaction again, the quiet pride inside. Love yourself. Love who you are. Let yourself feel proud.

* *

Celebrate the sexuality in your life, all the satisfying times. Create times, or remember times, in which your sexuality fills you with pleasure. Imagine this pleasure occuring now. Give yourself permission to enjoy your fantasies. Whatever others may think, give yourself the gift of appreciating the pleasure of your sexuality.

* *

Bring to your awareness friends, family, lovers in your life who cared for you, who you cared for. If this care wasn't expressed, imagine as though it were. Acknowledge what you share with each of these people. Appreciate once again what each of these relationships means to you. Bring one relationship to mind at a time. . . .Feel the care you shared. . . .Feel the joys. . . . .Acknowledge these people in your life. . . .Your life has been full. Celebrate. Enjoy once again all those times in which you've lived fully. . . .Fill yourself with the fullness of your life.

* *

When you're ready, bring to awareness all the beauty of the earth. Imagine being on a warm, sunny beach. The sand is warm, the air is salty. The gulls soar through the sky. The waves build, break, and roll up onto the beach. . . .Then there is the majesty of the mountains, their crisp air, and greenery. Their snow caps, and mountain streams. . . .The quiet beauty of the desert, with its vast skies. . . .The rolling tranquility of farmlands. . . .Rivers that run through the land, sometimes smooth, sometimes raging. . . .Fill your mind with visions of the beauty of the earth, places you've been, places you'd like to have been. . . .Create them in your mind's eye. Enjoy them. . . .Acknowledge the beauty of the earth.

* *

Bring to mind other things you've enjoyed: paintings, sculptures, concerts. All the different forms of music you've enjoyed. Flowers. Whatever you enjoy, imagine enjoying it again. Imagine it in detail. Recreate it, in your mind's eye. Enjoy it again. . . .Think of qualities you like: colors . . .softness . . .scents . . .Bring these qualities into awareness. You may want to imagine surrounding yourself in some quality you like. Maybe a color, or coolness, maybe a sound, or smell. Whatever quality you like, immerse yourself in it. Vividly imagine, create it. Breathe it into yourself, into your body.

* *

You may want to send it to different areas of your body, and nurture your body with this quality. Imagine as though this quality helps the area feel a bit better. Expect it to continue to feel a bit better. . . .Now suggest to yourself that you always sleep soundly, as soundly as a sleeping baby. . . .Imagine your breath bringing in all the oxygen your body needs. Imagine whatever your body needs, and feel it actually taking place. Pretend.

* *

Take time to continue imagining anything you didn't have time to get into in detail before.

* *

When you're ready, begin to finish what you're doing, and bring your attention back to my words. . . .Now, if you like, you can make yourself ready to come out to outer consciousness levels. Know that whenever you wish, you can comfort yourself with the goodness of life itself.

Know that you carry the goodness of life in your consciousness always. . . .All you need do is focus on these visions whenever you choose, and when you do, they will comfort you. . . .

* *

End with "Return to Waking Consciousness" (page 209).

Induction. *Use this to begin each of the five meditations given.*

Close your eyes and focus on your breathing, breathing fully, breathing easily, letting your breath be full and relaxed. . . .With each breath you relax more and more. With each breath your imagination becomes more fluid and free. Let your breath move through your body, caressing your body into a deep state of relaxation. . . .Imagine your tensions soaking down into the earth, like the rainwater soaks into the ground. Feel yourself relax more and more with each exhalation. . . .Feel yourself relaxing more and more, and know that your body will continue to relax more and more as you move through this meditation.

* *

*Imagine telling your body it can relax now. . . .As your body con-
tinues to relax, become aware of your mind. Imagine that your mind
is as vast as the sky, as in fact it is. Imagine as though your breath
were a breeze clearing your mind. . . .Let your mind relax, and know
that as your mind relaxes your thoughts become softer, easier, almost
as though they were like fluffy clouds that pass through an afternoon sky. You can watch all your thoughts pass through the sky of
your mind, lots of space for whatever moves through your mind. . . .It
feels good to let your mind relax, to let your thoughts become softer,
easier. Let your mind be open and clear. . . .Know your mind will
continue to relax as you move through this meditation. . . .Feel each
breath relaxing your mind more and more.*

* *

*Feel each breath making your imagination more vivid, more
clear. . . .As your mind continues to relax, become aware of how you
are feeling. Give yourself permission to relax emotionally. Imagine
letting all the anxieties, all the frustrations, and all the "shoulds"
soak down into the ground, with each exhalation of breath, just like
the rainwater soaks into the earth. And letting yourself feel emotionally safe and secure, emotionally relaxed, imagine this relaxation. . . .If you have any fears or anxieties, imagine them being
washed away by the rain, blown away by the wind, cleared by your
breath, just as the air is cleared after a storm. With each breath you
are more and more relaxed, your imagination more and more vivid.
Let your whole being be clear, relaxed, and alert. It feels good to relax. . . .Give yourself permission to relax emotionally. . . .Feel yourself quieting down inside.*

* *

*Now in a moment, I am going to count on a descending scale from
ten to one. At each descending count you will be able to feel yourself
relaxing even more than you now are, entering a very deep state of
consciousness, entering into a place of deep knowingness, the source*

of your awareness. Moving down deeper and deeper with each descending count, beginning to move further down into yourself.

Ten, relaxing, relaxing with each breath. . . .Nine, deeper and deeper relaxing, a little more, returning to yourself. . . .Eight, softly, gently, easing yourself down into who it is that you are. Moving down, deeper and deeper. . . .Seven, softly, gently, moving down, very calm, very clear. Moving down inside of yourself. . . .Six, feeling your breath take you deeper to the essence of who you are, deeper and deeper. . . .Five, moving down, down into your place of wisdom, whatever you sense that to be. Deeper and deeper into yourself. . . .Four, into the place where your knowingness will reveal to you your healing process. Deeper and deeper. . . .Three, moving down, down. Your imagination becoming increasingly vivid. Very, very deep, deeper and deeper, returning to yourself. . . .Two, moving down into the depths of knowingness itself. . . .One, you are centered at a very deep level of consciousness now. Your imagination is fluid and free. Here your imagination will reveal to you what you need. Know that you'll continue to remain alert and aware throughout this meditation.

Create now what you consider to be your own place of power, a very special place. Create it now with your imagination. Create a place of power. It may be deep down in the ground, or high up in the sky. It may be a place you've once been, or a place you've often been. Or maybe your place of power is solely a creation of your imagination. Wherever it is, imagine being there now. . . .Create it.

Let your breath breathe life into your place of power. . . .Imagine what would be all around you. . . .Create it. . . .Feel it. . . .Be there. . . .Experience this place charged with power, power that springs from the source of life itself. This place is potent. This place is alive with potential. Imagine this place in detail. . . .Sense it. . . .Hear it. . . .Feel it. . . .Smell it. Imagine as though this were the home of your spirit. Feel the magnetic core of your being vibrating with the spirit of this place. However you create it, feel it, know it, this is your place of power. . . .However you see it, sense it, hear it, this is your place of power. The power deep within you resonates with this place you create. . . .Imagine breathing in the quality of this place, the peacefulness, the potency. . . .From this centered place, you can tap the fullness of your personal powers. Here you can come to know yourself, and view your life with clarity. Here, you come to know your body, and how to heal yourself. Here, you can change yourself and your life any way that you want.

Affirmation of Gay Lifestyle*. *If you wish, use this passage as indicated in the meditations on "A Vision of a Healthy Immune System" and "Choosing the Best Lifestyle for Yourself."*

Feel yourself whole, experience yourself fully, believe in yourself, in your integrity, in your power. Acknowledge yourself for having the courage to be who you are. . . Appreciate yourself for having the courage to be different, the way in which you are special, you have the sensitivity to express who you truly are. . . Affirm the expression of your body, acknowledge, appreciate your gayness, your expressions of love, your sensuality, the celebration of life, of your body. Acknowledge, appreciate your gayness, how good it has felt to share with other men, how natural it feels to be drawn to other men. . .

If anything comes up that makes it difficult for you to love yourself, to appreciate who you are, to appreciate being gay, whatever stops you from doing that, just as you can let your tensions soak down into the ground, let any of those negative messages soak down into the earth, purge yourself, cleanse yourself of any self-hatred, let it soak down into the ground, fertilizing the earth, breathe it out, leaving you relaxed, loving yourself, loving who you are, leaving yourself whole and open. . . Celebrate who you are, who you share with. . . Let all of the ugliness of the world around you that has been aimed at you and your brothers who are gay, let all of it soak down into the ground. Let all the constricting denial of life soak into the ground, leaving you clear and strong.

* *

Now draw up from the earth the courage to be who you are. Draw in from your place of power the courage to accept variety of experience, the courage to express life as it moves through you. . . The courage to know that your sexuality is a natural expression of life itself, let yourself receive the support of the whole of the community and the

*Prepared with the help of Mica Kindman, Don Gorman, and Norm Crystar.

whole of the gay community in particular, this strength that we have together, the bond that we share. . . Receive that support. . . Let it strengthen you. . . Let it heal you. . . Accept support from the friends you have. . . Feel yourself a part of that strength, the collective strength of our gay community. The power of gay love guiding the straight community into seeing its own limitations, transcending them and becoming open.

Accept the goodness of yourself, of your friends and lovers, of the community, and let any residual hatred (of being gay) which is really a disease, soak into the ground, let it all soak down into the ground. . . .Feel yourself, cleansed, clear. . . .Let your consciousness emerge with strength, courage and sensitivity. Celebrating life, what it is that life has offered, knowing what there is to live for now.

* *

Let the spirit of being gay give you the strength to muster the courage to take charge of your life. Feel the spirit of life, the spirit of your life. . . .Loving yourself, experience your gayness as a privilege, as a gift from life itself, the spirit of gayness runs deep into your deepest spirit, into the very source of your life, and as you experience it, it heals you. View your gayness as a privilege, a way to learn, a way to know yourself, a way to experience yourself, your life, the joy within you. . . .

As you experience the spirit of gayness, the spirit of life itself, feel life percolating through your body.

* *

Feel your body's ability to heal itself, to take care of itself. Your body is a healing, self-replenishing system. It knows, it has a deep, innate wisdom of how to care for itself. . . .

Vitality of Life. *Use this passage as indicated in meditations on "A Vision of a Healthy Immune System" and "Treatment Choice."*

Feel the life that flows through you always, the spontaneous, inexhaustible energy, vibrant, radiant energy moving through you like a river that's never twice the same. Imagine this force of energy, the rhythm of this energy, energy which your life rides on from moment to moment. Feel it teeming in every cell of your body, through every pore, every organ, energy, radiant energy. Feel this energy's connection with all of life force energy, energy that permeates everything, the glow of the life force.

*   *   *

Feel the energy expanding, bursting forth, feel the celebration, celebration of life. Feel it surging through you, the movement of this energy. The dance, the sound, the rhythm, the music of this energy. Pulsating energy, moving through you. Feel all of this, celebrate life. . . Feel the wisdom of this energy, how it is that it always knows how to regenerate itself. Feel this energy's ability to heal, to return anything into a harmonious, balanced condition, fully vital, yet balanced, maintaining an equilibrium. Acknowledge the wisdom of life itself. Let yourself reside in the sanctity of life itself. . . The vitality of life itself resides in every cell of which you are composed. Every cell of which you are composed has a will to live, and is full of life.

Direct your awareness into your body now. As you do, sense, feel, see inside yourself, endeavor to experience your body in good health. You may wish to imagine yourself very tiny, as if your whole awareness were moving through your body. You may wish to imagine yourself riding a pinpoint of light, a light that illuminates the internal workings of your body. Know that it is fine, in fact it is good, to simply make up what it is like inside yourself. You need not imagine it literally. As you take this journey through your body, you may have your own way of imagining what is going on inside. Listen to these words only when they're helpful. Follow your own inclinations. Follow your own imagination. However you imagine it, is what is right for you.

Imagine the inside of your body as if it were a great landscape. Just as in the country, each creature, each plant is separate, alive, and yet part of the whole community. Inside your body there are all kinds of cells, each separate, each having its own job, yet all part of the greater community of life that percolates inside. Imagine the inside of your body like a great landscape. . . .Know that with each breath, the landscape comes into clearer focus. . . .The landscape of your body is full of life, sounds, colors, textures, smells. . . .Imagine your heart. Feel the pulse of life in your heart. . . .Hear it, alive with the rhythm of life. Out of your heart flow rivers of life blood, carrying nutrients throughout the reaches of your body, nourishing every cell of which you are composed, keeping every cell of which you are composed strong and healthy. . . .And your lungs move gracefully with the rhythm of life, bringing oxygen throughout your body, every cell of your body breathing in fresh air, cleansing and clearing your body, keeping you healthy and vibrant. . . .Rivers of blood, circulating throughout your body, nourishing every area, replenishing each and every cell of which you are composed. . . .Your lymphatic fluid smoothly flows along with your blood, cleansing and clearing, carrying away whatever is no longer needed, cleaning your body. Lymphatic fluid smoothly flowing along with your blood, carrying away any debris. . . .Life-giving blood traveling through your whole body. . . .Be aware now of your muscles giving the terrain of your body shape and movement. . . .of your bones giving you form. . . .of your nervous system keeping all the cells of which you are composed in clear communication. The landscape of your body is full of awareness, of consciousness. Sense your digestive system, transforming food into nourishment, into energy, into what you need for your life, for your health. Feel your sexual system full of energy, energy that celebrates life itself. . . .Imagine the whole of the landscape of your body, every cell of which you are composed is strong. Each cell has a strong membrane surrounding it, maintaining its autonomy, yet it's a part of the whole, doing its job well. With each breath you can experience the insides of your body more vividly.

Return to Waking Consciousness. *Use this passage to conclude each of the five meditations given.*

Make yourself ready to come out to outer conscious levels. In a moment, I am going to count from one to five. At the count of five, you will open your eyes, feeling refreshed.

One, coming up slowly. . . .Two, remembering all that you have learned in this meditation. . . .Three, knowing you can come back to this place on your own, any time you like. . . .Four, beginning to sense the room around you. . . .and Five, opening your eyes, feeling refreshed, revitalized, and full of health, ready and able to act on what you know is right for you.

Margo Adair's note:
The author acknowledges the San Francisco Shanti Project for its support of and participation in the writing of this material and the production of it onto audio-cassette tape.

Ed. note: The first meditation, "Vision of a Healthy Immune System," will prove powerful and effective for many readers. For others, it may smack too much of out-and-out militarism. If this is the case for you, you may wish to design an entirely original visualization, incorporating some of the accurate anatomical information contained within it.

Your own inner sensibility and imagination can create the perfect visualization for you. You don't even have to see pictures; have faith that what you are sensing, feeling, hearing, or knowing while regularly engaging in this process is working for you. Allow your imagination to find the perfect way to put the principles of psychoimmunity into practice.

Stephen Levine, author of *Who Dies?*, has suggested that instead of visualizing hunting down and killing cancer cells, we might want to imagine melting them with love. Stephanie Matthews-Simonton now draws her images far more from nature than from the vocabulary of the Pentagon. A naturalistic image, such as birds pecking at seeds—transforming matter as part of the natural order of things—might work for you.

You might wish to base your images on the material in the Psychoimmunity channeling which follows, which suggests that basically there is nothing to be immune against. You could see your T-cells and B-cells playing more of a digestive function, scouting around for things to eat. Were they to see a little HTLV-III coming down the pike, they might exclaim, "Goodness gracious, that's no bean sprout! Time to chew it up and spit it out!"

Let your imagination run free. Allow yourself to have a good time. One client of Louise Hay imagined that he was the conductor of a long freight train. At a certain juncture, he split the cargo in two, with him heading to New York City while the HTLV-III chugged along to Kansas. Trust yourself. Allowing yourself to feel good and to play is part of the healing process.

CHAPTER 12

SOME ADDITIONAL APPROACHES

This section presents material of relevance to our readers which was not considered essential for inclusion of the healing program of The Holisitic Group. It begins with a discussion of cleansing baths, which are especially important to healthy living in our polluted and stress-inducing environment, and includes a special bath for people experiencing immune dysfunction. The second part includes brief discussions of several organically-derived and chemical substances which are being used in the treatment of AIDS and other dis-ease states. The final part includes an extensive list of Flower Essences, generated through Richard Katz, Kevin Ryerson, and Irene Newmark, which may prove of benefit to people diagnosed with AIDS, ARC, or other immune dysfunction. By sensing the relationship between the mind-body-spirit imbalances associated with AIDS and the Flower Essences which have been suggested, readers and practitioners may receive guidance for intuiting which essences may be appropriate in other situations.

Cleansing Baths
There is a long history of the use of cleansing baths in Germany and in the naturopathic community. These baths are quite effective in the removal of environmental toxins, heavy metal deposits, and radiation, which in this period of history represent a frequently encountered low-grade and continuous drain on the immune system and on general body functioning.

Almost all of us have unknowingly accumulated a fair share of heavy metal deposits in our tissues, with the possible exception of people who regularly swim in chlorinated pools. (Hair analysis is one method frequently employed to help detect the presence of these heavy metals.) Because of nuclear fallout, radioactive proliferation, toxic dumps, etc., you may appear symptom-free, but in actuality carry within you "a silent time bomb," the internalized fallout of the weapons of war. If you've experienced numerous X-rays, surgery, or CAT scans, worked before computer terminals or with chemicals and fumes (e.g., photocopy equipment, printing presses, automobiles, street fumes), you can assume that you have a fair share of toxic "gunk" in your body. Taking a series of cleansing baths is an inexpensive and pleasant enough way to ensure the maintenance of your health.

Because baths can sometimes be experienced as temporarily draining, they are best taken before bedtime. Drinking extra fluids is recommended, especially if you sweat a lot after bathing. If you are in a state of ill health, or of weakened constitution, it is advised to replenish beneficial minerals which may be leached out through the bathing process by consuming seaweed or vegetables high in minerals, such as leafy greens, zucchini, parsley, green beans, or jicama, on the day following the bath. While most individuals simply experience the baths as a relaxing and downright delightful experience, some individuals may sometimes feel uncomfortable, irritable, or edgy after bathing. This is frequently the result of toxins being pulled out of the body, and is a sign that the baths are working for you.

When taking any of the following baths, fill the bath to the top, and immerse everything except your face and hair. If you get uncomfortable or dizzy while bathing, sit up for a while before returning to a reclining position; do not lengthen the recommended time for bathing. Experiment until you find the right warm temperature which is most conducive to pleasant bathing for you.

A list of the most commonly suggested cleansing baths follows. It includes a series of baths recommended for general health maintenance, and a cleansing bath for food.

Clorox® brand bleach bath
Purpose: Helps clear lymphatic congestion, some viral and bacterial conditions. Removes lead and other heavy metal residues, drug residues, and, to a limited extent, some forms of radio-

active toxicity. In general, these baths are most effective for removing heavy metals and cleansing the lymphatic system. Dosage: General dosage is ½ to 1 cup liquid Clorox® brand bleach in a medium hot bath, soaking 20 to 30 minutes. Average bath is usually one cup bleach for 25 minutes. It is essential to use Clorox® brand because of its greater purity and unique energy. A shower with soap is recommended afterward. Be sure to keep the bleach out of your eyes while bathing and not to immerse your scalp hair. Though these baths may sound scary, they will not bleach your body hair or burn you.

Seasalt and baking soda bath, either separate or combined
Purpose: Primarily clear radiation, cleanse the auric field, and clear lymphatic congestion. If concern is solely with clearing radiation, use baking soda alone.
Dosage: In combination, average is two pounds of each substance. If taking seasalt alone, average is three pounds. Baking soda baths average three to four pounds, and may go as high as six pounds. Soak for 20 to 30 minutes (average time is 25 minutes). Showering afterward is not necessary. Hotter water results in a stronger bath.

Epsom salts bath
Purpose: Broad spectrum cleanser, pretty heavy-duty. To clear lymphatic congestion, remove heavy metals and radiation. More powerful than seasalt and baking soda for cleansing lymphatics.
Dosage: Take a hot bath rather than warm. Average dosage, four pounds. Spend no more than 12 to 15 minutes in the tub. You may take two of these spaced a week apart.

Apple cider vinegar bath
Purpose: Good for infections, particularly bacterial, or for certain skin conditions. Helps to acidify the body, thus having an antibacterial effect. Useful for women with vaginal and bladder infections.
Dosage: One quart in a tub; soak for ½ hour using hot water.

Clay bath
Purpose: Clears the aura, clears the energy field, pulls some radiation out, good for certain skin conditions.
Dosage: One cup green clay in medium hot to hot bath for ½ hour. Average of two is recommended.

Essential oil bath
Purpose: Refer to literature on aroma therapy. These work as emotional, spiritual, and energetic harmonizers.
Dosage: Pure rose oil, rose/geranium oil, lavender, wintergreen, rosemary, sage, as recommended.

Lemon bath
Purpose: Helps decrystalize old and stuck mental patterns.
Dosage: Juice of three lemons in hot bath for 15 minutes. Average of six baths, one week apart.

Lime and tumeric powder bath
Purpose: Works as cleanser on the spiritual level. Also helps clear metalics, radiation, and drug residues.
Dosage: Four limes plus two teaspoons tumeric powder in a hot bath for 15 minutes. Average of six is recommended. The yellow bathtub stain can be removed afterward with bleach. Be sure to wash the stain off your body—scrubbing with a loofa helps. Paying particular attention to washing the soles of your feet is advised if you're about to step onto a nice white towel or floor.

A General Cleansing Program
Purpose: Just about everyone on the planet can benefit from a series of baths to remove radiation and heavy metal deposits, as well as to cleanse the lymphatics.
Dosage: Take 6 Clorox® brand bleach baths (1 cup—soak 20 minutes—take 1 to 2 per week), following this with 4 to 10 baking soda baths (3 to 4 lbs.—soak 20 minutes—take 1 to 2 per week), following the guidelines offered above. The frequency of bathing is determined by strength of constitution. If of a weakened constitution or in a deficient state, space the baths out to 1 per week. The number of baking soda baths neces-

sary to cleanse the body is determined by the amount of radiation you may have absorbed; this relates to where you live, your job, the number of X-rays you have undergone, and your past history.

Cleansing bath for food
Purpose: A very mild solution of Clorox® brand bleach can help remove pesticides and other toxins from fruits, vegetables, fish and fowl; it will also raise the vitality of any food.
Dosage: ½ tsp. Clorox® per gallon of water. Soak for 10 minutes (12 minutes for thick-skinned foods), then soak for 10 to 12 minutes in clear water.

Healing-Tonifying-Detoxifying bath for AIDS and immune dysfunction
Purpose: Reliever of mental and emotional tensions; stimulus to the immune system; general antiseptic; fungicide; general glandular tonic; cleanser of the lymphatic system.
Dosage: 1 tsp. of the following mixture in the bath. Soak 15 to 20 minutes in a hot bath perhaps 2 times a week for as many weeks as desired.
Specific Oil mixture:

Tonka bean oil:	4 drops
Tea tree (melaleuca alternifolia)	8 drops
Niaouli	9 drops
Thyme	11 drops
Juniper	5 drops
Hyssop	6 drops
Cypress	7 drops
Angelica	5 drops

Incorporate this mixture into a body massage oil format, in a ratio of 1:24 (mixture:base), so that the resultant mixture contains approximately 4% of the essential oil mixture listed above. Tiferet Essentials uses a massage oil format which include Almond or Apricot 30%, Safflower 30%, Olive 12%, Coconut 12%, Aloe Vera 5%, Jojoba 5%, Wheat Germ 4%, and vitamin E 2%. (For wholesale and retail ordering information, please contact the editor—see address in Resources.) While this mixture can be used as a massage oil, with special focus on all lymph areas, especially around inner thighs (skip the genitals) and under arms, we believe that its benefits are most fully realized as a bath oil.

Other Antiviral and Immune-Enhancing Substances

In order not to confuse the layperson with an infinite list of substances to choose from, The Holisitic Group has included in its Inquiry into the Prevention and Healing of Acquired Immune Deficiency Syndrome those vitamins and substances which it feels will prove most appropriate to the largest number of individuals. Since many programs, both holistic and allopathic, employ substances not discussed at length in the Inquiry, a few are listed below, along with the positive and negative comments of The Holisitic Group.

Pau d'Arco (taheebo, tajibo, lapacho morado). This inner bark of a tree native to the Andes of South America has gained quite a reputation as an "anticancer" substance. The Group believes that it is definitely antiviral, and can also help correct imbalances in the cellular memory and the genetic code (see discussion on Blue-Green Manna in the Inquiry). You can buy it in tablet or herb form in health food stores. If used in tea form, use one teaspoon per cup, steep overnight without boiling, and drink one quart per day.

Ginseng. This overall tonic stimulates the thymus and the overall immune system, and also stimulates the pituitary gland. Korean ginseng is often not recommended for people with AIDS, as Chinese practitioners view it as too hot, having an effect similar to putting oil on a fire. American ginseng is preferable, because it moistens the yin more than other forms. Some forms of ginseng are tonics; others are stimulants. Because too much ginseng can throw the body off balance, please consult with a practitioner of Chinese medicine before consuming it on a regular basis.

Shitake mushrooms. The Group believes these are primarily antiviral, working in a manner similar to echinacea. Russell M. Jaffe, M.D., Ph.D. (see Resources) recommends Scientific Consultants, 5725 Chelton Avenue, Oakland, CA 94611, (415) 632-

2370, as a source of consistently high quality mushrooms. You can also buy mushrooms in the store, or grow them at minimum expense on a log. It is suggested that you check to see if you are sensitive to them, in which case a small dosage might be most advisable. Ganoderma mushrooms also have antiviral properties, and are equally effective.

Thymosin. Produced by the thymus, this substance helps rejuvenate and restore the immune system. It specifically affects the T-cells and the white corpuscle count, and can help restimulate the spleen. Currently being examined and synthesized in laboratories, thymosin may be available either now or in the future.

Echinacea. The Holisitic Group believes that echinacea works mostly as an antiviral substance, and is good if you're feeling run down or off-balance, feel something coming on, or have been exposed to a virus. While it has no known toxicity, it has been discovered that in many cases a strong dosage is only effective for a short amount of time, at which point its effect tends to plateau and a smaller dosage is appropriate. It is best taken in small amounts several times a day. Should one choose to extract a tea directly from the herb, or from the root powder, it is imperative to obtain the finest quality available. One could take 1 gram of the herbal root powder daily, spreading it out in small dosages every two hours. It is also possible to put 1 oz. of the herb in one pint of boiling water, simmering it for 10 minutes, and then cooling it in a quart jar in the refrigerator. Take ½ cup of this mixture, 2 to 3 times a day.

The most convenient method for ingesting echinacea is through herbal tinctures available in many health food stores. Obtaining tinctures made from organic and wild-crafted (grown in the wild herbs) helps ensure that the potency and life-energy is the highest. For example, the "Bio-Botanica" brand of tinctures available in many health food stores is made from commercial herbs. Organic brands of herbal tinctures include Herbal Pharmaceuticals, the Herbpharm in Williams, Oregon, and the wildcrafted and organic herbs prepared by Christopher Hobbs and his Native Herb Company in Ben Lomand, California. (For information on mail ordering their tinctures of echinacea, as well as others applicable to healing immune dysfunction, see the Resources section.) In addition, The Holisitic Group feels good about the Bioforce brand "Echinaforce" imported from Switzerland, and the "Immu-stim" formula, whose active ingredient is echinacea, prepared by Brent Davis of Wildwood Botanicals of Pasadena, California.

Christopher Hobbs, whose credentials include teaching herbalism at Paul Lee's Platonic Academy of Herbal Studies, the Portland Naturopathic School, New College of San Francisco, and Dr. Christopher's Schools of Natural Healing in Washington, D.C., and England, offers the following protocol for ingesting echinacea tinctures: If you take a full dose (termed by herbalists as "material" dose), which might be 20 or even 30 drops every two waking hours, do it for 10 days, then drop to a maintenance dosage of 7 to 8 drops per day for a week, after which you may begin the cycle anew. This is of course a general protocol, and is not necessarily the optimal program for you. Consultation with an herbalist is recommended before wholesale ingestion of any of the herbs mentioned in the preceding article.

Echinacea and Blue-Green Manna, an immune-building algae which comprises part of The Holisitic Group's model program for the prevention and healing of Acquired Immune Deficiency, appear to be complementary substances, and can help potentiate each other. Please refer to the discussion in the Inquiry section of this book.

Brief Comments on some Chemical Substances

Vinblastine: This chemotherapy agent, derived from the severely poisonous periwinkle plant, is taken intravenously to limit the growth of KS lesions. The Group believes that with certain individuals, administered in very modest amounts by a holistically aware practitioner, and combined with tremendous detoxification (e.g., saunas three times a week, a cleansing diet, etc.), vinblastine may prove effective. However, it can be harsh on the immune system in the long run and even suppress it, thus compromising the drug's short-term effectiveness. A holistic alternative is a harmless homeopathic preparation of periwinkle; homeopathic serial dilutions of mistletoe might also prove effective against KS lesions.

DHPG: This drug is being used to fight CMV. From a holistic standpoint, the Group prefers a harmless homeopathic preparation of CMV in concentrations of 10MM or 30X. Believing that research will eventually show that CMV is a parallel virus to the AIDS virus, the Group asserts that the above remedy may be beneficial in the healing of AIDS.

Non-Oxynol-9: This spermicidal ingredient has been demonstrated to kill the AIDS virus in laboratory test tubes. Alas, it is believed that research on human beings, if carried out conscientiously, will reveal that such spermicides can disrupt the anal and vaginal tissues, possibly leaving the user more susceptible to penetration by the AIDS virus than before. Even occasional use, let us say once a week, cannot be endorsed. As noted earlier in the text, we do believe that the potentially damaging effects of non-oxynol-9 are mitigated if it is employed in non-hydrogenated-fat-containing lubricants.

Ribavirin: Of all the inhibitors of reverse transcriptase currently being examined, including HPA-23, Suramin and Lentinan, the Group believes that this substance can most effectively protect the immune system from further viral infection so that the body can generate its own states of remission. We endorse its use.

Isoprinosine: While this drug can boost the immune system, it can have unfortunate side effects, including damaging the liver. From a holistic standpoint, Blue-Green Manna, thymosin, etc., are preferable.

Ribavirin plus Isoprinosine: While many people with AIDS are experimenting with this drug combination, either in controlled studies or on their own, we believe that the potentially-negative effect of isoprinosine on the liver limits its viability as an immune system restorer. While some individuals may be able to tolerate such a combination, others will experience detrimental toxic effects. Those sensing that is doing more harm than good are encouraged to try ribavirin itself.

AL721: This substance dissolves the protective coating surrounding the HTLV-III virus. Providing that the immune system is not too suppressed by the injection of this substance or various other drugs, it can prove an effective treatment which can lead to remission. We suggest that it be taken in combination with other immune boosters, such as Blue-Green Manna or other blue-green algae, ribavirin, thymosin, ginseng, etc.

Flower Essences Useful for Healing Emotional Patterns Associated with AIDS
After each essence you will find a code which relates to the company which produces the essence. Their addresses, as well as specific ordering information for the Flower Essence Services essences, available in either stock bottles or dosage form, can be found in the Resources.

Thousand Petal Lotus (FES): Suggested by Tom MacPherson. An opener to one's spiritual light, reminds one of one's spiritual self, deepens meditative state, helps enhance other essences.
Rescue Remedy Combination (Bach): Temporary calming and centering; counteracting stress and trauma; a general nontranquilizing formula helpful for coping with life and stress in this transitional period of history.
Rock Rose (Bach) (also included in the Rescue Remedy): Courage to transcend fear and panic.
Walnut (Bach): Making transitions; freedom from hindering influences, letting go of old stuff.
Pink Yarrow (FES): Centering and grounding, emotional resilience, counteracting emotional oversensitivity and vulnerability.
Yarrow (FES): Integrity of self; strengthening against negativity; for oversensitivity and vulnerability in general.
St. John's Wort (FES): Helps release fears from the subconscious.

Chapparal (FES): Facilitates healing; aids in connecting with higher inspiration for healing.

Aloe Vera (FES): A helpful adjunct to any sort of healing; helps with skin conditions, ulcers, tumors, leukemia, and cancerous conditions, nerve diseases, digestive and brain imbalances; improves reflexology treatment when rubbed on feet.

Self-Heal (FES): "I have a healer within myself;" helps to facilitate confidence in one's inner healing forces.

Penstemon (FES): Inner strength through adversity, overcoming self-doubt.

Morning Glory (FES): Facilitates energy flow in the body; vitality, alertness, freshness; helps one overcome negative, compulsive, and addictive habits and energy.

California Wild Rose (FES): Vitality, rejuvenation on all levels, love of life.

Sweet Chestnut (Bach): Rekindling of hope, faith, and optimism amid despair.

Borage (FES): Confidence and courage in facing danger and challenge; especially helpful in overcoming grief and discouragment.

Cherry: Vitality, cheerfulness.

While some individuals prefer to take flower essences directly from the stock bottle, an alternative is to prepare your own 1-ounce dosage bottles as follows: Cleanse the dosage bottle and dropper with boiling spring or purified water, and then fill it most of the way with same. Add 1 teaspoon brandy (omit if alcoholic) as a preservative. Then add 2 drops of each stock essence you wish to consume, up to 5 in a bottle. Shake it a good 100 times, say a prayer, and it's yours. (Note: Use 4 drops of Rescue Remedy stock concentrate when preparing a RR dosage bottle.) You may want to carry RR around with you at all times, to have on hand for yourself and friends in times of stress. I (Jason) once rescued half of the backstage crew of a San Francisco Lesbian/Gay Freedom Day Celebration with my trusty dosage bottle.

You can consume flower essences at any time, but try to separate them by 15 minutes from food or non-H2O drink. Shake the bottle a good 7 times before using. Place them on or under your tongue, or sip from a small glass of water. Keep the liquid in your mouth for a short time before swallowing. Try not to touch your mouth with the dropper, as this may contaminate the mixture. (That's why it's a good idea to carry a dosage bottle around rather than the stock mixture. Friends always seem to want to touch the dropper with their tongue.) For more information, contact the Flower Essence Society and see Gurudas' *Flower Essences*. The Flower Essence Society mail orders 1 oz. glass dosage bottles (12 for $7.00). Please see ordering information in Resources.

PART III

KEVIN RYERSON'S TRANCE CHANNELINGS

CHAPTER 13

INTRODUCTION TO KEVIN RYERSON'S TRANCE CHANNELINGS

Kevin Ryerson is a fully accredited trance channel, having perfected his craft through study at Richard Ireland's University of Life in Phoenix, Arizona, and matriculating with a degree as a Mediator.

Kevin's work is twofold: As a trance channel he works very much in the spirit and tradition of Edgar Cayce and Jane Roberts, allowing his normal waking consciousness to be set aside so that various Spirit Entities—Beings of Disincarnate Intelligence—may teach and guide through him. And as a gifted teacher and lecturer in his own right, Kevin has devoted his life since 1972 to sharing his knowledge of the field of parapsychology.

Trance channeling is primarily a means of accessing information. The source of the information is a vast reservoir of knowledge, variously termed the Universal Mind or Akaschic Records. The Universal Mind is comparable to C.G. Jung's theory of the collective unconscious. Jung states that all of humankind's evolved higher systems of thought (e.g., art, philosophy, technology, etc.) survive throughout all time and space. In his state of altered consciousness, Kevin is able to tap into the vast reservoir of the Universal Mind. Subject material as diverse as natural health therapies, the laws of physics, career direction, Atlantis, the Pyramids, the life of Jesus, and reincarnation are expounded upon by the Spirit Entities flowing through the channel.

Edgar Cayce, the most well-known channel of the recent past, focused most of his work not on predictions of earthquakes and other natural disasters, but on issues of health and well-being. Cayce often did readings for people whom he never spoke to or met—people who lived great distances from his center in Virginia Beach, Virginia. Follow-up research into his health analyses and recommendations yields, among those case histories which can be traced and verified, an accuracy rate of 92%, a figure which might justifiably arouse the wonder and envy of most traditional practitioners. Kevin Ryerson follows in this tradition, and is one of many mediators and psychics who have participated in long-distance channelings arranged through the Center for Applied Intuition in San Francisco.

Kevin's actual trance sessions usually last from 60 to 90 minutes, though his research group channelings, such as the one which follows, may last up to two hours. During this period Kevin sets aside his normal waking consciousness and "goes away" into the trance state, allowing Spirit Entities with clearly defined voices and personalities to communicate through him. In trance, Kevin remains seated with eyes closed, often reflecting through hand motions and facial gestures the distinct personalities of the Entities speaking through him. Capable of achieving a deep trance state in a short amount of time, he returns from his sessions unaware of the events that have occurred during his absence.

You may already be acquainted with Kevin's work through reading Shirley MacLaine's *Out on a Limb* or *Dancing in the Light,* or seeing Kevin play himself in her TV mini-series, *Out on a Limb* (broadcast in the fall of 1986). A reading of *Flower Essences* or *Gem Tinctures and Vibrational Healing,* edited by Gurudas and based on material channeled through Kevin, evidences his capability to channel both great spiritual wisdom and material that is highly detailed and technical in nature. Kevin's channelings are graced by such depth and clarity because he allows himself to serve as an "instrument" for higher knowledge, willingly detaching his ego from the information that Spirit chooses to communicate through him. As one who has been working with Kevin since at least December 1980—long before his *Out on a Limb* fame—I have learned to trust his work because of the intelligence, ease, and detachment which evidence his spiritual dedication, and because, most importantly, the information imparted through him makes sense to me.

The two Spirit Entities who address the group in the channelings in this book are the two who most frequently speak through Kevin. Biographical sketches of their lives while in the body (before they disincarnated and chose to channel information through Kevin and perhaps through other "instruments") are incomplete, due to their commitment to focus less on their personalities and former life-

times than on the material they can share with us. John, Son of Ze-
bedee, lived 2,000 years ago as an Essene (Hebrew) follower of Christ,
and has been linked by students of theology to John the Beloved,
author of the Book of Revelations. John's speech tends to the formal
and archaic, with his presentation always even and soft spoken. His
messages are filled with spiritual insight, drawing upon the teachings not only of Christ but of other great Spiritual Masters, and on
occasion contain references to the prophecy contained in the Book
of Revelations and its fulfillment in our present time period.

Tom MacPherson, in sharp contrast, led an extremely colorful
existence as an Irishman some 400 years ago. From information
pieced together by Kevin (from conversations with people who have
questioned Tom about this lifetime of his), we have learned that Tom
MacPherson became a "guerilla street merchant" (i.e., a pickpocket)
between the ages of 13 and 15 while living in London. Graduating
from this line of work, he apprenticed to a silversmith somewhere
between the ages of 21 and 25, during which time he also studied
alchemy. He led a multifaceted and Bohemian existence for the re-
mainder of his life, centering his activities around the Shakespear-
ian stage and the Elizabethan court. At times Tom worked as a
"freelance rogue," an avocation with some equivalence to that of a
private detective. Skilled in many areas, it is perhaps best to say that
he was a very colorful figure who valued his freedom, and who cul-
tivated and interfaced with many powerful friends in high places.

What is most important to us is not Tom's exploits and karma,
but the fact that he can share so much truth with us now that he
has left the body. Much more "familiar" and droll than John, he often intersperses his communications with a wit and humor which
are an absolute delight. Though he tends to be a bit more "practical" in his communications than John, both they and the many other
Entities who choose Kevin as an instrument can share information
ranging from the construction of the Pyramids and the life of the
great channel Madame Blavatsky to advice for the lovelorn and the
best foods to eat for breakfast.

The channeling which follows, "The Nature of the Healing Process," was conducted specifically for this book at Kevin's San Francisco apartment on May 29, 1985. Because the transmission was one
of the clearest I have experienced through him, only minimal editing was employed in preparing it for this volume.

The channeling begins with John's discussion of the nature of
mind, body, spirit, and the soul; this leads into his discourse on the
nature of the healing process. The explanation of these terms, which

is included in the beginning Introduction to this book, might prove of assistance in assimilating fully the essence of John's teachings.

Among the individuals whose presence made possible the depth and clarity of the material which follows are: Alan Brickman, M.A., transpersonal psychologist, facilitator of a support group for people healing of AIDS, and author of a forthcoming book which presents a counseling approach channeled through Kevin Ryerson; Yurii Cachero, counselor with Hospice of San Francisco, working with people with Acquired Immune Deficiency; Elaine Chiodi, secretary/xeroxer/human being extraordinare; Misha Cohen, C.A., co-founder of the Quan Yin Center of Chinese Medicine and the San Francisco AIDS Alternative Healing Project; Doug Fraser, masseur and bodyworker; Danaan Lahey, student of Zen Buddhism, homeopathy, and healing; Carolyn North, healer through dance, writer, and co-author of a forthcoming book on the endocrine system; D.R., a person healing of Acquired Immune Deficiency who is familiar with the channelings of Edgar Cayce; Michael Rabinoff, N.D., of the San Francisco AIDS Alternative Healing Project; Irene Smith, M.T., contributor to this book and founder of the massage program for Hospice of San Francisco and people diagnosed with AIDS; Paul Steutzer, N.D., student of acupuncture and Chinese herbs. Present in spirit but absent because of a shiatsu and Breema bodywork teaching commitment was Irene Newmark, certified acupuncturist and Chinese herbalist, nutritional consultant, and selfless healer, whose work with Gurudas, Kevin Ryerson, and others contributed to the channeling and development of many flower essences. She must be credited with helping to focus the proceedings and, along with Kevin, guiding the evolution of this entire book.

CHAPTER 14

EXCERPT FROM *THE SOUL'S PATH:*

A Group Channeling with Kevin Ryerson, October 9, 1985

Question: *Is there a relationship between suppressing specific emotions and cancerous cells?*

Answer: *Oh, absolutely.*

Question: *Which ones?*

Answer: *Generally, jealousy, fear, and anger. They're all natural, but when they're not expressed correctly, and are suppressed in the body, they can contribute to cancer.*

For instance, jealousy is a form of covetousness, but actually it is the desire to promote the well-being of other individuals, because true jealousy would be that a parent would be jealous for the concerns of the infant—do you understand this? So ultimately the flip side of jealousy is that it can be benignly channeled.

Anger is little more than the ability to feel one's frustrations. And if one cannot feel one's frustrations, they are suppressed, until eventually they become a disorder. So actually it's positive to be able to feel it, as long as it is channeled properly, because you can then rid yourself of the frustrations.

Fear is probably the biggest crippler of all. Faith in the Mother-Father God usually gets rid of that one.

Question: *Would that same reference also have to do with the area of the body? Would the place where a dis-ease manifests be a key to what the suppression might be?*

Answer: *Most definitely. The dysfunctional tissues have been isolated in many theories as having very specific meaning. For example, the associa-*

tion with Acquired Immune Deficiency is a complete collapse of the thymus, the central factor in the immune system.

This is because Acquired Immune Deficiency truly becomes active among parts of the populace whom the rest of the social order have disinvested or shunted off or turned their hearts off to.

And it truly becomes even worse when they turn their hearts off to themselves. It's the issue of keeping the commandment of loving your neighbor as yourself. The best form of healing is embracing God within your life to start with.

CHAPTER 15

THE NATURE
OF THE HEALING PROCESS

The Channeling:

John: *Hail.*

Group: *Hail, John.*

Jason: *Before we begin the channeling on the healing process, I'm wondering if you have some specific things to say to us as a group or to the individuals in this group.*

John: *This particular group has, indeed, seen, or crossed paths before. The predominant factor is, of course, the common factor of being healers. But, above all else, seeking the spiritual process involved in healing.*
    You have seen common days together in both Atlantis and Egypt during the days of Iknahton and Imhotep. Also during the days of the developing Mycenian kingdoms, in the regions of Crete, and the Therapuutae (the early physicians) of Greece, the Essenes and other points of incarnation.
    The prevalence of the common denominator of the healer is that you have the beginning, the focus, and the nexus of a core group of healers who are indeed as though, a generation of healers who shall see in the next seven-year cycle the beginnings of transitions that shall bring about the transformation of the whole of the healing institution itself. Do not think of "medical institution," but moreso "healing institutions," for that is indeed what the individuals persevere for; not medicine, but healing itself, which we sense you desire discourse upon, and we shall proceed with at this time.
    State general outline of desired discourse.

Jason: *We would like three separate discourses, each with a question and answer period. The first discourse would be on the nature of the healing process; the second one on the issues of immunity and psychoimmunity; and the third and final discourse on how all of the above relates to the specific case history of the health crisis of our time, Acquired Immune Deficiency.*

John: *As such. First, you would find that the healing process itself is the alignment of the physical, the mental, and indeed the spiritual dimensions. These three interlocking dimensions of the individual are literally alignment of three levels of consciousness. For even now it is being discovered that the physical body is a conscious entity in itself, and that each cell possesses a conscious factor within itself. This particular factor of consciousness is critical, and indeed, is the healing process itself. For all dis-ease itself is a break or a dysfunction within this consciousness process.*

For ye would find that, philosophically, the spirit is the life, the mind is the builder, and the physical is the result. So thus, in application to disease, all disease originates in a state of consciousness, whereas though, for purposes of definition, the physical body itself is merely as though a dense or biochemical or bio-energy form or state of consciousness. It is not truly even a seat of consciousness, but is a state of consciousness.

The mind is indeed a more refined state of consciousness that has the capacity to experience a broader range of memory and a broader sense of awareness.

Finally, then, the spiritual dimension is a function or a phenomenon of consciousness that can exist in a more intangible state. Here we have two models to suggest: one model is that the spirit is but a phenomenon of superconsciousness, or the intangible qualities that affect any collective mind, group dynamic or other accord. These can be cultural, societal, religious, psychological in the sense of group dynamics, peer group pressures, and various other accords.

And then there is a second model: it is the ability of consciousness to function independent of a physical framework. These are evidenced in such phenomena as telepathy, out-of-body experience, near-death experience, past-life recall, and other accords.

With these three defined states of self, we would give further definition for the sake of our discourse. The physical body is the subconscious. It is a state of consciousness that lies just beyond the perimeters of the conscious mind, which, as already established, is a greater range of awareness. The conscious mind is the mental, the intellectual or the personal framework of reference that an individual has personal awareness of concerning their conscious activities and behavioral patterns. Finally, the spiritual is a state of hyperextension of consciousness or, simply expressed, the superconscious.

In this framework, then, the healing model is the alignment of all three levels of these states of consciousness. First, the most easily stated in misalignment is the subconscious. This is corrected by restoring alignment in the body physical—the subconscious framework throughout the muscular tissues, individual cellular memory, the neurological tissues, and the various other specialized tissues which are best related to in the Oriental systems of consciousness. Even various specialized tissues such as heart, lungs, and kidneys store—let us be specific here—specialized ranges of awareness.

When there is a mis-rapport between that which is consciously perceived and that which indeed is consciously stored in the subconscious—when they become misaligned—then indeed the effects are cumulative and able to bring about cellular dysfunction in the sympathetic conscious dimensions. For instance, in the heart are stored predominantly issues concerning the parent image known as the father, issues of harmony, and other accords. In the kidneys, primarily unreasonable fears, or hidden fears. In the abdomen, here we deal with issues of the maternal (the mother) and other accords. The intention of this discourse is not to outline all the specialized function of the tissues, but merely to make suggestion.

When there is suppression of the conscious dimensions of any traumas that are stored in the specialized tissues, eventually dis-ease will enter the physical body, not through any outside invading organism, but by the susceptibility of the specialized tissues because of their entering into a state of conscious dysfunction, through a principal of suppression.

For health itself is a continuous and ever-expanding state of consciousness. Dis-ease is the suppression of consciousness; the healing process is the restoration of flows of consciousness and increasing awareness. This is observed in mundane psychologies and is noted as "psychosomatic illness." Many allergies are noted, for instance, as being psychosomatic in nature, even to the point of, again, specialized tissue dysfunction, which we would state as moreso synonomous with consciousness or awareness dysfunction.

In ordinary psychologies, it is considered that the roots of consciousness lay in events that have occurred, shaping certain natural and instinctual energies in the body physical, such as the maternal, the sexual, often as though some of the natural emotions, such as jealousy, fear of falling, anger, and other accords in the same. Traumatized events become stored in the specialized tissues and then lead to later psychosomatic illness.

It is generally noted that stress may leave the body physical open to many invading outside organisms. We would agree with this principle, that indeed dis-ease may be aggravated by outside organisms, such as viruses, bacterias, and other accords. But the true statement is that the lack of expanding awareness is the true seat of all illness and dis-ease.

Having outlined the familiar territories of psychosomatic illness, we would then begin to state the final primary area of discourse: psychospiritual dysfunction. This particular aspect we would find in the following: All disease has its roots in that which is termed as "karma," or conscious acts taken within the superconscious dimension. Trauma that has carried over from issues such as past lives or past life recall from the collective unconscious, may bear as much influence cumulatively upon an individual as any trauma or actions that had occurred in their childhood. For even as events in childhood may shape the adult personality, events in past lives may shape entire lifetimes. This is the true roots of all dis-ease. Here again, the ceasing of the expansion of the awareness is the primary disorder wherein disease may enter and reach the seat of the physical framework called the body physical.

But here is the question: When is dis-ease? When it lies in the mind, or only when it reaches the physical body? Expanding this definition, when is dis-ease, when it lies in the spirit, the mind, or only when it reaches the body physical?

Collectively speaking, we have also defined that the spiritual dimension, or mind existing independent of the physical framework, is that disease may indeed originate in social dysfunctions. The socially disinvested, for instance, are as a primary example of issues involved in some case histories, that poverty, social isolation and other accords are primary examples of the ceasing of expanding awareness. Prejudices are stagnation in the consciousness process; these would be as though primary examples of the origins of social dis-eases.

Having laid down these definitions, then, we would state that the healing process is the alignment of mind-body-spirit, or increasing awareness upon the conscious level from two sources: superconscious and subconscious. First, the acceptance of any given history that the individual has experienced, becoming consciously aware that it is indeed the roots in the dynamics of, not the person's character, but their behavior, for character and behavior are not synonomous. Behavior is peripheral. Character is the core, or the nature or the id of the individual. Dis-ease often enters in when conditional behaviors are associated with character.

Finally, then, the other source is superconscious. Full integration into a social, cultural and ethnic orientation, indeed, is critical to the healing process, but also, then, in the second model, the knowledge that an individual has infinite potential brings in transcendence of the dis-ease state, for a party, knowing that indeed they have the capacity of infinite potential, often will transcend social limitation or social disinvestment. They will transcend even physical limitations or mental limitations.

So thus the healing process is increasing awareness of the true nature of the self, which includes mind, body, and spirit, or the alignment of su-

perconscious, conscious, and subconscious. Methods and techniques to align same would be meditation, for meditation is a learned process. Body-mind theories integrating the mind and the physical form through such techniques as acupressure, acupuncture, diet, biofeedback, stress reduction and other accords are indeed enhancers to the learning of the true meditative process, and eventually these phenomena should be internalized, to where the person becomes self-healing (or self-actualizing), integrating mind, body, and spirit. For that is the healing process.

The pathways through which this integration occurs are through such phenomena as the meridian systems, the spiritual centers known as the chakras (which are the mild biomagnetic fields surrounding the seats of the specialized tissues, aligning along the primary spinal column, or the physio-kundalini passageways), and a gaining in a superior understanding that indeed it is as though energy fields which stimulate cellular memory, versus those energy fields that are a byproduct of cellular function. For instance, it is becoming slowly noted that the neurological tissues precede the healing of other specialized tissues; for it is the electrical fluidiums that stimulate the cellular consciousness and stimulates the healing process on the physical level.

But, mind ye, the neurological tissues, what then stimulate them? The meridians, for they follow the meridians, and the ethereal fluidiums are the biomagnetic fields of the body physical. For we would state the following: The human aura, or the biomagnetic fields, are functions of consciousness independent of the physical body; so, in turn, are the chakras. For the meridians are the nervous system of the superconscious, whereas the neurological tissues are the nervous system of the conscious mind, or the physioconscious mind, and the body physical is the subconscious, through cellular memory. Alignment of these three processes is the healing process. Meditation is the key here.

Further question?

Jason: *When you say "meditation," could you be more specific as to what you mean?*

John: *Alignment of mind-body-spirit.*

Jason: *So, meditation could include, for example, sitting and counting one's breath, or it also could be listening to a Louise Hay tape or Margo Adair or Emmett Miller. . . anything that aligns.*

John: *Correct.*

Jason: *Would you please define what a healer is.*

John: *One who facilitates a meditative process. One who aligns mind-body-spirit, through the many tools: Nutrition, for instance. Superior nutrition often in its first advantages alleviates stress. Stress in the body physical is often toxins and allergic reactions from inappropriately-digested foods. One is never truly allergic to food. For food does not act on the body; the body acts on the food. And in this you would find it is not an allergic reaction to the food; it is the inappropriate digestion of the food, probably finding its link in the salivic, the pancreatic, or the liver's areas of dysfunction, enzymal dysfunction, or the phenomena of the hydrochloric acids. Perhaps the highest gift of the spirit is healing, for it begets harmony and allows the person then to mend the temple in whence they would go to meditate and contemplate their own nature.*

Misha: *I was wondering if a macrobiotic diet is the most appropriate diet, or what type of diet would be the most appropriate diet for people with immune deficiencies?*

John: *Primarily, that which detoxifies. This, of course, is highly specialized to each unique individual, and each individual, we would suggest, would not go to extremes but to singular disciplines to isolate any allergies. But we would suggest that macrobiotics could indeed be as one of the better understood general dietary patterns that could be pursued, although with a careful increase in the amounts of fruits in the diet, particularly those highly enzymal, for purposes of detoxification. And careful monitoring of fasting would also be wise, in the same. To bring clarity to initial point, allergies lead to stress; nutrition leads to reduction of allergies, and thus to stress, thus accomplishing a superior integration of mind and body, and also then, spirit.*

Jason: *Ecton, the Spirit Entity who comes through San Diego-based trance channel Richard Lavin, recently suggested that to say that someone needs healing is to say that there's something imperfect with them, that people don't need "healing." Can you talk about that in relationship to what it is to be a healer, and what it means "to heal?"*

John: *To heal means to love, to have altruism. For initally the healer is the highly altruistic individual, who would seek, even if it is at their own expense, to promote the well-being of another. So thus is means to be a loving being. And it means to recognize the perfection in another, and desire to see that perfection manifest.*

Jason: *God bless. Thank you. People who are not familiar with the concept of karma might infer from your previous comments that we did something wrong in our past life and are now paying for our mistakes in this one. That is, people bring to the principle of karma a guilt-blame mentality. Please discuss this.*

John: *Simply expressed, even as you would not judge harshly the actions of a child—at least those with patience would not do so—so in turn each lifetime is but an event in the childhood of the soul. So karma does not exist as a punitive measure; no one is punished through karma. It is merely the repetition of corresponding or similar events that allow an individual to note that there is a harmonious system by which indeed they may experience themselves in actions in exact measure that they have accordingly taken, either in childhood and/or even in past lives. And in this, then, karma exists for one reason only: that karma and understanding are synonomous. Ye should never judge thyself by results, particularly physical results. Ye should only judge thyself by the process and to the degree to which ye have improved thyself. Karma and result-based thinking are highly similar.*

Never judge thyself by karma, for it exists only for ye to gain understanding. And all that ye must understand is that ye are part of a greater and infinite sense and order of things, and that thy karma must be experienced into that relationship or that greater order. For simply, ye are part of God and God is love. Experience everything uncompromisingly as an opportunity to increase thy understanding and to increase and learn to restore harmony to all things. And then there is no karma; there is only learning. So judge not any lifetime, for it is but an event in the childhood of the soul.

Jason: *That could not be clearer, John. Thank you. Your discussion of karma and judgment led me to think about abortion. Would you briefly address this subject?*

John: *Does not abortion occur in nature? Do ye not call this miscarriage? This is said then that perhaps it was God's will and that the child of the Soul had not yet decided to incarnate. When the parent perhaps decided that they are not fully matured in their adult perspective, and to carry the child to term may not be either in the best interest of the child or of the parent, and a medically-induced abortion is incurred, this is not synonomous with murder. Indeed, it was also aligned as a choice of the Soul to perhaps have the experience of that particular choice on the part of the par-*

ent. The Soul itself will eventually incarnate at the appropriate moment of incarnation.

The Higher Wisdom we would suggest is indeed to carry to full term, within the given emotional status of the parents as to a mature decision. If then the parents decide it is not within their full capacity to raise the child to full term, then perhaps it is wise to proceed with adoption to those parents who may bring the child to a fuller maturity.

Jason: *What kind of an experience would the Soul get from choosing to be aborted?*

John: *Often the state of the womb is a state of perfection, and may temporarily complete a conscious link with the earth plane to necessitate the final links of karma. Or it may prove to be a preliminary state before the final incarnation. But it is generally linked to karma, and karma begets understanding.*

Jason: *When is a fetus inhabited by the Soul?*

John: *It varies. Generally around the fourth or fifth month. But sometimes not until after birth.*

Jason: *Why might the Soul not inhabit the body until after birth?*

John: *Why not? Ensoulment is a process—the same that waking up in the morning is a process. Your desire to remain comfy and unawakened is perhaps the Soul coming in slowly, fingernails dragging.*

Jason: *What is the purpose of the Soul coming in slowly to the physical body?*

John: *Sometimes the knowingness that the Soul is bringing in is so tremendous that to bring about ensoulment suddenly would result in the tissues not being able to handle it. Einstein was such an individual. That's why he didn't speak until he was 3.*

Jason: *Now that we're on the subject of "choice" and "responsibility," I wonder if you could address these issues as they relate to dis-ease? One difficulty in conveying to people what these concepts mean is that when one talks about choosing what happens in one's lifetime or specifically about "choosing one's illnesses," many people again get caught up in Judaeo-Christian guilt and "blame" themselves for "choosing their illness." Perhaps there are words other than "choice" that are more suitable for conveying the judgment-less essence of this concept.*

John: *There is only one choice: that is, to indeed experience the event directly as it may occur, and gain understanding. For the only thing that you learn is how little you knew before; and all that which is not worth learning is preserved in books. So do not concern yourself here, either. It is not issues of choice.*

If a person wishes to alleviate issues of guilt, it is but that they must take note of the following: Love God, with all thy heart, mind, strength, and soul, and thy neighbor as thyself, and you can break no other law. Ye can transgress against no one. So therefore you must love self, rather than as though burdening self with guilt. For then ye may as though keep all the commandments, all the natural laws—these including social laws, divine laws, personal ethics and others—if ye come from this understanding, this one center of self.

Jason: *What about the issue of responsibility, as it relates, for example, to taking resoponsibility for one's own healing process, as opposed to looking for someone to give you the magic pill or shot that will make you well?*

John: *It is wise to discriminate those who have wisdom in the ways of healing, for this is an issue of right fellowship. The individual will also find that much of their healing can be dependent upon issues of right fellowship: not only as though seeking those individuals knowledgeable in ways in which they may promote and facilitate their healing process, but also those who would facilitate their other needs of general well-being. For the appropriate thought form is not that they are dying of a dis-ease, but they are living with it. And to live to the fullest extent is the integration of mind, body, and spirit, and so, therefore, is the healing process. So seek the fellowship of those who promote thy capacity to live, as though within a harmonious orientation, as to how you would perceive self and meeting thy true needs. Is this to your understanding?*

Jason: *Yes, thank you.*

Misha: *To return to the issue of karma—in Tibetan medicine, karma is considered only one aspect of dis-ease; there are other aspects, including evil spirits, and illness that comes just in this lifetime. Please clarify what you said about all dis-eases being a result of karma.*

John: *Is not karma actions taken in a conscious context?*

Misha: *Yes.*

John: *Are not so-called "ill spirits" simply conscious entities? (Yes.) Are they not as though but a collection of actions taken in a conscious context? (I believe so.) So therefore, is not karma "actions taken in a conscious context?" So, therefore, ye would only attract unto self those particular thoughts or thought-beings that are synonymous with thy karma. So thus, karma itself, or actions taken in a conscious context, may be stated as the root of the dis-ease itself. Is this to your understanding?*

Misha: *Thank you.*

Carolyn: *I wonder if what you are referring to as "cellular memory" is the same thing as what you have at other times referred to as "genetic memory," and if you could explain how cell memory is shaped and its relation to DNA in the cell nucleus?*

John: *What is the pattern that the kundalini traverses? Is it not the shape of two intertwining serpents? (Yes.) Is not the kundalini, when all the chakras open, the sum total of the spiritual revelation when the crown is open? (Yes, that is my understanding.) So therefore it may be said that the intertwining serpents indeed are as perhaps a model of, or a pattern of, superconsciousness. Would this be tenable? (Yes.)*

Then, in genetic function, is not then the DNA an aspect of cellular memory, or genetic memory? (I would think so.) What is the shape of the DNA modicule? (The same as the shape of the kundalini.) Correct. So therefore it is as though the ever-infinitely more finely crystallized, specialized cellular memory are as though reflections of the higher self, the consciousness. (Yes.) So therefore remember this: Matter follows thought; *and indeed, if final thought is the shape and the passageway of the kundalini, would it not then stand to reason, that matter would be shaped in its own similar image? (Exactly.) Behold: "Let us make man and woman in our image, even to the cells of their being." Is this to your understanding?*

So thus, even intuitively, medical science's greatest triumph was known by the ancients. Cellular memory is but a reflection of what the soul knows. For indeed, if the kundalini is the opening of those spiritual centers, it traverses in a similar double spiral helix; so in turn it is but a reflection of the phenomenon of the Spirit's activity. The cell is a carrier of a level of expression. Even as the cell may reproduce the whole of the physical be-

ing, so in turn does a single thought of the Spirit reproduce and contain the whole of the higher self.

Cellular memory thus means the ability of the body to reach a full level of illumination and to participate, in the sense that each single cell may hold that (illumined) knowingness, and may express it—it is not contained in, but may be expressed—through such phenomena as the genetic code or genetic memory, as a tool of that expression.

Jason: *And a way to achieve this kind of illumination and consciousness is through meditation?*

John: *Correct. Does not the mind extend itself to all quadrants of the body physical? Cannot the heartbeat be stilled? Cannot a single cell be commanded to multiply? Is this to your understanding?*

Jason: *We would now like a discourse on issues of immunity and psychoimmunity.*

John: *Psychoimmunity should be specifically linked to the issues of—where there is dysfunction in the conscious mind—to either subconscious or superconscious states, bearing along the following principles: In subconscious, ye animate or activate as though the principle of suppression. Through suppression, which is primarily as though simply expressed, the principle of denial, tensions come to be held in specialized areas of the tissues in the body physical. (Again, to the paternal, the heart; to the maternal, the abdomen; to paranoias and hidden fears, the kidneys.) Various combinations of these dysfunctions, or principles of denial, enter into the phenomenon known as psychosomatic illness.*

We would state, or further advance the model, that the tissues are so highly specialized that individual patterns of tissue dysfunctions are synonymous with consciousness dysfunction, through a principle of suppression or denial—usually through cumulative events that have occurred in childhood. These continuing patterns of consciousness dysfunction can eventually allow other organisms of a similar vibratory principle to enter into the body physical and further aggravate the cellular memory or the cellular function, which then medical science would finally recognize as dis-ease. This is the issue, then, that eventually is considered as an overall phenomenon known as general immune dysfunction, or low immunity, or involving issues of stress.

We find next, then, that in our secondary model of psychospiritual immune dysfunction, we address and deal with the issue of transcendency—

the refusal to work with the higher ideals or the higher memory function of the individual. For instance, in the manic depressive state, it is not so much an individual dwelling upon the negative, but indeed is moreso a refusal to accept a higher persepective of self. It is not low self esteem; it is the lack of spiritual sense of self. A transcendent principle, a lack of ability to perceive of a higher future state for self. This indeed is a spiritual dysfunction; it is the inability to bridge to a broader social context. It is as though there is a disinheritance, perhaps of ethnic context, cultural context, and other accords; these in turn may be used to restore the phenomenon of self-esteem.

So, once again we have issues of consciousness dysfunction. Also, it may be as though in our second model of superconsciousness, a dysfunction to come to learn a karmic lesson, and to transcend that lesson and bring in a higher understanding of self. So, once again, we would find as though that psychoimmunity is a skillful integration of mind-body-spirit for increasing awareness of one's self.

Further question?

Jason: We've seen a real rise in dis-eases that have at their core immune dysfunction, such as AIDS, arthritis, allergies, and candida; the list seems to go on and on. Why are we seeing such a rise in immune suppression at this time?

John: Because, when there is a cutting off of any particular individual and/or group from a higher collective consciousness, this becomes as though synonymous with issues involving consciousness dysfunction, which we say is synonymous with dis-ease itself. For, take careful note, here we have two extremely isolated sectors of two extremely different populaces. One is those whose sexual orientations are considered as though to be homosexual in nature. This socially disinvested group, because of rising social pressures in same, has become as though subject to the phenomenon of dis-ease, by being cut off from a sense of being socially integrated and accepted as a collective entity by a large populant sector. And there is a slow and graduating dis-ease rate in that populace because they are cut off from that larger social awareness. An increasing phenomenon of self-esteem, and other accords listed earlier in the discourse (would help reverse this process).

A secondary populace to whom there are exact and parallel histories of dis-ease and dysfunction are black communities, isolated in southeastern regions of the country, who, although more upon a basis of a heterosexual community, suffer exact parallel dis-ease case histories. Common *denominator— socially disinherited, cut out as though from an increasing perspective of themselves as being psychologically integrated into the collective consciousness. Remember again, collective consciousness in the physical model is one model of superconsciousness.*

Also, these abilities then convolute and turn a normally outward perspective and examination of the self to an inward and internal, first analytical, and then eventually self-destructive conscious process. Common phenomenon: consciousness dysfunction—blockages in expanding awareness of self in sense of citizenship, social framework, and also the beginning to spiritually disinvest themselves. And so thus entering in issues of the disease state and the breaking down of the natural state of their psychology, or harmonious psychology, and the ceasing of self-actualization. And thus, immune dysfunction, a psychoimmune dysfunction.

Alan: *John, you have explained that the subconscious is synonymous with the body, and that things from a person's childhood, when denied, can get stored in the subconscious, therefore inducing dis-ease in the body. You presented a similar model in terms of the superconscious, saying that disease can come about from our collective past life experiences, manifesting through the vehicle of the chakras. Would some of these superconscious informations, if denied, also lodge in the body?*

John: *Correct. The means in which they lodge in the body is that often, as though, the events in the childhood are as though collectively synchronistic with events that have occurred in past lives. That is the mechanism by which the two forces become lodged or cease their conscious expansion at the cellular level. Is this to your understanding?*

Alan: *I think so. Now, as the chakras are working all the time, we're always integrating this information. If there is suppression in the adult life, this also, then, would be dis-ease-producing, and would eventually manifest in the body. (Correct.) Is there a way that a healer can differentiate between material that is subconscious in origin and material that's superconscious in origin?*

John: *There is no need to differentiate. It is that the individual should integrate both, in same. However, as a general rule of thumb, usually past-life is superconscious, and events that coordinate with the historical events in this lifetime are subconscious. Is this to your understanding?*

Alan: *Thank you.*

Misha: *John, you said earlier, in terms of the collective consciousness, that dis-ease can be generated by situations of social, cultural, economic and/or political disinheritance and disinvestment. What would you see as the vehicle for redirecting the collective consciousness in order to help those who are cut off from the collective consciousness?*

John: *First, the acceptance uncompromisingly that all are human beings. You're not dealing in civil rights issues or other accords in the collective and social framework; ye are dealing with human issues. So thus the uncompromising acceptance of all as human beings, unconditional of race, unconditional of sexual orientation, unconditional of gender, unconditional of any accord, but accepting all as human beings. And, then carefully reviewing the wisdoms that each individual or each collective group of individuals have, as though, preserved. These would then be higher degrees of social tolerance, high degrees of ethnic tolerance, and other higher ideals, thus preserving cultural contexts and others which may have an extreme degree of value to personal identity. Is this to your understanding?*

Misha: *Yes, it is. Thank you.*

Jason: *I feel that I need to ask one of my questions again, John. Herpes, candida, and AIDS are three dis-ease states that have really—certainly in the United States—taken over public consciousness, and seem to be running rampant. Can you talk about why they are manifesting at this time, from the perspective of mind, body and spirit?*

John: *First, many of these dis-eases are considered, as though, to be sexually transmitted within same. There is a great desire for intimacy on the part of individuals, or to share intimately in same. This is connected with the process of the lower chakras, in same. Greater intimacies and greater freedoms on the part of individuals concerning the issues of their sexuality is a use of the lower chakras as though to force and break down social taboos, and to allow the inter-mixtures of individuals. For by many years, the suppression of the rights of individuals concerning human issues in sexuality, or rights of intimacy and other accords, have been as used to separate races, suppress persons of specific sexual orientations, and other accords in same. This is the first burst of this generation to break down those barriers, phenomenas of exploring the accord, simultaneously holding down an overinvestment in medical models—to be able, as though, to clear self of what was felt to be, as though, medical conditions, in same—made individuals lacking in greater sensitivity towards intimate partners and other accords, in some basic issues, such as hygienes and other accords, in same.*

Slowly but surely, a returning of the state of balance is not only, as though, an issue of hygiene, but moreso an increased sensitivity towards other parties and persons, not as a moral issue, but as an issue of sensitivity in the human dimension, and even as a pragmatic issue. Thus, spiritually, the link to the lower chakras—issues of freedom, creativity, and sensitivity, and understanding, the first three chakras. Now that there is, as though, a stabilization, ye have entered a period of preservation. For ye have only one of two choices in the increase of what ye call these dis-ease states, and they are consciousness issues. Ye have a choice of fear and isolation, which medically you call quarantine, and is often excuse for others to not have to further expand their consciousness concerning the phenomena of their brothers and sisters and their other fellow human beings; or ye have the choice of understanding, and knowing that there is a deep need for increased *sensitivity, particularly again to those of the socially disinvested, to whom, as though, these states or conditions are not punitive, but indeed to whom these states and conditions feed upon.*

And until you learn that you are thy brother's and thy sister's keeper, ask not for whom the bell tolls, even as thy sage has said. For this dis-ease will not be as though contained, it must be confronted, and understanding and sensitivity and altruism and love and embracing the spiritually, the culturally, the socially disinvested are *the keys. For you do not live in a physical environment, you live in an environment of people, as a social and spiritual order. For even as ye have, as though, many thoughts, yet only one mind, so in turn there are many souls, yet only one God. For each of ye is a thought within the Divine Mind, and the Divine is simply love, and that is all ye need to understand.*

Jason: *On this note, would you please discuss both the phenomena of human sexuality and its specific manifestation as homosexual attraction between two men or two women.*

John: *Human sexuality and human relationships are practically synonymous, in that human sexuality is not to be found in the sexual act itself, but as a whole stage and a continuous energy with each and every individual. Human sexuality was stimulated within the physical form for the express purpose of drawing persons into, and negotiating, levels of intimacy. Sexuality is not desired as any form of barrier which would create self-conciousness within the self; moreso, it is designed to draw all individuals into human relationship. For human relationship is where ye have negotiated levels of intimacy with each other. Ye would find that negotiated intimacy and open intimacy are the very cornerstones by which ye have interactivity* with each other, which indeed is life itself. And one of the cornerstones is that magnetic force and attraction which is human sexuality.

To understand human sexuality, each person must take it upon themselves to become at one with their own sexuality. The only way to obtain this is not by dividing selves into roles of male and female, but moreso to merge those roles totally within the self. For it is only when the androgynous state comes upon the individual, where the individual accepts the self as both male and female, that both the self, and therefore everything about the individual, becomes liberated.

In the struggle of humankind, the first great oppression is that of sexuality. Having kindled one of the stronger human instincts within the self—the desire to have intimacy, to nurture, and reproduce—herein this translates into powerful, tangible political and social forces, by binding up the roles of male and female, and proclaiming, for instance, that only males may be the succeedors to properties, or only females may be the true source through which lineages pass, or by bonding persons in marriage that goes beyond free will, or binding persons' sexualities as though they become worthy of only various levels of imprisonment. It is only when each person becomes androgynous within their own right, and non-judgmental of other personage's sexuality and its expression (as long as it is of the consenting element), and all the diversifications of human sexuality merge and find a common path in the expression, that sexuality becomes the liberating influence, and yet the bond which is common to all.

Human sexuality is a magnetic fluidium that flows forth from all persons. It acts as an attractive force, not only upon a biological principle, but upon a literal magnetic principle as well, creating a continuous force to draw individuals into constant areas of human relationships, and then negotiating those relationships as is appropriate for each individual.

Homosexuality is but a sharing of intimacy. The division into male and female created human sexuality, crossing all lines of the experience—heterosexuality, homosexuality, and bisexuality. Each pattern is equal in the lesson. What is important is that each individual in their sexual expression, or rather, the intimacies of human relationship that they are drawn into, are balanced and loving and altruistic.

Sexuality is the attraction between two individuals of a likemindedness according to karmatic patterns, both upon the level of the soul, as well as upon patterns established by the mental, which is the pattern of the personality. The personality is shaped by the immediate environment of this particular lifetime. The principle of reincarnation also is a factor here, in that sexuality, in many rights, is shaped by those things past or from past lives.

Homosexuality, whether it manifests in the relationship between man *and man, or woman and woman, or the desire of copulation of two body physicals of the same sex, is manifested not so much on the level of the body's consciousness, but moreso upon the level of the soul through the body's consciousness. The basic principle of sexuality upon whatever level or system of thought is the dialogue of the body physical in his desire of communication with a system of intimacy. For the completion of any form of sexuality is intimacy between two shared body physicals.*

Homosexuality is neither a case of good or of evil—it is but the functioning of the bodies' dialogues to and with each other. Each body physical has its own means, its own dialogue and its own expression, desiring not so much sex itself, which is copulation between two individuals, but moreso desiring companionship and intimacy upon the levels of the body's own dialogue, from its own consciousness, manifested through the personality, but moreso upon the levels of the soul.

All things come from God, and all things return to God. The nature of sexuality is but a perception and a manifestation in the accord of the spirit. The balance with all these things is upon the level of the soul, and the manifestation of the karmatic pattern may be in any form, including homosexuality, in order to bring forth balance in the nature of one within all.

There are no divisions in God. There is neither male nor female. There is only one God, one love, which is harmony. And harmony is that which must be established between all.

Jason: *Why are so many gays artists, sensitives, and creative people?*

John: *Because as androgynous beings, there's a breakdown of the ego that allows for higher thought to flow in.*

Jason: *Do you consider lesbians and gay men by their very nature more androgynous?*

John: *Correct.*

Jason: *Sometimes they may deny that, but if they're willing to go within and look at their own nature, they will discover in fact that androgyny exists.*

John: *Correct.*

Jason: *Some gay people, instead of positively embracing their homosexuality as a wonderful gift, or as a unique choice of their soul—an experience that affords them a unique vantage point from which they can learn things that they might not be able to learn if they were heterosexual—tend to re-*

sign themselves to the experience. They say, "Well, I don't know if it's a genetic imbalance, or my mother, or what—but whatever it is, for better or worse, this is the way I am."

John: *It is well that there is the acceptance. It is the natural stages of death and dying—the letting go of archetypes from the straight models that have been inbred in them—and a death in the ego. It is moreso that ye are looking upon this that there should be a celebration of the spirit, because ye are spiritually inspired. If they were so spiritually inspired, they would then see all of their extensions of activities—not only their homosexuality, but all their affairs—in that light.*

Jason: *Thank you, John. Let us move on to the third discourse, which of course has already begun, on how all of the above relates specifically to the AIDS phenomenon.*

John: *Indeed, many of the points have already been reviewed. First, in the issue of Acquired Immune Deficiency, an individual must first have, as though, a predisposition of a lowered immune system. This is already beginning to be advanced in certain medical models. That predisposition comes from, as though, simply expressed, stress. Sources of stress: generally, cultural, social or physical disinvestment.*

Channel speaking would suggest spiritual disinvestment is the most crippling. Because of a rise of fundamentalism within religious beliefs, many groups have come to be spiritually disinherited. This fundamentalism cuts across all religious lines. There has also come to be fundamentalisms in issues of race, culture, ethnic, social orientation, and other accords. In other words, crystallizations of thought; not a desire for clarity, but a desire for definition, no matter what that definition. These lead, rather than to an expansion of consciousness, to a convoluted and not even introspective but self-critical and negative-based thinking. First, in communities, then amongst individuals, leading as though to disinvestment, again, in collective consciousness.

This allows then, for constantly mutating organisms to eventually enter one of these singularly isolated collective consciousnesses, where the predisposition of stress from the sources already quoted may begin to prey upon, alter, and eventually mutate to a point where it becomes again a specifically recognizable dis-ease state. Ordinarily benign microorganisms then become malignant, not of their own accord but because of, again, consciousness disinheritance or dysfunction. Ye then label it as dis-ease state when the question should be asked, where does the dis-ease truly lie? It is in the collective consciousness. It is in the spirit of the peoples. That is from whence ye have acquired the immune dysfunction. It is in the mind, and only then in the physical.

Is this to your understanding?

Jason: *Yes. Is HTLV-III, the AIDS virus, ordinarily benign?*

John: *It remains as either in a state of dormancy, for the unique social conditions in its accord had not existed until current planetary and social conditions have existed, in same.*

Jason: *So, it's been hanging around for a long time but it hasn't surfaced because the psychospiritual basis for the dis-ease surfacing wasn't there?*

John: *Correct. No process of incubation.*

Jason: *Thank you.*

Paul: *I use iridology, or frontal eye analysis, in my practice. Are there any signs or ways of determining an AIDS condition by using this procedure?*

John: *Correct. First, are there not, as though, central organisms that are the first to go into a state of dysfunction in the presence of acquired immune deficiency? (Yes.) Isolate that pattern of organs, then, as though relate that pattern to the method of iridology, and you'll have a diagnostic tool; particularly centering upon the thymus, the spleen, adrenals, and pancreas, for these are all the most sensitive organs to have high stress conditions, as well as two of the critical organs to go into a state of dysfunction in actual presence of virus isolated. Is this to your understanding?*

Paul: *Yes, it is. Thank you.*

Misha: *John, I have some questions relating to acupuncture and traditional Oriental medicine, which you have said would be very efficacious in the treatment of AIDS and immune deficiency. Which Chinese herbs are the most efficacious in the treatment of immune deficiency and AIDS?*

John: *I believe some of this information has already been assembled by The Holisitic Group. We would recommend, particularly in the female, the phenomenon known as dong quai. Ginseng in general. And dietary measures, mushrooms, as these are medicinal in nature. Also we would recommend a careful dietary pattern that balances both the yin and the yang, for note that there are both present: night sweats and also chills, for it is a balance in both the energies that is necessary.*

D.R.: *What kind of mushrooms?*

John: *Specifically, those known as the black mushrooms. And those which are first picked, with the smaller caps.*

Misha: *Which acupuncture points and methods would be the best for treatment of people with AIDS?*

John: *Primarily, think moreso in the predominant meridians; however, particularly the meridians associated with the spleen, those known as the triple warmer, and the heart, which also stimulates the thymus.*

Misha: *I've been doing a lot of work with analyzing the syndromes that people diagnosed with AIDS have in terms of Chinese medicine. I would like to name the syndromes that I've come up with, and I'm wondering if you can correct me or add me to the particular syndrome? They are: deficient kidney-jing, deficient kidney-yin, deficient kidney-yang, deficient spleen-chi, deficient lung-chi, deficient lung-yin, and of course toxic heat.*

John: *Look, also, to note deficiency in the heart regions of yang. This would as though complete the syndrome. Is this to your understanding?*

Misha: *Yes, thank you.*

Jason: *Alison, the head nurse on Ward 5-B, the renowned "AIDS ward" at San Francisco General Hospital (now Ward 5-A), asked a question that all of us wish to ask. How can people working with people diagnosed with AIDS help them to open themselves and be receptive to their own healing power?*

John: *The very calming presence that the healer brings by altruism or love is the first step. For love is the healing power, in itself, and the very ability to calm fears is the first healing step. As the healer facilitates understanding they may give gentle positive reinforcement; but do not overstep the bounds, for the individual may withdraw. An increase in the expansion of their awareness, by the very reduction of their fear—that is the first step.*
    Then encourage the individual to live with the dis-ease or the state, rather than, as though, dying from it—this is, then, the second psychological step. Acceptance of the condition, rather than resistance.
    Thirdly, then, facilitate a constant pattern of stress-reduction, then facilitate introductions to the various alternatives that would finally appeal

to the individual as to the models of healing that they would desire to pursue. We would suggest that, since the question centers upon their own abilities of healing, centering upon the phenomenon known as psychoimmunity, as related to creative imagery, would be one of the critical issues, because it is generally accepted that the power of mind is one of the more popular concepts in the collective consciousness to appeal to the broadest number of individuals. So thus creative imagery. Think of phenomenas of psychoimmunity, along with diet and nutrition, stress-reduction, and slowly build the alternatives and case histories. For often the critical turning point to the power to heal is often linked to the popular concept in the collective consciousness, of the ability of mind to heal.

So, thus, improve first their condition of mind through the methods spoken of, then expand their newly-found ability to discriminate and again self-reason, expose them to the broader number of alternatives, depending upon the individual practices of the individual healer. Then on to self-healing, creative imagery, meditation, stress-reduction, and the philosophical concept of living with the dis-ease. Is this to your understanding?

Jason: Yes. Why have so many people with AIDS chosen to leave the body, as opposed to living with the dis-ease, healing, and regaining a unity of mind, body, and spirit in this lifetime?

John: Because it becomes a mechanism perhaps to escape an order of things from which they feel disinvested, and they associate, as though, that with a leaving of the focus—the physical body—that allows them to participate in the experience.

Jason: Anne Strack, who is counseling people at the Pacific Center in the East Bay, says that one of the big fears of people diagnosed with AIDS is of going crazy from the dis-ease's neurological complications. They're scared of the possibility of losing their minds. What particular comfort or information can she provide to them?

John: First, point out the rarity of the phenomenon, even in the most advanced dis-ease states associated with AIDS. Secondarily, if the individuals work with meditation and other accords outlined in the manuscript, these states can indeed be thrown into remission. We find that individuals do not suffer issues of insanity or even coherence, but rather experience more of an Alzheimer effect. This involves a slow remission of personality and a more passive nature. Even if they were to suffer the full range of the affliction, it is not unlike the karma of the stripping away of the ego, and the entering into the deeper and more passive states—retaining, however, a still similar command and lucid consciousness.

Jason: *Are you suggesting that people with Alzheimer's do not suffer because they do not really know what is happening to them?*

John: *It is not a loss of sanity, but rather less and less function in various ranges of the personality. There are archetypes of highly productive individuals in the social order who display similar specialized intelligences and contribute to the well-being of the social order. Individuals who have concern about the loss of their own clarity of consciousness should do work with those whom are born in this manner, and see how those with specialized intelligence—those whom ye would normally call the retarded—contribute to the social order.*

Jason: *I am concerned about people with advanced Alzheimer's. To what extent are these people suffering, or even aware of their condition? Or is this rather a case of the stripping away of the ego?*

John: *It is a biologically enforced stripping away of the ego, and a progressive letting go of the personality and of the physical form.*

Jason: *What does the opportunistic infection cryptococcal meningitis represent in terms of the neurological system?*

John: *It represents the wearing away of the central, sympathetic, and parasympathetic nervous systems. Such conditions are the first examples through which one may begin to discover the critical relationship between the central neurological tissues and the parasympathetic neurological tissues as a function of the immune system. Study the channeling on Psychoimmunity, and the heavy emphasis upon the neurological tissues as a function of the immune system.*

Jason: *Michael, who is present here tonight, has been working in San Francisco to set up a holistic program for healing AIDS on a model, which is very similar to the model that The Holisitic Group presents in this book. He finds that he'll go up to people and tell them that the Macrobiotic Center in New York has been working with a group of people with AIDS for two years, and has 29 of these 30 people either stabilized or in remission, and Russell Jaffe in Vienna, Virginia, has 18 out of 19 people with AIDS in remission. Yet people seem to discount these successes by saying, "Yeah, and I wonder if isoprinosine will work." They just don't seem to focus on these holistic healing successes at all. It seems that people are very much attached to AIDS being a fatal dis-ease, and that it can be cured only through*

Western (allopathic) medicine. Please discuss this belief system, which seems to be clung to so strongly by many people diagnosed with AIDS, the medical establishment and the research establishment?

John: *First, you must understand that the community of healers is a community that must, as though, integrate itself into the framework of other communities. Merely because two communities may be similarly socially disinvested does not mean that there's an immediate psychological agreeance, or that they are allies. You must, perhaps, suggest that they would run their models parallel to each other, in same. Because, if there is a forcefulness to present one absolute choice of either medical or holistic, then as though this is an inappropriate psychology. For is not thy approach to integrate? Allow the individual the capacity to integrate both models, that you would be more quickly progressive. Is this to your understanding?*

Michael: *Well, that partly answers it. I really strongly feel, when I'm talking to people about setting up something like this, a blockage to hearing the idea. . . .*

John: *Pause. Entity desiring to speak. (Tom's voice comes in.)*

Tom: *Tip of the hat to you. MacPherson here, Tom MacPherson. How are you doing there?*

Jason: *We're doing fine. Aren't we? (Yes.)*

Tom: *I'd have to say that quite frankly I think we're dealing in issues of blarney, or selling a position. Is that not correct?*

Michael: *Well, trying to get people to hear it.*

Tom: *That is correct. That is known as blarney. Being Irish, I have a bit of expertise in that area, so I use the term positively. Describe your phenomenon more exactly.*

Michael: *When I try to explain the results that other people have gotten using holistic methods, there's a level of resistance where people cannot hear it—it's like not real to their mind. The conventional medical treatments will produce almost certain death for these people, and these alternative treatments will be getting good results with people who have AIDS. And they can't hear that fact.*

Tom: *Well, again you'll note that your very wording does not allow for the process John spoke of. You tell them that the medical model will produce certain death, do you understand this? So immediately you're telling them that their only choice is your choice. That is not a decision, and there is nothing to hear. And that is the very resistance process that you're experiencing. What you should probably do is isolate those particular medical models that are the most benign [e.g. interferon, thymosin, and Ribavirin]. Perhaps suggest the individuals run a holistic model, parallel to the more benign medical models, and isolate in the community holistic medical physicians. And I think you would then gain a much more sympathetic ear from these individuals, and that they would be able to entertain your models by taking a more integrated approach. Do you understand this?*

Michael: *I have worked with medical doctors who do utilize holistic methods, and they run into the same resistance when trying to present these alternative approaches. They just don't get very much positive response. On a psychic level, what is this resistance about?*

Tom: *First of all, massive news coverage. You might call it a cultural trance. It is your position that you are working from a strictly educational position, offering straight information. I suggest you're working more from a* deprogramming *position. And so therefore you have to present yourself as even more logical than logic demands.*

In other words, forewarned is forearmed. The more relaxed you are, the more you will have individuals open to the approaches and—I'm not certain—perhaps even regain some of your medical physicians, who are also waving the deathbed approach, saying that it's certain death to go that route. And I am suggesting that you must expand *and allow the individual to feel the sense of what you are, which is an alternative. And a wise person in a position of being an alternative, presents as sympathetic a view of their opponent as possible, so that the person feels they have a choice. Otherwise you are no longer an alternative; you are merely one more person trying to dictate their decision, and that is what the resistance process is. Do you see this, then?*

And you must also work patiently. Once you have presented your alternative, you cannot expect them to make an immediate decision, but present it so that they can mull it over and think about it. Once they start reviewing the information they will probably start being more sympathetic to your educational process. Plus, your particular initial efforts in these areas are probably only 24 months old, do you understand this? And you're coming up against a cultural trance that's anywhere from 20 to 30 years. Plus, your own papers, educational materials are just now beginning to be well-

read and well-received. So I think you should pat yourself on the back for the measure of success you have had to date, and know that your position will only improve, rather than deteriorate.

D.R.: *I'm a person with AIDS, Tom, and I have sort of embraced the holistic approach. . . .I have faith in it. I know that chemotherapy is not in the long run beneficial. But I was wondering, with this embraceable approach to holistics, would it benefit someone like myself to try, for example, vinblastine, in accordance with accepting the holistic approach?*

Tom: *Please describe the blastine process (the word itself almost sounds like blasphemy, doesn't it?)*

Jason: *It's been used a lot in treatment of Kaposi's sarcoma, and they claim it has a high remission rate.*

D.R.: *I believe it's taken intravenously in the hand. It prevents lesions from appearing, or reduces their appearance to, for example, four or five a year in a patient who had 50 or 60 and they were growing rapidly. Of course, these people were using stress reduction and everything else, in accordance with a macrobiotic diet or whatever.*

Paul: *I believe vinblastine comes from the periwinkle plant, vinca. . . .*

Misha: *. . . .which is severly poisionous.*

D.R.: *They do measure it out against your white blood cells, I believe, before they give it to you. So you would get, maybe, 7 cc's once a week, in accordance to how your blood cell count is each time you go. Because if it is poisonous, then it's killing something, and they adjust it.*

Tom: *First of all, the herbalists who are present: Would you have recommended ways of taking the periwinkle plant?*

Paul: *I think the plant is too poisonous to take as a tea.*

Tom: *Yes, but how about homeopathically? (Yes, you can use it homeopathically.) Very good. I would suggest that with certain individuals, in modest amounts, with tremendous detoxification, such as saunas and things to this effect, it might, in chemotherapy form, in the hands of, again, a very— running parallel—sympathetic medical practitioner, it probably could prove to be a degree of an effective therapy. The only key thing is, because of its* *toxic level, it could lead to immune suppression, do you understand this? But again, with tremendous detoxification, in some individual case histories, it could be worked out, but I'd lean more towards a homeopathic preparation. Do you understand this?*

Paul: *Yes. Rudolf Steiner had worked on the mistletoe plant, which is also a poisonous plant, but had given it homeopathically. In fact, the mistletoe is being used in Germany at the present moment for cancerous conditions. How would this react on Kaposi's sarcoma?*

Tom: *Restate your case, here, and list more the symptoms also.*

Paul: *Because of the "principle of similars," the mistletoe, which is a parasitic plant, has been used by Rudolf Steiner and Anthroposophic School to reduce swellings and tumors. This research was done over a hundred years ago. It is now being researched in Europe, and being given homeopathically in serial dilutions to reduce swellings. Since the Kaposi's sarcoma is also a type of lesion, would it work in this case?*

Tom: *Yes. There's even a bit of "doctrine of signatures," because when the mistletoe is removed from its host, it leaves deep lesions in its host plant. So there's even a more parallel "similar." Yes, it would prove to be an effective means, again prepared homeopathically.*

Jason: *I know we've talked a lot about a homeopathic preparation of CMV, which you say is a parallel virus to HTLV-III, and its benefits for people diagnosed with AIDS. Do you have any other specific homeopathic preparations you'd like to mention at this time?*

Dannon: *I want to ask about the miasmic root of AIDS. It seems to me that there's a strong tubercular root.*

Tom: *I would agree with the tubercular root, as it's linked to the emotional framework. But I would say that the true miasmic roots must also be linked to the syphilitic miasm, because the end results are almost highly similar; as well as you are dealing with a two-fold process. This is a virus that mutates in the system. So there are two definite, distinct stages of the dis-ease: tubercular, or the first, is the "context" of the dis-ease, then there's the "final" dis-ease itself, which is more syphilitic in nature.*

Dannon: *Would both tuberculinum and syphilinum be valuable in the treatment of this?*

Tom: *I think you'd find the syphilinum would be more appropriate as the dis-ease reaches its final stages, whereas with those who possibly show immunology signs of the dis-ease, such as, oh, certain T-cell counts, etc. Do you understand this? For carriers, you'd find the tubercular miasmic treatment would be more in order.*

Dannon: *And mercury could also be used, then, or would syphilinum, the germ actually taken from syphilis itself, be better?*

Tom: *Both would be equally effective. Oh, by the way, on expanding your table of elements: the more radioactive radium, and uranium, would also prove highly effective here, with the syphilitic stage.*

Dannon: *Plutonium, also?*

Tom: *Too deadly.*

Dannon: *Too deadly, even homeopathically?*

Tom: *That is correct. Stick with the radium, and the uranium, particularly locked into their "ore states." Finally, for the tubercular states: nitrogen, carbon dioxide.*

Jason: *Basic homeopathic theory asserts that what a substance causes in overdose, it will cure in microdose. Dana Ullman, co-author of* Everybody's Guide to Homeopathic Medicines, *is one of many who have noted the similarity between the symptoms of penicillin overdose and those of AIDS. He wants to know if a homeopathic dose of penicillin would be beneficial in the healing of AIDS.*

Tom: *Correct. Specific usage is up to a homeopath.*

Jason: *How about a homeopathic dosage of cyclosporin, a drug that is known to suppress the immune system?*

Tom: *It may prove beneficial.*

Jason: *It was stated in a previous channeling that if a dosage of penicillin were to suppress the immune system, it would do so for no more than 6 months. Are antibiotics and penicillin a significant co-factor in AIDS if used more than, let's say, four times a year? Or six times a year? Or eight times?*

Tom: *We do not see it as a major issue.*

Jason: *So even if one had recurrent syphilis, and were treated four times in the course of a year with megadoses of penicillin, the penicillin would not be a major factor in immune suppression.*

Tom: *Correct. Except in extremely isolated case histories.*

Jason: *If someone has an allergy to penicillin and antibiotics, would taking them impair the functioning of the immune system?*

Tom: *Some effects. . . .Many allergic reactions, however, can be greatly reduced by a detoxifying diet.*

Jason: *Got it. And of course this detoxifying diet would in turn help boost the immune system.*

Tom: *Correct.*

D.R.: *Are castor oil packs of use in the treatment of AIDS? They're mentioned a lot by Edgar Cayce.*

Tom: *Absolutely. They are excellent cleaners for both the liver and the entire intestinal tract, also allowing for a complete detoxification of the skin's tissue.*

D.R.: *Placed, as Cayce perhaps had mentioned, over the lower right side of the abdomen?*

Tom: *That would be correct. Oh, by the way, in detoxification, another good point to work in this area is just about the fleshy part between the index finger and thumb, extremely effective when working the castor oil pack, as it helps flush the entire intestinal tract.*

D.R.: *How would you do that?*

Tom: *Oh, merely hold it for about 2 to 3 minutes, do you understand this? And make certain the restroom door isn't locked from the inside.*

D.R.: *The castor oil packs would be heated on the surface of the skin?*

Tom: *That is correct.*

D.R.: *And when would you stimulate the area just mentioned, before, after or during?*

Tom: *You may hold during if you'd like.*

Jason: *Tom, you recommended, as a method of healing Kaposi's sarcoma and its lesions, ingesting a selenium solution composed of aloe gel, selenium, and organically bound silicon, plus applying a pack of this directly to the skin. Could you talk about the proportions of the aloe gels, the selenium, and the organically bound silicon?*

Tom: *The selenium and the silicon can probably be gained from sea vegetables, such as kelp. If you want to make a fairly traditional herbal poultice, you could just merely steep the sea vegetables, and place a good two fingers or so smear of aloe vera—having perhaps shredded the sea vegetables—over the general area of affliction, and the skin is a rather mild digestive organism, do you understand this?*

Jason: *Yes, so smear a little aloe vera gel on the lesion, and then throw on some sea vegetables?*

Tom: *That is correct. Or you can dry them. If you wish more exact proportions, I would suggest two fingers—for all of you old-time healers out there—two fingers of aloe vera or—for you more specific types—about three fluid ounces, along with, then, about three to six grams of dried kelp or dulse, or approximately half a fluid ounce of liquid dulse. Mix thoroughly, and then that may be applied to the lesions. Finally, when working with the powdered kelp intermixed with the aloe vera gels, it should be allowed to dry.*

Jason: *When HTLV-III mutates, so that it is no longer recognizable in the physical form, what does it mutate into?*

Tom: *It no longer is just reproducing itself. It finally integrates itself almost totally into the genetic tissues, or the individual specialized cells, that are then in a state of dysfunction.*

Jason: *Ribavirin is an inhibitor of reverse transcriptase that is now being given experimentally to people diagnosed with AIDS. Is Ribavirin in fact a medical model that is an approach to cure?*

Tom: *You say again the word "cure." It can be a process to stimulate the immune, to then generate eventually the body's own states of remission.*

Jason: *And it is valid in that form?*

Tom: *Most definitely.*

Jason: *How would it compare in effectiveness to something like Blue-Green Manna?*

Tom: *Again, we don't wish to compare degrees of effectiveness. It sets up systems that sound like they're competing with each other, when it's a careful integration of them that we desire.*

Jason: *But, in fact, either of them would be able to do that, or to facilitate that process?*

Tom: *That is correct.*

Jason: *You told me that non-oxynol-9, the ingredient in spermicides that has been shown to kill the AIDS virus in laboratory tests, can seriously irritate the anal tissues, perhaps contributing to ulcerations of the anal lining that would leave one quite open to penetration by the AIDS virus. Does it also irritate the vaginal tissues?*

Tom: *That is correct.*

Jason: *Do you have specific things to say to D.R., about the lesions that have been surfacing on his body, besides following the approach outlined by The Holisitic Group?*

Tom: *I think his case history is fairly typical. I believe we examined his case history, and running the parallel on the medical model that he was examining, vinblastine is something he could entertain for himself, provided the amounts were fairly modest. And again massive detoxification, such as saunas three times weekly.*

Jason: *Would it be more efficacious for him to approach it homeopathically?*

Tom: *I would suggest introducing the homeopathics. And since the real concern is certain advancements in lesions, I would suggest treating the surface lesions in manners already outlined. . . .I think his lesions would show a favorable remission.*

Jason: *You had said that echinacea is basically anti-viral. Paul Lee, for*

*example, said that echinacea was 80 percent as effective as interferon, and
directly stimulated the T-cells. Why did you say that echinacea was more
anti-viral, while Blue-Green Manna was more an immune enhancer? What
is the difference there?*

Tom: *Echinacea, you say, stimulates T-cells?*

Jason: *That's what Paul said, he said it directly stimulated the T-cells.
You might disagree with that.*

Tom: *No, I would find running parallels to that, and would agree with
it, and that would parallel exactly my statement as being anti-viral, do you
understand this? (Okay.) The issue of the Blue-Green Manna, you would
find, generally boosts the immune system, in that it stimulates the spleen,
thymus and various other factors in the immune system.*

Dannon: *Can I just ask quickly about phytolacca, or poke root? In terms
of homeopathic principles, it's got a lot of syphilitic manifestations: lesions,
and internal hemmorhages and bleedings, and things like that.*

Tom: *It would prove particularly valuable where the lesions have gone internal.*

Dannon: *Into the bowel?*

Tom: *That is correct.*

Paul: *There is a substance found in Oregon called sacred carrot, known
in Latin as* leptotaenia, *which is supposed to be very effective as an antibiotic, or anti-viral, substance. Might it be useful in treating AIDS?*

Tom: *Do you mean to be taken physically, or homeopathically?*

Paul: *Physically, as a tincture, or as a tea.*

Tom: *Yes, I do believe it would be good for fighting off secondary inflammations, which can often drain the body's immune forces to muster itself
against the major factor, do you understand this?*

Paul: *Yes.*

Tom: *I do believe we're going to have to go soon, since we do not want to drain the instrument. It's been very pleasant speaking with the lot of you, and I do hope we've been of aid. Saints be looking after you. God Bless You.*

Group: *God Bless You, Tom.*

John: *Hail. Seek to be at peace with those things that you receive from Spirit, for you'd find they are to further thy Father's works, and indeed, ye are that work. Walk in this, the Father/Mother God's Light. God Bless You. Amen.*

Kevin *(returning): Hello. Greetings. How are you all doing?*

Another Channeling, April 1986:

Jason: *Tom, Joan McKenna of the Institute for Thermobaric Repatterning has been researching syphilis and the presence of what she has termed the large amount of "previously undetected syphilis" in both people diagnosed with AIDS and the general gay population. With your assistance, The Holisitic Group has already investigated the presence of syphilis in people with AIDS, explaining it in terms of the surfacing of the ordinarily benign syphilitic miasm. I now have some further inquiries on the subject.*

It seems that 14% to 25% of people with syphilis are asymptomatic, and may escape diagnosis altogether, or at least until late in the progression of the dis-ease. Even when people are tested for syphilis, 1% to 2% of the blood tests are false negative. Since 60% to 80% of the individuals who do test positive for syphilis, at least in this area, are gay men, this indicates that there may be a lot of undetected syphilis undermining the health of the gay community and larger human community.

To confound the issue, it seems that people who use a lot of antibiotics or recreational drugs skew up the tests for syphilis, and often register false negative. Joan believes that if one has a long latency period for syphilis, topped off by chemical dependency on drugs or antibiotics, the syphilis may remain isolated from the blood and lodge in the lymphatic or neurological systems, the eye, or even an organ, thereby escaping detection entirely. This all seems quite dreadful.

If it is true that people who are immuno-suppressed by drugs or even HTLV-III may not produce the antibodies to syphilis that would be detected by current tests, how can one accurately diagnose them?

Tom: *The antibodies are still present in the system and can be detected. Furthermore, we would suggest that an allergic reaction to penicillin could connote the presence of syphilis in the system.*

Jason: *Is it usually the case that allergies to penicillin may provide evidence for syphilis?*

Tom: *Correct.*

Jason: *So how do you treat someone for syphilis if they're allergic to penicillin?*

Tom: *For one thing, the syphilis in many of these individuals would be dormant in their system, and present only as the syphilitic miasm. In that case, it could be treated homeopathically.*

Jason: *I'm a little confused here. It seems that the definition of "miasm" in Joan's dictionary is of "latent microorganism." Does this mean that the syphilis itself was in fact always present in a latent state?*

Tom: *A miasm in homeopathic terms means that a person has an inherited disposition to several archetypal dis-ease states. When homeopaths use the term "miasm," it refers to a pre-disposition to a microorganism or, more accurately, to a pre-disposition to a pattern of acute and chronic illness. Anyone versed in homeopathy can explain the distinction.*

Jason: *So do you believe that a lot of the people who show up false negative for syphilis have only the syphilitic miasm, as opposed to having active syphilis in their system?*

Tom: *There is a physiological cause, but it is existing benignly in a safely suppressed state in the system.*

Jason: *If someone has the syphilitic miasm, and then experiences immunosuppression because of AIDS, that miasm may surface in the body in an active state, and often as tertiary syphilis. I assume that one must first get rid of the syphilis before one can successfully heal the person of AIDS.*

Tom: *Correct.*

Jason: *What are alternatives to penicillin to rid the body of syphilis—especially if one is allergic to it?*

Tom: *First of all, the person should explore natural penicillin as an alternative to the synthetic form which is usually used. Secondly, if the person enters a detox program, and then goes on a high vegetarian diet for six months—since syphilis is such a slow progressive dis-ease, and takes years to overwhelm the body, such a complete program of detoxification may in many cases be undertaken—they could overcome the allergic reaction to penicillin.*

Jason: *And that kind of detoxification would certainly be beneficial to a person diagnosed with AIDS.*

Tom: *Precisely. It would run parallel to the program in the book. This in fact is a general way to deal with anyone who has an allergic reaction to penicillin. Penicillin is one of the superior antibiotics around because it is naturally derived. One could even, as an alternative, take in minute quantities of natural, organically-bound penicillin as a dietary discipline, and eventually it would prove effective, with little or no allergic response whatsoever.*

Jason: *What are good natural sources of penicillin?*

Tom: *Basically you could just grow it in the molds and things—not put it through the isolation process—and then take it in minute quantities by incorporating it into the diet. This is a perspective that individuals familiar with nutritional and other alternative approaches to healing will understand.*

Jason: *To backtrack just a bit, I think one of the problems we're dealing with, aside from possible allergic reactions to penicillin, is that people who use a lot of drugs or other antibiotics skew up the test for syphilis, so that even if they do in fact have antibodies to syphilis, these will not be detected.*

Tom: *We would suggest that they fast for several days, while abstaining from the drugs during the diagnostic period. Then the test should work.*

Jason: *What kind of fast would one need?*

Tom: *Ideally a fast of three to seven days, on juice and/or water. Grape juice would prove most beneficial.*

Jason: *Thank you, Tom.*

Jason: *Irene Smith, who has probably massaged more people diagnosed with AIDS than anyone else on the planet, feels that any deep pressure on the skin can cause complications in people with AIDS or AIDS-Related Condition (ARC). In her wonderful workshop for bodyworkers working with people diagnosed with AIDS, she expressed her reluctance to put any deep pressure on KS lesions, for fear of exacerbating the condition. It seems that KS lesions, an official indicator of AIDS, sometimes only manifest internally, and thus escape diagnosis. There are now documented cases of individuals who never manifested KS lesions or any of the other officially-recognized indicators of AIDS, and who died of what appeared to be an AIDS-Related Condition; upon autopsy, they were found to have been manifesting AIDS all along in the form of internal KS lesions. All this leads Irene to believe that, because you can't always tell if a person has KS or not, it is best to avoid deep pressure work on anyone diagnosed with AIDS or chronic AIDS-Related Condition.*

Can one do deep bodywork, such as postural integration, rolfing, or even deep shiatsu on people diagnosed with AIDS or ARC?

Tom: *It depends upon the amount of pressure that is applied, and how it is applied. If you get these bone-cracking therapists who drag out all the screws and hammers and tongs and iron maidens and everything else in their practice, then yes it could be a problem. But if a person practices steady pressure with deep tissue work, or such disciplines as Tragering. . . .in general the pressure work should be steady as you go. It is important to examine the situation on a case by case basis. If lesions are known to be present, either internally or externally, apply the pressure over a longer period of time. There is no way to standardize this. . . .the intuition of the practitioner is the key here.*

The alternative is to use non-force techniques of deep bodywork. One could, for example, use shiatsu, but simply apply the pressure more gradually. When you work the pressure points along the spine, have the person work with breath to expand the bone and muscle. Your job then is simply to guide and facilitate using a non-force technique. Using breath and non-force techniques, you can have just as effective results.

Jason: *So you might even be able to put pressure on the lesions without hurting someone.*

Tom: *Correct. Their own breath is doing the work. If a practitioner has an intuitive sense that deep work is called for in a certain area, simply work on the area longer, and have the person work with a lot of breath. You know when you stick your finger in sand, you part the surface, but the pressure actually extends down much further. . . .in a similar manner, if you apply the pressure steadily, and then have the person work with breath, merely the constant application of a steady pressure is going to get as deeply into the tissue as if you apply a lot of pressure. You're just going to get there sooner when you apply a lot of pressure. And you can even hook the tissue and move, as in postural integration or rolfing.*

Jason: *Aztec healing clay with Bentonite has been used to stop the pain associated with some cases of KS lesions. Is the less expensive red or white clay also effective.*

Tom: *We do not feel there is much of a difference.*

Jason: *Practitioners on the last two holistic healing panels I've either spoken on or covered for The Sentinel are saying that we can definitely keep people alive "until the cure comes," but they don't seem to be willing to say that we can totally rid the body of the virus.*

Tom: *That is true. What one must do is use the word "remission." A holistic program can hold the AIDS virus in remission—period. When it's in remission for X amount of time, and they go in for their tests and it's not there, then that's it—they are healed. This is the wise way for a holistic practitioner to phrase it. When you start using words like "cure" you get in all kinds of hot water.*

Jason: *Does one need to wear gloves if massaging a person diagnosed with AIDS who has open, encrusted, or oozing KS lesions?*

Tom: *If you cover the hands with oil, and always have the oil glide over the surface of the skin, and then you cleanse your hands thoroughly afterwards, this is as good as any gloves.*

Jason: *So I could massage oozing or encrusted lesions?*

Tom: *As long as you work with oils over your hands—but you shouldn't be massaging the lesions anyway, you should be working pressure points about them. Work the blood flows right up to the lesions. Push the blood flows toward the lesions, rather than working them per se.*

Jason: *Why this particular technique?*

Tom: *Because it will promote the energy flowing up towards the lesions.*

Jason: *Well, the lesions are hemorrhages under the skin. Does this mean that by moving the blood flows toward them you help move the blood through the hemorrhages?*

Tom: *That is correct.*

Jason: *And if the lesions aren't open, one can do massage strokes over them?*

Tom: *Quite right.*

Jason: *Are the disinfectants Betadine or Hibiclens, which Irene Smith uses, recommended when massaging a person with herpes, or open lesions, or questionable rashes? Or are the chemicals in them harmful?*

Tom: *They are excellent.*

Jason: *Chinese medical practitioner Misha Cohen said that she has someone who has applied for participation in the San Francisco AIDS Alternative Healing Project program who is taking the sulfur drug pentamidine in prophylactic dosages on the advice of his physician to reduce the possibility of reinfection by pneumocystis. It seems like something like this is just plain detrimental to the body's immune system.*

Tom: *We do not find this advisable. The holistic approach is not to continually dispense antibiotics over a long period of time into the system.*

Jason: *You've said that antibiotics are not a significant co-factor in the rise of AIDS. They are however a significant co-factor in the rise of candida. This confuses me.*

Tom: *It would take a physiological textbook to explain this medically. It's like saying, if two people are identical twins and one caught a cold and the other one didn't, why? You'd have to go through whole medical history of the person, isolate it, etc. . . . .*

Jason: *So, to put it simply, candida works differently in the body than HTLV-III.*

Tom: *Exactly. And this relates to the fact that candida is found more naturally in the body than is HTLV-III.*

Jason: *I've heard some talk of the benefit of ginger foot baths for people diagnosed with AIDS.*

Tom: *Ginger is a stimulant. It stimulates the neurological tissues on the high reflex pressure points on the bottom of the feet, so therefore is an overall stimulus to the entire immune system. Caffeine foot baths will do the same thing, though ginger or jasmine are better on the nervous system.*

Jason: *Irene Smith has massaged some people in advanced stages of AIDS who are experiencing neurological complications which manifest as an Alzheimer's-like state. She has found, upon talking to them, that some of their apparent confusion when, for example, call her their mommy or daddy, is part of them working out "unfinished business" (as Elisabeth Kübler-Ross would put it) from their childhood.*

Tom: *This occurs when the neurons associated with the memory are affected. . . .stress-related issues would come up for clearing. This is part of the letting go.*

Jason: *Do pain-killing drugs such as morphine interfere with this final clearing-out process before death?*

Tom: *No.*

Jason: *Can you comment on the use of oil of melaleuca for the healing of skin lesions.*

Tom: *We do believe that it is applicable to lesions in general.*

Jason: *In parts of Africa, where AIDS is of epidemic proportions, it appears to be mainly a heterosexual phenomenon. Seventy-five percent of all African AIDS cases in fact involve heterosexual women. This transmission of AIDS amongst heterosexuals in Africa (and Haiti for that matter) is usually attributed either to scarification rituals or to the widespread use of shared needles in the injection of penicillin.*

Tom: *Some of that is accurate, but we believe that the majority of cases are attributable to lacerations acquired due to the form of sexual practices of intercourse before the full clitoral or other stimulus or lubrication on the part of the female.*

Jason: *You are referring to a tendency among men to engage in heterosexual intercourse before the woman is fully lubricated?*

Tom: *That is correct. Plus, of course, the element of the higher degree of stress of women in a disinvested culture is operating here, making them more susceptible to the AIDS virus once it enters the bloodstream through vaginal tears.*

In terms of scarification rituals, it would be found that women do not participate in scarification rituals. While some cases of AIDS are spread through shared needles, AIDS will be found amongst people with whom that is not the case.

Jason: *There's a new study that suggests that the exchange of semen in oral sex isn't a significant factor in the spread of AIDS, and that most sexually-transmitted cases amongst gay men are spread when semen enters anal fissures during anal intercourse. I believe that the researchers followed a group of gay men who engaged exclusively in oral sex, and that only one member of that group developed positive antibodies to HTLV-III. Furthermore, it was found that the man who developed positive antibodies had in fact also participated in anal intercourse as the receptive partner.*

Tom: *That is correct.*

Jason: *Is the primary sexual way that the virus is transmitted through the entrance of semen into the bloodstream through anal (and vaginal) intercourse?*

Tom: *That is correct.*

Jason: *Nonetheless, swallowing semen is "risky business."*

Tom: *That is correct.*

Jason: *Will there come a time "after AIDS" when gay men can safely engage in oral and anal sex without the use of condoms?*

Tom: *These are wise sexual practices to begin with, merely to cause drops in other forms of "social" dis-eases.*

Jason: *So the trainings that people have been doing to eroticize "safe sex" and condoms will continue to be beneficial?*

Tom: *That is correct.*

Jason: *I've noticed since the rise of AIDS the emergence of studies suggesting that human seminal plasma and spermatozoa themselves can suppress immunity. According to a section on this subject in a recent book on the immune system, the biological "reason" for the alleged immunosuppressive nature of sperm is to enable them to travel through the "hostile" territory of the female reproductive tract. It is suggested that a woman's system senses sperm as foreign invaders, or antigens, and resists them by attacking them with antibodies; these in turn must be fought off by the sperm in order for them to survive their mission of fertilization of the egg.*

This book goes on to suggest that when a man repeatedly exposes himself to many different sperm through sex with multiple partners, it is as though he is confronting many different antigens. Some researchers suggest that this may be a predisposing factor for AIDS, owing to the formation of "antibodies which cross react with lymphoid cells" and Circulating Immune Complexes, or CIC's. Gay men diagnosed with AIDS, as well as gay men not showing signs of the dis-ease, frequently evidence both sperm antibodies and CIC's in their blood.

Tom: *The implication is that sperm reduces the immune system. It is correct. It is a very temporary response. It's also partly due to the trauma of the penetration—the stress associated with the sexual act until there is a release in climax.*

Jason: *Is the same stress associated with vaginal intercourse?*

Tom: *To the uninitiated, and to those who have so-called hang-ups around it, yes.*

Jason: *But in anal sex there tends to be more of a trauma?*

Tom: *That is correct. . . . .mostly because of the value judgment placed on the act.*

Jason: *Since it's a temporary and benign effect, it doesn't in the long run weaken a gay man's immune system if he engages in anal sex?*

Tom: *That is correct.*

Jason: *And if he has anal sex, let us say, once a day with several different men, it doesn't necessarily lower it.*

Tom: *That is correct.*

Jason: *And condoms would be suggested, with or without the threat of AIDS, as a general safeguard against dis-ease transmission.*

Tom: *That is also correct.*

Jason: *It has also been suggested that the anus itself is not adapted to receive the "assault" of antigen-like bodies, otherwise known as sperm. The implication here, as I hear it, is that anal sex is unnatural, and that the human body is not made for it.*

Tom: *No, I think you are projecting Fundamentalist things of unnatural acts and crimes against nature on a very simple statement that the anus has a low immune factor quality. I hardly see that in the same category. For instance, when one swallows, the hydrochloric acids in the stomach are part of the immune system. When one breathes, the sinus passages immediately rid and sort out such things. The anal passage is primarily designed for the body's own excrements that have already been treated. Merely what is being stated is the idea that the injection of an immune suppressant, as they argue semen is, in combination with the virus—that particular orifice is not particularly geared to handle such a substance.*

Jason: *And there is truth in that? But isn't the immune suppressing factor of semen itself temporary and benign?*

Tom: *That is correct. The silliness of the argument is that neither is the mouth necessarily designed to receive a penis; neither is the tongue necessarily designed to stimulate a clitoris. Human creativity does what it does with each natural appendage. The hands were never originally designed to grip a steering wheel, but that does not keep you from whizzing about in your chariots. Do you understand this, then?*

Jason: *Yes.*

Tom: *So I would have to pronounce you guilty of your own projection and reaction to the statement. It is merely a very clear medical statement. I think you were reacting to it from a Fundamentalist aspect.*

Jason: *Thank you, Tom. I accept your critique. I do have one final query on the subject of semen and anal intercourse. A study that is frequently cited by researchers to support the belief that semen inserted into the anus can lower the immune response of the receptive partner involves a series of eyebrow-raising experiments on laboratory animals. To be specific, weekly deposition of pooled rabbit semen into the rectums of healthy male rabbits was shown to modify their immune response.*

Tom: *What is transpiring is that there is a reflexive action in the coccyx that stimulates a pouring out of adrenalin into the system, of which a quick boost can temporarily lower the immunity.*

Jason: *So that's what they're picking up with the rabbits, because they're probably doing this frequently to them.*

Tom: *Most definitely. . . .as well as rabbits are very high strung creatures to begin with. I do imagine if someone threatened to stick* anything *unwanted up one's rear posterior, so to say, that is going to lower something.*

Jason: *But in the long run it's not a problem.*

Tom: *Quite right.*

Jason: *Tom, I'd like to ask either you or John if you have any final message for the readers of this manuscript.*

Tom: *(Pause. Entity desiring to speak.)*

John: *Hail.*

Jason: *Hail, John.*

Jason: *John, I'm wondering if you have any concluding remarks you'd like to address to the readers of this manuscript.*

John: *To the community as a whole. . . .it is when they are as a house divided that they cannot stand. They should let no element or sector of their social order or their brotherhoods or sisterhoods become divided. For it is when they are a house divided that they indeed serve two masters, and they must love one and hate the other. And this bends them to hate some aspect of their own appendage, their own being. For they are as though the morning stars that must again shout as one. And in this then they must find their unity. For in it they find that element which binds them all together, which indeed is the common spirit which they call love. For without this, they are but as the dust that they tread beneath the earth from whence they come and whence they will return.*

For that which providest life (and that is what they must do—provide life one unto the other) is through their unity, through their full embracement, through the acceptance of their humanity, and their binding together in mind, body, and spirit. They must take upon themselves the yoke and find that their own burden is not more heavy but indeed lightened as they move toward a common goal of a unity amongst all humankind.

Seek to be at peace with those things that you receive from Spirit, for you find they are to further thy Father's works, and indeed, ye are that work. Walk in this, thy Father/Mother God's Light. God Bless You. Amen.

Jason: *God Bless you, John. Thank you.*

CHAPTER 16

EXCERPT FROM *THE SOUL'S PATH*

A Group Channeling with Kevin Ryerson, October 9, 1985

The questioner is D.R., a person healing of AIDS.

Question: *I have a feeling that part of my soul's journey this lifetime around is to contract AIDS and then heal myself of it, so that I may show myself that I can alter my negative belief systems and overcome fear, and so that I can teach what I learn about the power of conscious thought to other people.*
Answer: *What do ye believe?*
Question: *That AIDS can be overcome.*
Answer: *(Repeating with emphasis) What do ye believe?*
Question: *I believe it can happen.*
Answer: *What would ye teach? Do you believe ye are God?*
Question: *Yes.*
Answer: *And if ye are God, are not all things with God as possible?*
Question: *Yes.*
Answer: *So therefore, indeed, if thy belief is that ye are God, this is all ye must articulate—but also then ye must express. For what ye are truly saying is: Have faith. For faith is evidence of things unseen. And yet if God embraces all things, then all things work toward the common whole and the common good. Give as though a single point to thy faith, that ye are God, and then all things are rendered unto thee. Is this to your understanding?*
Question: *Yes.*
Answer: *So it is not a matter of belief systems; it is a matter of the* fact *that ye are God. Is this to your understanding?*

CHAPTER 17

EXCERPT FROM
A CELEBRATION OF UNITY:

A Group Trance Channeling with Richard Lavin (who channels "Ecton") and Richard Wolinsky (who channels "Martenard"), December 27, 1985

Martenard: *As for your dis-ease AIDS, in the next year or two—and it is not clear—there will be a cure. The time frame is still mutable.*

Ecton: *But before this cure, so shall there come the perceptions of that which some entities call "Psychoimmunity." Knowing fully well and deeply within themselves that the only person responsible for their own health, or for their dis-ease, is the person who has, or does not have this particular dis-ease. For there is no germ in this world—no virus—that can affect you adversely unless there's unconscious permission given. And the lessons to be learned from these unconscious permissions are truly profound—even if it means the death of some of your brothers and sisters in this world.*

Martenard: *Understand that they form their reality, and they have their reasons for it—and trust those reasons. People do not choose it because they are the "victims" of other belief systems—because they are the victims of a germ or a virus. They do not choose it because they are the victims of anything. They choose it for their own reasons. And who are you to assume you understand? And to some degree you do not understand your own choices, so why make judgments on them?*

Ecton: *And as you allow yourselves to see the immensity of your creativity, so will it be that much easier to accept the choices made in relation to a child contracting a dis-ease—knowing full well that this child does not consciously say to him- or herself, "It's time for a dis-ease." But look beyond the surface—the circumstance of the issues—into the truth that rests beneath—for that is the dimension of the reality that each and every entity is moving toward remembering.*

CHAPTER 18

PSYCHOIMMUNITY

A Channeling through Kevin Ryerson, Mediator

Introduction

The focus of this channeling is on psychoimmunity, the capacity of the mind to use visualization as a major tool for effecting health and well-being in mind, body, and spirit. It contains a wealth of information, much of which is not currently understood by modern science, concerning the evolution of the heart and the immune system, the functions of the thymus and of the adrenals, and the nature of the aging process.

This channeling was originally generated in the spring of 1984, at the time when immune dysfunction was becoming a major health issue in the United States. To facilitate reader comprehension, minimal editing has been employed; a synopsis has been included, which follows the channeling.

The following notes may prove of assistance while you read. You will find that the Spirit often uses the singular verb "is" when referring to the singular level of either mind, body or spirit, and employs "are" to indicate that whatever is being discussed is operating on all three levels. This principle often operates with other verbs, nouns and adjectives, and explains in part the apparently "incorrect" grammar of the channeling.

One aspect of John the Beloved's idiosyncratic speech is his frequent repitition of the phrase "in same." While I have omitted this phrase on most occasions, I have found that John often uses "in same" to clarify his meaning, and have gained insight into the material by rereading sentences with this in mind.

Kevin Ryerson has supplied me with definitions of a few key terms employed in this channeling. "Cell memory" may be understood as "whatever stimulates a cell to reproduce itself." The cell memory includes the DNA, or "genetic memory," which contributes to cell reproduction. It also includes the process of mitosis, the specialized cell memory by which genes intertwine and separate, enabling the cell to reproduce itself. When there is a breakdown of cell memory and the mitosis process, dis-eases such as Acquired Immune Deficiency Syndrome may result.

The "electrical fluidiums" can be measured in terms of the bio-chemical electrical response in the nervous system and the galvanic skin response on the surface of the skin. These electrical fluidiums usually coordinate with the acupuncture meridians of Chinese medicine.

You are encouraged to give yourself time to digest this materi-al. The information contained herein grounds any discussion of the visualization process in the actual physiology of the human body, and supports current understanding of the key role of psychoim-munity in the healing process.

On April 19, 1986, Kevin Ryerson generated the following material on psychoimmunity. This material is excerpted from "The Emerging Mind: Knowing and Being in the Nineties," a channel-ing which is available from the Center for Applied Intuition (see Resources).

John: *There shall be within the next five years thorough documentation of the psychoimmunity principle. This would be a quality of mind so thoroughly integrated into every cellular level of the body to be able to even-tually, by means of your advanced technologies, to observe the actual bend-ing of the genetic code itself through mind—not merely the generation of antibiotics, the regulation of heartbeat, and anatomical levels, but project-ing not only to the cellular but to the molecular level itself.*

This will begin when it is found that there is no other pathway except through that which is called the meridians. You will be able to truly ob-serve the phenomena of mind as an agency independent of even the phenome-non of psychophysiology itself. For you will truly discover that mind is either advanced or suppressed as a conductive energy. The so-called current phys-ical models, even the chemical models, merely suppress or advance conduc-tivity of the energy that is mind in itself. And the behavioral alterations are not chemical in nature, or as the result, but merely advance or block neurological and meridian activities which, when both integrated, create the phenomenon of the integration of both conscious and superconscious mind, which again is the evolutionary force.

This is best observable under hypnotic states, whereby a phenomena which you currently label in medical phenomena as stigmata will generate a capacity of physiological surgery, where it is documentable that individuals entering into ecstatic states, and/or may through psychotraumas, make reappearances of welts or other blows suffered in childhood on command. By exploring these phenomena under more controlled conditions through meditative, hypnotic, and not drug-induced, but sound-induced or light-induced or vocally-induced altered states, these will lead to new capacities to generate principles of psychoimmunity, and even phenomena that is now currently called, as controversial as it may be, psychic surgery. For you may consciously induce these states, and then apply them as advances, rather than as though being scoffed at as unachievable within Western physiological and anatomical disciplines.

The Channeling:
John: *Hail.*

Questioner: *Hail, John.*

John: *State nature of inquiry.*

Questioner: *The inquiry is into the process of psychoimmunity, including an overview of psychoimmunity and a specific inquiry into the adrenals and psychoimmunity.*

John: *As such. You will take and find that the various elements of psychoimmunity are a culmination of perhaps three or even four forces within the body's physiology. These would come about as through the process of the mental forces which are stored in the cranium or in the various diverse portions of the left and right brain hemispheres, that there here is instored capacities of low voltage electrical energies, and that through direct focus—through visualization—there is the ability to channel these mild electrical forces and their stimulus abilities through to specific portions of the body physical, aiding in the actual tissue stimulus of various internal organs that would be as associated with the necessary buildings of the immunities expressed within the body physical in its own right.*

You would take and find that all disease levels that function in the body physical is a dysfunction within the physical framework itself and not so much from invading organisms in same. For you would find that it is only that the body prepares itself as a host for these invading organisms. These, of course, would be inflammatory or bacterial or virus stimulus within the body physical, or the inability of the body physical to eliminate various tox-

emias from in same, which may also in turn lead to the wearing upon the tissues of the body physical.

A very key element of psychoimmunity is that it is a tissue rebuilding process, or a tissue stimulus process, even down to the finer levels of that which may be considered as a pre-tissue status of various proteins and other sources that go into the enzymal properties and the make-up of antibiotic properties. So therefore, you would take and find that the very key to psychoimmunity itself would be the observed results of low voltage electrical forces in the body physical that find their source as first as a battery or storage capacity in the cranium itself, then the projection of these forces into internal organs and the internal glandular structures necessary to bring about stimulus of both their tissues and the function of those tissues. For you would take and find that health in the body physical is a by-product of the integration of, again, all these forces; but the triggering mechanism of psychoimmunity itself is balancing indeed the body's electrical forces. (It is not so much the biochemistry of the body physical itself but, indeed, directly again the electrical forces of the body physical.)

The nervous system is not only a system of messengers, denoting to the body physical its capacity of sending messages from various portions, such as in the coordination of the various motor nerves and various messages to the body physical in same; indeed, it is the physiological passage through which energy, integrating into the body physical through again the form of low voltage electricities, actually stimulates the cells into growth through the prodding of a physiological source of energy, as you would understand it, as in the flow of electrical forces or electrons in same. So therefore, the nervous tissues, or the nerve tissues in same, and all their passages, both sympathetic and autonomic, are not only messengers again for those tissues but are a source of energy that helps us maintain them.

Often the rapid deterioration, for instance, that is observed when there is the cutting off of neurological flows is not so much only from the inactivity of the tissues, but actually the lack of electrical stimulation of those tissues. For it is the capacity of constant stimulus from both the neurological accord, as well as the normal physiological integration upon the biochemical levels, that actually become the functions of the tissues. For instance, even as you study the capacity of tissue regeneration generated by mild voltages of electricity from electrode implants in those tissues, these in turn of course are amplifications of what the nerve tissues in their own right are a direct function of same. So to understand psychoimmunity and its mechanism, the individual must expand their concepts of the functions of the nerve tissues.

The major process of psychoimmunity in these days, it is sensed, is the capacity of the mental forces to increase the neurological activities, or stimulus, to various key internal organs through a process of focused visioning or visualization.

It must also be understood that not only is there the force of the stimulus of the direct electrical fluidium in its own right (or the direct flow of the electrons), but the by-products of their mild electro-magnetism. It is the increase of these forces that increase the capacities of the blood fluids to carry forth their functions. Within the red corpuscles these would be found to be the high concentration of iron that become the carrier of the electromagnetic charge to other portions of the cell memory of tissues. Within the white corpuscles it is high concentrations of the mineral substance known as magnetite that become the carrier of these forces. For also it can be observed that exposure of all forms of cell tissues to mild magnetic fields helps increase the stimulus of these forces so as to allow greater enhancements for patterns of cell division and, therefore, tissue regeneration, increasing by ten to twenty per cent new generations of cell tissues.

Also, when there is a single thought or singular pattern held within the capacity of the cranium, that single thought as a magnetic pattern—or moreso as an electromagnetic pattern—is transferred to those forces in its own right, directly to the blood flows, beginning as to shape the cell memories along the lines of the desired electromagnetic pattern. So, therefore, this is an extension of the function of the nerve tissues, wherein the cranium or the tissues of the cranial function—that is, the flesh brain itself—becomes a direct organ internalized for the function and process of stimulating within the blood cells themselves a specific pattern of electromagnetic stimulus of the cell memory, so as to produce the necessary antibiotic properties through the agencies mentioned of the iron and the magnetite. For just the subtle alteration of this element and mineral substance within these specific cell tissues, or substances moreso, are the source of psychoimmunity that, when they integrate into the activities of the spleen, become the source or the pattern for the necessary antibiotic properties in same. This would be the key agency for the manufacturing of various custom forms of immunity within the body physical.

Breakdowns in the immune system, in areas of reneeding of stimulus or de-stimulus, find their forces centered in the adrenals, the spleen, the thymus, the thyroid and the pituitary, in its functions in same. Also, both the coccyx and the medulla oblongata are second carriers of the neurological tissues' functions, being transformers or builders of neurological energy, particularly in meditative processes, and then their transfer distribution throughout again both the sympathetic and autonomic nervous systems— also that portion of the anatomy which would be the parasympathetic ganglion finding its entry in the throat. These are the carriers in same that the functions, again, that are suggested that the neurological tissues are indeed an active force in tissue regeneration and growth — not just the exercise of the tissues and then the neurological tissues carrying those messages as of the conditions, but moreso contributing directly to the conditions, by being the stimulus and a source of energy — not food substance as in biochemical, but a direct source of energy that stimulates the cell memory process through the forces described earlier.

It would be found (as again suggested) that the blood flows supply greater capacity to the cranial energies for two-fold function. It is through the increased biochemical activities in the brain itself that there is the generation of an internal system in the neurological tissues, and that a portion of the function of electrical synapses in the brain continues to the benevolence of the biochemical process of the body physical itself as an agency critical to the physiological process, in stimulating continuously the proper functions of each internal organ. The agencies of the coccyx and the medulla oblongata are of central importance because they are expanded areas of concentrations of neurological energy to be carried for stimulus purposes of the internal organs of the endocrine systems, and their critical stimulus in balancing the metabolism as a whole. The medulla oblongata acts as a stimulus and storer of energy specifically for the functions of the thyroid, and specifically for the functions of the parasympathetic ganglion. The coccyx acts as a specific storer of energy for the activities of the adrenals.

In part, why there is atrophying of the thymus is that formerly the heart acted moreso as a concentration of neurological tissues, rather than muscular tissues, in the anatomy of man. The thymus, when in a nonatrophied state, functioned as the perfect regulator central to the immune system, that when man integrated in dietary accords of a non-toxic nature there is no great need for the concentrations of the muscular tissues now known as the heart.

The heart functioned and developed through an evolutionary process of the need for eliminating various toxins from the body physical, and developed also a strengthening of the adrenals in their need and capacity and functions in the body physical. The heart, as a muscular tissue, now in turn responds to toxins and others in the body physical in the enaminations, due to these radical alterations in dietary patterns — particularly the taking of solid substances into the body physical. Notations made in the dietary accords of individuals would also find that athletes of both vegetarian and highly active accord have lesser needs of the dynamics of the heart's functions in its regulatory flows, and that even though as strengthened as a muscular tissues, the heartbeat remains at lower rates in same. Also be found in similar athletes, that due to the increased neurological stimulus upon the heart from the athletics, there would be an increase of the generation of cells of the thymus. For therefore the heart tissues, as suggested by the channel speaking, have evolved from originally a neurological mass, directly responsible for stimulus of the thymus, to now moreso a mass of muscular tissues, with the functions described and the purposes described in same.

The key element in restimulating balances with the immune system would be to seek to restimulate the functions of the thymus. Are these things to your understanding?

Questioner: *In the original state, were you saying there was a lesser need for blood flows due to less toxins in the body?*

John: *As such.*

Questioner: *Could you clarify how the thymus originally functioned and how the thymus can be restimulated to function as it did originally?*

John: *First, its function is practically identical with the functions it has now; it is as the central stimulator of the immune system. However, you would find that originally the function of immune system is moreso for the proper digestion of elements in the endocrine system, not so much as a system for immunity from invading dis-eases. For when the body physical is in a proper state of health there is no invasion of dis-ease forces; there is merely the passing, through the body physical as a host, of various life forms that connect man, as a physical being or moreso as a biological being, with the elements of the planet itself. This is merely a process of incubus; the passing of these forces through the body physical, as a contributor rather than a taker, to the biological functions of the planet, or to that which ye term as the food-chain.*

Therefore, the original forces in the body physical would be moreso likened to the functions of digestion of proper elements of minerals and other substances from man's original dietary accord, which again, is suggested as fruitarian and vegetarian. The thymus was critical to maintaining these functions in same; even as in these days it is discovered that proper nutrition is one of the key elements necessary for the building of specific antibiotic properties for the fending off of dis-eases within the body physical.

The very term "immune" is in and of itself defensive and offensive. Moreso the body physical should be in a state of harmony. Of course, this calls for radical alterations of the philosophical accord of the individual. But, even as that philosophy within an individual, as an organized rational system of ethics, may lead to de-intensification of tension that may lead, for instance, to such tensions that could cause both pre-cancerous, pre-ulcerous and various other conditions in the body physical, so, in turn was this philosophy of the body physical and its functions applied towards the thymus—that as man deviated further and further in his mental forces, in philosophy, actual active logic and rational function—lesser the altruistic nature—the thymus became dysfunctional. Toxins then built in the body physical, only due to the faculties of the destimulus of the thymus. For toxins are but material that the body physical cannot integrate into its own bio-chemistry and so therefore must build an immunity to them. The dysfunction of the philosophy within man upon the rational and meditative levels led to the dysfunction of the thymus, then to the evolutionary force mentioned within the heart tissues (the muscular tissues in same), and has been a continuing natural force within man.

With the restimulation of the thymus within the body physical there would begin to be the more proper function of the entire endocrine system as a digestive aid, rather than being thought of as separate and independent functions in the body physical of balancing various dis-ease states or making war upon various dis-ease states. Restimulus of the thymus. . . .this would come first by increasing the body physical's own abilities of electrical forces. These would come, first, through a process of meditation and alterations of the philosophies or the ethics by which an individual conducts themselves in daily life functions, beginning by bringing forth systems of nutrition and diet that may aid in these processes; then through a permanent and institutionalized meditation centering upon the thymus, that would serve to increase the functions of both the neurologial electrical flows reaching the thymus, and other forces in same. Other techniques of increasing these neurological stimulus are along the accord, of course, of acupuncture, acupressure, electromagnetic supply to the general area and the stimulus of the thymus.

Indeed, the very functions of this centralmost of internal organs could be the key to stopping of the aging process. For the aging process is but a destimulus of both the electrical functions and the physiological functions of the thymus and its ability to ingest properly the nutritional qualities of the body physical. Is this to your understanding?

Questioner: *Could you amplify how the body ages through the improper digestion of nutrient substances due to the dysfunction of the thymus?*

John: *This is a two-fold process. The aging process is a process of destimulus of the neurological tissues in their ability to restimulate the cell growth, through the processes described before, in stimulating the cell memory in increasing new generations of the cell tissues. These are not a breakdown in the genetic patterns or the genetic messages, for these have been moreso almost as a mechanical function; it is the direct breakdown in the cell mem-*

ory itself, which is electrical in nature. The other part of this process involves the dysfunction of the thymus. The thymus is the centralmost coordinator of the stimulation and harmonizer of all the elements of the immune system itself. It was the physiological coordinator of cell growth in putting forth systems of biochemical or hormonal accord in coordinating all the functions within the body physical and harmonizing them. This duty now falls moreso to the capacity of the pituitary, which has come to be associated as the master gland. The pituitary remains in a proper state of stimulus being that it finds its feet and its center where it obtains this necessary neurological stimulation constantly, whereas the thymus has lost its centermost portion of stimulation. So therefore there is the coordination of two influences—the chemical activity itself, and, with the lack of interjection of the chemical forces created by the thymus, the eventual breakdown in the chemical process itself, leading eventually to the dysfunction of the neurological tissues and their capacity to stimulate those generations in same. Is this to your understanding?

Questioner: *Yes, it is. Could you discourse now specifically on the adrenals and their relationship to psychoimmunity?*

John: *Pause. . . .entity desiring to speak.*

(Tom MacPherson enters.)

Tom: *Hello. Tip o' the hat to you.*

Questioner: *Hi, Tom.*

Tom: *How are you doing there?*

Questioner: *Fine.*

Tom: *Bit of interesting information, would you agree?*

Questioner: *Yes, especially as regards the aging process. Is it being suggested that the restimulation of the thymus gland is the key to stopping the aging process?*

Tom: *Most definitely. Although, at this time we would like to put it more modestly: it's retarding, and, in some cases, possibly even reversing.*

Questioner: *Now, perhaps you could run it by me one more time. I under-*

stand that there is breakdown in the cellular pattern which eventually influences the nervous system in its ability to stimulate the cell tissue, but how does this breakdown in cellular tissue arise? Is it the excess of toxins that are undigested?

Tom: *In many ways, yes . . .the forces are many. It's basically the wearing of toxins on the body, which John points out are merely mismanaged chemical substances in the body that need elimination. So therefore the cells must concentrate on a twofold function: both intake and elimination of the quantities of toxins that formerly, with the functions of the thymus, were not necessary in proper nutritional elements, thus decreasing the longevity of the physical body. Even worse, the key element is that there has been a breakdown in the function of the thymus in stimulating the immune system to its full capacity—that is, the internal glandular functions of such things as the spleen, pancreas, so on and so forth. All these agencies should be looked upon as digestive agencies.*

Questioner: *Rather than immune agencies . . .?*

Tom: *Absolutely.*

Questioner: *Then, with the proper functioning of the thymus, what is the body's natural lifespan?*

Tom: *If it was to reach full capacity, several hundred years at least . . .possibly even approaching one thousand . . .with proper maintenance, so to say . . .but that's not likely anytime soon. I would say that with the proper functioning of the thymus . . .easily close to the age of 125, the same way that you are now reaching 72 years of age, and closer to 200 with the current collective consciousness. By current collective consciousness I mean the patterns of life . . .the current philosophy . . .the current social forces.*

Questioner: *I was wondering, in terms of cell memory, if there was a direct correlation between emotional states and personality and the correct stimulation of certain organs, as expressed in the five elements theory of Chinese acupuncture. . . .That is, that certain emotional states correlate to the energies in certain organs.*

Tom: *Absolutely.*

Questioner: *I was wondering if there was a further correlation in how the mind may influence the genetic memory itself—if it may change the genetic memory itself? John was speaking of the area of the brain actually being able to send out an electrical stimulus to charge or to carry energies to certain organs. Please discuss the force of mind in genetic memory and how, exactly, that process of carrying energy to the various organs is stimulated by visualization.*

Tom: *First of all, yes, it is possible to alter the genetic memory. . . .Usually this is to the negative, and produces cancer cells. Cancer cells usually contain an extra quantity of magnetite, and therefore have an actual tendency to pick up the negative patterns and over-stimulus of electrical energy, to the point where the cell memory is overly-stimulated, or over-altered, by its continuous passage or over-stimulus through negative thoughts. There is usually a tendency to dwell on the negative, so this becomes an over-stimulation of electromagnetics held within the brain and the nervous system. As the blood cells pass through there, that over-stimulus of electromagnetic force is then passed on to those cell tissues holding too much magnetite, usually by a single molecule or two, and the cell memory becomes altered. The magnetite, as mineral substance in the body, is the key here.*

Questioner: *Does the cell memory actually become altered by its passage through that area of the brain, or does the cell memory become altered, say, as in the over-stimulation to the stomach, when one gets an ulcer?*

Tom: *Both, actually. An over-stimulation of focus of thought of a negative pattern extends down, shall we say, to the stomach. The stomach is also another one of those concentrations of nerve-endings that aided the thymus. This is again a bit esoteric, but simply stated: over-stimulation of the neurological tissues in their capacity of producing electrical fluidiums and electromagnetic fluidiums—when the magnetite in the cell tissue becomes overly stimulated with what would be the equivalent of a positive charge in the body—I'll stick my neck out and identify the charge itself as a positive charge—the cell tissues can become cancerous. And it is stored in the magnetite.*
    We would like to go into the isolated functions of the adrenals at this time. A moment please while we realign the instrument. Here we go. . . .

(John enters.)

John: *Hail.*

Questioner: *Hail, John.*

John: *In the isolated functions of the adrenals, as they contribute to the systems of immunology, as you understand them within thy current context of physiology, they would be found to have impact upon both the regulatory flows of the heart and the functions of the muscular tissues, and to be a mild stimulus for the entire endocrine system, which includes stimulating the functions of the pancreas and the spleen; the presence of the generated adrenals also stimulates pituitary actions. Overabundance of the adrenals have been easily observed to be contributors to various functions of heart dis-ease. Indeed, current physiological studies may even suggest contributions to diabetes and, after long periods of overstimulation of the adrenals, a deterioration of the function of the spleen.*

Subtler forms of stimulation of the adrenals, to the point where they actually become toxic, would be that over-stimulation or even dysfunction of the adrenals may at times be found to be present in individuals of a hyperallergenic condition. In dysfunction of the adrenals there is the incapacity of the heart to respond; it then becomes only toxins themselves that stimulate the heart, which is seeking to eliminate those things which become the source of the allergenic state.

Allergies are merely oversensitivities of the body physical's functions to exposure to more toxic elements and an inability to eliminate them, to wherein the toxins actually are adapted by the body to carry out the functions of the adrenals which are in a state of dysfunction. The body physical, having its activities in these accords and their functions, brings forth imbalances to wherein the body cannot acknowledge proper functions of the adrenals.

Overstimulation of the adrenals may also cause similiar activities if the body may seek too quickly to eliminate various nutrient supplements that could be properly digested into the body physical in its activities in same, thus stimulating over-elimination of that which should be properly absorbed nutrient values. These again overload the eliminative organs—both the kidneys and skin tissues. Other dis-ease states in association with these would be asthma and bronchitis.

These are but examples of the functions of the adrenals. Other accords include the causing of destimulation of the circulatory flows and thus the atrophying of other internal functions within the body physical and its anatomy. Stimulation of the adrenals, it will be found, causes as a collapsing, or a closure when over-exposed, of some forms of the vascular tissues of the blood veins. In that dis-ease state where as there is the atrophying of the blood vessels and the circulatory flows to various portions of the body physical, it could be as stated that there would be as found to be as a presence of overstimulation of the adrenals; this would be the source of the dis-ease state. Overstimulation of the adrenals also aids in the continuous storing of tension in all the internal anatomical functions, but particularly in the muscular tissues. These allow for the atrophying of circulatory flows throughout the body physical as a whole.

Understimulation of the adrenals allows for toxins, particularly those of the heavier metals, to the point where Vitamin C, Vitamin A and even Vitamin E may as become toxic to the body physical, leading to allergies. So thus all the theories of misfunctions in the circulatory system, and the progresses that various things of a healing nature concerning restoration of the circulatory flows through the theories of massage and reflexology, for such examples, may be balanced by balancing the adrenals.

The suggested areas of the adrenals, as in the process of psychoimmunity, is that it has direct relationship to one of the major reflexive points in the body physical. This would be as the coccyx. So, therefore, there is greater ease in attainment of the stimulus of this particular critical glandular function. The wisdom in the isolation of the treatment of this particular glandular function is that it is a simplistic matter of either stimulus or nonstimulus of the glandular function that leads either to the aid and the promoting of the health, or the return of its functions in full which are critical to such a broad variety of the body's physical functions in its current state of evolution. Is this to your understanding?

Questioner: *Yes, it is. In the collapse of the vascular tissues through over-stimulation of the adrenals. . . .is this due to the lack of proper nutritive values because the adrenals have stimulated so much shedding of toxins which deplete the body of its necessary nutrients?*

John: *As such.*

Questioner: *In the understimulation of the adrenals, the allergic states are due to the building up of toxins which then must be shed through the other organs, such as the skin, the kidneys and the liver?*

John: *As such.*

Questioner: *How does the over-stimulation of the adrenals contribute to the storing of tension in the muscles and, therefore, the atrophying of circulatory flow?*

John: *It is simply that the adrenals are, of course, the reflexive trigger of the survival instinct in same; that is, the adrenals are the direct stimulus for the functions of the expansion and the contraction of the muscular tissues. Over-stimulation of the adrenals would be a continuous biological message for the muscular tissues to hold themselves in a constant state of reflexive action, as if critical to the survival of the body physical itself. That reflexive response constantly puts the individual upon the levels of the muscular anatomy, in a constant state of threat to the functions of the body physical in its own right.*

These then lead to concentrations of blood flows to the muscular tissues for two functions: because of their constant state of biological readiness to respond to the survival instinct, plus the accord of the blood flows attempting to carry off the adrenals—which at this point have become a toxin within their own right—thus atrophying the proper flows of the blood flows to other portions of the body physical because of their concentrations in these areas. Is this to your understanding?

Questioner: *Yes, it is.*

John: *Pause. Entity desiring to speak.*

(Tom MacPherson enters.)

Tom: *How are you doing there?*

Questioner: *We seem to be leading in the direction of an understanding of how the overstimulation or the understimulation of the adrenals affects certain states of health in the body.*

Tom: *Quite right.*

Questioner: *I suppose the next logical step would be a program that is directed toward the stimulation or non-stimulation of the adrenals for certain dis-ease states.*

Tom: *We believe that now you have your "White Paper" on the carriers of psychoimmunity. So I believe what we would like to do at this time is cut off the flow of the information. We believe it is currently packaged to provide food for thought, describing exactly the carriers of psychoimmunity, which is currently not understood.*

Very pleasant speaking with you then. Saints be lookin' after you. God bless you.

(John enters.)

John: *Hail.*

Questioner: *Hail, John.*

John: *Seek to be at peace with those things that you receive from Spirit, for you will find they are to further thy Father's works and, indeed, ye are that work. Walk in this thy Father's light. God bless you. Amen.*
End of Channeling

Synopsis of Channeling:

The Electrical Flows.

Psychoimmunity, the capacity of the mind to utilize visualization (focused visioning) to increase the neurological stimulus to various key internal organs, is made possible by the operation of three or four different forces operating within the human organism. The psychoimmunity process facilitates the channeling of the low voltage electrical energies stored in the cranium—the left and right brain hemispheres—to specific areas of the body, thereby aiding in the actual stimulus and rebuilding of the various organs and tissues which compose the body's immune system.

Psychoimmunity operates from the principle that dis-ease is caused, not so much from invading organisms such as bacteria and viruses, or from toxic substances, as from dysfunctions which cause the body to leave itself open to these invading substances. The psychoimmunity process involves the projection of the low voltage electrical forces of the body, initially stored in the cranium, into the organs and glands of the immune system. It allows one to balance the body's electrical forces, thereby stimulating and rebuilding tissues. This process extends down to the pre-tissue status of various proteins and other sources which contribute to the enzymal properties and make-up of antibiotic forces within the body.

By channeling the electrical forces of the body through the nervous system into these tissues, physical dysfunctions are corrected in the body and healing can occur.

The nervous system, both sympathetic and autonomic, serves a dual function: it is both a system of messengers for the body, and the physiological passageway through which the low voltage electrical energies travel to stimulate cell growth. These flows of electrical energies are the key to cell growth within the body. The rapid tissue deterioration which can be observed when a neurological flow has been cut off from the body's tissues results mainly from a lack of electrical stimulation from them, as opposed to their inactivity. Validation for this point can be found in experiments which demonstrate that mild voltages of electricity generated by electrode implants in the body can bring about tissue generation. Again, the nerve tissues function not only as a messenger system but also as a source of the electrical energy that helps maintain them.

The capacity of the body's fluids to carry on their functions is increased not only by direct electrical stimulation, but by the by-products of their mild electromagnetism. Within the red corpuscles, a high concentration of iron becomes the carrier of the electromagnetic charge to other portions of the cell memory of the body's tissues. Within the white corpuscles, a high concentration of magnetite carries these electromagnetic charges. Exposure of cell tissues to mild magnetic fields stimulates them, thereby promoting cell division and increasing new generation of cell tissues by ten to twenty percent.

In the visualization process, when a single thought or image is held in the mind, it is transferred as an electromagnetic pattern through the blood directly to the body's cells, shaping their cell memories. The brain thus complements the work of the nervous system, and functions as an extension of it. It can stimulate, by means of the electromagnetic charge carried by the iron and magnetite within the blood cells, the cell memory of the cells which produce the appropriate antibodies to effect healing. Thus, psychoimmunity hinges on the subtle alteration of the iron and magnetite in the cells, which, when they integrate into the activities of the spleen, produce the antibodies necessary to build immunity in the body.

Breakdowns in the immune system, whether due to a need for greater or lesser stimulus of these antibiotic properties, are centered in the adrenals, spleen, thymus, pituitary, and thyroid.

The coccyx and medulla oblongata, two reflex points which can be stimulated through chiropractic manipulation, also contribute to the building of immunity in the body. These points build neurological energy, particularly through meditation, and transfer it by means of the sympathetic and autonomic nervous systems, and through the parasympathetic ganglia which connect to the throat, to specific organs and cells of the body, thereby stimulating cell memory and actively regenerating and rebuilding tissues. Necessary to the operation of this process is the principle, mentioned above, that the neurological tissues serve not only as messengers but as a direct source of the electromagnetic energy necessary to stimulate the cell memory and produce immunity.

The brain serves a dual function. Not only is it responsible for thought and memory, etc., but, through its biochemical activity, it generates the electrical currents within the nerves which stimulate the proper function of each bodily organ. The coccyx and medulla oblongata specifically serve as the concentrations of nerve tissues which carry these electrical currents to the organs of the endocrine system responsible for balancing the body's metabolism. The medulla oblongata stores the energy which stimulates the thyroid and parasympathetic ganglia, while the coccyx stores the energy which stimulates the adrenals.

The Heart, the Thymus and the Immune System

One of the reasons why the thymus shrinks and atrophies early in life relates to its connection with the heart. In an earlier state of evolution, the heart served as a concentration of neurological tissue, rather than its present status as a concentration of muscular tissue. During this period, when the thymus was non-atrophied, it served as the perfect central regulator of the immune system.

The heart in fact evolved from the need to eliminate toxins from the body, and to augment the function of the adrenals.

When the diet is non-toxic, as it originally was, it is not necessary for the heart to function as a muscular organ. This is because when there are fewer toxins in the body, there is less
need for blood flows, and consequently less need for the heart
to function as a muscular organ. If, for example, we observe
the heartbeat of athletes and vegetarians, we will find that it
is slower than that of other human beings. This is attributable
to the fact that athletes and vegetarians have a lesser need to
eliminate toxins from the body. Athletes also demonstrate an
increase in the generation of thymus cells. Again, this is because the heart is more able to function as it was originally
intended, as a neurological mass which was directly responsible for stimulating the thymus, as opposed to a muscular
mass which regulates blood flows.

The thymus has always functioned as the central stimula-
tor/regulator of the immune system. As will be described below, it is the changing nature of the immune system itself that
has dictated change in the thymus. The key to restimulating
balances within the immune system, and promoting tissue
rebuilding and cell growth within the body, is to restimulate
the functions of the thymus.

The immune system's original function was to bring about
the proper digestion of elements in the endocrine system,
rather than to effect immunity from invading dis-ease-carrying
organisms or toxic substances. When the body is healthy, dis-
ease forces do not invade it. In such a state, substances are
simply digested by the body, and then excreted to rejoin the
food chain from which they came. When in an earlier state
of evolution the diet was essentially fruitarian and vegetarian,
the thymus performed its initial critical function of maintaining the digestive process of the immune system, and excreting that which was taken in.

When the body is in its ideal state of harmony, there is
no need for "immunity." In such a state of harmony and balance, the thymus functions properly as the central regulator
for the proper digestion of elements, and all that is taken into
the body is digested and excreted. The dysfunction of the thymus can be directly traced to a change in the philosophy (the
actual active logic and rational functioning) of mankind, away

from the original altruistic nature. (The connection between the location of the thymus in the heart chakra, and the energy of the heart chakra as that of love, is the key to an understanding of this concept.)

Thymal dysfunction in turn allowed the build-up of toxins. Toxins may be understood as "mis-managed chemical substances," material that the body cannot integrate into its own biochemistry, and thus must eliminate. Toxic build-up demanded that the body develop a means of building immunity to these toxins. This led to the development of the heart as a muscular organ.

When the thymus is restimulated, the entire endocrine system can begin to function properly as a digestive aid, rather than as a separate and independent system in the body which balances dis-eases and wages war upon various dis-ease states. The spleen, pancreas and other organs of the immune system are thus stimulated by the thymus to perform their ideal functions as agencies of digestion. Thymal restimulation can be brought about by increasing the electrical flows to it through meditation, a change in philosophy and ethics, and an improvement in diet and nutritional intake. Acupuncture, acupressure and all systems which produce electromagnetic stimulation of the thymus and the region around it can also increase the neurological electrical stimulus to the thymus.

Aging and the Thymus
The thymus is the key to stopping and even reversing the aging process in the body. Aging is nothing more than a lessening of the electrical and physiological functions of the thymus, and the lessening of its ability to properly digest substances taken into the body.

Aging, when viewed from this perspective, can be seen as a two-fold process. It is a wearing down of the body, due to the thymus' inability to digest substances taken into the body. It is also the progressive inability of the nervous tissues to restimulate cell growth through stimulation of the cellular memory. As discussed earlier, the neurological tissues carry low voltage electrical currents to the cells, thereby stimulating the cellular memory to generate new cell tissues. When aging occurs, there is a direct breakdown in the cell memory itself, which is electrical in nature. (Cellular memory may be contrasted with the genetic patterns or genetic messages, which, as opposed to being electrical in nature, are almost a mechanical function.)

The thymus originally coordinated and harmonized all of the body's functions, producing the hormones and biochemical substances necessary for proper cell growth. The pituitary has since inherited this function, and is now considered the "master gland." As opposed to the thymus, the pituitary is located in a place in the body where it can continue to obtain the constant neurological stimulation necessary to its continued and proper functioning.

With proper functioning of the thymus, a person could easily live to 125. Given the current growth in collective consciousness, lifespan will in fact approach 200. And, while it's not likely anytime soon, with the thymus functioning to its full capacity and maintained properly, the body could in fact approach 1000 years of age.

The Power of Thought
There is a direct correlation between emotional states and personality and the energies in certain organs. An understanding of this relationship is expressed in the Five Elements theory of Chinese medicine and acupuncture.

It is possible to alter genetic memory through thought patterns. When the thought patterns are negative, this process can be a negative one, producing cancer cells. Cells which tend to become cancerous are those which contain an extra quantity of magnetite, even by a molecule or two. Through negative thought patterns, such cancerous cells have an actual tendency to pick up both the negative patterns and overstimulus of electrical energy, to the point where the cell memory is over-stimulated and over-altered. Negative thinking overstimulates the flow of electrical energy which is initially stored in the brain and the nervous system, passing it through the blood as a positive charge to those cell tissues which contain an extra quantity of magnetite, thereby altering the cellular memory to the point where the cell becomes dangerous. The magnetite is the key element of this process.

The Adrenals

The functions of the adrenals include: affecting the regulatory flows of the heart, affecting the functions of the heart's muscular tissues, and serving as a mild stimulus for the entire endocrine system (which includes the functions of the pancreas, spleen and pituitary). Overstimulation of the adrenals contributes to various kinds of heart dis-ease. Current research also indicates that adrenal overstimulation may contribute to diabetes. In addition, long periods of adrenal overstimulation may contribute to a deterioration of the functions of the spleen.

Individuals with hyper-allergenic conditions often evidence overstimulation of the adrenals, or the dysfunction of the adrenals to the point where they become toxic. In such a situation, the heart, which seeks to eliminate the sources of the allergic state—the toxins—by digesting them, cannot adequately respond to the situation. This results in the toxins themselves stimulating the heart to perform its digestive functions.

Allergies are merely oversensitivities of the body, caused by its overexposure to the toxic elements which it is unable to eliminate. In such a situation, because the adrenals are in a state of dysfunction, and the body cannot acknowledge their proper functions, the toxins are actually adapted by the body to carry out the functions of the adrenals.

Overstimulation of the adrenals may also result in allergies if the body too quickly seeks to eliminate various nutrient substances that are ideally digested by it. This results in an over-elimination of nutrient values that are ideally properly absorbed, to the point of overloading the eliminative organs of the kidneys and the skin tissues. Asthma and bronchitis can be traced to this phenomenon.

Overstimulation of the adrenals can destimulate circulatory flows. This impaired circulation can result in the atrophy of some of the body's internal functions, causing collapse or closure of some of the vascular tissues in the veins. In arteriosclerosis, or in any dis-ease where there is the atrophying of the blood vessels and the circulatory flows to various portions of the body, an overstimulation of the adrenals will be found as its source. Finally, overstimulation of the adrenals also contributes to storage of tension in all parts of the internal anatomy and specifically in the muscular tissues. This allows for the atrophying of circulatory flows throughout the body.

Understimulation of the adrenals can lead to toxic accumulations, especially of heavy metals, to the point where even Vitamins C, A and E can become toxic; this again leads to allergies. In such a situation, the skin, kidneys and liver, among other organs, are pressed into the task of eliminating these toxins.

Malfunctioning circulatory flows may be brought into balance by balancing the adrenals. Massage and reflexology are examples of healing systems employed to restore the circulatory flows.

The key relationship of the adrenals to the process of psychoimmunity lies in the direct relationship of the adrenals to the coccyx, which, as discussed earlier, is one of the major reflex points in the body. By stimulating or destimulating the reflex point of the coccyx (the first chakra), adrenal function can be brought into balance. [Ed. note: Herein lies the importance of chiropractic adjustment in the healing of immune dysfunction and other dis-ease states.] Proper functioning of the adrenals is critical to a broad variety of bodily functions, and necessary to maintaining balance and health.

The adrenals are the reflexive trigger of the survival instinct—the fight-or-flight syndrome—in the body. The adrenals stimulate the expansion and contraction of muscular tissue. When the adrenals are overstimulated, the muscles receive a continuous message to hold themselves in a constant state of reflexive action, or tension, as a means of maintaining physical survival. This survival response, which maintains the body in a constant state of tension and readiness, creates over-concentration of blood flows to the muscular tissues. These blood flows attempt to carry off the toxins which are created by the overstimulated adrenals. This can lead to atrophying of the blood flows to other portions of the body, to circulatory problems and vascular collapse, as well as to the depletion of necessary nutrients due to their over-elimination from the body.

CHAPTER 19

AIDS AND THE HEALING PROCESS: A FURTHER EXPLORATION

A Channeling with Kevin Ryerson

Present at the channeling were Misha Cohen, D.O.M., C.A., co-founder of the San Francisco AIDS Alternative Healing Project; Irene Newmark, C.A., eclectic practitioner of natural medicines and health consultant for many people diagnosed with AIDS; Alan Brickman, M.A., C.HT., trans-personal psychologist who has counseled many people diagnosed with AIDS; "Samuel," a man recently diagnosed with AIDS; and the editor, Jason Serinus.

Jason: *Hail, John. I'd like to begin by asking for clarification on a few of the points that are made in the book. Current scientific opinion is that semen and vaginal secretions can transmit the AIDS virus. Is it true that vaginal secretions can also transmit the AIDS virus?*

John: *Not without actual open skin abrasions.*

Jason: *So, in terms of a woman transmitting it to a man, there would have to be abrasions on the penis?*

John: *Correct.*

Jason: *And what happens if there was male oral to female genital contact?*

John: *Again, concern if open abrasions.*

Jason: *But basically when we talked about men and gay sex, my sense was that pre-seminal fluid wasn't really a problem; it was basically the semen itself.*

John: *This is the major concern, correct.*

Jason: *Great! They're also saying that the virus can incubate for five years or longer, and it is transmissible during this time. What I thought you said in a previous channeling was that the period of incubation is eight to 22 months at most. I therefore concluded that if it took longer for the virus to surface, it had been successfully rendered into a dorman state and was not transmissible in that dormant state. Is it or is it not transmissible while it's dormant?*

John: *It may prove transmissible directly through the activities in a more concentrated state such as in so-called direct exchanges of blood fluids, such as in direct transfusions, and/or as in direct open abrasions. However, in the activities of lesser exchanges in the seminal fluids, not till after 22 months do we find that the dis-ease is transmissible. Is this to your understanding?*

Jason: *No.*

John: *After 22 months, the incubation phase is complete and the virus then becomes transmissible. Note in the five-year cycle of incubation currently referred to by medical researchers it would be after the initial 22 months that the virus would then become transmissible; the researchers add another 24 to 32 months to this initial incubation period. The researchers measure this additional three-year cycle as consonant to an incubation cycle. We say the incubation cycle is as 18 to 22 months at most and then after that indeed the virus is transmissible. It is transmissible in activities in its dormant state in the first 22 months, but only generally either through blood transfusions and/or as through open or direct abrasions.*

Jason: *So for the first, let's say 22 months, it is dormant. After 22 months, at most, it would be incubating. And it still might not surface as a dis-ease for five years.*

John: *This is closer to a correct perspective.*

Jason: *And if someone then goes into remission, they could then render the virus into the dormant state after the dis-ease surfaced. Is this correct?*

John: *Correct.*

Jason: *In that case, would the virus be transmissible?*

John: *After a three-year period of dormancy—not transmissible.*

Jason: *So they'd have to be in remission with no symptoms for three years?*

John: *Correct.*

Jason: *I misinterpreted some of that information when I edited the Inquiry of the Holistic Group. Hopefully this will clarify matters.*
  We've talked about the fact that people can develop antibodies to the AIDS virus (HIV), not by coming in direct contact with the virus, but simply by coming in contact with another person's antibodies. What I've been told is that the test is titered in such a way that those people would not register positive to the test. Is that true?

John: *This depends on whether their own body, in reaction to the antibodies passed on, stimulated or duplicated precisely their own antibiotic response.*

Jason: *So some of those people will test positive, and some will test negative?*

John: *Correct.*

Jason: *OK. My last question concerning material in the Inquiry section conerns sexual conduct. You basically suggested that sexual abstinence was beneficial for people with AIDS. Is that correct?*

John: *It depends uniquely upon one case history to the next. Some activities, as long, however, as the individuals are integrated into what would be considered stress-reducing and/or loving environments, would prove harmonious. But for some individuals, a period of abstinence may actually remove from them feelings of guilt—feelings that perhaps they might act as an agent in passing on the virus to other individuals. For such a period of time, abstinence in this manner could reduce more subliminal stresses that could be placed upon the individual, because of guilt associated with that framework of possibility.*

Jason: *Thank you. A well-intentioned reviewer suggested that The Holistic Group was making moral judgments by suggesting abstinence. Your response clarifies the loving concern from whence such advice comes.*
  This leads into a discussion of the issues of responsibility and blame. What some people think is that holistic health advocates blame people for

their illness. They think we're suggesting that if persons diagnosed with AIDS had been "good," if they had taken care of themselves, if they had loved themselves "well enough" and "good enough," then they wouldn't have AIDS.

Misha, you mentioned the controversy about metaphysical counselor Louise Hay, who has been such a magnificent source of inspiration and hope for so many of us.

Misha: *Louise Hay has been accused of saying that the reason why people diagnosed with AIDS are ill is because they have made themselves ill through self-hatred, and that the only way to heal is through self-love. As a result, many people who don't become well—who don't heal themselves and die—often die feeling guilty.*

John: *Describe source of controversy.*

Jason: *I think people feel that if they try to do things to heal themselves and they end up dying that they've done something wrong, and are at fault. They think that they are to blame for getting AIDS—that they're at fault for being dis-eased and not healing.*

John: *Is there truth in this?*

Jason: *What I understand is that we create our own reality and our own unique experiences. But we don't do that because we're "good or bad" or "right or wrong." We simply create the perfect set of experiences from which to learn.*

John: *The question is: Do ye desire to address controversy or do ye desire to seek to increase thy own understanding?*

Jason: *The second. Louise Hay is not the issue here. The real issue concerns the fundamental nature of the healing process.*

John: *We suggest that the individual should accept the potential in the issues of death and dying. For in accepting and making death the ally, they live each life to the fullest and love themselves to the fullest of each day— that by that method, they may extend their lives amidst a loving fellowship.*
For while it is true that an individual is learning to accept themselves, indeed as that for which they are, we would find that the individuals would be able to do so only within the context of "right fellowship." For it is where two are gathered, so in turn also is the Father/Mother God's loving presence. So thus, it is in a fellowship—a loving heart and a loving mind. That

if they choose to pass this plane, perhaps it was done so out of a great love that they have for their brothers and sisters to raise *the awareness, so that they are no longer disinvested from the fellowship that is the greater society.*

So if indeed they did "choose their reality," is it not then the issue of the manner of how they experience *death and dying, that no greater love hath any man or any woman than they who would give their life for their brother or their sister? Is this to your understanding?*

Jason: *Yes. I've sensed that a lot of people diagnosed with AIDS have really chosen to serve as our teachers. It's almost as though they've taken on the dis-ease as a means of bringing together in love the people around them.*

John: *Correct. Add thy own insight, and that summary, and you will have addressed so-called controversy. Controversy is merely a divergency from the truth. It is confusing what they associate as "fact," as though fact is synonymous with truth. It is a house built on sand.*

Jason: *Thank you. Could you talk more about the issue of self-responsibility in healing?*

John: *This merely means taking to the degree of full responsibility that one may.* Responsibility and blame are not synonymous. *Responsibility means executing choices and changes in lifestyle to live life to its fullest, no matter to what degree or longevity that life may be lived. Blame, in its negativity, must be affixed in a judgment. For remember, "thou shalt not judge." If you are to say the individual is not to judge themselves and none are to judge them, that is then taking full responsibility for one's activities—for one's own healing. Is this to your understanding?*

Jason: *Yes. And if one attempts to take responsibility and discovers themselves leaving the body, then it isn't a question of having failed themselves.*

John: *No, for there is no success or failure. There is only the experience of the experience.*

Irene: *Are there any common soul lessons when someone does leave the body and has taken the path of alternative healing and spiritual growth?*

John: *If they are surrounded by loving friends when passing over, that is the lesson. For they have drawn the very community of individuals together whom at first perhaps sought to reject them. Is this to your understanding?*

Jason: *Yes. Does anyone have any more questions on that issue, because it's the key topic that's coming around? Think about your clients and the people you've worked with.*

Misha: *A lot of people come to me questioning the meaning of "responsibility." I think of "responsibility" as being what someone can do once they are diagnosed or once they discover that they want to do something for themselves. It means that they can take responsibility and create something for themselves.*

This is the antithesis of seeing "responsibility" as an indictment, as a judgment. It's the opposite of the idea that when one is not conscious, one is always making one's self ill, and that one is to blame for the illness.

Some people see red when it is suggested that they are responsible for every single thing that they do, and that they create their own illness—that's where people come up with the idea of blame. They don't understand that responsibility means that once you say, "I want to take responsibility for my health," that you will do everything possible to regain health, and possibly if you don't regain health, you will have learned something in that whole process. Can you talk about that?

John: *What is the final model for health? If the final model of health is a joyous being, who shares indeed joyously with others, even unto the point of their physical passing, then they have achieved a state of mind and well-being. It is moreso taking responsibilitly for how one lives life, and life philosophy, versus any issue of dis-ease. Study the works of Elisabeth Kubler-Ross here.*

Jason: *As concerns the whole notion that "we create our own reality," how would we go about introducing people to what this means?*

John: *It is simply the factor that even as though events in childhood shape the adult personality, so then can we say that character is fate. Make the argument no more complex than that. It is then the quality of the thought that the individual chooses to emphasize in their life that becomes character then becomes fate. Is this to your understanding?*

Jason: *Yes. Samuel, who is here tonight, was diagnosed with KS and AIDS less than two weeks ago. He's just come from a health consultation with Irene, who came up with some interesting information about the karmatic nature of this experience for him. Would you be willing to share this, Samuel?*

Samuel: *Sure, and jump in, Irene, if I'm not explaining it well. It seems that there's someone I've been in relationship with in as many as six past lives who has a lot of hate and resentment toward me. It seems that these unresolved issues of love are manifesting in my heart chakra and thymus as AIDS. What can I consciously do to achieve some peace and harmony within myself?*

John: *All revelation is subjective to the individual so each case history often is entirely unique. As the issue of love and rejection functions as a collective consciousness, these have been pointed out in earlier discourses. With Samuel in particular, as we scan the whole of both thy ethereal and physical anatomy, we find no particular being from past lives attached to self. Moreso there has been an activation of the heart chakra, which is centered in the thymus, and the beginning of the opening of an examination of thyself from all elements of thy being.*

It is not unusual for individuals to undergo what Elisabeth Kubler-Ross refers to as the so-called "five stages of death and dying" within the context of so-called "ego death." Because of your diagnosis, there is an outpouring upon yourself to have to examine the disciplines that indeed a loving heart may be. This is to allow the self to be in correct and loving fellowships, and to open the wholeness of thy heart to self, as well as to allow others to love thee also. In this very sharing of thyself here in such a highly personal manner—that even though thy name may be kept anonymous—this is a loving and open act—to share so much of thyself personally with other parties. This is the lesson for self. Is this to your understanding?

Samuel: *Yes.*

Jason: *So in terms of the person in past lives, it could be that what you're referring to is a pattern of love and relationship with another. In this lifetime, Samuel is learning more about loving others and loving self. And that's the karmatic connection with the past relationship.*

John: *And remember, karma simply means "actions taken." Karma is merely the events of the childhood of the soul.*

Jason: *Well, if there is the pattern of not accepting this personality and a lack of love and closing one's heart off in past lifetimes . . .*

John: *The entity that must be accepted is the entity of self. The issue that is sensed is the opening of the heart of the individual or the heart chakra.*

Jason: *Thank you. Can you share some specific techniques for getting in touch with one's higher self and getting answers to questions? When faced with the plethora of material in this book and other books, plus everything that everybody is saying, people diagnosed with AIDS often say, "Oh my God, what should I do?" And when one responds with, "You have to ask your higher self for the answers," that becomes a meaningless cliché for them because they simply don't know how to go about connecting with their higher self. Could you share a particular visualization or a meditation technique for tapping into one's own inner wisdom?*

John: *All persons in the room, close their eyes . . . Meditate upon white light for precisely 10 seconds . . . Slightly clear the thoughts, and then ponder a moment the full potential of God's unlimited love . . . Draw a deep breath, and think of a moment when ye were deeply loved and deeply nurtured. Think of a person's face by whom you were deeply loved and deeply nurtured . . . Allow that feeling to flow through thy being . . . Breathe it deeply . . . For any moment—any thought—which nurtures is God's love. Any person who nurtures is attuned to the higher self . . . Draw in a deep breath . . . Relax a moment and ponder the clarity of mind that is now possessed. Perhaps note a slightly increased intuitive state. And it is from this context then that a person would ask the so-called "higher self."*

For the higher self is the God-spark. It is there to teach—it resides in each individual. It is not an esoteric state of consciousness; indeed, it is the very foundation of the person's consciousness. It is their own highest potential as a spiritual being. It is clarity. It is light. It is love. It is the very ability to nurture. It is the ability to acknowledge the sacredness of one's own being—the ability to conceive of themselves as of the substance of the divine.

So by entering into that state where they can conceive of themselves as the same substance as the divine, by seeing the harmonious way of nature, and in that moment—in that inspiration—it is then that they shall ask and then receive. They shall knock and it shall be opened.

Jason: *Thank you. You said at the recent San Francisco Whole Life Expo channeling that we will begin to have faculties of mind in which a person will become their own physician. Would you like to elaborate on that?*

John: *The manuscript that ye have put forth is the first step in that direction. Latter discourses shall add to it. Companion pieces are as, of course, beginning to be set in place, such as* Spiritual Nutrition *by Gabriel Cousens, M.D., and by the other author (who is yet to be) who is currently present [Alan Brickman], who's working on the issues of chakras and of the nurturing of individuals upon case-by-case studies.*

Jason: *Thank you. I want to ask about the differing ways in which the opportunistic infections associated with AIDS emerge. For example, hemophiliacs never seem to get KS, while gays come down with it a lot. A man with AIDS who had intended to be with us tonight has had pneumocystis pneumonia seven times, but has never had KS. Other people develop KS but never get pneumocystis. What is the psycho-spiritual basis for these patterns?*

John: *Physical basis for the hemophiliac is that there is a unique composition in the protein make-ups of the cell walls that contribute a synthesis of the condition for the purposes of the bleeding. In these activities, then, the virus cannot bond. Is this to your understanding?*

Irene: *From past channelings you've talked about the virus mutating and becoming more inherently a part of the cell and the connective tissue and the skin and that's related to the manifestation of KS. Are you saying that process doesn't happen with hemophiliacs?*

John: *Correct.*

Jason: *OK. Why will some people who are not hemophiliacs develop pneumocystis as opposed to KS?*

John: *On the spiritual or physical levels?*

Jason: *Spiritual level and physical level.*

John: *Genetically, it varies from one case history to the next. There is the capacity that the AIDS virus would be affected slightly genetically from one case history to the next. The selective properties that break down in the autoimmune system differ from one person to the next, and the virus in some individuals cannot break down the complete functions of the autoimmune system.*

Jason: *And that accounts for the difference?*

John: *Correct.*

Jason: *What about on the spiritual level?*

John: *We would also point out that each individual's spiritual lessons are different.*

Jason: *And this would have to do with why some people develop AIDS as pneumocystis and some people KS and some people toxoplasmosis?*

John: *Correct.*

Jason: *Because of the different quality of the experience and the lessons.*

John: *Correct. Remember, all revelation is subjective.*

Jason: *Thank you.*

Misha: *Would you say that people that have KS—as opposed to pneumocystis—have stronger immune systems? People with KS often don't develop pneumocystis for very long periods of time.*

John: *Moreso it is a selective process. The immune system has been weakened in specific areas.*

Jason: *Is there some other immune dysfunction such as, for example, Epstein-Barr virus, which you could talk about in terms of the psycho-spiritual pattern at its root?*

John: *The attempt to break these down into individual spiritual patterns eventually would create merely a complex apothecary of so-called psycho-spiritual issues. It is wiser to look at the overall pattern of the phenomena, not in the generalization, or in a vagary, but as the specific same methodologies can be applied to each individual. Where as you would desire to break it down in each right, it is wiser to institute that individuals work with meditation to be able to isolate their own lessons from their dis-ease, which are subjective to each case and every history. Is this to your understanding?*

Jason: *Great. Thank you. There is a new theory on the roots of male homosexuality from Lee Ellis of State University at North Dakota at Minot. This theory says stress in the mother during pregnancy triggers a surge of maternal hormones which enter into the fetal bloodstream and ultimately interfere with the production of fetal testosterone, when they instead "should be masculinizing the brain." When studies were conducted with the mothers of gay men, they reported two and a half times the levels of stressful events during pregnancy. I'm wondering if this is true? [General laughter] Well, it's headline news, it's the "new theory." So is this true? Does the "maternal stress" affect the hormone levels and does it have to do with homosexuality? (I haven't gone off my rocker, kids.) [Laughter]*

John: *Describe both your sense or feeling of this theory.*

Jason: *My sense is that it doesn't matter one bit, since homosexuality is primarily the choice of the soul. If the mother's stress in fact contributes to homosexuality, and the soul desires a homosexual lifetime, then it simply might choose to have a mother who experiences "maternal stress." Besides, who gives a damn? That's my feeling. [Laughter]*

John: *There's a slight physiological base to the insight; while there is truth in the insights being offered, there is a greater degree of activity involved in establishing a homosexual orientation. But the true key here would be that they would finally establish that indeed homosexuality is conceived in the pre-natal states, so therefore is a physiological and psychological phenomenon. This shows that the issue of homosexuality indeed is a phenomenon that is there and occurs in birth, and therefore occurs in nature. So therefore homosexuality is a* natural *phenomenon. Is this to your understanding?*

Jason: *Yes. The man who came up with this theory says he is doing everything possible to make sure his wife doesn't go through any stress so that they don't end up having a homosexual child.*

John: *Perhaps the individual's very stress around having a homosexual child will produce the stress in same. [Laughter]*

Jason: *Yes. We're all looking forward to that child. [more laughter]*

Alan: *Why has negative feeling on the part of society toward homosexuality, although not in every culture, been such a common factor in our human existence?*

John: *It is linked truly to the issue of fear of death and dying, in the sense that it is of course the myth of the concept that parties engaged in the so-called homosexual activity do not as though perpetuate the species or the particular peoples. It is wrapped in the fears and the superstitions of mortality and death and dying.*

Jason: *More so than the fear of not being a "full man" or being a "full woman"?*

John: *We speak of the collective fear.*

Jason: *Thank you. Because we're in a channeling right now, I'd appreciate your comments on another theory on homosexuality being transmitted by a rather dramatic entity who is attracting a large number of people. Here we go!*

It is suggested that in development of God-man and, I presume, God-woman, that women were judged less than God by their male soul-mates because they bore children. Male soul-mates did not understand the pain of birthing, and felt their female soul-mates were not God because they were experiencing pain while giving birth. While the first should only mated with their soul-mates, they later began to experiment with other non-soul-mate partners; the result was that both sexes then felt abandoned. Women began to seek for the "right man" to love them; men began to "go through" women looking for the "perfect one" who was the mate of their soul. As women were used and abused, they decided to come back as males to escape rejection by men. These former women manifested effeminate male bodies and were judged less equal than other males. Some continued to come back as males. When they eventually decided to cross over again and incarnate as women, their bodies carried the cellular memory of making love with women so they became lovers of women, or lesbians.

The males, on the other hand, who crossed over into women's bodies out of guilt for how they had treated women, eventually became lovers of men. When they later crossed over again to reincarnate in male bodies, they too carried with them the cellular memory of making love with men and became lovers of men, or homosexuals. [Laughter]

Control yourselves, children [more laughter]. People take this stuff seriously. There are all these people who consider themselves "New Age" out there reading this book who believe this is why we are who we are.

John: *The channel speaking would invest no words in that which would be considered convolutions or tortured logic. The very time spent in addressing such pseudo-controversies is incorrect.*

Yet within the "Gordian knot" just presented indeed there is some element of truth upon a case-by-case basis. However, moreso it is that the soul wishes to experience its own full range of activities, and the implication that homosexuality indeed does not occur in nature is an incorrect balance. There are at times indeed those who had long feminine incarnations then became men and carried over then with them the cellular memory.

However, to sever the "Gordian knot," ye simply must know that all souls are androgynous. All souls contain the God-spark. As ye are then naturally bonded and wedded to love each other, each according to their own nature, it then becomes clear that the variety that has been created in human nature is merely for ye to have the experience to overcome limitations, superstitions, and fears. That is the only reason for these experiences . . . to see humanity in all and God in all, and each to be according to their own nature, but filled and have their natures shaped by the love that is God. Is this to your understanding?

Jason: *Yes. Very clearly so.*

Alan: *John, I think that without discounting human suffering, most of us have felt an incredible advancement of consciousness since the rise of AIDS amongst us. The AIDS issue on an individual and community basis has really been an extraordinary thing. I at least imagine that the coming together of people, the opening of communication and love that we're experiencing will only continue to happen.*

I'm wondering if you would like to make some general remarks on this situation at this time, two years after our last group channeling. I feel that the atmosphere is different; some of the groundwork for this new understanding has already been laid.

John: *Describe area of insight desired.*

Alan: *It seems as though the nature of AIDS is changing. For example, we may be closer to a medical break-through—there's a lot more information—there are a lot more people to go to. I think there's been a lot of dialogue (though there could certainly be more) between the so-called heterosexual and so-called homosexual communities, as well as a lot of dialogue within the so-called gay community. I'm trying to establish some kind of global overview here.*

John: *The only global overview is that the major thing that AIDS has accomplished is to open a human dialogue. Where once there were walls between the communities, AIDS has now broken those things down—for the human dialogue that is now open is just that. It creates new fellowships, it creates new bonds, new empathy.*

When a people as a whole separate themselves one from the other, they lose track that all are part of the body that is a part of the whole. AIDS is accomplishing an opening of a human dialogue that is best opened by first opening the heart. For when ye may see a blossoming of the humanity of others, as in your current state of affairs where even those whose hearts are perhaps the hardest are eventually growing to be intolerant of those who will not conceive of the humanity of others, you are witnessing a greater capacity—a greater human dialogue.

When eventually this so-called "plague" passes, you will be a stronger and a more loving peoples. For that is, indeed, the revelation. Is this to your understanding? (Yes.)

Misha: *Is the relationship of AIDS in Africa the same?*

John: *Correct. AIDS transcends across all racial issues, all socio-economic lines, and all other accords. In Africa, we find those again who have been disinvested are the ones whom the dis-ease seems to prey upon.*

Jason: *When are other times when AIDS has surfaced in history—when the psycho-spiritual pre-conditions have been there?*

John: *There were brief times in the periods of the Greeks that are historically preserved, and once in Egypt. Also in the activities in the histories of India.*

Jason: *The lesson or the learning of breaking down barriers and loving each other with an open heart is always the lesson, in whatever form it takes. But why has it taken the form of AIDS at this particular point in history? We've been learning the same lesson throughout all of human existence. Learning to love each other and ourselves, and to be totally one in the moment, is what Jesus, Buddha and all the great spiritual masters came to teach. Why are we learning the lesson this way—through the medium of AIDS—at this particular time?*

John: *Because ye do not keep the laws of the prophets. What is the heart of law? Love the lord God with all thy strength, heart, mind, and soul, and thy neighbor as thyself. Ye keep this and ye can break no other commandment. The laws of the prophets command and reveal that ye live in a harmonious community.*

Jason: *Yes, but John, we broke that law 100 years ago as well, but AIDS didn't surface at that time. What is the reason why it's here now and not then?*

John: *What was thy suffering 100 years past? What was thy suffereing 100 years before that?*

Jason: *The same.*

John: *If ye but ponder a thousand upon a thousand lifetimes, what is thy suffering? Thy suffering is as when ye do not recognize God within others. For when ye live as though as a harmonious people, none of these dis-eases shall visit thee.*

What is the suffering? Each in each and every of its own time. Has there not been the groundswell in the most recent of days that indeed ye see that the suffering of races leads to the suffering of nations? [Ed. Note: John is referring to both discrimination against gays and lesbians and to the suffering and rebellion in apartheid South Africa.] It is how in this period of time that there came to be into the foreground by both political will and activities an increase that now perhaps one of the few minorities that is left to be persecuted by the collective consciousness are those of the so-called gay community.

Jason: *And also the black community.*

John: *Correct. But in these activities you would find that these again are the socially disinvested. Follow the pattern in the theory of the socially disinvested, which is a lack of love, and you will follow precisely the course and the activities of the so-called "plague" known as AIDS.*
What then, again, is the plague? It is always the lack of love.

Jason: *So, the specific reason why we are experiencing this dis-ease at this point in history is because of our need to raise our consciousness around the disinvested. In terms of our current historical context—at this crucial moment of transition into the New Age—AIDS is the experience that is teaching us the necessity to transcend the illusion of separateness and "againstness" and to open our hearts one to another.*

John: *Correct. For this is always these conditions; this is always the need.*

Jason: *We would now like to talk more specifically about some approaches and substances being used to heal AIDS.*

Misha: *AL721 is being tested now in the National Institutes of Health. Lots of people are experimenting with different home-made versions of it. According to certain sources, this is going to be the drug for AIDS. Is that true?*

John: *Describe its inherent properties, or its formulation as currently stated.*

Jason: *It's a natural, apparently non-toxic substance made primarily from lecithin that has shown remarkable promise in healing people diagnosed with AIDS. It's very inexpensive and easy to make. The problem in obtaining it arises from the fact that until the FDA finally approves it as a safe "drug,"*

*the company holding the patent on it can only distribute it as a "food." Be-
cause that company stands to make a lot more money if it can sell AL721
as a "drug," it has been withholding distribution of the substance. As a result, many different parties are gaining access to and formulating alternative home formulas which we believe will achieve the same results as the
official hard-to-get substance.*

*AL721 seems to fluidize the membranes of T-4 cells allowing receptors
to become more mobile and discriminating, which makes it more difficult
for the virus to get through. It may also act against the virus directly by
disturbing the lipid coating (we're not sure). The first question is: Does it
work directly against the virus?*

John: *Correct.*

Jason: *Secondly, you have said previously that in fact if people didn't have
a reaction to it, or weren't allergic to it, that AL721 could lead to states
of remission that could eventually be considered cure. How effective is it
against the AIDS virus, and in healing?*

John: *It will vary of course from one case history to the next. And the substance will have to go through several generations of formulation. But we
would isolate that the principles that they are researching and working upon
here—of working directly with the T-cells within* culture—*within the
formula—then returned to the blood fluids, will be the final formulation
that can allow for the ability of the body's own forces to begin to resist the
virus.* As well as then taking the substance directly into the bloodstream
itself, acting directly upon the virus by the breaking down of its outer protein shell, particularly when diagnosed in the early phase, or dormant phases
of the first 22 months. Is this to your understanding?*

**[Ed. Note: John is making reference to experiments currently being con-
ducted by Dr. Jay Levy, M.D., at the University of California Medical Center in San Francisco. Dr. Levy has determined that it is the so-called
T-suppressor cells which control the HIV virus in the blood, and prevent
the virus from growing. "In several different laboratory tests, the virus could
grow in helper T-cells only if the suppressor T-cells were removed." By with-
drawing the blood, removing the T-suppressor cells and working with them,
and then returning them to the blood stream, it seems possible to remove
the virus from the bloodstream. John is suggesting to culture the blood within
the medium of AL721 before returning the blood to the body.]*

Jason: *Yes, now are you talking about taking AL721 directly into the bloodstream?*

John: *Yes.*

Jason: *Do you mean taking it intravenously or ingesting it orally?*

John: *Both.*

Jason: *There are various formulas for it, including the initial formula from Israel. It seems many people are not even certain of the proportions of the ingredients in that formulation. Some formulations use egg oil, others use PC-55. It has even been suggested that these formulas would prove more effective with the addition of mixed ascorbate. Could you suggest the most ideal formula?*

John: *Not in this particular session, but within 20 days.*

Misha: *That's when a shipment of one of the substitute substances, which I believe will be marketed as "Lively Lipids," is due to arrive!*

Jason: *Is there time for another follow-up session on specific technical substances with you?*

John: *In this period of time?*

Jason: *Yes. In 20 days?*

John: *Correct.*

Jason: *OK, great. In the time we have left for this channeling, what would you feel is most important to concentrate on?*

John: *Ye seem most concerned with the phenomenon of thought forms.*

Jason: *That's what I chose to begin with. Then I wanted to move on into healing modalities and specific substances. I have pages and pages of substances and techniques to ask about.*

John: *Begin list of so-called substances.*

Jason: *A homeopath in Orinda, Ben Hole, M.D., is using blood autonosodes for his 25 clients with AIDS. Are blood autonosodes an effective homeopathic treatment for AIDS?*

John: *Describe potency.*

Irene: *A few drops of blood are taken and the preparation is taken up either to a 6X diluted 1:10 or 6 times or 1:100 6 times, and then with the possibility of taking it up further, but usually starting out as starting out as 6X or 6C.*

John: *Within the ranges of homeopathy to work as a singular treatment we find these to be effective, but more effective if combined with other suggested homeopathic compounds.*

Jason: *Such as the ones that you've already discussed.*

John: *Correct. [Ed. Note: See earlier channeling.]*

Jason: *I've heard that Merc Sal 30X works very well for pneumocystis. Is that true?*

John: *Correct.*

Jason: *And two others that have been suggested are homeopathic preparations of cyclosporin and typhoidinum.*

John: *Again, we isolate that these factors, if used in combination with other substances, can prove correct. Remember, the effect of the virus is over such a broad range, that attempting to check it at any point in its process, as it goes through its series of mutations, is part of why there is such a broad variety of so-called effective methods.*

Jason: *So you're saying that since the virus is in different stages of progression at different times and affecting different areas, we'd want to use a combination of approaches—and homeopathy would be of them?*

John: *Correct.*

Jason: *I understand that there's been a discourse on neurological complications that Tom gave to another party. Could you talk some about neurological complications associated with AIDS?*

John: *In part ye would find that in some individuals, in the rare circumstances where the virus actually finally invades the autoimmune system itself, it is because the virus functions and replicates in one of its points of mutation the precise DNA pattern, not unlike a so-called neuropeptide. It is in these particular cases that some of the medical case histories will finally be able to link the neurological tissues with the phenomenon of function of neuroblast being linked to activities of the immune system itself and more specialized cell tissues.*

So therefore, in specialized case histories, the genetic make-up of individuals as their own neuropeptides function, are close to the virus as it functions in one of its points of mutation. If the virus passes through that phase of mutation and does not in that temporary moment while inhabiting the body physical invade the neurological tissues, it will not do so in same. Is this to your understanding?

Jason: *Yes, and in that particular moment, should the virus pass through that mutation—what are other substances besides Blue-Green Manna and Super Blue-Green that would work to stop it from moving on to the neurological level?*

John: *This has been thoroughly discoursed upon already. [Ed. Note: See amino acid discussion in The Holistic Group's Inquiry.]*

Jason: *Candice Pert, who's a researcher with the National Institute of Mental Health, says that HIV may act like a drug and fool the brain into thinking it's a hormone. I think that this confusion of symptoms could be responsible for some of the neurological complications. She says that the brain and the immune system have the same molecules. Is this true?*

John: *In the function described specifically as neuropeptide, correct.*

Jason: *She's also discovered a new neuropeptide called Substance-T or Peptide-T, which seems to block the entry of the AIDS virus into both T-4 (helper) immune cells and brain cells. I'm wondering if this is a valid mode of exploration?*

John: *This is a valid mode of exploration, in particular where the virus has gone through that series of generations and into the neurological tissues.*

Jason: *Does Substance-T naturally occur in the brain?*

John: *If it correctly is isolated as we sense it has been as a functional neuropeptide, correct.*

Jason: *Is it found in certain natural substances, such as Blue-Green Manna, and are there others that one could use to help at this point?*

John: *We find it occurs in nature. Yes, it is in so-called Blue-Green Manna. Also within certain spectrums normally referred to, as in grains—in particular wheat germ. It also occurs in so-called macadamia nuts.*

Jason: *Samuel has been considering using DNCB for his KS.*

John: *Describe as understood.*

Misha: *It's a photographic chemical that can be brushed onto the skin. It's supposed to increase the immune system, particularly the blood work.*

Jason: *It originally was used for warts. It creates a raised patch on the skin. It seems to bolster the immune system, and to specifically fight KS.*

John: *As directly applied to the areas of the lesions?*

Samuel: *Correct. Or just painted on the skin to elicit an immune response.*

John: *To what degree, and how many times is the substance applied to the body physical?*

Samuel: *Solutions of 2/15ths of 1% in Vaseline Intensive Care Lotion® are applied in very small doses directly to the lesions, I believe once a day, I'm not certain.*

John: *As such. If stimulated through covering no more than approximately 20% of the surface areas of the skins, we see that there can be a balance here. Perhaps we would suggest that in higher portions, we would have some concerns that it eventually may have a mild toxic effect on the skin's tissues.*

Jason: *Are there other substances that you would find more in harmony holistically in terms of dealing with the lesions? I know we gave some formulas that are in the book. I know of one man in Seattle who has successfully used one of the formulas to shrink his KS lesions. There are a lot of other chemical substances that are being used now. We could go through the whole list but I don't know how much time we have left with you. Is there anything you'd like to isolate specifically at this time?*

John: *No, not at this time.*

Jason: *Do you have any predictions as to when there will really be a breakthrough that can contribute to mass remission from and healing of AIDS?*

John: *The phenomenon known as AZT is one that indeed extends the longevity of the individuals when finally given in correct dosages. This was as though a first phase. [Up to May, 1987] Second phase shall be when they learn there is the capacity of cultivating the body's own T-cells within a formula such as AZT, and/or through the formulations of the process that has been isolated from so-called lecithin. These will be the final so-called breakthroughs.*

Jason: *Ah, so that's what you talked about earlier. It involves taking the blood out, running it through a culture of AL721 (or a more appropriate formulation derived from lecithin) and/or AZT, thereby enabling it to interact with the T-cells, and then returning the cleansed T-cells to the blood and the body.* *

John: *Correct. Seek to be at peace with those things which you receive from Spirit for ye would find that they are to further the Father/Mother God's works, and indeed ye are that work. Walk in this the Father/Mother God's light. God bless you. Amen.*

Jason: *God bless you, John.*

Kevin: *Hello.*

The Group: *Hi, Kevin.*

Kevin: *How are you doing?*

The Group: *Good.*

End of Channeling

*[Editor's note: At the time of the actual channeling, I may not have completely understood the possibilities suggested by John. The most likely scenario involves removing the T-suppressor cells from the blood (the cells which seem to block reproduction of AIDS virus), culturing and reproducing them within the medium of an AL721 formula and/or a substance such as AZT, and then returning them to the bloodstream to fight the virus. A less likely possibilty, but one worth investigating, involves removing the T-4 helper cells, running them through the substances mentioned above, and then returning them to the body. Further research will clarify the situation, and ideally produce the breakthrough we have all been creating through our prayers.]

Addendum

The follow-up session suggested by John could not be scheduled before this material went to press. It is my hope that such a channeling, which will concentrate on treatment modalities and protocols, healing substances, and immune dysfunctions (including Epstein-Barr, ITP and AIDS) will have been conducted by the time you read this. To obtain the transcript, please send a self-addressed stamped legal size envelope plus $5.00 to The Holistic Group, P.O. Box 3073, Oakland, CA 94609-0073. California residents please add 7% sales tax. Checks will be returned if not available. Please allow up to 10 weeks for delivery. Orders outside U.S.A., add $3.00 for postage and handling. No telephone inquiries, please.

PUTTING PSYCHOIMMUNITY INTO PRACTICE

by Jason Serinus

All prices quoted below are subject to change; changes are not the responsibility of the editor or publisher. California sales tax fluctuates between 6% and 7%, depending upon the county in which the sale is made.

Among the gifted healers achieving impressive results in facilitating the healing of cancer, Acquired Immune Deficiency, and other dis-ease states is the Santa Monica-based metaphysical counselor, teacher, lecturer, and Science of Mind Minister *Louise L. Hay*. I was first introduced to Louise's work by Tom Chaudoin, whose interview appears earlier in this book. I am grateful to them both, because a weekend with Louise at Wildwood Ranch/Resort, followed up by daily use of one of her meditation tapes, has led to important breakthroughs in my life.

Louise L. Hay healed herself of supposedly fatal vaginal cancer through techniques of visualization and self-love, and she has committed herself to sharing this work with others. Her cassette tape, "AIDS: A Positive Approach," was first produced in 1983, when many of the gay men she had worked with began to call her to ask what they could say to their friends who had just been diagnosed with Acquired Immune Deficiency. Examining the dis-ease, and intuitively understanding that it has roots in a lack of love and self-love, Louise produced her tape to be able to reach as many people as possible with her inspired words of healing.

Since that time, Louise Hay has become a source of inspiration and hope to countless thousands of people worldwide. She has worked individually and collectively with thousands of people diagnosed with AIDS, and touched the hearts of many others. The love she puts into her work is palpable to anyone allowing themselves to truly listen to and take in the experience of her tape, and I cannot recommend it highly enough. For many men, it has been Louise's wise and healing voice that has led them to their own healing power.

Louise believes that almost everyone on this planet suffers from self-hatred and guilt to some degree. Gay men in particular, she finds, often carry a heavy load of rejection and oppression from parents and society. Her work involves accepting oneself and embracing the totality of one's being with self-love. By helping people to dissolve the hatred and oppression within them and to absolve themselves of all guilt, Louise helps her clients get in touch with the healing power of love. As she explains, "When you love yourself, everything in life improves, and you strengthen yourself inwardly. I teach people that there is nothing wrong with them—that we are all wonderful beings. I do this with everyone who comes to me, regardless of the imbalance or dis-ease."

Louise Hay explains that "the word 'incurable,' which is so frightening to so many people, means that we must go within to effect a cure." By going within, and changing the mental patterns which are at the root of dis-ease, healing can be achieved. "Just as we have the ability to create atmospheres where we can become ill, so do we have the ability to create atmospheres where we can become well. Dis-ease is our body's way of telling us that we have a false idea in our consciousness, and this idea needs to be changed." By changing our belief systems, "we change the experiences that are going on around us and within us. Everything we experience in life we create by our thinking/feeling patterns. What we choose to create right here at this moment is going to create our future."

Louise finds that the people with Acquired Immune Deficiency she has met who adopt the conventional medical approach to dealing with Acquired Immune Deficiency usually do the poorest, while people employing alternative approaches do the best. "Healing," she asserts, "comes from a willingness to change inside. I can almost tell when people first come to me if they're going to make it or not. I look at their attitude toward themselves and their willingness to commit themselves to whatever they must do to heal themselves. We have to be willing to fight our fear, which dissolves when we allow the love that is within all of us to surface."

When asked for an example of someone she met whom she realized was not willing to change, she cited one person with Acquired Immune Deficiency whose reaction to a cleansing diet was to whine: "I don't like the taste of the food."

Certainly the most well publicized of Louise Hay's clients, as of this writing, is Louie Nassaney, who was featured as the cover story in *People* (11/18/85). Diagnosed with AIDS in May 1983, Louie's eventual realization that his rapidly deteriorating condition was linked to his image of himself as a "victim of AIDS" had impelled him to make, in Louise Hay's words, "drastic changes" in his life. By coming out to his parents, altering his diet, reducing stress, and working with Louise, Louie's "devastated" condition improved to the point that he was entered into a gay "Superman '86" contest by the AIDS Project of Los Angeles as an example of someone in remission from the disease. During the semifinal round of the contest, when each contestant was asked "What is your fondest memory?" Louie answered without hesitation, "The day I was diagnosed with AIDS and got my family together to tell them." This choice to turn his potentially permanent "victim" status into an opportunity for transformation and self-affirmation can be understood as key to his healing.

Louise Hay told a huge San Francisco audience tha Nassaney dedicated himself to 1½ hours of visualization a day during his healing process. Because rabbits have a propensity to multiply indiscriminately, he visualized his T-cells multiplying "like little white rabbits happily copulating away," thereby experiencing his T-cell count going up and up. He also thought of his KS lesions as pencil marks, and held in his mind an image of a large pencil erasing them (he literally rubbed his lesions with a pencil eraser to deepen the impact of this visualization).

Shortly before appearing with Louise on Los Angeles television, Louie was quoted as saying that "my metaphysical therapy has given me such a sense of well-being that I am convinced this is what has saved me. I certainly would recommend it to anybody, although no one can promise it will work for a specific person. All I know is that it has worked for me."

Louie Nassaney and your editor have appeared on several panels and events together in 1987. I have the deepest respect for this beautiful man's dedication to healing himself and his brothers.

Louise Hay's busy schedule includes lectures and workshops around the world, private consultations, television appearances, and a weekly healing group in Los Angeles. Louise held a very successful evening and all-day workshop in San Francisco in September 1985, co-sponsored by yours truly, which made a deep and lasting impact on the community. The 450 attendees at her talk, "AIDS: A Positive Approach," gave substantial evidence of the large number of individuals who are embracing the positive approach to healing espoused by Louise and the contributors to this book. The healing circles and organizations which were spawned by her visit are indeed allowing people with AIDS in the Bay Area to give themselves permission to heal.

Louise Hay's books include *You Can Heal Your Life* ($10.00), *You Can Heal Your Body: The Metaphysical Causes of Illness* ($3.00), *I Love My Body* ($5.00), a 30-day affirmation guide to a healthy body, *Your Personal Colors & Numbers* ($3.95), which your editor uses to tune into the special energy of each particular day, and the long-awaited *A Positive Approach to AIDS* (1988), which includes accounts from people who are using Louise's affirmations, meditations and visualizations to aid them in their healing. Her cassette tapes include: *Morning and Evening Meditations; AIDS: A Positive Approach; Cancer; Your Healing Power; Self-Healing;* and *What I Believe/Deep Relaxation* ($10.00 each). I recommend the last tape listed for people who may not be concerned with healing a specific illness or affliction. Filled with positive things about who we are and what we can be, playing this tape nightly can facilitate fundamental changes in one's thought patterns, thereby allowing goodness, health, and prosperity to manifest.

Louise's fans, and especially attendees at her regular Wednesday night meetings at West Hollywood's Plummer Park or monthly Hay Rides in San Francisco, will want to own some of her song and meditation tapes. *Loving Yourself* ($10.00) contains songs and meditations by Louise and Jai Josephs, including the popular "I Love Myself The Way I Am" and "I Love Money." It also has a beautiful Mother/Father/Child Meditation and Ocean of Prosperity Meditation. Newer are *Songs of Affirmation* with Louise and Joshua Leeds, including "Doors Opening," and *Gift of the Present: Songs of Affirmation Vol. II* (extended play, $10.95 each).

Louise has made available her *You Can Heal Your Life Study Course*, an at-home workshop designed for in-depth study. It is available in either audio cassette or video cassette format, with the option of her book *You Can Heal Your Life*. Cost is $25.00 for the two audio cassettes ($30.00 with the book) or $50.00 for the two video cassettes in either VHS or Beta formats ($55.00 with the book). A recent offering is a 55-minute video tape, *Doors Opening: A Positive Approach to AIDS* ($35.00 in either VHS or Beta formats), an intimate view of her Wednesday night AIDS group. This group, which began in her living room in January 1985 with 6 men now attracts almost 400 people a week. As Louise explains, the principles taught in this video "transcend the issue of AIDS. They speak to the need for healing in all of us. This video is not just about AIDS. It is a bringing together: a balancing of body, mind, and spirit in an atmosphere of love and acceptance. Here healing is approached from a holistic level. This video is a testimony for the power of love to heal." Most recently released is *Conversations On Living: Your Thoughts Create Your Life!*, a 1 hour video of Louise's lecture at a recent health symposium in Los Angeles ($29.95, VHS or BETA). "Filled with insights on how we create health and dis-ease, this video is an enlightening discussion about how the subconscious retains and responds to our long-standing thoughts." A step-by-step description of each part of the body and the mental and emotional causation for illness each represents and a questions and answer sharing time round out the video.

After visiting the homes of several friends, and finding positive affirmations tacked to the bathroom mirror, refrigerator, and goodness knows where else, I am persuaded to include Louise's 11x17 full color poster of 10 positive statements, *How to Love Yourself*, ($5.00), the greeting card version ($1.25), the truly beautiful *Loving Treatment* poster (24x36—$8.00, 11x17—$3.00), the greeting card ($1.00), and, yes, far more meaningful than your standard vacation throw-away of a bikini-clad buxom bombshell holding some ripe fruit, the Loving Treatment postcard ($ .60).

Hay House is also distributing several important books and tapes by other individuals and groups. Among these are the much-lauded *Love Your Disease* by John Harrison, which has been highly recommended to me by numerous sources ($12.00), *When Someone You Love Has AIDS* by BettyClare Moffat ($9.95), *As Someone Dies* by Elizabeth A. Johnson ($6.95), with an introduction by Louise, and *Looking Good and Feeling Good* by Bill Roberts (Video—VHS or BETA—$29.95, audio—$10.00), an excellent exercise program by a fine man which "will inspire you to energize your body and appreciate who you are." Also available are songs and chants from Stephen Longfellow Fiske, Alliance, and other musicians (write for information).

To order any of the above, or to contact Louise's office about working with her, write Hay House, Dept. JS, 3029 Wilshire Blvd. #206, Santa Monica, CA 90404. Include the following handling charges with your order: up to $5.00, add $2.00; up to $15.00, add $3.00; up to $25.00, add $4.00; up to $50.00, add $5.00; up to $100.00, add $6.00; above $100.00, add $8.00. Canadian and Mexican residents, add $1.00 to the appropriate handling charge, while residents outside North America must add 10% of the total order to the printed handling charge for surface mail, and 30% of the total order to the printed handling charge for air mail. California residents add 6½% sales tax. Make your check or money order payable in U.S. funds to Hay House.

To reach Louise's office by phone, call (213) 828-3666. Please mention this book, and leave her a message that Jason loves her.

Russell M. Jaffe, M.D., Ph.D., who runs ACT Technologies Corp., an allergy testing laboratory in Vienna, VA, made San Francisco Bay Area headlines in February 1985, after presenting evidence to a gathering of orthomolecular physicians that 18 of 19 people with Acquired Immune Deficiency who have volunteered to work with him have been experiencing remission for at least one year. What is most heartening about Jaffe's work is that it combines both physical, emotional, and spiritual approaches, ranging from megadoses of vitamins and detoxification of heavy metals and environmental poisons to Mobilizing Inner Healing Mechanisms through peer co-counseling, visualization, *A Course In Miracles,* and Intensive Journal Techniques. Jaffe's use of vitamin C, zinc, selenium, relaxation, and stress reduction techniques, immuno-enhancing substances, saunas, and visualization, is in total harmony with the approach of The Holisitic Group. We find his work exciting and validating. You can reach Russell M. Jaffe at 2177 Chain Bridge Road, Vienna, VA 22180, or by calling (703) 255-9834.

Many physicians in the San Francisco Bay Area employ elements of Russell Jaffe's approach and our own in the treatment of AIDS. *Keith Barton, M.D.*, whose frontispiece graces this book, practices at 3099 Telegraph Ave., Berkeley, CA 94605, (415) 845-4430. Keith has been quite active in educating the community about the need for a holistic approach to the treatment of AIDS and other dis-eases, and has published some excellent articles in the San Francisco *Sentinel USA* and the *New York Native.*

Richard Shames, M.D., a family practitioner who has also endorsed this text, has done pioneering work in the field of holistic health and nutrition for many years. The author of *Healing with Mind Power,* a contributing editor to the *International Journal of Holistic Health and Medicine,* and former Chief of Health Services at the Edgar Cayce Medical Clinic, Richard has an exceptionally positive attitude toward the treatment of people diagnosed with AIDS or ARC.

One of Richard Shames' first patients diagnosed with AIDS was William Calderon, whose accounts of achieving "complete recovery" graced the cover of *New Realities* magazine (March/April 1985). Using visualization and megavitamin therapy, totally cleaning up his diet, and especially getting involved with *A Course In Miracles,* William managed to eliminate totally the KS lesions that covered much of his body and lined his esophagus and rectum. Calderon died on May 10, 1986, three and a half years after his initial diagnosis. Richard Shames expressed his belief that, had his patient continued to minimize stress as he did during the first years of his illness, rather than exposing himself to the "immune-suppressing" rigors of television interviews, phone calls, letters, and seminars, he might still be alive today. (See discussion concluding Chapter 4.)

Richard Shames, M.D. can be reached at 232 E. Blithedale Ave., Mill Valley, CA 94941, (415) 383-1262.

Shirley B. Scott, M.D., a Bay Area holistic practitioner who has reviewed the material in this book, recently appeared on an AIDS and Immunity healing panel with myself and Misha Cohen, C.A., of the San Francisco AIDS Alternative Healing Project. Shirley maintains a private practice which includes, in addition to people diagnosed with AIDS, many women healing candida and other immune-related dis-eases. She can be reached at 3698 California St., San Francisco, CA 94118, (415) 431-9241.

Laurence E. Badgley, M.D. is an alternative medical doctor who uses the natural therapies of homeopathy, vitamins, minerals, and acupuncture. His co-worker *Laura Bushnell* trains people in using biofeedback and visualization. Laurence has been treating many people diagnosed with AIDS, and was a key organizer of the major two-day San Francisco conference (8/23-24/86), "Talks on Natural Therapies for Chronic Viral Diseases." Both Louise Hay and myself spoke at this conference. He is the author of *Healing AIDS Naturally* (Human Energy Press), an extensive volume which in many ways complements this book. Contact him at Ste. D, 370 W. San Bruno Ave., San Bruno, CA 94066, (415) 873-4076.

A further resource for practitioners who take a nutritional approach to health is the *Orthomolecular Medical Society*, headquartered at 6151 W. Century Blvd., #1114, Los Angeles, CA 90045.

Promising results in the treatment of nearly 30 people with Acquired Immune Deficiency have been reported at the New York Institute of Applied Biology, headed by the Rumanian-born octogenarian-plus *Emanuel Revici, M.D.* Revici's research into the role of lipids in the body's immune system, and treatment of people with cancer, schizophrenia, drug addiction, and other dis-ease states, has dominated his work for the last 65 years.

Clinical application of Revici's research, employing more than a dozen medications he has developed, began in late 1982, and as of July 1985, only 2 deaths had been reported—one a suicide and the other due to bacterial pneumonia in a patient who refused hospitalization. Revici's first patient with Acquired Immune Deficiency, who came to him with pneumocystis pneumonia, was still alive and well in July 1985, although he left treatment on multiple occasions for as long as 6 months and continued a sexually promiscuous lifestyle.

Dr. Revici's work, initally praised for its success in the treatment of cancer, began to meet with hostile reaction around the time of of World War II, when chemotherapy was developed under the auspices of the Army's Chemical Warfare Department. He is currently involved in litigation with the FDA, which is attempting to restrict his practice. As Dwight L. McKee, M.D., explained shortly before joining Revici's staff in New York City, the motives for trying to suppress findings "totally compatible with mainstream science" are simple: "If cancer treatment was subtracted from the American hospital system (as it could be if treatment results were swift and sure), the system would collapse."

The Institute of Applied Biology is located at 164 East 91st Street, New York, NY 10128 (212) 876-9669. Dr. Lynn Anderson, 21 N. Holly, Medford, OR 97501, is a practitioner of Dr. Revici's work on the West Coast, while Marcia Smith at #8 Muriel, Fairfax, CA 94930, (415) 459-5013, serves as the West Coast liaison.

The *Gerson Institute* in California was begun by the late Max Gerson, who spent over 50 years working with cancer patients, claiming thousands of successes with "incurable" diagnoses. His program involves cutting down the amount of work the body must do to digest food, and involves consuming vegetables and fruits, juiced and pressed, sometimes on an hourly basis. The Institute will not take patients who have received chemotherapy, believing that their immune systems have been compromised beyond help; their treatment of people with Acquired Immune Deficiency is temporarily limited to outpatients because of current difficulties with Mexican medical authorities, compounded by homophobia, which could threaten their Mexican operations.

Max Gerson's book, *A Cancer Therapy: Results of Fifty Cases*, provides information for home treatment, and is available for $9.95 plus $2.00 handling and 6% sales tax. Contact The Gerson Institute, Box 430, Bonita, CA 92002 (619) 267-1150.

The Institute for Thermobaric Studies, located in Berkeley, CA, orients itself around the work of Joan McKenna, who holds an O.M. (Order of Merit) from the London School of Economics. McKenna's unique approach to the prevention and healing of dis-ease states has shown successful results in the treatment of cancer, herpes, and AIDS, and has gained the attention of many San Francisco Bay Area physicians.

McKenna believes that the thermodynamic patterns of heat, pressure, and motion are the key to what is happening healthwise in the body, and that the only way a virus can enter healthy cells is if the cells are overheated. After examining the heat patterns of a dis-ease such as pneumocystis pneumonia, she puts people on a program which includes rehydrating the system with deionized water, detoxification and cleansing diets, the use of cooling foods, "physical repatterning" (including stress reduction, yoga, visualization, empowerment to heal, and taking responsibility for one's health), and a regimen which normalizes the body's heat distribution patterns. This regimen results in a temporary lowering of the body's temperature, similar to what is experienced when a fever breaks, which can lead to healing. Since McKenna sees a direct relationship between overheating in the body and stress, the stress reduction techniques which are discussed in this book play an essential part in her Institute's program.

While the work of the Institute is still in its infancy, The Holisitic Group believes that Joan McKenna's approach is valid. Especially when combined with stress reduction techniques, lowering the body's temperature can in fact kill cancer cells. It is essential to point out that the consistency with which this program is instituted and adhered to by both practitioner and patient determines its ultimate effectiveness. The Group also feels impelled to note that there are elements of the Institute's programs which form a closed system—a set of laws, principles, and ways of being complete unto itself—with which we are uncomfortable. (Contradictions are perhaps inevitable whenever a given healing system, be it Chinese Medicine, Macrobiotics, or Thermodynamic Repatterning, sets up laws which may shut out other equally valid healing methods.) In particular, the Institute has suggested that saunas, because of their heating effect, are detrimental to people with AIDS. We disagree, and feel that saunas can play an important detoxifying role in the prevention and healing of AIDS.

Reservations aside, the Institute for Thermobaric Studies appears to be doing valuable work. Contact the Institute at 2919 4th St., Berkeley, CA 94710, (415) 644-2635.

The successful work of the above practitioners, and of many other practitioners, some of whom protect themselves in a climate of political conservatism by choosing not to make the headlines, validates the holistic approach to healing presented in this book. You may discover in your explorations individual practitioners who suggest vitamins, immuno-enhancers, detoxifiers, stress-reduction techniques, and spiritual approaches not mentioned herein. Differences are not necessarily contradictions; all healing substances and techniques are merely avenues by which you can allow the love you have within you to surface so that you can heal yourself. The Holisitic Group strongly believes that it is not necessary or even desirable to pack your bags and run to Virginia or California, New York or Los Angeles, Mexico or the Bahamas, in order to heal yourself. You can do the work you need to do beginning with this moment, right where you are. The reports of people who are healing themselves of Acquired Immune Deficiency confirm that the approach offered herein is applicable, not only to Acquired Immune Deficiency, but to a wide variety of immune dysfunctions, cancers, and other dis-ease states.

The AIDS Mastery, led by Sally Fisher, co-director of the Actor's Institute, is a workshop especially designed for people diagnosed with AIDS or ARC, and for those closely associated with them. A special adaptation of a workshop originally conceived by Dan Fauci, founder of the Actors Institute, The AIDS Mastery is a powerful and potentially transformative experience.

This two-and-a-half-day workshop is designed to "unleash your power, creativity, and self-love so that you can directly affect the quality of your life. The quality of life is not determined by circumstances, but by how we hold the circumstances. . . .The AIDS Mastery puts you in touch with choice; with the will to see and exercise options. . . .Life is about choosing to live in the present. If you see the possibilities in everything, then anything is possible."

I joyfully participated in the AIDS Mastery in San Francisco in 1986, and cried my heart out on the last day. Not only did I experience a deep emotional clearing that is allowing me to live my life more fully, but I was blown away by the willingness of the other attendees to delve deeply into the depths of their own hearts and souls. As one of the participants said to us at the close of the first evening,

"Living in the moment is something I've read about, but it just feels different when I hear it here."

As for Sally Fisher, it is no secret that I think she's the best thing to come along since chocolate chip cookies. Dynamic, sometimes outrageous, very "out there" in a totally positive sense, and absolutely inspiring, she alone is worth any price of admission. Like Louise Hay, Sally has had an intimate experience with the power of the mind to heal. When her son Fisher Stevens, a nationally-known actor, was diagnosed with Hodgkin's Disease, it was a combination of individual consultation with Louise Hay, inner work and visualization, plus allopathic treatment that did the trick. As a result, Sally like Louise, brings total conviction to her work, and I've seen it pay off in the quality of the AIDS Mastery experience.

Rather than attempt to give you rundown of what may transpire during the AIDS Mastery, let me simply repeat Sally's favorite quote from Swami Muktananda that "Transformation and enlightenment happen the moment we recognize who we are." If you are ready for that recognition, or at least intrigued by it, the Mastery is a good place to peel away some of the layers between your ego and your God-self.

In addition to taking the AIDS Mastery around the country, Sally has prepared six cassettes: "Body Talk;" "Breaking Patterns;" "Completing Relationships;" "Relationships: Sex & Intimacy;" "AIDS: Anger Incorrectly Directed at the Self (Redirecting);" and "Self Love." These tapes retail for $10.95, and $5.00 for people diagnosed with AIDS experiencing financial hardship. NY State residents, please add the appropriate sales tax. Contact Northern Lights Alternatives, Dept. J, 5 W. 19th St., 3rd floor, New York, NY 10011, (212) 924-8888.

The Experience Weekend, facilitated by Robert Eichberg, Ph.D., is for women and men, 18 years or older, who are willing to take responsibility to improve the quality of their lives. The 2-day weekend, founded by the late David Goodstein, owner/publisher of the gay "Advocate" and Rob Eichberg, provides a means for people to discover and experience their own power, and the choices available to them.

Rob Eichberg is one of the few openly gay men who is conducting seminars on healing and empowerment on a national level. Although I have not yet had the opportunity to experience his Experience, my initial meeting with him convinced me that he is an inspiring teacher motivated by deep concern for the community and the planet. I encourage you to explore his work.

Rob has also been facilitating an evening workshop, *Being Powerful in the Face of AIDS*. This is sometimes presented as a fundraiser for AIDS service organizations. You can contact him at 116 N. Robertson Blvd., Ste. 801, Los Angeles, CA 90048, (213) 659-2307.

AIDS & KS: A Holistic Approach, the original research paper of The Holisitic Group, is available by mail for those who would like to examine the roots of the information contained in the Inquiry section of this manuscript. Derived from a single meeting of a research group with Kevin Ryerson on April 10, 1983, supplemented by additional inquiries on June 2 of that year, this material will be found to be not only fairly accurate, but highly prophetic in nature. It is available postpaid for $5.00 plus 7% California sales tax when applicable from The Holisitic Group, P.O. Box 3073, Oakland, CA 94609.

"Living with AIDS", a July/August 1987 *Yoga Journal* article by Susan Jacobs with myself, is the most complete and affirming account of the positive and transformative aspects of the AIDS phenomenon now available. Filled with page after page of positive testimony from people diagnosed with the dis-ease and their open-hearted supporters, it is an ESSENTIAL supplement to the material contained herein. This article was specifically invisioned to counteract the notion that the AIDS experience is only about pain, suffering, despair and fatality. It is especially recommended for individuals who are willing to open their eyes to the opportunities for individual and planetary transformation that this dis-ease presents to us. Reprints are available for $3. (Note that this issue also features articles on Yoga and AIDS and material by Stephen Levine.) Contact *Yoga Journal*, 2054 University Ave., Berkeley, CA 94794, (415) 841-9200.

"AIDS: The Promise of Alternative Treatments," a September 1986 *East West Magazine* article by Carolyn Reuben, is the most complete and affirming account of holistic approaches to healing AIDS yet published in magazine format. For reprint information, contact them at 17 Station Street, Box 1200, Brookline, MA 02147, (617) 232-1000.

Healing AIDS, a newsletter of healing tools, resources and aids, is published and edited in San Francisco by Ed Sibbett and Doug Yagaloff. It not only is the most complete guide to holistically-oriented AIDS special events, groups, programs, workshops and classes in the Bay Area, but it contains a continually-updated list of videos, cassettes and books, healers and counselors, and "new finds" which will be of interest to all. Most importantly, the short articles that head-line each issue, such as "Rebirthing and AIDS," "How Much Can Life be Enjoyed?," "Take Charge of Your Healing," and "The Healing Power of Affirmations" are an excellent and easy way to introduce someone you love to the myriad resources and holistic healing options currently available. Yearly subscriptions are $7 for people with AIDS/ARC and low income, $12 for others. Advertising and classifieds are welcome, and articles, resources and healing tools are sought for publication. Contact Healing AIDS, 3835 20th St., San Francisco, CA 94114, (415) 647-3156.

The AIDS Treatment News, published biweekly by John S. James, reports on experimental and alternative treatments, especially those available now. It collects information from medical journals and interviews with scientists, physicians, health practitioners and persons diagnosed with AIDS or ARC. Its goals are to increase the options for treatment, disseminate hard-to-get treatment information, and examine the ethical and public-policy issues around AIDS treatment and research.

John James has done a magnificent service by assembling information on AL721, DNCB, lentinan, BHT, coenzyme Q, naltrexone, AZT, aerosol pentamidine and other treatment options in a format that tells us what we need to know and what some people might wish us not to hear. Subscriptions are $25 per quarter, or $8 for PWA/PWARC, and include copies of the most important back issues covering the substances listed above. A complete set of back issues is available for $30. Contact John S. James, P.O. Box 411256, San Francisco, CA 94141, (415) 282-0110.

The *People with AIDS Coalition Newsline*, published monthly by the New York PWA Coalition, is the most complete and moving document of its kind in the world. A whopping 48 pages, as befits the Big Apple, it is filled with supportive personal testimony from PWAs, medical and holistic update, book reviews, and photos. Thanks to the good graces of Michael Hirsch and staff, it is available free to PWAs and PWARCs, and by $20 subscription to others.

The PWA Coalition has also made available a 160-page publication *Surviving and Thriving with AIDS*. Filled with stories of how people have coped with and lived beyond their initial diagnosis of AIDS and ARC, it has been designed specifically to answer the questions of and provide support to people who have just been diagnosed. It is available at no charge to PWAs and PWARCs, and for $5 to others. (Although I was not asked to write this, I hasten to add that I'm sure donations to support the publication and dissemination of this free material will be gratefully welcome and accepted.) Contact the PWA Coalition, 263A West 19th Street, New York, N.Y. 10011, (212) 627-1810.

Margo Adair, developer of Applied Meditation, does consulting with agencies, conducts trainings in the community at large, and works with individuals on a one-on-one basis. For people diagnosed with AIDS, ARC, or other life-threatening dis-eases, she teaches intuitive problem solving, stress reduction, visualization and healing skills. For people who are providing support services for such individuals, she teaches how to: stay centered emotionally and avoid burnout, design visualizations, avoid the victim/rescuer mentality, develop and maintain sensitivity to cross-cultural differences and develop methods for mutual support.

Margo's work is always conducted with an awareness of the social condition in which we live. Her empowerment workshops are specifically designed to transform limiting patterns that are a result of such cultural condition as homophobia, racism, etc.....

Margo Adair has prepared two sets of audio-cassette tapes of guided visualizations for people diagnosed with AIDS and for the Worried Well. Each set comes with a booklet explaining the process of visualization and offering specific guidelines for using the tapes. The visualizations begin with the assumption that each of us is his/her own best judge of what is best for us: They provide a context for each person to choose their own ways of living well.

For people with AIDS, there are two cassettes with the following four meditations: *Envisioning a Healthy Immune System; Healing and Treatment Choice; Respite: Enlightening the Heart and Relieving Pain;* and *Wise Self: Courage to Keep Up the Fight and/or Let Go.*

For the Worried Well, there is one cassette with two meditations on it: *Envisioning a Healthy Immune System* and *Cultivating Wellness in Your Life.*

All tapes are co-produced by the Shanti Project and Tools for Change, and include music by Stepfan Dasho. The set for people with AIDS (the two cassettes with four meditations and instruction booklet) is available for $12.75 plus $1.40 postage (California residents add .90 tax). The tape for the Worried Well is available for $8.50 plus $1.40 postage (California residents add .60 tax). Make checks payable to Tools for Change and mail to: Tools for Change, Dept. P, P.O. Box 14141, San Francisco, CA 94114.

Margo's book, *Working Inside Out: Tools for Change,* contains a rich assortment of applied meditations. It is a step-by-step guide that teaches a person to relax. It is available at your local bookstore (tell them it is published by Wingbow Press and distributed by BOOK-PEOPLE in Berkeley, California—(800) 277-1516 or (415) 549-3030). If you want to order the book yourself, not through a bookstore, then send $12.00 (postpaid) to Tools for Change, Dept. P, P.O. Box 14141, San Francisco, CA 94114.

In addition to these, Margo also has a complete, excellent set of generalized applied meditation tapes called the "Working Inside Out" tape series:

Tape 1: Relaxing / Cultivate Desired Attributes

Tape 2: Stress Reduction / Affirmations / Centering for the Day

Tape 3: Rehearsing the Future / Creativity Flowing

Tape 4: Mental House Cleaning / Tapping Universal Energy / Self Protection / Stretching the Imagination

Tape 5: Stretching Your Confidence / Fear as Challenge

Tape 6: Listen To and Heal Your Body / Create Your Own Healthful Routine

Tape 7: Meeting Overwhelming Challenge and / or Life Threatening Illness / Enlighten the Heart, Relieve Pain

Tape 8: Sexuality / Enjoyment / Bring Forth What Is Needed

Tape 9A & 9B: Cultivating Your Best (available using male or female pronoun) / Exploring Your Life

Tape 10: Liberate Yourself / From Trauma to Wisdom

Tape 11: Getting Unstuck / Habit Control

Tape 12: Move Beyond Alienation / Enriching Connections

Tape 13: Cultivate Community / Turn Anger into a Positive Force

Tape 14: Crystal Clear Communication / Family: Create a Loving Future

Tape 15: Letting Go / Manifesting Your Highest Values

Tape 16: Caring Acts Heal the Planet / Towards A Balanced World

Tape 17: Sustaining Our Work Towards Peace & Justice / Surpassing Culturally Imposed Limitations

Tape 18: Embracing Cultural Diversity / Healing the Organization

Tape 19: Reclaim Your Emotional Life (for men) / How to Discover Who Profits

Tape 20: Reclaiming Your Power (for women) / Patience, Endurance, & Courage

PRICE LIST
(Available *only* in the following quantities.)

		Shipping and Handling* 4th Class	
		Mail	U.P.S.
One Tape @	$10.95	$1.75	$2.75
Two Tapes @	$ 9.95=$19.90	$1.75	$2.75
Three Tapes @	$ 8.95=$26.85	$1.75	$2.75
Five Tapes @	$ 7.95=$39.75	$1.75	$2.75
Ten Tapes @	$ 6.95=$69.50	$2.00	$3.25
Fifteen Tapes @	$ 5.95=$89.25	$2.50	$3.50
Full Set or 20 Tapes	$ 4.95=$99.00	$2.50	$4.00

Add 6% or 7% Sales Tax if inside California

*Prices based upon April 15, 1987 rates. Please check with the United States Postal Service, or United Parcel Service, to ascertain the correct rates if you believe there's been a change.

To order these tapes, calculate the amount from the table above and send a list of the tapes you would like along with a cashier's check or money order for the calculated amount to: Tools For Change, Dept. P, P.O. Box 14141, San Francisco, CA 94114, (415) 861-6838.

Emmett E. Miller, M.D., has made some of the finest healing, stress reduction, and behavior modification tapes to be found. Several of his tapes, including "The Healing Journey" and "Letting Go of Stress," are considered classics, and are recommended by Elisabeth Kübler-Ross's organization.

Emmett's tapes include "Healing Journey" (#16) (Ed. note: the music by Raphael is fabulous); "Letting Go of Stress (#23, music by Stephen Halpern, Ph.D.), "Rainbow Butterfly (#11, music by Georgia Kelly—aids one's ability to visualize and deepen meditative skills, further self-esteem, aid in personal transformation, helps improve a bad day or lighten a mood—great for children); "An Answer to Cancer" (#29); "Change the Channel on Pain" (#46, managing pain successfully); "Accepting Change—Moving On" (#48, for coping with death, dying, divorce, or feeling stuck and wanting to move on); "10-Minute Stress Manager" (#53); "Imagine Yourself Slim" (#19); "Easing Into Sleep" (#20), and "Healing Your Back" (#05). "Healing the Planet," a new cassette, employs both narration and beautiful music in a transformative visualization which allows one to move the energy of self-healing outward to the larger task of communal and planetary transformation. This and all single cassettes retail for $10.95.

In addition, you can order such two-tape sets as "Successful Surgery and Recovery" (#203) and "Writing Your Own Script" (#202, an aid to changing behavior patterns, redoing old scripts, dropping negative patterns and behavior, and facilitating change), which retail for $18.95. Also available is Dr. Miller's book, *Self-Imagery: Creating Your Own Good Health* ($7.95) which presents case histories illustrating the benefits of his methods in improving and maintaining mental and physical health, and which is accompanied by a free full-length audio cassette, "Introduction to Software for the Mind," which includes sample excerpts from many of Dr. Miller's most popular tape programs.

All of Emmett Miller's tapes are available from Source Cassettes, Dept. M176, P.O. Box W, Stanford, CA 94305. Include $1.50 postage and handling for the first item in the continental U.S., $3.00 for Canada, Hawaii, and Alaska, and $5.00 for overseas locations; for additional items, add .50 each. California residents add 6½% sales tax. Note that 10% discounts are available for orders of 3 to 5 items; 15% discount for orders of 6 or more items.

Mary Richards has prepared a wonderful series of "Master Your Mind" visualization and relaxation cassettes, two of which specifically deal with AIDS. As of this writing, I have had the opportunity to audition the self-hypnosis sides of "AIDS...A Self Healing Process" and "Opt for Vibrant Health in this Age of AIDS" (designed for the Worried Well). Featuring both Mary's soothing voice and the seductively inviting voice of Dennis McMillan (a great idea!), with fine music and those familiar New Age birds twittering away, these well-crafted tapes will quickly earn their place next to the indispensible masterpieces of Louise Hay.

The above tapes are part of Mary Richards' Self Hypnosis/Subliminal Series 2000, which features audible programming on one side and the same information recorded subliminally on the other. Other tapes in this format include "Making the Transition," "Freedom from Addiction," "Stress Reduction," "Spiritual Cleansing," and "Your Inner Healing." Her Subliminal Impact Series includes "Strong Immune System," which my friend Van Ault has used successfully to rebalance himself when he felt a cold or some other dis-ease coming on. Other titles in various formats include "Be All That You Are," "Find the Joy Within," "Successful Woman," "Relaxed in the Dentist Chair," "Successful Surgery," "Fighting the Cancer," and "Supporting your Recovery," "Release Discomfort," and "Self Healing Sleep."

The Children's Series includes "I AM a Happy child" (I sure could have used that one way back), "I AM Whatever I Want To Be" (hmmm...), and, yes, "I AM proud...My Bed is Dry." Of all of Mary's tapes, the tape that one part of me says I "should" buy is "Letting Go of Chocolate," while the other part of me, which resists all shoulds, is gearing up for another late-night raid at the local junk food store.

Mary Richards healed herself from a brain concussion, serious back and neck injuries, and her doctors' diagnoses of permanent inability to work by doing deep-relaxation meditation and accessing her own inner answers 4 hours a day for a period of 6 months. She writes, "My accident gave me an opportunity to heal the effects of burnout and create a healthier flow in all areas of my life. In time, I realized that my accident had been a blessing in disguise, for all of my guided relaxation tapes come from my own life experience and healing as well as my work with clients." Mary's healing crisis, like that of Louise Hay or Sally Fisher's son, has blessed us with some wonderful tools for transformation.

All of Mary's tapes are $12.95 each, except the Children's Series, which goes for $10.95. Add $1.60 for postage and handling, plus up to 7% sales tax for California residents. Contact Master Your Mind, Dept. W, 881 Hawthorne Drive, Walnut Creek, CA 94596.

The Simonton Center practices and promotes the pioneering work of O. Carl Simonton, M.D. His classic work, *Getting Well Again* (Bantam paperback), co-authored with Stephanie Matthews-Simonton and James L. Creighton, has contributed immeasurably to popular acceptance of the power of the mind to effect healing.

Located in Southern California, the Center offers five day New Patient Session programs which use group process to empower patients to make changes in their lives which will facilitate the healing process. A prerequisite for consideration for these programs, which are held approximately each month, is reading *Getting Well Again* and beginning the relaxation, mental imagery (creative thinking) and self-help program described in the book. The Simonton Cancer Center also offers individual counseling with their staff therapists at a charge of $100.00 per hour. People with AIDS are welcome in new patient sessions, and individual sessions. For further information, call (213) 459-4434.

New patients considering using any part of the Simonton approach are encouraged to begin with the following 4 items:

(1) *Getting Well Again* ($3.95);

(2) "Relaxation and Mental Imagery as Applies to Cancer Therapy" (#312, $10.00), a cassette tape which includes instructions on use of the mental imagery process specific to cancer patients plus much guided relaxation and visualization;

(3) "Role of Belief in Cancer Therapy," (#400, $40.00), a four-cassette public lecture series, delivered by O. Carl Simonton at the Crystal Cathedral, including questions and answers from the audience;

(4) "Hope, Hopelessness, Purpose and Trust" (#404, $10.00), a 1985 talk by Dr. Simonton.

All books and tapes are available by sending your check or money order, U.S. funds only, to Simonton Cancer Center, Dept. W, P.O. Box 1055, Azle, TX 76020. Include $1.00 per item for all orders within the U.S., Canada, or Mexico, and $1.50 for overseas airmail or rush handling.

The Metaphysical Alliance, founded by Michael Zonta, holds monthly donate-if-you-can healing services for the Bay Area AIDS community. These services, which begin with the daily 5-minute 7PM meditation for the healing of AIDS, which is observed worldwide in local time zones, have inspired many who are on the healing path.

Tapes of some of the excellent speakers and panels at these services are available at nominal cost. I consider the two panels, "AIDS Survivors and Thrivers Parts I and II," which featured 6 heroic men, half of whom have lived with AIDS for at least 5 years, *indispensible* to anyone wishing to understand the mind-body-spirit essence of the healing process. Also available are moving talks by Louise Hay and Sally Fisher, two by Irene Smith (Part I on touch, Part II on Elisabeth Kübler-Ross's appraoch to emotional growth), a nutritional panel with Misha Cohen, D.O.M., C.A., Denise Buzbuzian, nutritionist, and Tom O'Connor, author of *Living with AIDS*, and an evening with long-term AIDS thriver Louie Nassaney. Donations of $7 are requested for audio tapes, and $10 for videotapes. Contact the Metaphysical Alliance, 2261 Market Street #465, San Francisco, CA 94114, (415) 431-8708.

Patricia Sun deserves her international reputation as a "must see" New Age healer and teacher. I have attended several of her Bay Area evening presentations, and, making allowances for the heterosexual framework from which she tends to reference, have found her work and her famed healing tones a continued source of renewal and inspiration. Director of the Institute of Communication for Understanding, Patricia teaches a new style of conflict resolution based upon a win/win philosophy and the creation of new options for communication. I think she's great.

In November of 1986, at a talk co-sponsored by the San Francisco group Expect a Miracle, Patricia Sun created an invaluable perspective from which to understand the process of dis-ease and the nature of healing. The 2-tape set of this talk, "Empowering Healing," (#38–$20.00), makes reference to AIDS, cancer and autoimmune dis-eases. I consider this tape an invaluable addition to the material contained in this book, and have incorporated some of the ideas I received from Patricia into my own seminars.

Other tapes by Patricia which seem most appropriate to this book's subject matter include her "All sounds and meditation" (#1–$10.00), which will give you 60-minutes of Patricia's unique healing tones and meditations; "Well-being Meditation tape" (#12–$15.00), created to heal the locked stress and emotional energy in the body—includes a mind/body relationship meditation and Patricia's sounds; "Introductory tape" (#15–$10.00); and "The Wisdom of our Bodies" (#35–$15.00), a vibrant workshop on healing tapes at the Stanford School of Medicine. You may also want to explore tapes dealing with

"Compulsive Behavior" (#16—$20.00) (oh no, it's 11PM and I'm still writing!), "Overweight Workshop Parts I and II (#27 and 28, $20.00 each)—"Excess weight is the depression of personal power; a fear of surrendering to one's power and clarity"; "Women and Relationships" (#20—$20.00), "Personal and Planetary Peace" (#33—$20.00), and "Personal Power to Heal the World" (#34—$20.00). California residents, please include up to 7% sales tax with your order. Write Patricia Sun, Dept. 30, P.O. Box 7065, Berkeley, CA 94707.

The Cancer Support & Education Center of Menlo Park, CA, has a whole series of tapes available. Write them for information at 250 Oak Grove Avenue, Menlo Park, CA 94025.

"Getting Well Healing Imagery: A Guided Visualization" is a cassette tape by *Wendy Allen*. Tom Chaudoin who is interviewed in this book found this tape in a health food store and recommended it to me. Order the tape from Guided Visualization, P.O. Box 28504, San Jose, CA 95159. The cost is $10.00 each, postpaid. All California residents may now recite the 6% sales tax mantra, and pray that it does not increase in 1986.

Dick Sutphen, an author of self-help books, hypnotist and seminar leader has recorded a huge catalogue's worth of books and self-hypnosis tapes on almost any conceivable subject. I auditioned his "A Strong Immune System" tape (HPO30—$12.50, free to anyone testing HIV-positive who can't afford it), and consider it of value for people healing immune dysfunction, ARC or AIDS.

My initial reaction to the tape was disappointment in the absence of music and a discovery that I personally do not resonate well with Dick's voice. Choosing to let go of those feelings, I found Dick's self-hypnosis induction masterful and effective. The program itself allows the listener to construct both their own vision of how the immune system might optimally function and their actual healing process. For those readers who have their own ideas about these matters, and want some space of their own between the suggestions of most tape narrators, this will provide the perfect opportunity to create exactly what they want.

Other Dick Sutphen tapes recommended to me by D.R., a person diagnosed with AIDS who contributed to some of the channelings in this book, are "Stress Control" (HP002—$12.50), "Eliminating Fear & Worry" (HP003—$12.50), "How to Rapidly Develop Psychic Ability" (2 tapes, C837—$24.95), and "Healing Acceleration" (C830—$24.95). All these tapes are recorded in both self-hypnosis backed by subliminal versions, and often allow you to either continue with your day or work in your sleep. Shipping charges: Order up to $15.00, add $1.50 up to $25.00, add $2.00; up to $35.00, add $3.25; up to $45.00, add $3.75; up to $55.00, add $4.50; up to $65.00, add $5.25; up to $75.00, add $6.00; up to $100.00, add $7.50. Canadian orders, include $7.50 extra in U.S. funds. California residents add sales tax. Contact Valley of the Sun Publishing, Dept. S, Box 3004, Agoura Hills, CA 91301. Please mention this book.

"Zodiac Suite" is a cassette tape by *Steven Halpern,* which I follow up the scale while doing my musical chakra meditation. Steven's "Spectrum Suite" is a pioneering piece of music designed for relaxation and stress reduction, and is also available on LP. If you cannot find these at your favorite New Age music outlet, write Halpern Sounds, 1775 Old Country Road, #9, Belmont, CA 94002, or call (415) 592-4900 for more information.

A Way to Survive the AIDS Epidemic, a lovely little book based on the Metaphysical Teachings of the Ancient Masters, has been assembled by *Thomas Alan Berg.* Thomas healed a tumor by studying the ancient art of self-healing and the spiritual teachings of Christ, Buddha, and other Masters. The book has been described by its editor as "a meditation on inner soul potential for self-healing," and is comprised mainly of short excerpts from great spiritual works, interspersed with the editor's commentary. Order from Palm Publications, 1850 Union Street, #294-B, San Francisco, CA 94123; $4.95 plus 6½% sales tax for California residents, postpaid.

"Exploring the Heart of Healing in AIDS" was the title of January 1986 San Francisco presentation by *Stephen Levine,* former director of the Hanuman Foundation Dying Project and author of *Who Dies?* and *Ram Dass,* author of *Be Here Now, Grist for the Mill* (with Stephen Levine) and *How Can I Help* (with Paul Gorman). The event, which marked the first time that these two noted spiritual teachers joined together for a public talk about AIDS, addressed issues arising from the high death rate from the dis-ease. Among the subjects covered were the possibility of healing one's life regardless of physical recovery, burnout among health care workers, learning "to touch with mercy that which we have touched and experienced with anger and fear," and the spiritual nature of our physical existence. Multiple references were made to what these men had learned from working with Elisabeth Kübler-Ross, M.D., contributor to this volume.

This memorable afternoon, which included an invaluable 20-minute meditation on sensation and pain led by Stephen Levine, has been captured on both audio cassette and videotape. The two audio cassettes are available for $17.00 ($18.00 for California residents, which includes sales tax). Videotapes are available for $65.00 in ½-inch VHS format ($70.00 for California residents including sales tax); $75.oo in ½-inch BETA ($80.00 for California residents); and $90.00 in ¾-inch format ($100.00 for California residents). Make checks payable to "The Access Group, Ltd.," and send to Daniel Barnes, c/o The Access Group, Ltd., Dept. A, 4 Cielo Lane, Building 4, Unit D, Novato, CA 94947.

Stephen Levine's books, *Who Dies?* ($9.95), *Meetings at the Edge* ($7.95), and *Gradual Awakening* ($5.95) complement the works of Elisabeth Kübler-Ross and others. Order from Alan Klein, Dept. SL, 1034 Page Street, San Francisco, CA 94117. Enclose $1.50 per book for postage and handling. California residents add 6½% sales tax. U.S. and Canadian orders only in U.S. funds, please.

Easy Death: Talks and Essays on the Inherent and Ultimate Transcendence of Death and Everything Else, by Da Free John, has been termed a masterpiece by no less an authority than Elisabeth Kübler-Ross. This work was recommended to me by a person with Acquired Immune Deficiency whom I entertained on the San Francisco General Hospital AIDS ward, who reported that reading it had enabled him to accept for the first time the blessings and fullness of his life.

Not only was *Celestial Arts* the only publisher besides Stillpoint willing to consider publishing this book, but it has made available some of the finest New Age books on healing and inspiration to be found today. I want to especially recommend *How Shall I Live: Transforming Surgery or Any Health Crisis into Greater Aliveness*, by Richard Moss, M.D. This book, along with the talk of Patricia Sun listed in this section, has greatly expanded my understanding of the healing process.

Also available from Celestial Arts are such books as *Loving Someone Gay* by Don Clark, Ph.D., *Sound Medicine* and *Companions in Spirit* by Laeh Maggie Garfield, *Choose to Be Healthy* by Susan Smith Jones, *The Essential Alan Watts, Self Imagery* by Emmett E. Miller, M.D., *The Black Butterfly* and *The I That Is We* by Richard Moss, M.D., all of the rebirthing books and relationships books by Sondra Ray, *Love is Letting Go of Fear* by Gerald G. Jampolsky, M.D., all of Virginia Satir's books, *The Bum Back Book* by Michael Reed Gach, and *Headaches: The Drugless Way to Lasting Relief* by Harry C. Ehrmantraut, Ph.D. Need

I say more? Contact Celestial Arts, P.O. Box 7327, Berkeley, CA 94707. For customer service and all orders, call (415) 524-1801.

Psychoimmunity and the Healing Process can be purchased in quantity at a discount by organizations and individuals who wish to make books available to clients or people in need, or who would like to sell them to raise funds for service work. Please contact myself, Jason Serinus, c/o The Holistic Group, P.O. Box 3073, Oakland, CA 94609. For bookstore orders, please contact Celestial Arts (see listing above). Readers wishing additional single copies shipped directly to themselves or friends may order directly from me. Copies of this Second Edition are $10.95 each plus $1.50 for postage and handling. For First Class postage, please send $3.25/book. (Orders outside USA: surface mail, $2.50 postage and handling. Airmail is $4.00 for Canada, $7.00 elsewhere). California residents add 7% (77¢) per book. Please make checks payable to The Holistic Group, and allow up to 8 weeks for delivery.

Paul Reed, my editor at Celestial Arts, is a novelist, critic and essayist who has written extensively about AIDS, safesex, and health for several years. He was one of the first writers to do a series on safesex, published as "Looking for Mr. Safesex" in the San Francisco *Bay Area Reporter* way back in 1983. His book, *Facing It: A Novel of AIDS* (Gay Sunshine Press—$7.95) has established itself as the only serious novel about the AIDS crisis so far in print. First released in 1984, it chronicles one man's struggle with AIDS in the frightening early years of the epidemic, way before an alternative support system existed.

Paul has continued to write about safesex, and has given evidence of his compassionate concern for his brothers in his many critical reviews of the current AIDS literature. In 1987 he co-authored (with Patti Breitman and Kim Knutson) the short, sex-positive book, *How To Persuade Your Lover To Use a Condom—And Why You Should* ($4.95). If you feel you may have difficulty in convincing your sexual partners to use condoms and have safesex, this book contains actual scripts upon which you can base your dialogue with them. This material will also help you initiate your own inner dialogue with any resistance you may have to protecting yourself and others.

Paul's book *Serenity* (Celestial Arts—$5.95), available beginning October 1987, is designed to help gay men cope with the everyday stress of living in the midst of the AIDS epidemic. He tells me that his approach is "more psychoanalytic than holistic," and that he in fact "takes a few shots at the logical potholes in the holistic model." Hoping that he has remembered that healing is a spiritual act, and therefore transcends the limitations of Western logical empiricism, I recommend this book to you. If it supplies fodder to my own critics, some of whom believe that anyone who advocates that healing of AIDS is possible is irresponsible and "dangerous," I hereby remind Paul that this author also writes book reviews.

Paul Reed lives in San Francisco with his beautiful lover Tom. His 1987 projects include another novel and a nonfiction book about questions of sexual identity, hope, loss, and survival. If your local bookstore doesn't have enough foresight to stock his works, you can order them directly from him at P.O. Box 14793, San Francisco, CA 94114. Please include $2.00 for postage and handling (California residents add 6½% sales tax), and send him a little wink from yours truly.

I have been very fortunate to have as my editor a sympathetic gay brother who has chosen to work with such an open-minded and life-affirming publisher as Celestial Arts. My thanks to all.

Nan Fuch's book, *The Nutrition Detective*, comes highly recommended from two fine practitioners, Misha Cohen, O.M.D., C.A. of San Francisco and Elaine Stocker, D.N., a practitioner of Naprapathy, cranial manipulation, nutrition and exercise counseling in the Chicago area. Although Nan's book focuses mainly on women's health, its information is of great value for all people.

Nan has been doing "The Nutrition Detective" workshops in the L.A. area, helping individuals get in touch with their own inner guidance concerning nutritional matters. A tape from Channel Light Productions will be available sometime in 1987. Contact Nan Fuchs, 3124-C Colorado Ave., Santa Monica, CA, (213) 829-4130.

Flower essences are a simple, safe, and effective tool for protection and transformation which operate on the levels of mind, body, and spirit (see Inquiry for detailed discussion). Information on the Bach Flower Remedies can be found in *The Handbook of the Bach Flower Remedies* by Dr. Philip M. Chancellor, *A Guide to the Bach Flower Remedies* by Julian Barnard (both published by C.W. Daniel Co., Ltd., England), and in Dr. Bach's own *The Bach Flower Remedies*, a compilation of his books. *The Medical Discoveries of Edward Bach, Physician,* by Nora Weeks, is perhaps the only current available biography of Dr. Bach. In addition, information on Flower Essences, channeled through

Kevin Ryerson, is available in *Flower Essences* by Gurudas (Brotherhood of Life).

The Flower Essence Society of Richard Katz and Patricia Kaminski was founded in 1979 to stimulate an educational and research network among flower essence practitioners and to encourage the study and use of local essences. The society can mail order their Stock Kits #1, 2, and 3, each of which contains 24 stock bottles of their line of flower essences, and which come in either 1 dram ($60), 2 dram (7.4 ml., $80) or 1 ounce ($160) sizes. In addition, they sell individual stock bottles, including many of the essences marked "FES," (see Chapter 12) which may prove beneficial in a preventive/healing program for AIDS. These are available in sizes of 1 dram ($3), 2 dram ($4), and 1 ounce ($8). Newly available in 1986 is an introductory kit of 12 of their most frequently requested essences, which comes in 1 dram ($33), 2 dram ($44), and 1 ounce ($88) sizes.

Readers who prefer to purchase their essences at dosage dilution rather than at the stock level of concentration (a dosage bottle is made by mixing 2 drops from the stock bottle into a 1 oz. dosage bottle filled with distilled water and a little brandy—see explanation in *Flower Essences* and other literature) can purchase 1 oz. ready-to-use dosage bottles of desired essences at $5 each. In addition, the Society offers three highly concentrated flower fragrance oils by Omar: lavender oil ($5/bottle), white rose oil ($7/bottle), and red rose oil ($7/bottle).

The above flower essence offerings are available from Flower Essence Services, P.O. Box 586-J, Nevada City, CA 95959. For surface orders under $15, add $2.00, orders $15 or more, add $4.00. Rush orders, receiving first priority in shipping, add $3.00 to charges. For air mail charges, which can run considerably higher, write them for information. California residents add 6% sales tax.

The Flower Essence Society itself publishes a members' newsletter, and mail orders many books on plant study and lore, spiritual science, and Dr. Bach. Among their offerings are several books by "spiritual scientist" Rudolf Steiner, an "anthroposophist" whose teachings are often suggested for study by the Entities who speak through Kevin Ryerson. Steiner has proven one of the few individuals in recent history to apply successfully the discipline and clarity of scientific thinking to the investigation of the invisible realm of spirit. Contact them at P.O. Box 459-J, Nevada City, CA 95959. (Note that the address for printed matter differs from the address for oils and essences.)

Richard Katz of the Flower Essence Society would like to hear from both practitioners working with AIDS as well as individuals healing AIDS and ARC who have found flower essences a useful part of their programs. Please contact him at the above address.

Bach Flower Remedies may be ordered by contacting Ellon, Inc., Woodmere, NY 11598. Flower essences prepared by Gurudas are available through *Pegasus Products*, P.O. Box 228, Boulder, CO 80306. Joy Persetti of Hawaii, who has also consulted with Kevin Ryerson, has prepared flower essences available through *Joy's Hawaiian Flower Essences*, Dept. J, Pualana, P.O. Box 682, Haiku, HI 96708.

The Native Herb Company of Christopher Hobbs, an internationally respected herbalist, botanist, and teacher, is one reliable source of potent herbal tinctures and formulas made from organic and wild-crafted herbs (see Paul Lee's article). Those which The Holisitic Group finds specifically helpful in tincture form, and which are available in 1 oz. amber dropper bottles, include Echinacea ($6.20 retail, $4.00 wholesale), Milk Thistle ($6.20 retail, $4.00 wholesale—good for the liver), Pau D'Arco ($5.20 retail, $3.50 wholesale), and Siberian Ginseng ($5.20 retail, $3.50 wholesale). Also available are two herbal formulas: Candida Cleanse, a very potent 4 to 1 extract combining Pau d'Arco, Echinacea, Astragalus, Black Walnut, Nettles, Horsetail, Spirulina, Biotin, and Gentian ($13.95), and Vita-mune, combining Echinacea, Astragalus, Silybum, Avena, Asarum, Coliolus, Aralia, and Usnea ($6.75 retail, $4.35 wholesale). Wholesale prices are offered to both stores and practitioners using the tinctures in their practice, and to individuals who place orders over $50.00.

Christopher Hobbs has completed a book, *Superimmunity: Herbs and Other Natural Remedies for a Healthy Immune System*, which may be available from his Botanica Press at this time. As well as detailed herbal information, the book includes information on human biology and the functioning of the immune system, and can serve as a basic primer for lay readers. Botanica Press is also distributing other alternative information which may prove of interest to you, including the book *Internal Cleansing: A Practical Guide to Colon Health* by Linda Berry, D.C. ($3.95).

Christopher Hobbs's offerings are available from the Native Herb Co., Box 742-S, Capitola, CA 95010. Shipping charges are: up to $15, add $1.25; $15.01-$30, add $1.75; $30.01 and up, add $2.25. California residents add 6% sales tax.

Paul A. Lee's Platonic Academy of Herbal Studies, a professional training school for herbalists, offers both resident and correspondence courses. A former teaching assistant to Paul Tillich at Harvard University, Paul has published Tillich's *The Meaning of Health: The Relation of Religion and Health* through North Atlantic Books, Richmond, CA. High on his list of recommended readings are *The Herb Book* by John Lust, *The Way of Herbs* by Michael Tierra (East/West Books), *A Modern Herbal* by Grieve, and *Medicines from the Earth* by Dr. Thomson, as well as Tillich's teachings. Write Paul Lee at P.O. Box 409, Santa Cruz, CA 95061, (408) 423-7923 or (408) 426-8810.

Readers desiring further information on homeopathy are referred to *Everybody's Guide to Homeopathic Medicine,* co-authored by *Dana Ullman,* director of Homeopathic Educational Services, 2124 Kittredge St., Berkeley, CA 94704, (415) 653-9270.

Full-Spectrum Light Therapy is an exciting new system of healing, currently being developed and practiced by John Downing, Ph.D., a biomedical scientist from Mill Valley, CA. While Downing's emphasis is on using this method of treatment for people with functional optic nerve problems, full-spectrum light therapy in our opinion holds great promise for the treatment of AIDS and other immune dysfunctions; it deserves consideration by all readers and health practitioners.

In the visually healthy individual, the optic nerve assimilates equally each color component of the full spectrum of light, i.e., red, orange, yellow, green, blue, indigo, and violet. Downing tests the optic nerve to see to what degree it transfers the light information entering through the eyes back to the brain, and to ascertain what colors it is not fully assimilating. He then stimulates the neurovisual system with "bioresonant light." Downing developed bioresonant light by electromagnetically activating ordinary visible light, and feels that this light is much more characteristic of the bioelectric energy of the body than is ordinary light. This enhancement of the electromagnetic field of the light particle makes it more compatible and thus more assimilable into the human organism. Through what is described by neurological science as the Law of Facilitation, this stimulation reactivates dormant neural pathways from the eye to the brain.

The importance of this treatment for people with immune dysfunction is that the eyes, as well as the skin, are access points to the endocrine system. Light coming in through the eyes stimulates the visual pathways; some of these lead into the hypothalamus—the major control center in the brain—by means of the inferior accessory optical tract. Since the hypothalamus essentially regulates all the glands and organs in the body—specifically the pituitary (which hangs down from it), the thymus, and the adrenals—visible light directly affects the functioning of the immune system.

Fritz Hollwich, M.D., in his seminal work *The Influence of Ocular Light Perception on Metabolism in Man and in Animal* (New York: Springer-Verlag), expands upon this idea that light coming through the eyes affects our metabolism, our endocrine system, and our electrical/chemical balance. The author cites an experiment in which blood samples were taken of cataract patients before and after surgery. The researcher discovered that when the cataracts were removed, and more light was allowed to enter through the patients' eyes, they evidenced a significantly more balanced body chemistry in all the glands and organs. Downing's work supports such findings, in that he has witnessed many imbalances in the body clear up as a "side effect" of his full-spectrum light therapy. He specifically reports on several patients with allergies (an immune dysfunction) who were treated with bioresonant light for visual problems. In most cases, the allergy symptoms were significantly reduced; one patient was even able to discontinue allergy medication completely.

We believe that human beings have altered the body's ability to fight dis-ease by spending much time under artificial or filtered light. Downing's work offers much promise, not only for those with visual problems, but for people experiencing immune dysfunction. He is currently preparing several articles and a book on this subject which, along with his bioresonant light source, should be available and in use by licensed health practitioners by the time you read this. Contact John Downing, O.D., Ph.D. at the Neurophotonic Institute, 448 Ignacio Blvd., Ste. 337, Novato, CA 94947, (415) 883-5102.

Irene Newmark is an eclectic practitioner of natural medicines whose San Francisco-based practice began in 1977. A certified acupuncturist, Chinese herbalist, teacher and practitioner of shiatsu and breema bodywork, flower essence practitioner and nutritional consultant, Irene brings all of her skills and knowledge to her unique one-on-one health assessment and nutritional evaluation sessions. Her clients receive very specific programs of foods, supplements, flower essences, and therapeutic baths designed to optimize the body's ability to heal itself. Bodywork and acupuncture sessions are arranged when appropriate.

Irene Newmark has helped me survive the stress of multiple careers for years. Her help was indispensible in bringing this work into print, and clarifying some of the material contained herein. She can be reached at 181 Noe, San Francisco, CA 94114, (415) 552-3813. If you choose to phone her, please leave times when she can call you back, and if you're calling long distance, a number where she can call you collect. I cannot recommend this dedicated woman's work highly enough.

Jack Schwarz is available for lectures and private consultations. He has at last realized a long-held dream to establish his own health training center by opening the Aletheia H.E.A.R.T. (Health, Education, Assessment, Research, Training) Center in Oregon. Programs at the Center include three-day and five-day personal health assessments, internships with Jack and his staff, weekend workshops, etc. To learn more about his work, or to receive ordering information for his books, taped lectures, or tapes of chakra exercises, meditation and self-hypnosis techniques, and tools for self-regulation, contact the Aletheia Foundation, 1809 N. Highway 99, Ashland, OR 97520, (503) 488-0709.

Lynn Johnson, co-creator of the Meditations in this book, currently teaches groups and individual clients how to discover their own powers and access their own personal answers to problematic situations. Contact him at: (415) 626-6565.

Irene Smith, M.T., conducts her invaluable trainings for bodyworkers caring for people diagnosed with AIDS and all life-threatening dis-eases in cities around the country, including Seattle, San Francisco and Minneapolis. She has also assembled a booklet, "Guidelines for Massaging PWAs," which may be ordered from her organization, Balance. Irene both assists at some of the Elisabeth Kübler-Ross Center's LDT workshops when they are held in California, and co-facilitates emotional externalization weekends of her own. For further information, please contact her at Balance, 41 Carl St. #C, San Francisco, CA 94117.

For help in starting a massage service for persons diagnosed with AIDS in your community, you may also wish to contact *Stuart Holland,* who is helping set up and network massage volunteers on a national level. You may reach him at The Massage Studio, 2507 Blaisdell Avenue South, Minneapolis, MN 55404.

Elisabeth Kübler-Ross, M.D.'s organization Shanti Nilaya, with its administrative offices now called the Elisabeth Kübler-Ross Center, has been relocated from California to Elisabeth's new farm/center in the Shenandoah Valley near Head Waters, Virginia. One of Elisabeth's goals, in addition to holding some of her workshops at this new Center, is to build a residential care facility on the site for homeless, rejected, or dying children with AIDS. (Although Elisabeth has found the fear which accompanies the AIDS thought form a temporary obstacle to the construction of this facility, you can be sure that the love and determination of this dedicated woman will create the means by which her home for children can be realized. Meanwhile, she has been placing the children in the private homes of people who will adopt them, and setting up hospices for them. *Please* contact her if you can provide a home for an abandoned child diagnosed with AIDS.)

The Center publishes an excellent newsletter, which will keep you informed of Elisabeth's work, her lecture and workshop schedule, and the many "Friends of Elisabeth Kübler-Ross" groups which have formed around the country. It also features an excellent list of mail order books, tapes, and videotapes, which includes all of her works. (I especially recommend *The Quiet Mind*, sayings of White Eagle, which is available through the Center. Portions of this little book were read by hand analyst friend Anastasia Furst to my mother on her deathbed, and were of great value in her acceptance of her imminent passing.) Write the Center at South Rt. 616, Head Waters, VA 24442, or call (703) 396-3441.

Kevin Ryerson is based in California, and offers classes, retreats, intensives, private consultations, and occasional public presentations. His schedule often includes visits to Los Angeles, Santa Barbara, San Francisco, Sacramento, and Hawaii, with occasional jaunts to other U.S. cities and foreign countries made possible by special arrangement.

Kevin Ryerson's channelings and knowledge are currently featured in *Flower Essences* (Brotherhood of Life) and *Gem Elixirs and Vibrational Healing* (Cassandra Press), edited by Gurudas; *Out on a Limb* and *Dancing in the Light* (Bantam) by Shirley MacLaine—I recommend that you read *Out on a Limb* first—this volume, *Spiritual Nutrition and the Rainbow Diet* (Cassandra Press) by Gabriel Cousens, M.D., and *Channeling: The Intuitive Connection* (Harper & Row), edited by Melanie Branon and William H. Kautz, Sc.D. In addition, Stephanie

Harolde, a long and trusted associate of Kevin's, is assembling *Kevin Ryerson: The Ascendant Path* (tentative title) and several other works; Alan Brickman, M.A. is working on a manuscript based upon conversations with and through Kevin which will present a new holistic model of counseling; soul group member Elisabeth Ar has plans to publish *The Book of John*; and Essene Priest Leslie Goldman is planning manuscripts which will also feature the spiritual teachings and wisdom of the entity John. Last but not least, Kevin Ryerson himself is evolving several books of his own, one of which will feature himself and several other noteworthy trance channels.

Quality audio and video cassettes of Kevin's work are available. Some of these are records of Kevin's live events, promoted and recorded by yours truly, which include both Kevin's brilliant and invaluable lectures and the trance channelings and questions and answers which round out his teaching experience. Highly recommended are "Tantra and Human Sexuality: The Human Relationship," "The Soul's Path" (a wonderful introduction to metaphysics and our identity as mind, body and spirit), "An Evening of Prophecy" (12/86), and "Spirit Communication" (with Kevin at his most eloquent). The exclusive distributor for these tapes is Lisa Tate of Tate Enterprises, 32 West Anapamu, Suite 339, Santa Barbara, CA 93101.

To receive information on Kevin Ryerson's seminars, Life Purpose Intensives, and retreats, please write Lynn Tate and Kevin Ryerson, 3315 Sacramento Street, Ste. 603, San Francisco, CA 94118, (415) 751-9785.

In addition to the books mentioned above which feature Kevin's work, several books containing channeled information are in harmony with the approach of this book. Among those recommended by Kevin are *The Edgar Cayce Handbook for Health through Drugless Therapy*, edited by Reilly and Hagy-Brod (MacMillan), *The Roots of Consciousness* by Jeffrey Mishlove, *The Edgar Cayce Primer* edited by Herbert Puryear, Ph.D., *The Nature of Personal Reality* (a Seth book) by Jane Roberts, and *Man and His Symbols* by Carl G. Jung. There are of course many becoming available which feature channeled information. Some of these are quite excellent and reliable; others are somewhat weighted down by the beliefs and subconscious filtering of the instrument (channeler). By beginning your exploration with the trusted teaching of such channels as Edgar Cayce, Jane Roberts, and Kevin Ryerson, and tapping into your own inner knowledge with an open mind and a loving heart, you can develop the discrimination which will guide you to material of the highest quality.

The San Francisco-based *Center for Applied Intuition* is a network of intuitives and trance channels who work individually and collectively to create "a balanced, innovative approach to solving some of this planet's most serious problems." The Center maintains a list of gifted intuitives and trance channels whom they and Kevin Ryerson wholeheartedly recommend; arranges long-distance life readings for individuals in the United States, Japan, and abroad; sponsors conferences, channelings, lectures, and weekly forums; publishes a quarterly magazine, *Applied PSI* ($18 per year to individual and $32 per year to institutions); and can provide teams of expert intuitives to solve difficult technical problems encountered by scientific laboratories, businesses, communities, and other institutions.

CAI has many cassettes and transcripts available which may prove of interest to readers of this book. Among them are excerpts from their November 1984 conference "The Ultimate Journey: An Exploration of the Spiritual Dimensions of Death," including Kevin Ryerson's channeling, "Ascending the Spiritual Path" (transcript), Richard Lavin's trance channeling "View from the Other Side" (transcript—especially recommended—powerful and revelatory reading); Kenneth Ring's presentation, "Near Death/Far Death: The Experiential Data" (cassette); a "Portals to the Afterlife" panel of noted authorities (cassette); and Alan Shulak's "Death and Self-Transformation" presentation (cassette). They also have available an extensive annotated bibliography on "Death, Dying and Beyond" ($3).

CAI can mail order complete transcripts and cassettes of its 1985 conference, "The Development of Intuition in Elementary Education: A New Vision of Education." Available are four separate channelings through Kevin Ryerson, Richard Lavin, Jon Fox, and Verna Yater (cassettes and transcripts are available for each of the four channelings). It also has some individual channelings available, including Jon Fox's "The Horizons of Consciousness" (cassette), "States of Consciousness" (cassette), and "The Dynamics of Effective Psychotherapy" (cassette or transcript); Mary Gillis Reins's "Spirituality and Relationships" (cassette or transcript) and "Crisis of Spiritual Awakening" (cassette); and Verna Yater's "Reincarnation, Past Lives and Karma" (cassette).

Finally, CAI has made available tapes and transcripts of its 1986 conference, "The Intuitive Process," co-sponsored with San Francisco State University. Among the presentations at this conference was Kevin Ryerson's incomparable 75-minute channeling, "The Emerging Mind: Knowing and Being in the '90's" (transcript only). Including information on intuition, psychoimmunity, people of "specialized intelligence" (the so-called retarded), and the role of lesbians and gay men in the current planetary transformative process, this channeling is a mind-opener. (Contact CAI to find out in which formats this and other conference presentations are available.)

All CAI tapes and transcripts are $12 each, plus the obligatory 7% California sales tax for California residents. Contact Center for Applied Intuition, Dept. WH, 2046 Clement St., San Francisco, CA 94121.

Richard Lavin is a San Diego-based trance channel whose work has proven invaluable to me and many others on the spiritual path. Perhaps you caught his all-too-brief appearance with actress Joyce DeWitt and others on a February 1987 Phil Donahue show. Ecton, the nonphysical entity who speaks through Richard, is a loving, gentle, and empowering teacher, counselor and healer. Though the adjective I'm about to use may have been rendered ridiculous by one too many parodies of Valley Girls, I can find no word more appropriate to describe Ecton's gentle presence, wisdom, and facility with psychospiritual balancing and counseling than "awesome."

At the suggestion of spirit entity Tom MacPherson, I have helped promote some of Richard Lavin's Bay Area channeling events. These include the powerful and moving channeling on "The Gay and Lesbian Experience" and the mind-boggling and entertaining joint channeling, "A Celebration of Unity," which featured Richard Lavin and another fine channel associated with CAI, El Cerrito, CA-based Richard Wolinsky. (See Chapter 17 for an excerpt from this channeling). Single tapes of these and other channelings including "The Nature of Reality," "Inner Knowledge," "Clearing Blockages," and "Inner Child" are available for $10 plus 6% sales tax for California residents. Richard's two-tape sets include "Sexuality and Relationships," "Time," and "Channel Training" ($20 each). A complete list of the Ecton Cassette Tape Library, which includes brief descriptions of each offering, is available.

Richard Lavin offers evening and weekend intensives and private one-on-one consultations in San Diego, Los Angeles, the San Francisco Bay Area, and other locations. He has accompanied groups of seekers to Machu Pichu and to Belize, and will undoubtedly participate in further treks and quests. Contact Richard Lavin, Dept. E, 4616 Bay Summit Place, San Diego, CA 92117-6746, (619) 275-5757.

Jon Fox is a northern California-based electrical engineer, a staff intuitive working with CAI, and one of several dedicated individuals who channel the entity Hilarion. One of the most fascinating aspects of Jon's work is his construction of an "inert gas device," based upon Hilarion's instructions, which emits a very thin energy field which in just 3 minutes seems to at least temporarily clear negative thought forms from the mind of an individual lying beneath its beam. The inert gas device is a brass cylinder about 18 inches long containing a combination of the inert gases argon and krypton. Very strong electric and magnetic fields are applied to the cylinder, creating a strong and unique beam of energy, about ½-inch in diameter. This beam is directed 12 to 18 inches away from the physical body at the subtle energy fields which surround the physical body, and where it is believed that negative thought forms actually reside. Clairvoyants who have observed the effect of this beam on the subtle body have actually been able to see negative thought forms dissipate.

Jon is quick to point out that the inert gas device is hardly the fast-food answer to long-term psychotherapy. A helpful adjunct to other therapies, Jon has discovered that if a person does not fundamentally change their mental patterns, their negative thought forms will return in a couple of days. But the interim period of freedom which this device seems to make possible allows an individual clearly to identify their negative thought patterns, and to see the work they must do in order to clear them from their consciousness. It is speculated that by clarifying and defining negative thought patterns which are the root of dis-ease, the inert gas device can serve as a powerful tool to catalyze healing.

Jon Fox is currently experimenting with different group formats in which to use the inert gas device, including a Wednesday evening in which each group member is zapped, followed by an all-day Saturday intensive at which Jon, his wife Deki, and Hilarion can assist participants in initiating lasting change. I participated in the first group of this kind, and discovered myself, after the initial 3-minute exposure, blithely writing several pages of the most positive affirmations that have ever flowed from my frequently cluttered brain.

Jon Fox has a host of audio cassettes and video cassettes available of his counselings. Among them are "Relationships: Reflection, Power, Harmony," "Relating with Yourself," "Being Love: Opening the Heart," "Children: Parenting the Future," "Guilt: The Human Experience," "Worry: Energy We Don't Know What to Do With," "Work and Self Growth," "Receiving Money in the Helping Professions," "Meaningful Work," "Economics in the New Age," "A New Vision of Education," "Past Lives and How Do We Use Them," "Mineral Rebalancing through Hair Analysis," "Humanity's Responsibility in Space," and "Space Beings and Other Dimensional Realities." Audio cassettes are $7.50, while video cassettes (specify VHS or BETA format) are $35.00. Write Jon Fox, Dept. WH, P.O. Box 1025, San Rafael, CA 94915. California residents add 6% sales tax.

Several 150 to 300 page books of Hilarion's teachings have been channeled through Maurice Cook of Toronto. Write Marcus Books, 195 Randolph Road, Toronto M4G 3S6, Canada, for a complete list.

Caroline M. Myss, medical clairvoyant, author, journalist and editor at Stillpoint Publishing has been promoting individual and planetary healing ever since a nonphysical entity named Genesis began to speak through her. Her 3 years of work with C. Norman Shealey, M.D., Ph.D. has produced a collaborative package, *The Challenge of AIDS*. This offering combines medical knowledge, clairvoyant knowledge and holistic health approach to assist in the healing of AIDS. It also discusses the spiritual significance of AIDS in terms of global consciousness. The package contains an approximately 70-page booklet, with case histories of many PWAs on the healing path, and the story of a remarkable man who "completely healed" AIDS. It also includes 3 cassette tapes designed to empower healing, break through the fears that can attract AIDS to someone, and help heal the mental and emotional aspects of the dis-ease. It costs approximately $29.95.

This material, at least in written form, will also be included in *The Creation of Health: The Merger of Traditional Medicine with Clairvoyant Insight*, by Caroline M. Myss and C. Norman Shealey, M.D., Ph.D., due out toward the end of 1987. This book is a culmination of three years of collaboration by the authors, and features stories of how people have responded to and healed from their combination of insight and practice. Contact Caroline M. Myss, Stillpoint Publishing, Dept. G, P.O. Box 640, Walpole, NH 03608. Please, please mention this book, and the undying love of Jason for Caroline.

[Note: While *The Challenge of AIDS* should be available as you read these words, it was not yet in final form as I reached my deadline for the second edition of *Psychoimmunity*. I have, however, reviewed Caroline's earlier Genesis material on AIDS. While differing in some respects from the information and program offered herein, it did contain much deep insight, and certainly paralleled this book's approach. Especially knowing the heart of this wonderful woman, I can only recommend that you investigate her new offerings.]

Body Electric School of Massage and Rebirthing. This school in Oakland, CA, offers a professional bodywork certificate program, classes in healing and eroticism, and trainings in bodywork for people with a life-threatening illness.

Founded in 1984, Body Electric is dedicated to creating a homophobic-free environment for bodywork and healing trainings. Although the school is especially focused for gay men and lesbians, all persons are welcome to study at Body Electric. The school has a special emphasis on dealing with constrictions and fears due to AIDS, and offers discounts to people volunteering with AIDS organizations.

Healing the Earth Bodywork Training is a 150-hour, California state approved certificate program consisting of 9 individual courses: Swedish-Esalen massage, acupressure, shiatsu, Reichian bodywork, rebirthing (conscious breathing), anatomy, stretching and bioenergetics, massage therapy, and successful business practices.

Healing the Body Erotic is a 150-hour training for gay and bisexual men. This program in healing and eroticism includes classes in masturbation and erotic massage from a Taoist and Reichian perspective, anal pleasure and health, Taoist erotic spiritual practices, healing the heart-genital connection, self-erotic massage, and Tantric sex. These classes taught by Joseph Kramer are about loving and healing yourself and others.

Massage therapist Irene Smith (a contributor to this book) offers trainings to bodyworkers serving people with life-threatening illnesses. These classes help healers and bodyworkers to examine their own issues around death and dying as well as teaching specific techniques for working with clients both in the hospital and in their homes. Over 200 bodyworkers trained by Irene Smith and the Body Electric staff are now providing healing touch to people with AIDS/ARC and other life-threatening illnesses.

Joseph Kramer, Irene Smith, and the Body Electric staff regularly offer trainings in the San Francisco Bay Area and in other parts of the country. For more information and class schedules, contact Body Electric School of Massage and Rebirthing, 6527A Telegraph Avenue, Box E, Oakland, CA 94609, (415) 653-1594.

Intimate Explorations for Men is a powerful weekend workshop designed to help men love themselves and others. Facilitated by Floyd E. Goff, this workshop explores male sexuality and spirituality. With an emphasis on honesty, clear communication, loving unconditionally, dealing with fear, anger, and loneliness, as well as on touching, sensuality, erotic massage (there will be some nudity), this experience is designed to help men get their wants, needs, and desires met.

These workshops, lasting from Friday evening to Sunday afternoon, began in San Francisco in 1984 and are currently being facilitated by Floyd in other cities around the country. I participated in the first of these groups, and found it (as well as groups at the Body Electric School) a positive and healing experience. Those interested in participating in the Bay Area, or in arranging for Floyd to do his work in their own community, may contact I.E.M. at 66 Levant St., Dept. F, San Francisco, CA 94114, (415) 431-3899.

I.E.M. also sponsors men's drop-in groups in San Francisco on the first and third Wednesdays of each month, which emphasize interpersonal exploration and intimate sharing.

Facilitator Floyd E. Goff is a certified hypnotherapist, relationship counselor, sexologist, and past-life regression specialist. His work derives in part from his long-time association with Stan Dale, a highly respected producer of human sexuality and relationships workshops.

The Center for Attitudinal Healing was started by Dr. Jerald Jampolsky, author of *Love is Letting Go of Fear* and a tireless promoter of *A Course in Miracles.* Jampolsky is currently traveling worldwide and working independently of the Center, while the Center's work is currently being directed by Pam Harris.

Attitudinal healing is the process of letting go of painful, fearful attitudes. When we let go of the fear, only love remains. The Center defines health as "inner peace" and healing as "the process of letting go of fear." As their brochure explains, "It's possible to choose peace rather than conflict and love rather than fear. We believe that love is the most important healing force in the world." Pam further explained to me via telephone that the focus of the Center is not on "body healing" but on "healing life independent of whatever physical conditions we may have." Whether or not the outcome of this process is physical life or death, the goal of the Center's work is peace of mind and peace of heart.

The Center's work feels harmonious with that of Elisabeth Kübler-Ross, Louise Hay, and the unifying concepts of this book. You may contact the Center for Attitudinal Healing at 21 Main Street, Tiburon, CA 94920, or by calling (415) 435-5022. They can put you in contact with some of the groups around the country sharing similar philosophies.

The Shanti Project offers counseling and support services for San Francisco Bay Area residents facing life-threatening illness or coping with Acquired Immune Deficiency. They are located at 890 Hayes,

San Francisco, CA 94117, (415) 558-9644. A similar group has begun in Los Angeles, and others exist around the country. Becoming a volunteer counselor is a wonderful way to serve others and yourself. Professional accredited trainings are held regularly.

The San Francisco Shanti Project has a set of videotape training materials available which offer (along with a manual) a complete guide to Shanti's volunteer counselor training. For more information on the videotapes, costs, etc., write to them for their brochure at the address given above.

The Access Group, Ltd., the group that sponsored the remarkable joint San Francisco AIDS presentation by Stephen Levine and Ram Dass, was organized by clinicians working on the AIDS Ward at San Francisco General Hospital (5B, renamed 5A). In addition to providing AIDS-related consultations, The Access Group offers clinical and educational support services to health care providers, persons diagnosed with AIDS or ARC, and the larger community. They offer a variety of workshops, programs and materials integrating the best available clinical knowledge with the awareness that healing means more than simply changing the nature of the body. Projected plans for this group include putting on panels and workshops in various cities around the country. For more information, contact them at The Access Group, Ltd., c/o Daniel Barnes, Dept. A, 4 Cielo Lane, Building 4, Unit D, Novato, CA 94947.

The San Francisco D.A.I.R. organization (The Documentation of AIDS Issues & Research Foundation, Inc.) has amassed an important archive, which increases daily, from a broad variety of sources on virtually any AIDS issue. This archive includes published and unpublished research papers, tabloids, periodicals, and other printed AIDS and AIDS-related information. It also includes book titles about AIDS and immunology as well as audio and audiovisual tapes of seminars. D.A.I.R. sponsors forums in the San Francisco Bay Area on AIDS, including holistic approaches and research, and has committees working on parasites and poppers as predisposing co-factors to the dis-ease. They are committed to the education of health care providers, sending them the most current periodicals available on various AIDS-related topics, and are in the process of developing a survey of researchers active in AIDS research. Contact them at 2336 Market Street, Suite 33, San Francisco, CA 94114.

The San Francisco AIDS Alternative Healing Project provides and gathers information, maintains a telephone referral service for alternative and holistic practitioners and resources, and sponsors the Comprehensive Program for People Recently Diagnosed with AIDS/ARC. Practitioners in the program have included Misha Cohen, O.M.D., C.A., Alan Brickman, M.A., Sue Clemente, C.A., Dan Phillips, C.HT., and Ann West, MFCC.

The project's program reads like a page out of this book, and includes meditation, visualization, detoxification, herbal prescriptions, nutritional supplements, acupuncture, massage, health-promoting diet and lifestyle changes, emotional counseling, and support group. Volunteers and tax-deductible donations for their scholarship fund are always welcome. Contact the SFAAHP at 513 Valencia St., San Francisco, CA 94110, (415) 558-9292.

Quan Yin Acupuncture and Herb Center of San Francisco is a community clinic dedicated to accessible and affordable primary health care. Offering acupuncture, Chinese and Western herbs, classical homeopathy, shiatsu, massage, Rosen method bodywork, hypnotherapy etc...., it accepts payment on a sliding scale as well as Medi-Cal and insurance. Founded by Misha Cohen, O.M.D., C.A., who was present at two of the channelings contained herein, it is staffed by mostly lesbian and gay practitioners who have worked extensively with people diagnosed with AIDS and ARC. It also has a non-profit Healing Arts Center which includes classes from all realms of Mind/Body/Spirit. Contact them at 513 Valencia St., San Francisco, CA 94110, (415) 861-1101.

Mermaid Productions has a library of AIDS information videotapes available in VHS, BETA, and ¾" formats, including seminars focusing on alternative treatment and political issues. Two of the tapes currently available feature myself in panel discussions on holistic treatment of AIDS. The forum at San Francisco State University, shared with Ted Smith of The Healing Project, is especially recommended for its balanced content and comprehensive approach. Write them at 3623 18th Street, San Francisco, CA 94110, (415) 626-4240. (You might inquire about using their tapes for continuing education credits for nurses.)

Shared Visions and Sound Choices are spaces created by Will Nofke in Berkeley, CA, which feature New Age lectures, workshops, music, books, and tapes. Will also hosts "New Horizons" every Friday from 12:00 noon to 1:00 p.m. on KPFA, 94FM, listener-sponsored Pacifica Radio Broadcasting from Berekeley (where else?), which features interviews with people on the cutting edge of planetary/spiritual transformation. Tapes of many of these excellent broadcasts are available; their range and depth is unparalleled. Kevin Ryerson has done several evenings at Shared Visions, and Jack Schwarz often presents programs there. Stop by or call Shared Visions at 2512 San Pablo, Berkeley, CA 94707, (415) 845-2216.

Project Cure is a nonprofit organization that educates, lobbies, and demands of the U.S. Congress recognition of the validity of nonorthodox treatments for cancer. Its founder, Robert DeBragga, was diagnosed with terminal lung cancer in October 1978. After receiving minimal orthodox treatment, he began to research all aspects of medical literature, including alternative treatments both in the United States and abroad. In September 1979, DeBragga began a stringent nutritional program receiving as many as 300 vitamins, minerals, and glandular extracts per day. He is currently employing another type of nontoxic treatment composed of various selenium compounds (see the selenium solution for KS lesions, applicable to all forms of skin cancer, discussed in "The Nature of the Healing Process" in Part III of this book) developed by Emanuel Revici, M.D., of New York. To the amazement of his physicians, his condition remains stable, while his political activities proceed tirelessly.

Robert DeBragga writes in one of his fundraising/sign-this-petition-to-Congress appeals, "Almost every 'nonconventional' cancer therapy which has shown promise in the quest for cure and prevention of cancer (usually less expensive) has been shunned by the big medical establishment as quackery." The organization has much information available, and is currently defending the right of Dr. Revici to continue his healing work in the face of FDA opposition. Project Cure can certainly inform you of the refusal of the National Cancer Institute, the American Cancer Society, the American Medical Association, and the FDA to support the work of Linus Pauling, Max Gerson, the late Wilhelm Reich, and almost every nutritional and nonallopathic approach to healing one might care to examine. Contributions to this organization are tax deductible, and they deserve your support. Write Project Cure at 2020 K Street N.W., Suite 350, Washington, DC 20007.

Ann Wigmore is undoubtedly the most well-known and tireless exponent of the role of eating only living foods as a means of healing the body. Formerly associated with the Hippocrates Health Institute, and now the head of her own foundation, Dr. Ann has been having great success with people diagnosed with AIDS, cancer, and a host of other dis-eases.

The basic principle underlying the living foods movement is the fact that all foods, and all living things, have a specific life energy or vital energy. Chemically processing food, or even cooking it, alters and often destroys this life energy. Not only does each of us have a specific life energy or vibrational field, which interacts with and affects those around us, but the foods we eat, and the people we associate with, in turn affect our own energy field. Some people literally light up a room, and uplift our energy, by their mere presence; Ann Wigmore would suggest that a living food such as wheatgrass juice can help do the same thing from the inside. By combining the principles of eating only living foods with a regimen of detoxification and healing, Ann Wigmore has successfully put this principle into practice.

While Dr. Ann's regimen is a closed system like macrobiotics and Chinese medicine, and differs from the dietary recommendations of The Holistic Group, it does hold merit for those who are intuitively drawn to it. Certainly the principles of life energy, which are reflected in The Holistic Group's discussion of synthetic vitamins and avoidance of processed foods—and especially avoidance of such potential killers as white sugar and white flour—are vitally important to our health. For further information, contact The Ann Wigmore Foundation, 196 Commonwealth Ave., Boston, MA 02116, (617) 267-9424.

One final entry. Yours truly, *Jason Serinus*, has decided after much deliberation that this "Resources" section would be incomplete without some mention of my unique contributions to individual and planetary healing.

Those of you who have read the "Inquiry" of the Holistic Group may already have inferred that, after frequent prodding and unqualified endorsement from Tom MacPherson and John the Beloved, I have become a distributor of *Blue Green-Manna, Super Blue-Green*, and other remarkable nutritional products. If you'd like to follow up on Spirit's suggestion and explore them please contact me at the address which follows.

According to the entity John, I have been channeling healing energy through sound, touch, teaching and writing since my days of working on the pyramids in Egypt. At my 1985 birthday channeling, John presented me with a format for energy balancing/healing sessions which draws together all my various skills as a sound healer, bodyworker and teacher. Because these sessions affect all levels of one's being, I have appropriately entitled my work "Alignment of Mind, Body and Spirit."

My one-on-one "Alignment of Mind, Body and Spirit" sessions are highlighted by the channeling of my unique resonant tones produced by, of all things, my whistling! These tones, I am told, soar far beyond the "just put your lips together and blow" variety. It has been suggested that my pure, resonant tones, align people in a manner similar to the sounds of Patricia Sun, a counselor and healer known for her healing "sounds." (See listing in Resources above.) Without putting my pucker in peril by "making claims," I will simply note that when I work individually with people I seem to channel the tones most appropriate at that time for balancing energy and catalyzing growth and healing. I record these tones, along with a deep relaxation induction and healing imagery, on cassette, so that my clients leave with a meditation tool which they can use regularly to further the healing process.

My sessions continue with deep bodywork and/or Esalen-style massage, whose goal is to extend the alignment process to a muscular and tissue level. I conclude by guiding people through the spiral chakra meditation discussed earlier in this book. Specific affirmations and/or visualizations, words of guidance, and even suggested techniques for healing come through as needed at this time. Although I must honestly admit that the impact of my work goes far beyond the comprehension of my all-too-rational mind, ample testimony from my clients convinces me that John knew what he was talking about when he directed me to do this work.

I schedule sessions in the San Francisco Bay Area as my schedule allows, and occasionally do them on the road while I am conducting my seminars. I charge on a sliding scale for PWAs/PWARCs experiencing financial hardship, and welcome donations from readers which enable me to do my work for people in need without charge. (I also extend a note of thanks to Anne, Lee and others who have already supported this work.)

For those less esoterically inclined, I note that I also give full body energy balancing massages. To be perfectly frank, I have a wonderful touch.

That's not all, folks. For the mere price of this book you can own your very own one-of-a-kind cassette containing 16 whistled vocal gems, including many operatic classics. While it may not heal you of Acquired Immune Deficiency or athlete's foot, it is guaranteed to touch your heart and communicate some of the impassioned intensity of its unclassifiable creator. My cassette, a favorite of Lynn and Kevin Ryerson, Elisabeth Kübler-Ross, Paul Lee, Louise Hay, and other enlightened cognoscenti, can be yours for only $9.95 plus $1.50 for postage and handling (California residents please add 7% sales tax—70¢). See address and Note which follow.

It is rumored that in this very sentence I am putting out thought forms to distributors and producers of visualization/healing tapes that the time is right for me to record a special cassette designed for meditation and alignment. Way before hell freezes over, you will learn of this tape from your local outlet. Meanwhile, I can be cajoled into recording a tape consisting of a deep relaxation and healing tones especially for you on a high quality cassette. A short note about you, your photo, and $30 plus sales tax if applicable will do the trick.

I have begun to do "Psychoimmunity and the Healing Process" seminars in the United States, Canada, and abroad. These seminars allow me to share much up-to-date information about AIDS and healing, answer questions, play excerpts of material channeled through Kevin Ryerson, lead people in the powerful and aligning spiral chakra meditation, channel my healing tones and, most important of all, provide a lot of hope and inspiration. (There's a lot more from where this book came from.) My workshops are about healing—both understanding what it's about and actually experiencing it.

Sometimes sponsored by individual promoters, at other times by healing centers, AIDS and PWA groups, these seminars have been held in such cities as Seattle, Vancouver, New York, Philadelphia, Washington, D.C., Los Angeles, Santa Barbara, Tucson, Berkeley and San Francisco. Please contact me about leading one in your community.

Going on the road enables me to touch people directly with the vision of healing and love that has inspired this book and the articles I have published. It is a great joy, and a consumate privilege, to be able to share in the healing that so many of us are experiencning at this time.

To reach me, please write to Jason Serinus, c/o The Holistic Group, P.O. Box 3073, Oakland, CA 94609-0073. Please make out checks or money orders to "The Holistic Group." [Note: For tape orders to Canada and Mexico, please enclose $2.00 postage and handling for surface mail, and $4.00 for air mail. Other foreign orders, include $6.00 for air mail. Because of my traveling schedule, please allow 3-10 weeks for delivery.]

I would love to receive reports from individuals and practitioners who have found the material in this book useful for healing. There is a great need for testimony from long-term survivors, and for data and staatistics on those who are healing as a result of adopting a holistic approach. This material will be shared when appropriate, with anonymity assured if you so desire, through articles, networking, and speaking engagements.

It is wonderful to learn of all the wonderful new healing techniques and nutritional approaches emerging as a reuslt of this epidemic. AIDS is truly serving as a catalyst for transforming our healing institutions. While welcoming your letters, please note that I am neither equipped nor credentialed to answer health questions by phone or mail; nor can I routinely funnel them to Kevin Ryerson or his psychic dog Spot.

Please help express my gratitude to the people and centers mentioned throughout this volume by letting them know that you read about them, or were led to them, through this book.

NOTES ON CONTRIBUTORS

Margo Adair is the developer of "Applied Meditation," a means of directing consciousness for intuitive problem-solving. For 13 years she has been leading workshops across the United States, and counseling individuals, drawing upon spiritual, feminist, psychological, and political approaches. Margo developed her AIDS materials in consultation with professional counselors working full-time with people with AIDS. Her massive book *Working Inside Out: Tools for Change* is published by Wingbow Press in Berkeley, California.

Elizabeth Kübler-Ross, M.D., is undoubtedly the individual most responsible for bringing an awareness of life-death transition as a positive experience to public consciousness. Her book *On Death and Dying* has been followed by numerous books, tapes, and videotapes for adults and children. Elisabeth tirelessly lectures, counsels, and heals people worldwide and has established the Elisabeth Kübler-Ross Center in Virginia to make her workshops and services available to a larger number of individuals than ever before.

Paul Lee, Ph.D., founded and directed The Platonic Academy of Herbal Studies, a professional training school for herbalists in Santa Cruz, California. Dubbed "the Cheerleader of the Herbal Renaissance," he is a graduate of Harvard Divinity School and Harvard University, where he served as Paul Tillich's teaching assistant during the theologian's final two Harvard years. He has also served as Protestant Chaplain at Brandeis University, and taught at MIT and the University of California at Santa Cruz. Paul has published Tillich's *The Meaning of Health.*

Kevin Ryerson, Mediator, is a fully accredited trance channel in the tradition of Edgar Cayce and Jane Roberts. Kevin is dedicated to bridging the gap between science and spirituality. He has worked extensively with medical doctors, scientists, and other professionals to add perspective and knowledge to physics, issues of health, nutrition, and parapsychology. The subject of numerous televison and radio interviews, Kevin figures prominently in Shirley MacLaine's best-selling *Out on a Limb* and *Dancing in the Light,* and Gurudas' *Flower Essences* and *Gem Elixirs and Vibrational Healing.* He will make his television acting debut in November 1986 by playing himself in Shirley MacLaine's TV-miniseries *Out on a Limb.*

Jack Schwarz, N.D., is an internationally recognized authority on voluntary controls, human energy systems, and holistic health. His demonstrations at the Meninger Foundation—where he pierced his arm with a large needle, registered and felt no pain, and then healed himself immediately, leaving no evidence of the puncture—are well documented. Author of *The Path of Action, Voluntary Controls*, and *Human Energy Systems*, he travels around the world, teaching, lecturing, and offering private consultations and healings. In 1958 he founded the Aletheia Psycho-Physical Foundation, and has at last realized his dream of establishing a H.E.A.R.T. (Health Education Research Training) Center in southern Oregon.

Jason Serinus is an Independent Scholar *Cum Laude* graduate of Amherst College, with a Bachelor of Arts in American Studies. A master Postural Integrator and certified masseur in practice since 1973, he is first and foremost a healer, promoting health and harmony through the use of sound, bodywork, intuition, love, holistic and spiritual guidance. He currently writes, teaches, lectures, performs, promotes healing events, and maintains a private healing practice in the San Francisco Bay Area.

Irene Smith, M.T., is both a massage therapist in private practice in San Francisco and a volunteer assisting in workshops of the Elisabeth Kübler-Ross Center. Shortly after her life was totally transformed through exposure to the "Life, Death and Transition" work of Elisabeth Kübler-Ross, Irene introduced massage into the Hospice Movement of North California, and by example into the Hospice Movement of the entire country. She massaged her first AIDS client in July 1982, and in August 1983 began weekly room-to-room massage visits to the loving AIDS Ward of San Francisco General Hospital. Her work has since been enhanced by 16 AIDS massage volunteers and 10 additional home health massage volunteers whom she has trained through the Hospice of San Francisco. With support from the San Francisco AIDS Emergency Fund, Hospice, and the San Francisco Shanti Project, Irene Smith has lovingly touched the feet and hearts of more people with AIDS than perhaps anyone else on the planet.

INDEX

THE PUBLISHER RECOMMENDS . . .

SERENITY
by Paul Reed

For gay men and others losing friends, living with doubt, fearful of disease, and for therapists counseling the "worried well," here is a realistic and comforting approach to coping with the emotional stress of the AIDS epidemic. In beautifully written essays, Paul Reed shows how to deal with the paralysis of fear and go beyond it to get on with life in a positive, hopeful way. ISBN 0-89087-506-5, paperback, $5.95.

The New LOVING SOMEONE GAY, Revised and Updated
by Don Clark, Ph.D.

A gay therapist offers sensitive, intelligent guidance to gay people and those who care about them in this updated and revised edition of the classic originally published in 1977. Includes a completely new section on political gains, social changes, AIDS, and the growth of the gay community. ISBN 0-89087-505-7, paperback, $7.95

GUIDE TO STRESS REDUCTION
by L. John Mason, Ph.D.

From a stress reduction therapist, here is the outstanding book on the techniques of stress reduction used and recommended widely by doctors, holistic health practitioners, therapists, and counselors. With chapters on visualization, meditation, biofeedback, autogenics, desensitization, and progressive relaxation. ISBN 0-89087-452-2, paperback, $8.95.

To order any of these books, please send a check or money order for the amount shown, including $1.50 postage and handling for each book (California residents please add 6½% state sales tax to your order). Send your order to: CELESTIAL ARTS Special Orders, Dept. P, P.O. Box 7327, Berkeley, CA 94707. Please ask for a copy of our free catalog.